DATE DUE

			PRINTED IN U.S.A.

SOCCER UNDER THE SWASTIKA

SOCCER UNDER THE SWASTIKA

Stories of Survival and Resistance during the Holocaust

Kevin E. Simpson

ROWMAN & LITTLEFIELD
Lanham • Boulder • New York • London

Published by Rowman & Littlefield
A wholly owned subsidiary of The Rowman & Littlefield Publishing Group, Inc.
4501 Forbes Boulevard, Suite 200, Lanham, Maryland 20706
www.rowman.com

Unit A, Whitacre Mews, 26-34 Stannary Street, London SE11 4AB

British Library Cataloguing in Publication Information Available

Library of Congress Cataloging-in-Publication Data

Name: Simpson, Kevin E.
Title: Soccer under the Swastika : stories of survival and resistance during the Holocaust / Kevin E. Simpson.
Description: Lanham : Rowman & Littlefield, [2016] | Includes bibliographical references and index.
Identifiers: LCCN 2016010713 | ISBN 9781442261624 (hardcover : alk. paper)
Subjects: LCSH: Soccer—Europe—History—20th century. | Soccer and war—Europe—History—20th century. | Soccer—History—20th century. | World War, 1939–1945—Occupied territories. | National socialism and soccer. | Holocaust, Jewish (1939–1945) | Jewish soccer players—History—20th century. | Soccer players—History—20th century.
Classification: LCC GV944.E8 S55 2016 | DDC 796.334094—dc23 LC record available at https://lccn.loc.gov/2016010713

Printed in the United States of America

To the memory of Steven Tyrone Johns and
the innumerable "voiceless voices" lost to the Shoah

CONTENTS

ILLUSTRATIONS

Following page 134.

Cartoon postcard from the 1930s featuring a stereotypical Jewish Russian exile as a football being booted from the world. United States Holocaust Memorial Museum, courtesy of Wiener Library.

Reichssportführer Hans von Tschammer und Osten lecturing Germany's first-ever national team coach Otto Nerz and Fritz Szepan at Berlin's Olympic Stadium, 1936. The Granger Collection, New York.

Der Papierene: genius Austrian footballer Matthias Sindelar, 1932. Lothar Ruebelt-Ullstein Bild/The Granger Collection.

A mutually beneficial relationship. Schalke 04 captain Fritz Szepan meeting *Der Führer* at the Reich Chancellery in Berlin, October 1937. Heinrich Hoffman-Ullstein Bild/The Granger Collection.

Architect of the BreslauElf and wartime partner Sepp Herberger, who joined the Nazi Party in 1933 but eschewed politics in managing *Die Mannschaft* for over two decades, 1937. Schirner-Ullstein Bild/The Granger Collection.

Future German national team trainer of the 1974 World Cup champions and international player Helmut Schön in a friendly match against Denmark, a 1–0 win in Hamburg, 17 November 1940. The Granger Collection, New York.

The best of his generation: Fritz Walter, wearing the German shirt in the final year of international play under the Nazis (1942), would outlast Hitler, going on to captain a resurrected German national side at the Miracle of Berne in 1954. The Granger Collection, New York.

Polish pariah: *Volksdeutscher* Ernst Willimowski, Silesian-born star for Polish club and national teams, chooses football and identity with the German national team, 1942. The Granger Collection, New York.

The salute. England defeats Nazi Germany, 6–3, in Berlin in front of 110,000 people on May 14, 1938. The Granger Collection, New York.

Fritz Szepan of FC Schalke 04 scoring the first goal in a 2–0 win against First Vienna FC to claim the 1942 German domestic championship. The Granger Collection, New York.

Nazi propaganda photos of beleaguered prisoners playing at KZ-Dachau, June 10, 1933. Bundesarchiv, Bild 152-03-13 (top) and Bild 152-03-10 (bottom), photos by Friedrich Franz Bauer.

Sunday-afternoon soccer in the transit camp at Westerbork, Holland, 1943. Leader of the camp Jewish police force looks on. NIOD/Beeldbank.

League football match, started in summer 1943, played on the Westerbork assembly square. Yad Vashem.

Hand-drawn table of Liga Terezín from autumn 1943, author unknown. Champions: Köche (kitchen) team. Památník Terezín, copyright Zuzana Dvořáková.

Soccer match in the Poniatowa (Poland) labor camp, circa 1941–1944. Nearly every prisoner in the camp was eventually murdered. Ghetto Fighters' House Museum, Israel.

Handshakes at the start of the Nazi propaganda film *Liga Terezín* of the September 1, 1944, match featuring *Jugendfürsorge* (youth welfare) and *Kleiderkammer* (used clothing) squads. Chronos Media, Germany.

Play during *Liga Terezín*, September 1, 1944. Chronos Media, Germany.

Corner kick leading to a goal in *Liga Terezín*, September 1, 1944. Chronos Media, Germany.

Terezín ghetto favorite and former professional Czech goalkeeper Jirka Taussig in *Liga Terezín*, September 1, 1944. Taussig survived Theresienstadt and later Auschwitz. Chronos Media, Germany.

Souvenir poster from Terezín for team Aeskulap, signed by prisoners. Original color watercolor by W. Thalheimer, 1943–1944. Památník Terezín, copyright Zuzana Dvořáková.

Survivor of the Russian front Herbert Pohl dons the red shirt and black shorts of Dresdner SC in a 4–0 victory over LSV (Luftwaffe) Hamburg in Berlin's Olympic Stadium, June 18, 1944. The Granger Collection, New York.

Austrian civilians conscripted to offer a proper burial to the murdered on the former SS soccer field in the Mauthausen (Austria) concentration camp, May 10, 1945. USHMM, courtesy of Ray Buch.

Matches featuring survivors captivate throngs of fans in Munich after the war. Ghetto Fighters' House Museum, Israel; photo by Isak Sutin.

Matches were a popular diversion at the Zeilshcim DP camp (near Frankfurt), circa 1946–1947. Yad Vashem.

Jewish refugee Aaron Elster, hidden for two years in an attic in Poland, posing in the uniform of his youth team in the Neu Freimann DP camp near Munich, 1946. USHMM.

The rescued making the save for team Hatikvah (The Hope) in the Bergen-Belsen DP camp, the largest in Germany. Yad Vashem.

Inside the fence where a soccer pitch once stood. On the other side, the unloading ramp and the path to death. Auschwitz-Birkenau today, 2015. Courtesy of the author.

FOREWORD

Simon Kuper

The other day I had lunch with a man in his eighties who had survived the Holocaust. He has never told me much about what he went through, but it clearly continues to shape his view of the world. When he talked about the Syrian refugees now looking for somewhere to live, he reflected, "They are just like we were."

This man is one of the last survivors of the death camps. Before long, all direct links with the Holocaust will have died out. I saw the same happen with World War I. When I was a child in London in the 1970s, quite a lot of the old men you saw walking around were veterans of the Great War. Some of them were still known in everyday life as Captain This or Major That. By the time I reached adulthood, there were only a few of them left, mostly mute figures in old people's homes. In recent years the last few of them have been buried. Today, World War I is effectively dead, like the American Civil War: remembered by history buffs, but only vaguely by the public, and without its former power to influence human behavior today.

The same will happen with the Holocaust. Already, surveys by the Anti-Defamation League have found that growing numbers of young people have never heard of the death camps, or think they were faked as Zionist propaganda. As the late historian Tony Judt asked, "Can we preserve a European past that is now fading from memory into history? Are we not doomed to lose it, if only in part?" Judt wrote that on his last visit to Berlin's Memorial to the Murdered Jews of Europe; "bored schoolchildren on an obligatory outing were playing hide-and-seek among the stones."

People are forgetting. When I was writing about soccer and the Holocaust myself, I interviewed many survivors and saw how deeply the loss of that collective memory would pain them. The need to remember without living witnesses makes Kevin Simpson's well-written and compelling book all the more important.

It took until the 1960s for the Holocaust to be broadly discussed at all. Before then most Jews felt too scared or traumatized to speak, and few non-Jews were yet ready to hear them. Primo Levi's first Auschwitz memoir, *Se questo è un uomo* (*If This Is a Man*), was rejected by the big Italian publisher Einaudi in 1946 and was barely read when a small press finally published it.

Yet Levi, like many other witnesses, desperately wanted to be heard. "The intrinsic horror of this human condition . . . has imposed a kind of constraint on all testimony," he wrote. Telling the world about Auschwitz became the purpose of his life.

In 1999 I met the Dutch Holocaust survivor and soccer nut Meijer Stad, whose astonishing story also features in *Soccer under the Swastika*. Like Levi, Stad had written his memoirs, in his case on the advice of his doctor, who thought it might help cure his sleeplessness. But there were many stories Stad hadn't felt able to write. He told me one about a fellow prisoner who had eaten human flesh in the camp; after the war, back in Holland, Stad had once seen the man in the street. "Can you imagine that?" Stad asked me. "I'll tell you: it's terrible. If you hear the stories of survivors; you can't imagine it. . . . "

"It's unimaginable," I agreed, innocently.

"Don't you believe me?" asked Stad, shocked. It was a common worry among Holocaust survivors that their stories were so awful and bizarre that no one would believe them. Stad is now dead (like most survivors I met, he remained traumatized to the end), but I suspect he would be pleased to read about himself in Simpson's book.

Knowing about the Holocaust might help us fulfill the postwar injunction "Never again!" But knowing what happened is also quite simply a moral duty, a way of honoring the dead. That we know about at least some of the murdered people is thanks mainly to the innumerable memoirs of survivors. That so many memoirs were written is partly because of Jewish tradition: what happens to you when you die is vague and uncertain, there may not be a heaven or hell, and so the dead live on only in the memory of the living.

Every lost life in *Soccer under the Swastika* deserves to be remembered. Simpson writes movingly about the renowned Dutch soccer broadcaster Han Hollander, killed with his wife and children at Sobibor. In 2009, the German historian Thomas Schnitzler arranged for memorial stones to be laid outside Amstelkade 118 in Amsterdam, the Hollanders' old home. The stones were made and laid by the German artist Gunter Demnig, who has said, "A person is only forgotten when his name has been forgotten."

We know how people like Hollander died. Simpson's book tells an equally meaningful side of the story: how they lived, spoke, thought, played, and had fun, sometimes even just before dying, kicking a ball around in concentration camps. These soccer-mad people were among the first or second generation of continental Europeans to have embraced the game.

For that matter, many Nazis embraced it too. As Simpson documents, by the 1930s fascist regimes were using soccer as propaganda and as a tool of foreign policy. *Soccer under the Swastika* serves as evidence that the game isn't always ennobling. But for doomed people in concentration camps, or the Jewish boys playing against SS men on Gęsia Street in the Warsaw Ghetto (a scene described by the Ghetto diarist Chaim Kaplan as "a miracle"), sport offered a momentary escape from unimaginable torment. These people were killed (as was Kaplan), but they weren't just victims. They were alive, and that's how we must try to remember them.

And soccer brings us closer to them. Kicking a ball, sitting in the stands cheering, or listening to match commentaries on the radio, they are recognizable people like us, albeit in an unrecognizable time. The distance between them and us grows inexorably, their faces begin to fade, and a book like this helps to restore their humanity.

Simon Kuper (born in Kampala, Uganda, in 1969) was educated at Oxford University and Harvard. He has been working for the Financial Times *since 1994 and now writes a general column for the newspaper. He is British but lives with his wife and three children in Paris. He is the author of several books, including* Football Against the Enemy *(winner of the William Hill Prize for Sports Book of the Year in 1994),* Ajax, the

Dutch, the War: Football in Europe during the Second World War *(2003)*, The Football Men *(2011), and—with Stefan Szymanski—Soccernomics (2009). In 2008 he won the Manuel Vazquez Montalban Prize for Sportswriting, an award sponsored by FC Barcelona. In 2011 he was named Britain's Cultural Commentator of the Year in Editorial Intelligence's Comment Awards. In 2012 he was shortlisted for the Orwell Prize for political journalism.*

ACKNOWLEDGMENTS

The genesis of this book is the culmination of two kinds of inspiration. The first comes from playing and watching soccer from my earliest days through college. The other inspiration is the countless survivors of the catastrophe of the Holocaust, many of whom I met only recently as they have moved into their twilight years. Having the privilege to hear their stories moved me to write this book.

I am indebted to many people who contributed their expertise, time, and passions. Among the dozens of Holocaust scholars and teachers, survivors and perpetrators, and other witnesses I have encountered, a smaller number stand out for deserved praise. Each has offered guidance and primary source material, often going well beyond initial requests. Deserved thanks to Guido Abuys and Bas Kortholt at the Camp Westerbork Memorial Centre (the Netherlands); Marjan Dejevij at the Verzetsmuseum—the Dutch Resistance Museum; Christian Dürr, archivist and curator at KZ-Gedenkstätte Mauthausen Memorial Museum (Austria); and Markwart Herzog, master networker to German colleagues and sport historian from Schwaben Akademie Irsee (Germany). Many thanks to Albert Knoll at KZ-Gedenkstätte Dachau Memorial Museum; Aleksandra Kobielec, archivist at the Muzeum Gross-Rosen (Rogoźnica, Poland); Sven Löhr from the KZ-Buchenwald Memorial Foundation (Germany); Reimer Möller, archivist from the KZ-Gedenkstätte Neuengamme (Germany); and Eva Němcová, who worked diligently to provide rare photos, artwork, and testimonies from Ghetto Theresienstadt. She also serves as editor of the documentation department along with Martina Šiknerová at Památník Terezín (Czech Republic).

Thanks to Lorenz Peiffer, consultant to the Deutscher Fußball-Bund and sport science professor at Leibniz Universität in Hannover (Germany); Piotr Setkiewicz, director of the Centre for Research and archivist Adam Cyra from the Auschwitz-Birkenau State Museum (Poland); Klaus Tätzler from the KZ-Gedenkstätte Bergen-Belsen Memorial Museum (Germany); Olliver Tietz, director of the Deutscher Fußball-Bund (DFB) Kulturstiftung (Culture Foundation); Jim Tobias from the Nuremberg Institute for Holocaust Studies (Germany); and Ken Waltzer, emeritus director of the Jewish Studies Program at Michigan State University.

A special note of gratitude to the gifted writer and journalist Simon Kuper. Our shared interest in soccer at the intersection of history brought him to write the foreword for this book. His immediate and enthusiastic acceptance of my request is forever appreciated.

Deepest thanks to longtime friend, newsman, and surprisingly passionate newcomer to the game Les Linebarger for his invaluable comments on earlier drafts of the manuscript, offered always with a keen eye for audience and storytelling. My fascination with this oft-depressing topic was first nurtured by close friend and colleague JonDavid Wyneken. His reviews and historical insights added much needed perspective to a psychologist coming into this field as a one-time novice. Oded Breda at the Beit Terezín, the Theresienstadt Martyrs' Remembrance Association (Israel), helped revise the chapter on Terezín, offering important corrections and firsthand knowledge of the victim experience as the nephew of a prisoner-player murdered at Auschwitz. Faculty colleague and German-born artist Peter Pohle translated key German-language sources on players beholden to the Third Reich. Our fascinating conversations of his youth growing up behind the Berlin Wall helped deepen my understanding of life in postwar Germany. Another colleague at John Brown University, Simone Schroder, offered her eager and indispensable assistance as an acquisition librarian. My editor, Christen Karniski, also guided this first-time project to completion with patience and care.

I reviewed hundreds of pages of testimony, perpetrator reports, and original documents in the search for these hidden stories of soccer during the Holocaust. One fellowship laid the groundwork for these stories. The summer 2009 Silberman Seminar for University Faculty at the Center for Advanced Holocaust Studies at the United States Holocaust Memorial Museum, led by Peter Hayes of Northwestern University, opened up this field to me in a dynamic and powerful way. Professor Hayes will always hold a special place in my memory as a model scholar and dynamic teacher. Much of this book was influenced directly by my time spent among the vast archival resources of the USHMM and Yad Vashem (Israel).

I am indebted to my university and various Holocaust foundations for the travel support that took me to almost all of the European museums, memorials, and camps discussed in this book. There is something profoundly humbling about standing on the sites where so many suffered, to walk about in remote mass killing sites in eastern Poland that are now overgrown and largely forgotten.

My sincere gratitude to the gifted translators who so ably converted rare and recently uncovered testimonies, many of which were likely translated into English for the first time. These translators include Roswitha Cesarotto (German), Kasina Entzi (Dutch), Lydia and Naomi Koebele (Czech), and Kasia Vincent (Polish). Thanks to my students, who continue to inspire my teaching on the Holocaust. One such student, research assistant Courtney Padgett, was of great help as well.

To my children, Grace and Eli, I am grateful for your curiosity about this topic and for tolerating my fanatical absorption in completing this work. Footballers themselves, they endured my indoctrination in the beautiful game years ago. You are my travel buddies and my hope that the next generation will take seriously the call to "Never Forget." My deepest thanks and admiration to my wife, Stefanie, who unfailingly encourages my passions, tolerates long absences, and makes time and space for me to wander the world, all while keeping our home front running along flawlessly as I retreated into long-passed decades.

More than seventy years after the end of the Second World War, the importance of this subject was made strikingly evident to me one beautiful summer day in the nation's capital. On Wednesday, June 10, 2009, I made my way past the staff security checkpoint for entry into the United States Holocaust Memorial Museum. As a faculty fellow participating in a two-week seminar, I had been enjoying stimulating readings and engaging discussions when it came time to break for lunch. But the peace and calm of the solemn museum were shattered in an instant with the sound of gunshots. An elderly man had approached the front entrance when museum guard Stephen Tyrone Johns pulled the heavy glass door open for him. Officer Johns also helped us many mornings, offering a friendly greeting as we arrived for our work. On this tragic day, this kindness extended to a stranger was returned with violence when the visitor pulled a gun from beneath his coat and shot Officer Johns. In our basement meeting room, we hunkered down under tables in terror. The shooter, an avowed anti-Semite, white supremacist, and Holocaust denier, murdered Officer Johns in a rage-filled spasm of hate. Intending to strike fear into visitors, the gunman instead inspired defiance as visiting crowds grew significantly when the museum reopened two days later.

A note on the text: I use the terms *football* and *soccer* interchangeably here. *Soccer* is actually British in origin, a nineteenth-century slang term for "association football," shortened like *rugger* from rugby football. The terms *Holocaust* and *Shoah* (Hebrew for "calamity" or "catastrophe") are also equivalent, offering the reader a reminder of the distinctly (but not exclusively) Jewish focus of the Nazi genocide.

INTRODUCTION

"Everything I know surely about morality and the obligations of man,
I owe to football."—Albert Camus, onetime goalkeeper for Algerian
club Oran and 1957 Nobel laureate in literature[1]

A tattered postcard, a cherished family heirloom, held the faded signa-
tures of all of the winning members of the Karlsruhe FV soccer team,
which won the 1912 regional championship of southern Germany. Five
figures emerge from the front photo, looking dapper in their overcoats,
full suits, and fedoras. One man carries a cane, ornamental no doubt, as
he was an athlete in the prime of his life when the photo was taken. In
the center of the photo is Gottfried Fuchs, the tallest of the five men,
scorer of two goals in the 1912 final. To his left is his best friend and
fellow striker for Karlsruhe, Julius Hirsch, who netted four goals in the
team's 7–2 victory.

The postcard, sent by Julius Hirsch, had returned from oblivion,
hidden away in some attic or closet until nearly a century later, when
descendants of Hirsch found the treasure. At the time, the love-struck
Hirsch took extra care to address the postcard to his girlfriend's em-
ployer and not to her parents' home.

Both Gottfried Fuchs and Julius Hirsch were assimilated Jews, not
unlike many other Germans who discovered their passion for the game
of soccer in the waning days of imperial Germany. Fuchs became a
national footballing hero who catapulted into the limelight when he
scored ten goals in a 16–0 win against Russia in the 1912 Stockholm
Olympics. Julius Hirsch debuted with the German national team at age

eighteen in a match against Hungary and on the eve of World War I. Hirsch found his own fame as the first German player to score four goals in a single match, a feat he accomplished earlier in a thrilling 5–5 draw against the Netherlands. Fuchs and Hirsch were the first Jewish players ever to represent the German national team. There has not been a Jewish player since.

But Julius Hirsch suffered tremendously under the anti-Jewish measures of the new Nazi dictatorship in the 1930s, and he gradually slipped into an irredeemable decline. Fuchs would be exiled in the Nazi years, escaping eventually to Canada in 1937. Hirsch would not be so fortunate. A suicide attempt in late 1938 led to an extended disappearance from his family and two stints at a psychiatric hospital in France, totaling a year. The Nazis finally caught up with Julius Hirsch. Many years later, his daughter, Esther, remembered vividly the day of his deportation:

> On March 1, 1943, I accompanied my father, Julius Hirsch, to the central railway station in Karlsruhe, from where he was deported just in a normal railway carriage. It was one of the most horrible moments in my life.
>
> It was a bright, sunny day. Still today I cannot understand how the sun could shine on a day like that. We didn't believe that we would never see him again. My mother, my brother, and I woke up, all at the same time, in the middle of the night. We slept all together in the same room. We thought: "Something has happened."
>
> My father didn't believe that the Germans would harm him, as he had fought for Germany in the Great War and was on the German national football team. . . . It [deportation to forced labor] was such an indignity for him.[2]

The final days of Julius Hirsch were hastened with his expulsion to the Nazi empire's colonial east, to the extermination camp of Auschwitz-Birkenau. On the way, Hirsch managed to send Esther a short postcard in honor of her fifteenth birthday. Postmarked March 3, 1943, the last sign of life from Julius Hirsch must have been mailed while he was in transit. The inscription on the front of the note was brief and simple: "My dears, I'm fine and arrived safely. I'll come to Upper Silesia, still in Germany. Greetings and kisses, Juller."

Though no record exists of his arrival, Julius Hirsch likely met his end in Birkenau at the hands of his fellow German citizens, some of whom were undoubtedly the children of adoring fans from just a generation earlier. By the time Esther read her birthday card, "Juller" had been dead for about four days. Decades later, the German footballing community had entirely forgotten about Jewish players like Fuchs and Hirsch until a unique sort of postwar reckoning brought on by the awarding of the 2006 World Cup to Germany raised uncomfortable questions.

Early in twentieth-century Europe, soccer became a mass sensation and an instrument of international politics. The story of *Soccer under the Swastika* begins with the birth of the game in Germany and the emergence of powerhouse domestic teams in the southern and industrial western regions of the country. In the 1930s, soccer epitomized the struggles between political forces that swept the world into another world war. With the ascension of the Nazis to power in Germany, the Deutscher Fußball-Bund (DFB), the national football association, became forever tarnished by its association with fascism. Germany, the cultured nation of Goethe and Bach located in the heart of Europe, plunged into a fascist-led madness, the effects of which reverberate to this day.

The 1936 Berlin Olympic Games, the "birth" of the politicized spectacle of international sport, became the single greatest sporting feat of the Nazi regime, upon which Hitler lavished treasure and the attention of his propagandists. As the world turned a blind eye to Nazi persecution, the dictatorship secured badly needed prestige and legitimacy. Propaganda and sport came together like never before.

When the swastika flew alongside the Olympic flag, representing the best and brightest of amateur sport, Mussolini's fascists embraced football passionately, and the Italians' reward was the reflected glory of two World Cup championships won two years on either side of the "Nazi Olympics." In the dishonest decade of the 1930s, Europe's dictators made their "discovery" of propaganda and Germany shocked the world. In 1937, the BreslauElf, the best team Germany had ever fielded to date in international competition, thrashed Denmark 8–0 and went undefeated in eleven matches, winning ten of them. Strengthened with players from the dominant Schalke 04 football club, the BreslauElf would not sustain their brilliance and quickly faded in the politics of

Nazi expansion. For the better part of the decade, Austria's brilliant Wunderteam ruled the game, led by probably the best player of his generation, Matthias Sindelar, the genius footballer celebrated by Vienna's fabled coffeehouse society.

Soccer remained an irresistible force when the Nazis turned to conquering Europe. In Germany, the game was curiously played in the *Konzentrationslager*, the KZ—the German concentration camps established all over the Third Reich from the very founding of the dictatorship. In one bizarre turn of fate, players who were once loyal teammates on club side Hamburg SV found themselves on either side of the concentration camp fence, one as an SS guard and the other a camp inmate, facing each other down as bitter adversaries.

When war came to Poland, labor camps and killing centers were quickly established and soccer emerged in the killing fields of the colonial east. Soccer was played on the expansive grounds of infamous sites such as Auschwitz-Birkenau and the remote labor camp called Gross-Rosen. One makeshift soccer pitch at Birkenau, used by privileged prisoners granted a reprieve from death, was in sight of the loading ramp where thousands made their final walk to the gas chambers. But of all the matches that were played at the extermination center at Auschwitz, the most unfathomable featured a team of SS guards versus the *Sonderkommando*—the "special work detail" of prisoners who manned the gas chambers and crematory ovens—in the courtyard of Auschwitz crematorium II. The worst of the Nazi labor camps featured soccer as well: the Mauthausen camp situated at the foot of the Alps, in the idyllic countryside of Austria. Prisoners avoided deadly work in Mauthausen's quarries through the privilege of sport. The seemingly irresistible urge to play brought the game to many other labor camps across Germany and the eastern provinces.

The prize jewel in the Nazi empire, Ukraine, shared in this mania for football. Initially, Ukraine responded fiercely to Nazi invasion, but their humiliation was made complete on the battlefield by the overwhelming force of blitzkrieg warfare, and resistance took another form. Football in the capital of occupied Ukraine, Kiev, was led by a charismatic and brave goalkeeper named Nikolai Trusevich, who brought back a sense of dignity and a bright glimmer of self-determination in an otherwise brutal occupation.

Fabled football matches from this time of war and occupation continue to captivate. Contests pitting the occupied against the invaders, in which Ukraine's best footballers—erstwhile soldiers in the war against fascism and men who also featured for the excellent prewar Dynamo Kiev side—were matched up against a select side from the Nazi Luftwaffe. A fascinating blend of legend and valiant resistance came together in a final contest now known to history as the "Match of Death." The brutal aftermath of these matches involved imprisonment, torture, and for some, the ultimate penalty, death. Legend long held that all of the Ukrainian players were murdered at the infamous mass killing site at Babi Yar, a deep ravine located just outside of Kiev where tens of thousands were murdered. But the truth of the destinies of these heroic players has proven even more fascinating.

In Western Europe, nowhere was interest in football more fanatical and enthusiastic than in occupied Holland. While Poland and Ukraine suffered tremendously, the Netherlands relaxed under a largely peaceful occupation. Life often went on as if nothing had changed. Domestic football boomed in Holland and even in the transit camp at Westerbork, the oft-temporary point of departure for thousands sent to the East. While the deportations rolled on, so did the ball.

Soccer under the Swastika tells of the most unique ghetto-camp in all of Europe, where Jewish culture thrived and sport took on a prominent place in the daily lives of the imprisoned. One of the first nations to be subjugated under Nazi rule was Czechoslovakia, and in this country of deep German heritage and rich Slavic history, the passion for soccer drew thousands to watch league football in a ghetto called Theresienstadt (Terezín in Czech). Soccer in the ghetto was an inspiration to player and spectator alike. Prisoners dubbed their top league Liga Terezín, and thousands played wherever they found open spaces and courtyards behind ghetto walls. Residents of Terezín took to soccer with such fervor that their Nazi masters exploited the game by featuring it prominently in a notorious propaganda film created to hide Nazi crimes from the world. That Terezín was the antechamber to Auschwitz made such deceptions all the more diabolical.

The Second World War was the most lethal and costly war in human history, yet untold millions would die not only in battle but also as the result of murderous political policies of totalitarianism writ large. The rapid victories of the Wehrmacht, the German army, over all of its neighbors were swiftly followed by the arrest, deportation, and imprisonment of hundreds of thousands of additional prisoners. War and conquest delivered millions into German hands—Poles, Jews, their fellow Western Europeans.

In Eastern Europe, the Nazis set into practice their theories of racial superiority, collecting civilians and prisoners of war en masse for shipment to labor and detention camps. Laborers, even those at Auschwitz, had a chance to survive. Nazi victims would succumb to a death that was not possible without the war. The years between 1941 and 1942 were particularly lethal to those captive to the Third Reich, where mobile killing squads completed their murderous work by bullet and carbon monoxide gas, administered by the diesel engines of mobile vans brought to execution sites. Jews from every nation in Eastern Europe were shot on the edges of ditches and open pits.

The suffering and killing in the Nazi east was personal. Soldiers and police auxiliaries looked down the barrel of a gun at their victims, often while others held the person in place for the killing shot. Guards manned watchtowers as those below endured disease and starved to death. People were rounded up, placed on trains, and delivered to the gas chambers, often in a rush of angry commands and terror. Individuals were stripped of their belongings, separated from their loved ones, and sent to their wicked fates. This mass murder by bullets foreshadowed the industrial killing of the gas chambers.

Before it all ended, more than 95 percent of the Jews who would be killed between 1939 and 1945 lived outside Germany's prewar borders.[3] Hitler's war of territorial expansion, to create *lebensraum* (living space) for empire-minded Germany, was paired with a crusade of racial purification that consumed the European continent. War and genocide eventually brought about the destruction of a people and a civilization that had lived in and flourished across Europe for centuries.

The cataclysm of war left a continent in ruins, and individuals were forced to reassemble their lives as best they could. The final stories of *Soccer under the Swastika* follow what happened after the liberation of the camps and the collapse of the Nazi empire. The surviving remnant of Jews took up residence in one of the few places left accepting of their presence—refugee camps in Germany, on land where survivors said, "Jewish blood stained the soil." Called "displaced persons" camps, they were home to enthusiastic soccer players and fans who refused to bow to death and the supposed impossibility of rebuilding one's life. In these places of rebirth, we also find reconciliation and remembrance. Less than a decade after the war ended, Germany rose from the ashes and an entire generation of Germans would point to *Das Wunder von Bern* (at the 1954 World Cup) as the moment when the nation would reclaim a small measure of dignity and a step out of the shadow of a very dark but recent past.

This introduction closes with a look at three extraordinary lives, each representing a key element of football during the Holocaust: the perpetrator, the occupied, and the Jewish victim. The first of the three biographical sketches examines the life of Schalke 04 midfielder Fritz Szepan.

Born the son of Polish immigrants in the industrial Ruhr region of western Germany, Szepan was a gifted footballer from his earliest days. Slow of foot but possessing an elegant, technically gifted style and intelligence, the commanding center-half captained both his Schalke 04 club team and the German national team in the 1934 and 1938 World Cup tournaments. Schalke 04 dominated domestic football during the Nazi era, winning six national championships by playing a one-touch style dubbed the *Schalker Kreisel* ("the spinning top") that mesmerized opponents. The hardworking coal miners of the Ruhr adored Schalke. In turn, the Hitler dictatorship latched onto the successes of clubs like Schalke 04 as shining examples of the new Germany.

While all of Germany's national team players were honorary members of the NSDAP (Nazi Party), Fritz Szepan joined voluntarily in May 1937, on the same day as his brother-in-law and Schalke 04 teammate, striker Ernst Kuzorra. Szepan later benefited from the Nazis' criminal policy of "Aryanization" when he bought an undervalued textile business forcibly removed from its Jewish owners. And in the lead up to the sham elections held in neighboring Austria in spring 1938, Szepan found himself entwined with aggressive Nazi propaganda seeking to unite the two German-speaking nations. Though it is unlikely he wrote these words himself, this footballing hero of proletariat miners of Gelsenkirchen, his home city, endorsed the annexation of Austria into Hitler's greater Reich by declaring, "The enthusiasm of the football fans in the stadiums of the Third Reich are a testimony of the health and strength of our race. An eternal thanks to the leader of all Germans who secured the future in the arena of sports and games. An enthusiastic 'yes' to our Führer Adolf Hitler!"[4] The Jewish owners of the business Fritz Szepan bought were later deported to the ghetto in Riga, Latvia. Stripped of their livelihood, Sally Meyer and Julie Lichtmann were soon thereafter likely murdered by an *Einsatzgruppen* unit, one of the mobile death squads that roamed throughout Eastern Europe in the aftermath of the swift and decisive German military victories. Footballers like Fritz Szepan, who early on drew the favor of the Nazi Party, generally thrived in Germany until the fortunes of war brought the nation to ruin.

Other footballers found themselves caught in seemingly impossible circumstances when war engulfed Europe. Poland's most controversial player, Ernst Willimowski, a striker who once scored four goals in a 6–5 loss to Brazil in the 1938 World Cup, fled Nazi occupation of his country quickly. Hailing from Upper Silesia in southern Poland, Willimowski claimed German citizenship, going on to wear the white shirt of the German national side, then adorned with the swastika.

Then a pariah to the country for whom he scored 112 goals in 86 club matches, Willimowski opportunistically seized the chance to resume his career and, by joining a police unit, also avoided the military draft. While Poles and Jews were dying by the tens of thousands, the red-haired Willimowski was scoring goals for his club side 1860 Munich, including the first goal in the 1942 Tschammer-Pokal, the newly created German cup. He also scored twice on his debut for the German national team in 1941, going on to tally thirteen goals in only eight matches. But the prolific Willimowski was more than a rank opportunist. When his mother was deported to Auschwitz in 1944 for consorting with a Russian Jew, he used his connections to free her.

Such ambiguities reveal the fluid nature of national identity in these times. The supremely gifted striker was a living contradiction; Willimowski identified as an ethnic German but rejected National Socialism. Yet he was still despised in Poland. Willimowski survived the war but would never return home, living out his days in Germany, his adopted country, which would one day forget that he even played for the national side. German identity saved the life of Ernst Willimowski. But Jews in Nazi Germany and the rest of Europe had to be even more resourceful to survive the coming onslaught. One Dutch Jewish footballer proved to be particularly resilient and extraordinarily lucky.

The door on the cattle car carrying Meijer Stad and his fellow salt miners slid open, and bright sunshine poured into the dark carriage that had carried the men two hours away from their work camp. Beautiful countryside with rolling pasturelands unfolded before the men had their eyes adjusted to the light. The prisoners expected to be unloaded at their next and latest destination, Buchenwald concentration camp, in southeastern Germany. Instead, the peaceful scene was shattered by machine gun fire. Meijer Stad jumped from the train in panicked terror, feeling a burning pain before blacking out.[5]

The bodies of the executed were taken to Buchenwald for incineration, but nurses charged with the disposal of the dead were shocked to find Stad still alive. He had taken ten bullets in the arms, legs, and torso. One bullet had glanced off of his head. Swapping his wounded body for a corpse from the camp, a French prisoner, trained as a doctor, removed the bullets with a penknife and nurses treated his wounds with leftover rags.[6]

The road that led the Dutch Resistance figure to this moment was a long and winding one. Meijer Stad grew up in the Jewish Quarter of Rotterdam. In his youth, he learned that he was a decent footballer but an even more exceptional runner. He made his debut for top-division soccer club Xerxes in The Hague shortly after the German invasion in 1940. At the same time, Stad had joined the Celebes track club, which recruited heavily from members of the Dutch Resistance.[7] Refusing to wear the yellow star, Meijer Stad also took the name of his Christian stepfather, Bouwens, to evade capture as a Jew. In 1942, Stad went on to become the Dutch 3,000-meter champion, running against largely German competitors in Amsterdam's Olympic Stadium. In the resistance, Meijer Stad smuggled contraband, hid refugees (including, by his telling, the grandnephews of Albert Einstein), helped kill Dutch collaborators, and, on one occasion, with a friend drowned a pair of drunken German soldiers in a canal.

"Bouwens" laid low for four years until the spring of 1944, when he was denounced by a jilted lover. Interrogated and beaten, Meijer Stad was shipped off to the Vught internment camp, where he again used sport to stay alive, joining a camp soccer team there. Before liberation day, Stad passed through the camps at Westerbork, Bergen-Belsen, and eventually Buchenwald, where he was finally freed. Meijer Stad's astonishing story of survival includes one more intriguing footnote. After the

war, Stad became a successful advertising man in Holland. At a conference in 1974, Stad met up with an Argentine wine dealer looking to
place a highly gifted youth player with a Dutch club. This was the era of
Total Football, and the world adored the way the Dutch played the
game. Stad called upon his wide-ranging connections with the best
football clubs in the Netherlands. But FC Dan Haag, Sparta, Feyenoord, and even Ajax all turned him down cold. It was the mistake of a
lifetime. The young Argentine phenom was Diego Maradona.[8]

For these three prominent and talented footballers, survival links
their stories. Yet one might ask, why tell the story of soccer during the
Holocaust? Admittedly, the study of this history is unyieldingly grim.
The Holocaust was genocide on a scale never seen before—modern
technology and bureaucratic efficiency driven by primitive impulses. It
deserves our attention not as a remote or distant reality but as a means
for understanding ourselves. For it was ordinary people who were situated at the center of this catastrophe. They are not an unknowable
"other" removed by seventy years of time. Tragically, genocide continues to haunt the human story.

Soccer in the Nazi era reflected shared joys and ancient hatreds. Yet
stories such as these rarely find their way into most historical accounts
of the time. They are often deemed inconsequential. For almost every
concentration camp in the Nazi system, these hidden stories of soccer
as a pleasure pursuit, a means of survival, and a method of resistance
appear in victim testimonies. Sepia-toned photographs call out from
this past, showing inmates in tattered clothes chasing a football around
a dusty assembly square. Many of these records, diaries, and memoirs
have been forgotten or obscured by time as they languished in archives.
This work recalls the voices of the victims and those who knew them,
offering authenticated scenes of the most harrowing sites of torture and
murder the world has ever seen. *Soccer under the Swastika* casts a
penetrating light over the darkness that is the Holocaust by celebrating
the survivors who played the beautiful game.

The sheer numbers of victims lost to the Holocaust numb our sen-
sibilities. Worse yet, the incomprehensibility of these losses blunts our
sense of the individuality of each victim.[9] Amid the profound deprivation, suffering, and deaths of so many during the war, soccer shined as a
humanitarian response to brutality. This work is a call to remember,
especially, characters like Meijer Stad and Julius Hirsch, who would

have faded into oblivion if not for the recent efforts of the German footballing community devoted to honoring Hirsch's memory.

As modern-day world football struggles to combat racism and anti-Semitism in the terraces, the endurance of the human spirit embodied in the soccer players during this time offers insight for those committed to breaking down racial, ethnic, and religious barriers in the sport today. With the diminishing loss of firsthand memories of these events, time is of the essence in telling these stories of survival and resistance. This is the largely untold story of soccer in the most desperate of living situations, as Nazi genocide raged unrestrained.

I

SOCCER UNDER THE SWASTIKA

"In soccer, ritual sublimation of war, eleven men in shorts are the sword of the neighborhood, the city, or the nation. These warriors without weapons or armor exorcise the demons of the crowd and reaffirm its faith: in each confrontation between two sides, old hatreds and old loves passed from father to son enter into combat."— Uruguayan novelist and football historian Eduardo Galeano, from *Soccer in Sun and Shadow* [1]

Fritz Walter emerged from the back of a transport truck in the early winter of 1945 disoriented and confused after a long journey to an as-yet-unknown destination. He had surrendered along with an estimated forty thousand other German soldiers to the Red Army in the dying days of World War II. Walter had been one of the Red Fighter Pilots, a German Luftwaffe unit led by war hero, ace pilot, and Nazi propaganda darling Major Hermann Graf. As he jumped down from the transport truck, he overheard someone say they had arrived in Maramureş, Romania, in the Carpathian Mountains near the border with Ukraine. As a stopover on the way to their ultimate destination of a Siberian gulag, the Maramureş transport center was a welcome rest. By now, word had traveled to the Eastern Front that transport to any Soviet prisoner camp was a likely death sentence.

Filled with fear, Fritz Walter spent his time at the transport center waiting and watching as a few of the station guards organized impromptu soccer matches against the prisoners. One day, as Walter stood on the makeshift touchline in Maramureş, the ball rolled out of play. Passing it back in his heavy, ragged army boots, he was invited to join in; almost immediately his talent showed. As the teams paused for a half-time break, one of the Hungarian guards came over to Walter and whispered quietly, "I know you." Walter, unsure what would come next, froze in anticipation. He didn't want to draw the ire of the Soviet guards. Too many prisoners had been given "special treatment" as retribution for the millions of Soviet soldiers killed by Nazi Germany in the early days of the war—he'd heard stories of what that meant, especially for German POWs. But his tension ebbed when the guard quickly added, "Hungary v. Germany in Budapest, 1942. . . . *You* won 5–3." For on May 3, 1942, Walter had scored three sensational goals in a comeback win against Hungary that obviously had left an impression on at least one crucial admirer that day. The day after being recognized by the guard, Fritz Walter's name was removed from the transport list headed to Siberia, while the vast majority of those who continued on the journey would never return home to Germany.

Soccer had kept Fritz Walter alive. This son of a truck driver from Kaiserslautern said after the war that while he'd been a famous footballer, it hadn't mattered to him where a player was from or which country he fought for: "What do I care that the inside right is from Hungary? We're footballers and nothing else."[2] But the Nazi power elite did care about such things; before the war was over, football in Nazi Germany would inspire, corrupt, and serve both as an act of torture and as active resistance. The story of soccer in these times of war and genocide begins, however, with a brief look back at the Great War, which set into motion the events that led to the rise of the Nazi state.

As a defining event of the twentieth century, World War I set the stage for a number of major political and cultural upheavals that would reverberate into the decades that followed. Athletes from nearly every sport joined their nations' armies. Famously, football played in the trenches and behind the lines had relieved the tension of awaiting the next enemy charge and lightened the monotony of military life. Sport was already a mass phenomenon across Europe before the war, and when soldiers finally laid down their arms with the November 1918 Armistice, war-weary nations embraced football fervently, and German soldiers brought the game home in their rucksacks.[3]

As it did elsewhere in Europe, soccer boomed in Germany. Player registrations with the Deutscher Fußball-Bund (DFB), the German football association, spiked fivefold in just a few years, and overflow crowds filled stadia around the country. The clubs of western and southern Germany advanced most rapidly, playing in a cosmopolitan style that really meant the more sophisticated Scottish passing game imported by the many British coaches recruited to Germany. One unlikely club rose from Germany's rapidly growing industrial center. Known to supporters as their beloved *Die Knappen*—a term taken from the ancient German word for "miners"—Schalke 04's passionate and humble fan base would witness the club rise from the lowest ranks of German league football to challenge the established order and become the most dominant club of its era.

The national team would have to wait years until a coach was appointed, and fan support for the national side was weak, at best. The DFB remained a conservative organization with an entrenched ruling structure that did not adapt well to the explosion of interest in soccer in the interwar period. At the heart of the conservativism of the national football association was an adherence to the *Dolchstoss* legend, the "stab in the back" myth that held that Germany's defeat in World War I was the consequence of weak politicians and agitators back home who prevented the German military machine from winning the war. Communists were blamed by most, as the seeds of discontent and Bolshevist revolution were in the air all across Europe by the end of the war. This insidious myth found its way into the National Socialist political platform in the ensuing years. Despite having overcome the chaotic conditions of the now crumbled Wilhelmian monarchy, football in Germany remained laden with the political agendas of its elite, and soon these agendas would align with the increasingly dominant Nazi revolution.

THE DILEMMA OF THE DFB

Germany endured a de facto ban from international matches as the victors of World War I refused to play them. England even moved to expel Germany from FIFA (the Fédération Internationale de Football Association, the new governing body for world football) in 1920, and the only matches the German FA could drum up were against wartime allies, Austria, Hungary, and Finland, and the ever-neutral Switzerland. Consequently, the growth of the German national team foundered for nearly a decade while the domestic game flourished. Amateurism also factored into the isolation of Germany on the international stage, and because Hungary, France, and Austria certified payment for players, the DFB remained on the outside looking in at the world's game. In the chaotic years of the Weimar Republic, the future of German football ended up in the unlikely hands of three men who were rather different from each other, but who also shared a common vision of building a competitive German national team.

The isolation would soon change with the appointment of the first national team coach on July 1, 1926, against the wishes of the executive board of the DFB (and without official approval). The lone voice of dissent was a young DFB official installed as its association president in 1925, who rejected the dire assertion that the selection of a national team coach would be the first of many irrevocable steps down the slippery slope to professionalism. This young German FA official was Felix Linnemann, a onetime police inspector who valued discipline and order but who could also be a genial and calm character subject to fits of rage. Linnemann became a key progressive voice in the conservative and provincial DFB. The man chosen by Linnemann to be the very first national team coach was Otto Nerz. Nerz came from a working-class background and had made his way in the world, earning a degree and scaling the social ladder through industriousness and strength of will. Nerz was a physical education teacher who travelled to England as a young man to absorb the English style of play and surprisingly became the subject of a short newsreel feature: "German professor learns English football." A novelty to the gathered reporters who filmed their interview with Nerz in 1923, one can see the enthusiastic young trainer performing calisthenics barefoot as a guest of West Ham Football Club in London.

Otto Nerz was also a father figure to the third man integral to the creation of the national team, a young player named Joseph Herberger who was poor like Nerz and equally driven. Of the three men, Herberger was the much better player, and he showed his quality when he scored twice on his debut for the German national side in a 1921 friendly versus Finland. What the others lacked in understanding of human nature and of what motivated players, Herberger possessed in abundance. While Herberger was blessed with "street smarts," Otto Nerz was the embodiment of what one might expect of a German coach in this era: a cold, domineering figure, possessing a stern countenance, with close-cropped hair and steel-rimmed glasses.

As the head trainer, Nerz instilled in his team a grim determination. He demanded well-conditioned and disciplined players, and he showed a gift for strategy. But this coaching philosophy was met with resistance at first as regional and club loyalties among the players were much stronger. In the end, Nerz's rigid, calculated approach quickly proved successful in the first meaningful test for the squad. Germany won its opening match in the 1928 Olympics in Amsterdam against Switzerland, 4–0, a convincing win that featured a hat trick by Richard Hofmann, the future DSC Dresden star. Hofmann was likely the most naturally gifted player in German history (not named Beckenbauer), tallying twenty-four goals in twenty-five matches with the national team. Under the guidance of Linnemann, Nerz, and Herberger, momentum-building victories over Italy and Sweden in 1929 further burnished Germany's reputation as an emerging football nation.

As Europe descended into the Great Depression and political instability increased across the continent, totalitarianism rose to fill the void left by democracies unable to cope with the forceful, often violent demands of nationalist uprisings. With the German economy in total collapse and the government seemingly incapable of responding, the National Socialist Party, an obscure right-wing political party from Bavaria, brought an unprecedented politicization of all cultural life to Germany.

The Nazis eventually brought the full weight of their ultranationalist political ideology to bear on nearly every element of life in Germany. The dictatorship saw fit to intervene widely in society, to dominate the fields of education and medicine, art and music, and film and sport. Though no single country can be considered responsible for politicizing sport, two major sporting competitions from the 1930s stand out as the apex achievements of fascism for mobilizing ideology in sport: the 1934 World Cup hosted by Italy and the 1936 Berlin Olympic Games. The expansionist aims of both dictatorships challenged the feel-good, pacifist cosmopolitanism of both international events. As one astute observer would note many years later,

> International football came of age at precisely the moment that mass ultra-nationalist politics was at its height in Europe and Latin Ameri-

ca. More finely attuned to the manipulation of popular taste, more ready and able to intervene in mass culture than the bumbling empires of *fin de siècle* Europe, the new dictators and populists of the 1920s and 1930s took a close and active interest in the game and there was no one to stop them.[4]

Germany was a sporting pariah for most of the 1920s, but as the country was gradually welcomed back into full international status, a sporting transformation quickly followed suit. British and German club sides increased the frequency of competition against each other, setting the stage for full international matches as the tumultuous decade of the 1930s began. As the sense of isolationism cooled and British relations with Germany improved during the late 1920s, the time finally arrived for the first international match featuring England and Germany. England had lifted a decade-long ban against playing their old wartime foe. On May 10, 1930, in Berlin, the first match saw England effectively go down to ten men after twenty minutes following a particularly brutal collision between English teammates (the injured player, Billy Marsden, suffered a broken cervical vertebra, but he would not leave the match until halftime; Marsden would never play competitive soccer again). Initially, the teams traded goals, but after England took a 2–1 lead to the halftime interval, the Germans responded by netting two goals to take the lead.

All three German goals were scored by the inimitable Richard Hofmann, the first foreign player ever to tally a hat trick against England. England mounted a furious rally. With only seven minutes to play, short-handed England clawed back to level the score. Finishing with a 3–3 draw and earning the respect of the game's presumed "masters," the DFB and soccer-loving Germany would point to this match as the start of something important. A few weeks after the match, the first-ever World Cup was hosted and won by the tiny South American nation of Uruguay, setting into motion a quadrennial global footballing phenomenon.

Despite Germany's progress on the pitch, only one team in Europe was the equal of Uruguay in 1930. Austria had long played a cultured style of football built on a diverse ethos that celebrated the skilled and technically brilliant game played on the streets of the Danubian capitals of Vienna and Budapest. Players from these unassuming origins shined for the Austrian national team. Dubbed *Das Wunderteam* for their dominant victories over Europe's established elite, the Viennese eschewed strength and physically imposing play for an artistic, beautiful, and graceful style. These skillful players, who learned their football as schoolboys in the rough-and-tumble streets of Vienna's immigrant neighborhoods, took great pride in beating opponents with flair and joyful excitement. Such was Austria's dominance in 1931 that they easily dispatched the inexperienced Germans in two convincing shutout wins, 6–0 and 5–0. But the teams of the Danubian School also enjoyed a distinct advantage: they were all paid to play for their club teams. Amid the long-standing rivalries between the German-speaking countries of central Europe, the contentious issue of professionalism became the central dispute in Germany as FA officials debated how to respond as the DFB surveyed the ruins of the national team.

In the interwar years, the amateur ethos had long dominated the European game, and among the nations playing as professionals, there was a striking difference in ability. The DFB operated within principled theories of amateurism, which were very popular among Germany's educated upper class, many of whom had held the reins of the DFB since its inception.

Complicating matters further, DFB profits were kept in reserve (some say hoarded) rather than reinvested in the game, causing yet another rift between players, club managers, and national sport officials. But Germany, which had the highest number of registered players and clubs on the continent, remained ambivalent toward the "pay-to-play" scheme in football. Across the seven regional federations of the DFB, none were as tenacious in enforcing a rigid amateurism as the Westdeutschland Spielverein (WSV). With some unfortunate member clubs banned outright for competing against visiting professional clubs from outside their borders, the rising club Schalke 04 would soon run afoul of the powerful lords of the game in western Germany. A crisis loomed.

THE PEOPLE'S CLUB OR NAZI DARLINGS? SCHALKE 04 ASCENDANT

In the western part of Germany, football captivated the Ruhr region and especially the small coal mining town of Gelsenkirchen, an unimpressive part of a collection of cities between Dortmund and Duisburg. The manufacturing heart of the nation, the Ruhr was largely forgotten until the Industrial Revolution, when its new coal mines revealed their wealth to the fabricators of steel. Workers poured into the region, and mass migration from Poland, Silesia (then on the outskirts of the Austro-Hungarian Empire), and East Prussia filled the factories, mines, and housing settlements that quickly popped up.

Settling into small, crowded housing estates, these immigrants, many of Polish origin, rallied around the community-based football clubs like Schalke 04. Strong rivalries followed—to this day, these old allegiances remain for club teams separated usually by no more than twenty miles. Club players of the Ruhr were usually born in this industrial region, spoke the local dialect, and represented local passions. Schalke 04, representing Gelsenkirchen, eventually became famous across the country because it served as a successful substitute for a weak national side in 1930.[5] Schalke was also a projection of meaning beyond sport; labor movements in Germany had been largely destroyed by the time the National Socialists consolidated their power in the mid-1930s. Schalke 04, the workers' club, came to represent a lost identity, amid the "metropolitanization" of the game in the prewar years. Just two years after promotion to the top regional division, Schalke 04 christened a twenty-eight-thousand-seat stadium. Soon thereafter, the club dominated German football.

In Germany, schoolboys from the middle class and educated, often well-heeled gentlemen had bred the game originally as an amateur pursuit. But the pure amateurism of this era was soon swamped by a clandestine professionalism that reached a crisis point on August 25, 1930, when the DFB cracked down on the underhanded payment schemes and devious accounting practices practiced by business interests in support of their local clubs. As the economy fell while football grew in the years prior, unemployed players sought out teams that feigned amateurism, like Schalke 04. The club hardest hit by the DFB cleanup was indeed Schalke 04, which saw its entire first team effectively banned—fourteen players altogether—and the club was prevented from playing in DFB-sanctioned tournaments for a year. But little changed after the verdict. A year later, Schalke returned to the national championship league. Public support for Schalke remained unwavering, reaching a dizzying high when a crowd of seventy thousand showed up to their first game after reinstatement, a friendly against Fortuna Düsseldorf.

Behind the scenes, as the WSV was moving toward legalizing professionalism, the Nazis moved to take over German football, and with that all hopes of modernizing German football were extinguished. With blinding speed, Adolf Hitler and his Nazi Party crushed any lingering democratic impulses in the country, and German football found itself unable—and unwilling, as it turns out—to resist this force.

RISE OF THE NAZIS

Before it claimed the reins of the German government in January 1933, about 1.4 million people had already joined the NSDAP (Nationalsozialistische Deutsche Arbeiterpartei, the National Socialist German Workers' Party). Yet, in this nation of sixty million people, the National Socialists never commanded widespread majority support. NSDAP rallies were held in every corner of the country and were especially attractive to young middle-class men fostering an ideal image of masculinity and a social order built on strength and heroism. The rallies were high theater, encouraging a type of national grandeur with deeply meaningful symbols. Often these mass demonstrations of athletic performance were also sporting rituals, choreographed to accentuate the human body. These impressive spectacles of sport pageantry celebrating "Nordic" aesthetics and National Socialism's commitment to racial purity featured often in many sporting events during the Third Reich.

Physical education became a requisite in training the collective German body, especially in the eventual Hitler Youth. Hitler was fascinated with shaping the *Volkskörper*—the collective health of the German body—which he considered under threat by the Jew and the physically "inferior." The beautiful Aryan body also became the visual embodiment of Nazi propaganda. Physical strength and athletic achievement would equal political power. The horrific extension of these ideals eventually came through the exercise of war and genocide. The Holocaust began with cleansing the *Volkskörper* from within Germany; the physically and mentally disabled were targeted along with the psychiatrically impaired.

The pseudoscience of social Darwinism also reigned in the United States and Great Britain, where it was interpreted as the survival of the fittest individual, whereas in Germany it was seen as survival of the fittest race. These racial hygiene theories also claimed inferior races would corrupt the ability of the "people's sport" (soccer) to offer a remedy to this "disease." Particularly insidious was the influence of these ideas on German sporting officials. DFB officials, saturated with these racial policies since the organization's founding at the turn of the century, also viewed the *Volkskörper* as diseased and particularly vulnerable to the predations of professionals and their commercialization of the sport. Nazi officials further worried such a sporting culture encouraged passive consumption of the sport by the masses, further weakening physical fitness. Under such thinking, national soccer teams found that persistently losing would suggest a racial weakness. Therefore, sport would offer an ideal battleground to test these ideas: prevail on the football pitch as a nation, and it would demonstrate the superiority of one's "race."

Radical change became the answer to years of economic crisis and instability in Germany after 1929. Worries of a communist takeover of Germany helped fuel the rise of the Nazis. In July 1932, Hitler's National Socialist Party won 37 percent of the vote in parliamentary elections, setting the stage for a takeover of power once Hitler was appointed chancellor on January 30, 1933. With the help of conservatives, other nationalists, and powerful business interests, the Nazi Party kept the German left from power by forming a coalition government and calling for snap elections. In early March 1933, when the results were announced, the Nazis had vanquished the Social Democratic and Communist parties with 43.9 percent of the vote and nearly 45 percent of the seats in the Reichstag, Germany's parliament. The final piece for Hitler's seizure of absolute power was the "Enabling Act," passed in late March 1933, which gave him emergency powers he never relinquished. With a sweeping ferocity, the Nazis soon purged their coalition of all dissenting voices, monopolizing power and solidifying connections to essential grassroots organizations under the direction of a centralized propaganda apparatus.

The intensity of this political persecution continues to astound; almost simultaneous to the Nazi's consolidation of power, the concentration camp of Dachau outside of Munich (the first of its kind) opened on

March 20, 1933. Dachau was quickly readied to receive political prisoners within three weeks of the elections, holding the Nazi's enemies in what was called, euphemistically, "protective custody." Shockingly, the near complete capitulation of the pillars of German society to the regime would follow; churches, schools, and the law would all lie down before the menacing totalitarianism of Hitler's Nazi movement. Sport would also take its place in service to this dictatorship obsessed with expansionist totalitarian power.

Sporting organizations in Germany closely cooperated with multiple levels of government as the *Gleichschaltung* (or "forced coordination") marched on across all levels of Germany society. This process of "Nazification" was an extension of Nazi Party doctrine that originated in the late 1920s. It called for the synchronization of essential areas of life and leisure, including sport, under the supervision of trusted party officials. This coordination meant that football clubs from the amateur level all the way up to the national side would be placed under the direct influence of the NSDAP.

Sport would be but one of the paths by which Adolf Hitler and his government of criminals could break free from cultural isolation in Europe. Only the failing fortunes of war kept the Nazis from fully taking over the major European sports movements, especially the governing organization of world football, FIFA, which offered no significant opposition to the Nazis in the years prior to the outbreak of war.

NAZI SPORT: FOOTBALL UNDER THE FÜHRER

"German sport has only one task: to strengthen the character of the German people, imbuing it with the fighting spirit and steadfast camaraderie necessary in the struggle for its existence."—Joseph Goebbels, minister of propaganda, April 23, 1933[6]

The isolationism of much of Europe in the 1930s gave much greater importance to international matches than ever existed before. The rise of the propaganda age brought politics to sport and linked countries together, through radio, print, and film, that otherwise would have been sheltered from each other. Thousands poured into the major cities of Europe looking for work, and they brought with them a love for soccer. The mass appeal of sport was also well suited to a political era in which peak physical fitness was embraced as a natural virtue and a pathway to national greatness on the battlefield. Though initially suspicious of soccer immediately after the Great War, the Nazis and the Italian fascists soon accepted the game on its own merits, and by 1934 soccer was well established through increasingly popular domestic and international competitions across Germany and Italy.

Though the intervention of the state in German sport existed well before the arrival of the Nazis on the political scene, it was the National Socialists who capitalized most on the chaos in society at the time. After much debate in 1933 among the Nazi hierarchy in the immediate aftermath of their seizure of power, a new sport structure was agreed upon, modeled on Mussolini's fascist structure, which would soon raise Italy to the pinnacle of world football.[7]

At the helm of the new German sport hierarchy was Hans von Tschammer und Osten, a Nazi loyalist and an SA-*Obergruppenführer* (a top-ranking "Brownshirt"), who was named *Reichssportkommissar* in April 1933, a title that would be changed a few weeks later to *Reichssportführer*. In rapid succession, Tschammer gained control of nearly every area of sporting life in Germany as part of the "coordination" of previously democratically elected sports federations. Conspicuous in this takeover was the DFB, which, on July 9, 1933, formally submitted to the forced coordination policy. The DFB enjoyed a sizeable membership from across the political spectrum and employed strong regional structures that were seamlessly incorporated into the new political configuration demanded by the Nazi leadership.

Accordingly, German football was divided into sixteen *Gaue*, with one more region when Austria was added after the *Anschluss* in March 1938. *Gau* is an older German term first used in medieval times to mark a political boundary, usually a province or region. The Nazis loved these old German words as they hearkened back to a "pure" Germanic heritage steeped in tradition and nationalism. Along with the new league structure imposed by the Nazis (collectively called the *Gauligen*), the German Cup was introduced in 1935 and, unsurprisingly, named after the *Reichssportführer*. The Tschammer-Pokal (cup) was first awarded to 1.FC Nuremberg, and Schalke 04 was the first club to win "the double"—league and cup champions—in 1937; Austrian powerhouse Rapid Wien won it immediately after the *Anschluss* in 1938. This cup competition continued until the waning days of the war. It would not be until a decade after the war that the competition would resume. In 1953, the DFB-Pokal returned to the German game, shedding its Nazified name.

Sitting at the center of Nazi control of sport was Tschammer, who was also head of the sport office of the Kraft durch Freude ("Strength through Joy," abbreviated KdF), the massive state-operated leisure organization. Tschammer und Osten also served as chairman of the German Olympic committee, a powerful post ahead of the 1936 Olympic Games in Berlin.[8] The link between the state and sport strengthened further. The KdF was also part of the larger German Labour Front (*Deutsche Arbeitsfront*), the national German labor organization that took direction from Hitler's inner circle, most notably from Interior Minister Wilhelm Frick, who would one day face justice as a war criminal at the postwar Nuremberg Trials. The KdF directed the building of sports fields and the hiring of coaches to the extent that by 1940, eight million people played and competed under its direction.[9] Later, increasing numbers of players were lost to military service, and clubs could no longer field teams. Filling the gap, military-based clubs would soon pummel more established but weakened private football clubs.

When it came to competition on the football pitch, the *Reichssportführer* moved quickly to impose his vision. Early in 1933, Tschammer called for Nazi representatives to travel with teams on international assignment and to manage athletes and the national image while abroad. The Nazi Foreign Ministry also got involved in German international football by requiring the national anthem to be played at every foreign match, under the red swastika flag. Submission to the "new order" saw the Hitler salute made compulsory for players before international matches and the expulsion of Marxists and Jews from the national association. Such demands were meant to build racial and patriotic unity under the Nazi banner while acclimating foreign audiences to the spirit and symbols of the Nazi government, not yet sure of itself on the international stage.[10]

Mobilized to radically change German society, the Nazis engaged in a charm offensive in the first three years of their rule leading up to the 1936 Berlin Olympics. Less than three months after the Nazis seized power, on March 19, 1933, Germany played its first full international football match against France. Held in Berlin, amid calls for a boycott back home and fears of violence and harassment, the French team disembarked upon their arrival in Germany's capital to the sounds of an orchestra. At the football grounds, rather than inflicting beatings on political enemies, SA thugs were occupied with collecting alms for the poor. Before the kickoff, the French squad received a warm ovation from the fifty-five thousand gathered spectators. While the football entertained and the teams fought to a 3–3 draw, including a French comeback from a 3–1 deficit in the final ten minutes, the crowd was well behaved and enthusiastic in their support for both teams.

Reporters on hand for Nazi Germany's first international match against the French remarked that the home crowd took to listening politely to "La Marseillaise" before kickoff, a response unlikely to be repeated among French supporters in Paris upon hearing "Deutschland über Alles" now that the belligerent Hitler regime was in power. The Nazis even had help from the president of the French FA and the creator of the brand-new World Cup competition, Jules Rimet. So impressed was Rimet with his hosts that at a postmatch banquet, he promised to calm tensions back in France and to speak positively on behalf of Nazi Germany.[11]

Behind the political posturing, though, the Nazi regime moved quickly to implement the "racial cleansing" of the nation. June 2, 1933, is the date most historians cite as the moment when the persecution of Jews and so-called enemies of the state began in German sport. Following the pronouncement that day by Education and Culture Minister Bernhard Rust (an *AltKämpfer* or "old fighter" who joined the NSDAP in 1922), all Jews and Marxist athletes were purged from their clubs and national organizations. But the truth is even more sinister. Football clubs across Germany acted well in advance of this decree: FV Karlsruhe, FC Nürnberg, and Eintracht Frankfurt enthusiastically purged their memberships of players and supporters with a Jewish heritage or leftist political leanings well before June 2. The myth that carried forward in this authoritarian era was that "no one had a choice." Club histories continue to reflect this perspective. But, in reality, the Nazification of German clubs often advanced with no direct intervention by the state. Seeking favor in the new political reality, these purges often began five to ten weeks before Rust's decree as a measure of opportunism.

But some clubs were not caught up in the National Socialist madness. Legendary German club Bayern Munich did not voluntary expel their Jewish members; Bayern club president Kurt Landauer (a Jew who was later sent to Dachau and lived in exile in Geneva after his release) resigned against the will of the club. That a Jew would be the president of a Bavarian club was astounding, as Munich was the birthplace of the Nazi movement in the early 1920s. And to this day, the club 1860 Munich is seen as a working-class team, while their wealthy neighbors across town, Bayern, are viewed as upper class and bourgeois. In a bizarre twist of fate, the April 19, 1933, edition of *kicker* magazine (founded by DFB father and soccer-mad gentleman of Jewish descent Walter Bensemann) featured the official announcement by the DFB declaring that "members of the Jewish race, and persons who have turned out to be followers of the Marxist movement, are deemed unacceptable."[12]

With the Italian dictatorship as a successful model of "sports as politics," the Nazi regime watched the second World Cup tournament with keen interest as the upcoming hosts of the 1936 Olympics. Italy hosted the 1934 World Cup, and ahead of the competition, Italian dictator Benito Mussolini made no effort to mask his intentions of using the increasingly popular sporting event as a platform for his particular brand of fascism:

> You athletes of all Italy have particular duties. You must be tenacious, chivalrous, and daring. Remember that when you take part in contests beyond our borders, there is then entrusted to your muscles, and above all your spirit, the honour and prestige if the national sport. You must hence make use of all your energy and all your willpower in order to obtain primacy in all struggles on the earth, on the sea, and in the sky.[13]

Some nations, such as Britain and the Scandinavian countries, attempted to resist the increasing political influence of sport. After an overhyped and intensely politicized match against Italy in 1933, England's first-ever on the peninsula, the consequences of playing a nation whose political and sporting aims were deeply enmeshed were glaringly obvious. Britain's reluctance came to the forefront. The four teams representing the United Kingdom, despite an offer by their Italian hosts to pay their expenses, steadfastly refused to participate in the 1934 World Cup. Other nations also declined the invitation to play. Most prominent among them was defending world champion Uruguay, unable to travel to Italy because of the financial devastation of the global depression. Argentina also refused to compete in protest of the defection (i.e., recruitment) of a handful of their best players to the Italian team.

Back in Germany, international competitions like the World Cup were rejected by Nazi officials as an unacceptable ideological compromise to those nations elevating peace and internationalism. A few years earlier, the DFB had rejected the chance to host the 1930 World Cup and initially declined to take part in the larger dispute across Europe about competing against teams comprising professionals. But not all shared this view: Sepp Herberger and many other more progressively minded coaches and officials saw such positions as outdated. In the end, compromise won out and Germany participated in the 1934 World Cup, the first time the team played at a major competition as a representative of the new Nazi regime.

For a time, National Socialism became an irresistible force in the development of German football, but Nazi interest in the national team waned as winning results proved impossible to guarantee to a regime accustomed to controlling everything. A surprise third-place finish at this World Cup would only strengthen the dictatorship, and though it would be a few more years before state propaganda would become a driving force in the German game, the Nazis' vision of athletic competition meant that football in Germany could no longer enjoy any meaningful independence. In the twisted Nazi mindset, sport would make the nation fit, morale would be boosted, and victories on the field of competition would enhance the prestige of the German nation, a nation gradually building toward conquest of its neighbors.

As the Nazis' reach extended deeper and deeper into society, the national game felt the effects. Clearly, Germany was making striking progress on the football pitch, but after an opening-round 2–0 loss to Norway, with Adolf Hitler in attendance, the German FA would soon lose autonomy. The loss, which eliminated the host nation from the 1936 Olympic soccer tournament, meant that the DFB would also forfeit any meaningful influence over the national game in the ensuing years. With almost immediate effect, the Hitlerjugend (Hitler Youth) under the direction of Reichsjugendführer Baldur von Schirach would take over youth academy football (players between the ages of ten and sixteen) from the clubs at the behest of Reichssportführer Tschammer und Osten. Thereafter, for all practical purposes, the DFB ceased to exist; in 1940, the national football association was formally dissolved. But before the world would plunge into yet another world war, German supporters of *Die Nationalmannschaft* would witness one of the great teams in German history, the first to be managed by legendary German trainer Joseph "Sepp" Herberger, playing a style of football made famous by their archenemy, Great Britain.

THE BRESLAUELF

With all of the political maneuvering in sport in the mid-1930s, the game of soccer was also maturing. Tactical sophistication started to produce positive results on the field. One of the great tactical innovations of interwar European football was the WM formation (3–2–2–3; defensive positions listed first), built for the counterattack when the game was played more directly, through the center of the pitch. The WM was the brainchild of Herbert Chapman, the first modern manager and trainer of Arsenal FC in England. The WM formation allowed lightning-quick wingers, whose pace and crossing ability were essential, to be positioned slightly forward and released quickly on the break to exploit the space left behind the attacking team. As other teams struggled to cope with the innovation, Arsenal won five first-division titles and two FA cups during the 1930s.

On the continent, a few German club teams soon picked up on the WM, and when these players put on the national shirt of Nazi Germany, the results were impressive. When Germany faced off against Denmark on May 19, 1937, in Breslau (now Wrocław, Poland), the team would become among the most celebrated in German history. Longtime manager Otto Nerz had been removed as head coach shortly after the failure of the Berlin Olympics, though he stayed on as an assistant to help Herberger, his former understudy who became the *Reichstrainer*. Together, these men assembled a team that soon gained the admiration of Europe's established footballing elite. Loaded with players from rising German clubs Schalke 04, Bayern Munich, and other western Bavarian club teams, the Breslau XI (the BreslauElf, or Breslau Eleven) embraced the WM formation already in use across Europe. Herberger would remain the national team trainer for twenty-seven years, bringing the team from anonymity to the pinnacle of the game as first-time world champions in the postwar years. But it was Otto Nerz who would be credited with bringing this group of players together, many of whom played on the squad that beat Austria in the third-place match at the 1934 World Cup. Nerz, a stern tactician with a fascination with the English style of play—long balls and hard tackling—accepted the more fluid and entertaining style favored by Herberger, which he believed would bring Germany glory on the football field as its government intimidated the continent.

By now the team, manager, and federation officials were used to wearing the eagle-and-swastika badge on uniform and tracksuit. In the match against the Danes, contested at Breslau's Hermann-Göring-Sportfeld, Germany played with such verve, creativity, and technical brilliance that the normally solid Denmark squad had few answers for the combination play of the Germans. Germany utterly dismantled the Danes 8–0, with five goals in the first thirty minutes. Among the most memorable of the goals on the day was a fifty-five-yard pass delivered to the feet of Schalke 04 left winger Adolf Urban. Seeing center forward Otto Siffling breaking toward goal, Urban effortlessly passed to the forward, who slotted the ball home. The goal took all of a few seconds. Siffling, slight of build and imaginative in his play, preferred to run into space rather than play as a target man. His selfless work was rewarded when he scored the fourth of his five goals on the day, a brilliant build-up play started by the German defense. The eighth and final goal was a fine tally by team captain Fritz Szepan. Szepan was now the undisputed leader of a team of technically gifted German players, the best in the country's history. In Sepp Herberger's new configuration, Szepan moved out of the back where he played as a center half and into the inside forward position, capitalizing on his attacking skills.

With twelve minutes still remaining and the Danes visibly demoralized, the Germans began to toy with their guests. Such arrogance prompted the perfectionist Herberger to step to the touchline and deliver a severe but deserved reprimand. Spectators on hand reported that the score would have been much worse if not for the acrobatic play of Danish keeper Svend Jensen. Poorly prepared and fighting unseasonably hot conditions on the day, Denmark's loss remains the worst in their history.

Undefeated, the German team won ten of eleven matches in 1937. On paper, the BreslauElf would be invincible with the addition of the Austrians as Hitler moved to "reunite" Germany with his home country of Austria. But as the contemporary football writer Uli Hesse described it many years later, the *Anschluss* proved to be an own goal in Germany's quest to dominate European football.[14]

HITLER ON THE MARCH AND THE 1938 WORLD CUP

As the supposedly unified Reich team of Germans and Austrians stumbled into the 1938 World Cup hosted by France, a rising and confident Swiss team, their first-round matchup in Paris, was waiting. Tensions ran high as memories of the most recent match between the two teams a year earlier induced fan hostility that bordered on open revolt. Any goodwill was long forgotten well before the match. Traveling supporters were pelted with rotten fruit, and any fan carrying a flag with a swastika was targeted. The boisterous French crowd jeered the Hitler salute at kickoff and rained down abuse, glass bottles, and assorted rotten groceries throughout the match.

By this time, it was clear that DFB officials and head trainer Herberger were taking instructions in team selection from a higher authority. Herberger forced his squad of players from the BreslauElf and the Austrian Wunderteam to play together, and team spirit was strikingly absent. Any cohesion was spent on long-held animosities between the players. Yet the Nazi newspaper *Völkischer Beobachter*, the widely read daily paper of the party, declared ahead of the competition, "Sixty million Germans will play in Paris!" But the national side faltered under the pressure of expectations and after a 1–1 draw in the opening match against the Swiss; the replay five days later saw the Germans crash out of the World Cup 4–2. The Swiss newspaper *Zurich Sport* defiantly countered: "So 60 million Germans were playing. We only needed 11 footballers." *Die Nationalmannschaft* would lose again to Switzerland three years later, this time on Hitler's birthday, a national holiday in the Reich. Both losses to the Swiss confirmed the doubts the Nazi regime harbored about their ability to control football as an instrument of foreign policy.

The persecution at home in 1938 gained momentum. The autumn of that year would witness the most dire restrictions placed on Jewish citizens in Germany since the Nazi takeover five years earlier. Emboldened by foreign policy victories abroad, the regime moved against the civil rights and property of Jews. Up until this point, the government had promoted boycotts of Jewish businesses and fomented waves of anti-Jewish violence from the earliest moments of seizing power. The Nuremburg Laws of September 1935 further deprived Jews of citizenship rights, and just two days after the terror of the *Kristallnacht* ("The Night of Broken Glass") pogrom of November 9 and 10, 1938, Jews in Germany were ordered to liquidate their property to "Aryan" owners. This "Aryanization Decree," issued by Reichsmarschall Hermann Göring, required all shops, factories, homes, and valuable property to be sold in order to transfer ownership to Aryan hands. This government-sanctioned looting saw millions of dollars of assets sold at a massive loss. As we will learn later, Aryanization and domestic football in Germany shared an uneasy relationship.

Despite their failure in the World Cup, Germany rebounded by playing weaker footballing nations as the game's elite shunned the increasingly threatening Nazi regime. The quality of the BreslauElf reasserted itself in 1939 as Germany dominated Poland, Romania, and Belgium by identical 4–1 score lines in the uncertain months before World War II. In these matches, head coach Sepp Herberger would discover two brilliant young talents. The first was the supremely gifted player from Kaiserslautern, Fritz Walter. The other great discovery was a young Helmut Schön from the club DSC Dresden, a player who scored in each of these victories. Schön came from a cultured, aristocratic background and would go on to score sixteen goals in seventeen games before the war. That Schön idolized the Austrian great Matthias Sindelar showed that not every player harbored hostility to the once-adversarial players of Hitler's newly constituted national team. Sindelar, the sublimely gifted Austrian striker, represented the best of the technically gifted players, those who learned the Viennese style on the streets. The story of Matthias Sindelar mirrors the fall of Austria into the Nazi maelstrom in the ensuing years.

Herberger went on to manage the national side to a revenge win over Norway, 4–0, a resounding response to their shock defeat in the 1936 Olympics. A few weeks before the Norway match, Herberger inspired his boys to a narrow 3–2 loss in Florence to two-time defending world champion Italy. The win over Norway came on June 22, 1939, and exactly one year later France capitulated to the Germans at Compiègne, in the same railcar used for the 1918 armistice. As the world awaited Nazi Germany's next move, desperately hoping to avoid another war in Europe, the football continued with the start of new seasons all across the continent. Players and spectators alike could not foresee the catastrophe to come as August turned to the first day of September in the late summer of 1939.

FOOTBALL IN WARTIME

Europe was growing restless when the August 27, 1939, match featuring Hungary and Poland kicked off in Warsaw. Dubbed "The Last Match," it saw Poland run out as historic winners, securing a 4–2 victory over the "Mighty Magyars" after conceding the first two goals. The relatively unknown Polish striker Ernst Willimowski scored a hat trick on that day. Willimowski's story is as complex as the wartime occupation of Poland. An ethnic German who starred for the Polish national team, he later switched sides to play for Germany. The fate of Poland under German domination is intertwined with the fate of Willimowski. Exactly one month after this momentous match, with the city of Warsaw aflame and bombed out, the German army occupied Poland's capital. League football disappeared in Poland until 1947.

After September 1, 1939, the fires of war raged in Europe. Within days of the declaration of war, football across Germany came to a sudden halt. Immediately, national team trainer Sepp Herberger lost nine of his players to conscription, and many other players starring in the top domestic league soon joined the war effort. Neighboring Poland was the first country to fall, subdued in just three weeks by Blitzkrieg warfare, despite a courageous effort to push back the Nazi invaders. Only years later would the world learn that Hitler and Stalin had made a secret deal before the war. Called the Molotov-Ribbentrop Pact, the agreement ensured Poland's demise by partition between the Soviet Union and Nazi Germany. German foreign minister Joachim von Ribbentrop negotiated the deal, and from the earliest days of the war, the Reich envisioned football as an instrument of foreign policy. The Nazi regime sought to enhance its stature internationally by sending German football teams abroad and by hosting foreign teams in Germany. By October 1939, the Poles had been thoroughly defeated and completely occupied by Soviet and Germans forces. After a pause in active combat, and with Western Europe in Hitler's sights, football continued into the new year of 1940.

With the drumbeats of war ever increasing, Nazi politicians and propagandists worked tirelessly to unite sport with Nazi ideology. Both seized upon the feeling of *Kampfgeist*, the "spirit of the struggle," to claim a link between the football now being played at the international level and the impending march of German armies across Europe. Elevating the soldier as the nation's greatest role model was not unique to the Nazis. But the idea became deeply embedded in the German consciousness as years of rhetoric about the martial values of strength, bravery, and collective discipline came together in a single word to describe the new style of play in German football: *Kampf*.

It has been said that the playing style of a nation reflects the culture and consciousness of that nation. In contemporary terms, the Brazilians play the Samba-infused *jogo bonito*; Spain mesmerizes its opponents with the ball possession dominance of *tiki taka*; the Dutch are celebrated for their *total voetbal*; and the organized and defensive style of the Italians is often called the *catenaccio* (the "door bolt," invented, interestingly, by an Austrian coach in the 1930s), though it seems rather incompatible with conventional notions of Italian "joie de vivre," the carefree, upbeat, and decidedly anti-German style of life.

Before the Nazis, German football was not so easy to classify. It was respected as skillful but also thought much too slow and ponderous. But soon, industriousness and self-sacrifice to a hard, disciplined style became the preferred approach. As was their habit, the Nazis would confiscate all sorts of words for their "movement"; *Kampf* would now enhance the national football team with an aggressive and masculine élan. Strikingly, there was seamlessness to the new footballing philosophy and the Nazi view of the world where *Kampf* meant a tough, tireless battle for existence, a life-and-death struggle for the physical (and spiritual elevation) of the German *Volk*. The cult of the soldier, the glorified embodiment of *Kampf*, now became infused into the athletic mindset in the Nazi conquest of German football culture.

So indelible was this idea in the Nazi German psyche that the legendary Sepp Herberger frequently exhorted his players with impassioned calls to embrace *Kampf*. In a loss to Sweden in 1941, when the fortunes of war still favored Nazi Germany, Herberger exclaimed, "The forwards are too soft. No *Kampfer*! Against Sweden one can only win with strength and *Kampf*, speed and hardness."[15]

For the German national team, between 1939 and late 1942, the DFB tested this Nazified playing style by scheduling just over thirty international matches against teams allied or existing as satellite states to Nazi Germany. Nations such as Italy, Hungary, Romania, and Bulgaria featured regularly. The Italians also played on throughout the war, and despite the eventual Allied invasion of the peninsula in 1943, Serie A games continued. Neutral nations also offered themselves as opponents; Spain, Sweden, and the ever-reliable Swiss played the Nazi team. Interestingly, Sweden, as a neutral, agreed to play Germany during the escalating war but stood stoically, arms at their sides, as prematch introductions proceeded.

Domestic soccer continued in the Reich, primarily to keep up a sense of routine in times of great sacrifice. Players recalled that while there was no direct pressure to win international matches, the constant worry was that to play poorly meant being dropped. Any future call-up would then be jeopardized, and players would have to report back to their assignment or military unit. The worst-case scenario meant being sent to the front. If that meant to the Eastern Front, fighting against the Soviets, it meant a more likely death, especially in late 1942 and early 1943 when the war turned against Nazi Germany.

The Nazi war of conquest marched on in spring 1940 with the invasions of the Scandinavian countries. Norway held out for two months, but Denmark surrendered almost immediately. Because of this quick capitulation, the Danes managed to retain some autonomy through the nominal control of the government and security forces. In Denmark, as the football continued on, the Danes also fought a clandestine war against their Nazi occupiers, one that culminated in one of the largest collective acts of resistance ever achieved during the war. Denmark, with a coordinated effort that stands as a rare and shining example of humanitarianism, rescued over 7,200 Jews (over 90 percent of all the Jews living in Denmark at the time) by fishing boats, kayaks, and rowboats and sent them to Sweden. The rescue was completed on Rosh

Hashanah, the Jewish New Year, over two days on October 1 and 2, 1943.

The political and sporting situation in Norway was different but equally intriguing. After their defeat, a puppet government was installed with Norwegian fascist leader Vidkun Quisling taking over with an absolutist rule. Norway resisted the occupation and the football dictatorship that followed. After being forced to answer to a *sportführer*, the opposition and resistance was immediate. Across the country, Norway's athletes created a nationwide strike of all sports, spectators abandoned the grandstands, and players and coaches refused to compete. One semifinal match in the Norwegian cup in 1942 had just twenty-seven spectators.[16] Those who did play were allied to collaborationist governmental officials, but clandestine matches did spring up in the countryside, emblematic of the larger resistance. Across Europe, it is safe to say that the more an individual country offered resistance, especially through partisan activity and guerilla warfare, the less likely it was that the football continued.

By late June 1940, Belgium, Holland, and France fell to the Germans, the British endured a forced evacuation back across the English Channel, and the Soviets absorbed the Baltic states of Lithuania, Latvia, and Estonia along with part of Finland. Independent football would not return to the Baltics until after the fall of communism. After launching the war and swiftly conquering the Low Countries and France in 1940, the Third Reich moved to create a new order in international sport in these occupied lands. While some sporting federations readily submitted to Nazi demands, FIFA attempted to resist. FIFA president Jules Rimet, along with the French presidents of international ice hockey and swimming federations, directly opposed Nazi sports policy as directed by Reichssportführer Hans von Tschammer und Osten, but in the end, their opposition was inconsequential. As the war intensified, efforts to create a thoroughly Nazified international sports system faded away. After the occupation of France and the rest of Western Europe, FIFA was run by a lone individual, a German general secretary loyal to Nazi interests and headquartered in Zürich. FIFA would reclaim its independence in July 1946 when Rimet was reinstalled as president and planning began for the 1950 World Cup tournament to be held in Brazil.

The blindingly fast defeat of France and Western Europe through the all-encompassing Blitzkrieg warfare took hold in the German sporting press, which could immediately call upon the offensive brilliance of the BreslauElf. Reporters took special interest in highlighting dramatic and high-scoring matches, deliberately linking the successes of the Wehrmacht on the battlefield to the footballing drama playing out in front of them. Nazi sporting officials were equally quick to seize upon this military glory in calling for a new tactical formation to replace the WM, now seen as English (which meant too defensive), pacifist, democratic, and the worst charge of all, "Jewish."

One former player with the power to force a Nazi-approved change was Karl Oberhuber, a Bavarian regional sport official with deep connections in the government. Oberhuber refined his skills of "persuasion" in the paramilitary SA, and he is more aptly described as an enforcer who joined the Nazi Party very early on and who embraced the fusing of sport and politics. Oberhuber was active in the vanguard of the movement, which meant he fomented violence, and before an amnesty that came with Hitler's takeover of the government, Oberhuber was briefly imprisoned.

In his position under the *Reichsportssführer*, Oberhuber demanded the national team adopt an aggressively attacking style that was common to teams from southern Germany (often featuring a five-striker front line). Such demands were in line with the larger ideology running throughout German society at the time, and were it not for the arcane infighting of the various offices within the wide-ranging Nazi bureaucracy, Oberhuber would have prevailed. But he was no match for the diplomatic skills and popularity of Sepp Herberger, who artfully resisted the Hitlerian regime (when he himself was an apolitical man solely devoted to keeping football going), which would have otherwise claimed yet another victory over the "beautiful game." History would soon forget the hysterical, militant demands of Oberhuber: he disappeared into oblivion after 1941, losing a power struggle within the party. After the war, Oberhuber could be seen pushing a milk vending cart near the partial ruins of the Frauenkirche in Munich; at the same time, Herberger reclaimed the helm of the German national team, where he would lead the team to the world championship less than ten years after the war ended.

Domestic football in Germany was seen as more essential to the morale of the nation and thus was encouraged to continue. The workers' club from Gelsenkirchen continued to dominate during the war years. The ascendancy of Schalke 04 over the domestic game provided both inspiration and foil to the Nazi regime. Winners of six of the eleven league championships during the dictatorship, Schalke 04 teams were shining examples of the new Germany, strengthened by the common worker. Never mind that Schalke 04 represented predominately left-leaning supporters; the Nazis would feature such popular players as Fritz Szepan and Ernst Kuzorra in propaganda newsreels and photo ops, with the führer himself congratulating Schalke's winning sides.

In wartime, the most memorable matches on the German domestic scene reflected the rise and eventual fall of the German military. As the Wehrmacht appeared to be unstoppable in Europe and poised to conquer England, Schalke 04 met DSC Dresden in the 1940 German club championship. Prewar Dresden, the "Florence on the Elbe," was a sophisticated city situated exactly between Paris and Moscow and now had a football club that reflected its cosmopolitan flair. Schalke 04 could not be more different. Representing Gelsenkirchen, a city built haphazardly to meet the massive influx of immigrants seeking work in the local mines, Schalke 04 reflected a hardworking, blue-collar mentality.

But the 1940 final failed to live up to the hype as Schalke ran out 1–0 winners in a rather boring game, according to onlookers. DSC Dresden found a measure of revenge in winning the Tschammer-Pokal that same year over 1.FC Nuremberg, and in the league, they won twenty of twenty-two matches.[17] Schön's Dresden club stopped short of making the rematch with Schalke 04, losing to Rapid Wien (Vienna) 2–1.

Rare color newsreel footage of the final match featuring Rapid Wien and Schalke 04 shows relaxed Nazi officials and German soldiers cheering under a bright summer sun at Berlin's Olympiastadion. Reichsportssführer Tschammer is seen celebrating each Schalke goal with enthusiasm. A few of the ninety-five thousand fans in attendance even fashioned hats made from daily newspapers to shield the sun. On the pitch, the dominance of Schalke continued as Rapid Wien quickly went down 2–0 in the first eight minutes. The score held until the sixtieth minute, when Schalke scored a third, this one coming after Rapid's celebrated striker Franz Binder had missed a penalty kick. But no one would've predicted what would follow. Rapid Vienna mounted a comeback that is unequaled in German footballing history. Two minutes after Schalke's third goal, Rapid scored their first and, in a burst of inspiration—and probably unbelievably good fortune—Franz Binder scored another three goals in a nine-minute span: two were brilliant free kicks taken outside of the penalty box, scored either side of the third goal, a penalty kick. Schalke responded, but it would be too late.

To this day, one can find Schalke 04 fans who cry foul over this result, citing conspiracy theories that the Nazi regime wanted an Austrian champion, a winner from the Ostmark. Some even claimed that the führer himself, the ever-proud Austrian, was in the stands that day, but the evidence doesn't support either of these claims. Rapid had cleared a ball off of the line late in the game, and Schalke hit the woodwork in the game's final moments. Reporters after the match once again made comparisons to the Blitzkrieg style of attacking football on display in Berlin. Shots on goal arrived at "lightning speed," and players battled in heroic fashion, enduring the "blood-soaked" events on the pitch.

There is also a significant footnote to this historic match: the date of the final was June 22, 1941, the same day Germany invaded the Soviet Union. Known to history as Operation Barbarossa, the maneuver saw four million soldiers under the German high command storm across the Soviet border, signaling the beginning of Hitler's war of annihilation, which would sweep up countless millions in death and destruction. As the Nazis waged war mercilessly on the Soviets, they also pursued ethnic cleansing throughout Eastern Europe. Mass killings of Jews and Russian POWs at gunpoint by mobile death squads called *Einsatzgruppen* foreshadowed the industrialized killing that would follow in Poland. One horrific scene in a ravine called Babi Yar outside of Kiev over two days in late September saw 33,771 lives extinguished by one of these squads. Yet, in these places of the greatest suffering and death, football continued to be played, improbably but irresistibly.

Soviet losses in the war were catastrophic: fifteen million died in military service accompanied by another six to seven million civilian deaths. Such sacrifice meant that any pursuit other than the defense of the homeland was seen as obscenely futile. But isolated matches would be played during the war, often following victories against the Nazis. In one pyrrhic celebration after the monumental victory at Stalingrad in

1942, a Red Army select eleven featured against a hastily reconstituted Dinamo Tbilisi club side. And the fabled "Match of Death" in then-occupied Kiev that same year between a patchwork Dynamo Kiev and players from the German Luftwaffe would come to take on mythic meaning for the Ukrainian nation for decades to follow.

In harmony with the Nazi goals of "race and space" (*lebensraum*, "living space" for Germany's imperial ambitions), 1942 started with the most notorious administrative action of the war. Leaders of the Third Reich's state security, labor, diplomatic, and economic offices met at a lakeside villa in Berlin to lay out their plans for the "Final Solution" to the so-called Jewish Question in all territories held by the Reich. The Wannsee Conference on January 20 set into motion the disastrous killing centers in Poland that ultimately murdered more than 3.5 million people. The year 1942 was also pivotal in the war. The defeat of the Wehrmacht on two fronts would spell the beginning of the end. Rommel's Afrika Korps met defeat in North Africa to British and American forces growing in strength, while the devastating and complete loss of the German Sixth Army at Stalingrad in the winter of 1942 signaled a momentous change in the fortunes of war.

On the international football stage, a 3–2 loss to Sweden in Berlin, on Hitler's birthday in 1942, infuriated Propaganda Minister Goebbels. The team was slipping in quality, team rosters were erratic, and training inconsistent. Simply, football was no longer a top priority. Emblematic of this inconsistency, the secretary of foreign affairs wrote of the match, "100,000 have left the stadium depressed; and because victory in this football match is closer to these people's hearts than the capture of a city in the East, such an event must be prohibited for the sake of the national mood."[18] By the late summer, qualifying games in the first round of the German Cup (the Tschammer-Pokal) were suspended, but league matches would continue until October. As the year drew to a close, Germany avenged a loss to Slovakia played just five days before the invasion of Poland. The win on November 22, 1942, included a hat trick by unheralded August Klingler, a player who featured only five times for the national side. Two players from this match would be killed in combat within weeks, including Klingler.

The single-mindedness with which Sepp Herberger prepared his teams during the war years was at once admirable and lamentable. As more and more players were pressed into service (while others, like

Helmut Schön, were booed on the pitch for evading combat), Herberger contrived ways to bring players back from the front: he invented military honors to bestow on his favored boys. Many Germans were shipped off to concentration camps for much less, but Herberger successfully invented reasons to award Iron Crosses to players on leave. One such player was Fritz Walter, still considered by many to be the best German footballer ever. Walter would go on to become one of the heroes of the "Miracle at Berne" when the reconstituted German national team improbably won its first World Cup in 1954. Described by those who knew him as intensely focused, hardworking, modest, and loyal, Walter was unrelenting in his dedication as a player.

Making his debut for the national side in spectacular fashion with a hat trick in a 9–3 thrashing of Romania in July 1940, Walter went on to play in twenty-four of twenty-five games during the war. He would see most of Europe, island hopping the Mediterranean and fighting through Bohemia and Romania as a soldier in the Wehrmacht and another eight countries as a footballer. Walter, in his memoirs, remembers Herberger saying to him after the Romania match, "You didn't disappoint me. You can come again."[19]

The burden of war became more and more evident in the lives of most Germans. Severe rationing meant teams were restricted in their travel, and many of the trains used domestically were requisitioned to meet the reprehensible aims of the Nazi regime: transporting Europe's Jews to ghettos and death camps in the East. Fewer and fewer young men were available to play, and in these tumultuous times, many even questioned the appropriateness of playing games when so many were dying. But as the dominant team of the era, one could look at the Schalke 04 roster and not know there was a war on. For Schalke, with only few exceptions, players were kept safe and made available for matches as requested. Schalke 04 went on to win their final championship in 1942 over another Austrian team, First Vienna.

The final German cup competition of the war was played at the close of 1942. Held on November 15, the Tschammer-Pokal was won on two late goals by 1860 Munich, with the winner scored by Ernst Willimowski. The 2–0 defeat of Schalke 04 was something of a miracle given their near-absolute dominance in that era. Schalke's star left winger Adolf Urban played his last game for the club that day. Within a week, "Ala" Urban was sent to fight in the east. Germans would learn in May 1943 of the player's death from a mortar attack at Staraya Russa (the same town, near Saint Petersburg, that held the summer residence of the Russian novelist Fyodor Dostoyevsky) on a BBC German-language broadcast; he was the only player from the BreslauElf to die in combat.

Internationals featuring the German national team came to an end in late 1942 at the direction of Goebbels. Domestic soccer continued as if nothing in the daily lives of the average citizen had changed. Severe rationing, restrictions of travel, and the steady catastrophic losses of life and property gave the crumbling Third Reich a sense of foreboding about the outcome of the war.

GÖTTERDÄMMERUNG: THE ENDGAME

With the war clearly turning against Nazi Germany, the desperation among the leadership increased. On February 18, 1943, Propaganda Minister Joseph Goebbels made his famous "Total War" speech from the Sportpalast in Berlin, in which he called on all Germans to give themselves completely to a war of survival against the Russians. At the same time, the announcement came that there would be no more international sporting competitions; matches against Hungary, Spain, Italy, and Sweden were all scrapped after devastating defeats on the Eastern Front.

In the east, the subjugated finally mustered the strength to fight back. In Poland, the long-persecuted Jews held captive in the starvation-inducing ghettos resisted. In April 1943, the Warsaw Ghetto uprisings began; a handful of fighters held out for nearly a month before they were brutally crushed by the German army. Back in Germany, the tens of thousands of foreign workers, POWs, and forced laborers who were kept in concentration camps throughout the country fought back using any means at their disposal. Often, fighting back meant simply surviving. Once again, soccer provided a pathway for redemption, and in a few profound cases survival. Stark differences existed between prisoner groups, whether they were held inside Germany or in the colonies: sport for the captive Poles, Slavs, and other eastern workers was expressly prohibited. But in Germany, the opportunities varied widely, and in almost every concentration camp within Germany's traditional borders, soccer was being played. Local sport would continue, as it was most closely linked to the general mood and morale of the country. Public demands also kept the national soccer championship going as well.

By the close of 1943, Reichssportführer Tschammer was dead of pneumonia and DSC Dresden claimed the domestic championship of a country on the brink of collapse. The football being played across the land was farcical. Scores were lopsided, substitutes could not be found for injured players, and even damaged footballs could not be replaced. By now, Allied bombers could target any city in the Reich without much resistance. Propaganda attempted to assure the people that the tide of war would soon turn to Germany's favor. But few truly believed this. Almost every German family was touched by the death of a soldier or family member as Germany was soon encircled by its enemies. The June 1944 landings at Normandy and the advances of the Soviet army pushing through the Baltics and Belarus all signaled the beginning of the end of the Third Reich. On July 23, 1944, a few weeks after the landings at Normandy, the first death camp, Majdanek in eastern Poland, was liberated by the Red Army. Just a few months later, the most notorious of Poland's killing centers was finally freed. On January 17, 1945, Auschwitz-Birkenau was evacuated by the Germans, and the forced death marches commenced back into Germany. The camp was liberated ten days later.

As the war dragged on and fewer healthy young men were available to fill the rosters of established clubs, especially in Germany, service-related clubs began to dominate. German championships took place in almost all sports until 1944. Football was no exception. In 1944, DSC Dresden and Air Force Hamburg (LSV, or Luftwaffe, Hamburg) contested the final national championship of the Nazi era in Berlin's Olympiastadion in front of a reported seventy-five thousand spectators, though other accounts reported many empty seats. The changing room used by the players before the match also doubled as an air-raid shelter. The massive, monolithic Olympic Stadium, with its forty-foot-tall limestone walls, was an important symbolic place in the crumbling Nazi empire. But it also made an inviting target for Allied bombers, who had so far avoided it.

DSC Dresden defended their championship from the previous season, with an aging but still effective Richard Hofmann leading the attack. Another of Schön's teammates, Herbert Pohl, patrolled the midfield but without his left arm, lost to a Russian bomb in 1943. Pohl was a visible reminder of the losses sustained by the average German as the war turned against his country. Dresden's opponent, LSV Hamburg, played as a military club and benefited—as both clubs did—from political influence to ensure conscripted players were stationed close by.

As the cities of Dresden and Hamburg met on the football pitch, the regime kept up appearances that the war would still be won, that nothing had changed. Thousands gathered on the day to watch, and hundreds of thousands more listened on the radio. LSV Hamburg was favored in the match, but DSC Dresden took a 1–0 lead into halftime on a disputed offside call. Hamburg conceded again just five minutes into the second half. Hamburg's defense wilted under relentless pressure, and ten minutes later, Helmut Schön dribbled brilliantly past the Hamburg defense to tap in the ball for Dresden's third goal. The red-and-black-clad players of DSC Dresden later put the game well out of reach 4–0, and after the match, the winners even took a moment to write a celebratory postcard to a teammate held in an American POW camp. This last meaningful match of the Third Reich would be linked to the postwar transformation of German soccer. Many others playing as soldier-athletes in this match and across Hitler's Germany would contribute significantly to the rebuilding effort by coaching and developing emerging youth talent and, in Schön's case, going on to manage West Germany to World Cup victory in 1974.

By the end of the war, as Germany lay in ruins and was occupied by Allied forces, sport had been but one of many elements in German cultural life to succumb to ideology. The effect of propaganda in joining the increasingly popular sport of soccer to Nazi ideology was decidedly mixed in its success. Match results at the international level did not always follow the dictates of the dictatorship. But one propaganda effort stands out as the best example of joining sport with Nazi ideology: the sport film.

Well known is the Nazi film *Olympia*, documenting the 1936 Berlin Olympics. But few know about the soccer propaganda film released in the summer of 1942, *Das Grosse Spiel*. Based on the epic match played on the day of the invasion of the Soviet Union, June 22, 1941, between Rapid Vienna and Schalke 04, *Das Grosse Spiel* is the fictionalized tale of Gloria 03, a local soccer squad from the fictional town of Wupperbrück in the Ruhr region. The footballers are hardworking miners, and the values of cohesion among family, team, and nation are repeated throughout the film. Nazi symbolism is kept to a minimum. Reichstrainer Sepp Herberger scripted the soccer scenes, making a cameo along with nineteen of his national team players. *Das Grosse Spiel* artfully blends the messages of cultural integration, shared team spirit, and *Volksgemeinschaft* (national community) into a soccer-rich narrative. Gloria 03, an obvious stand-in for Schalke 04, goes on to win the national club championship 3–2 over "FC Nord."

Soccer unifies in this tale. Heroic are the hardworking people of the Ruhr, on and off of the soccer field. One of the Gloria 03 players returns from injury, hobbling back onto the field to score the game winner. The Nazi propaganda ministry had worked out the formula to persuade and manipulate through more understated means. By the time the film was released, the horrors of Stalingrad had not yet been realized. But the killing machinery designed to implement the Holocaust was in full operation, and the insidious impact of propaganda in building support, or at least quiet and passive acceptance, for the war and the so-called Final Solution was firmly entrenched in German society. The story of the Nazi integration of propaganda and sport would begin more than a decade before the "victory" of Gloria 03 in *Das Grosse Spiel*.

2

WAR MINUS THE SHOOTING

"In the actual act of deception, among all the preparations, the horror in the voice, expression, gestures, amid the striking scenery, the belief in themselves overcomes them. It is this that speaks so miraculously and convincingly to the onlookers."—Friedrich Nietzsche, German philosopher and Nazi inspiration [1]

The 1930s in Europe were a decade of deception. The dictators—Hitler, Mussolini, and Franco—and their "discovery" of propaganda would forever change their societies. Football was the leading spectator sport in this era, becoming a national obsession in many European countries still struggling to rise from the devastations of the global economic depression. Attendance at domestic and international matches exploded despite this time of economic austerity. Weekends were given to watching and playing the game, and the emerging influence of radio and motion pictures would bring matches featuring the national team into the homes and workplaces of fans all across Western Europe.

The decade witnessed the rise of the important international match, almost always played in the capitals of European football—London, Rome, Paris, and Berlin. In both democratic and totalitarian states, football entertained and moved politics. But football penetrated the daily lives of citizens especially in the fascist states. No nation would match the success of the Italian regime in exploiting football, which started at the domestic level and reached a pinnacle with the national side. Known as the Azzurri, the Italian national squad reached dizzying heights in the first of the newly initiated World Cup competitions of the

1930s. Olympic competitions also became increasingly important to spectator and government alike. When the athletes arrived in Berlin in the summer of 1936 for the Olympic competitions, Nazi Germany was ready to maximize the political benefits of hosting the games.

Football also served as a measuring stick: a nation's place in the global pecking order could be enhanced by wins over the game's traditional powers. A win against the English, the "masters of the game," would secure prestige for a new government. In the years that immediately followed the rise of the dictators, football under fascism became indistinguishable from other affairs of state. Before war would overwhelm the continent yet again, the English and the Germans would meet on the football pitch one last time as neutrals and the politics of appeasement in May 1938 would come to dominate. Football on the eve of war became more than just a game.

SPORT AND NAZI IDEOLOGY: THE "DISCOVERY" OF PROPAGANDA

The widespread use of propaganda at the start of the twentieth century by all of the major Western powers shaped the popular understanding of the time. Adolf Hitler studied the tactics used by Germany's adversaries during the Great War. Learning most from British and American propaganda, he believed this new political advantage was a primary cause for Germany's defeat. Especially emblematic of the propaganda employed by the Allies was the atrocity story, the alleged cruelty performed by enemy soldiers on innocent civilians or captured soldiers.[2] Hitler viewed World War I as a war of persuasion. As he sat in a German prison cell in 1925 for trying to overthrow the government, the failed artist wrote his philosophical autobiography, *Mein Kampf*, a cynical, hate-filled treatise on how to manipulate the masses. As one of the most bought, least read books in Germany, Hitler's manifesto anticipated the primary role propaganda would later play in the Third Reich. In it, he boldly proclaims propaganda to be "a truly terrible weapon in the hands of an expert."[3]

Soon, Hitler would prove himself to be just such an expert. The Nazi use of mass persuasion is cemented in the popular imagination as destructive, cynical, and outright evil. The perils of propaganda in the

Nazi era—in gaining popular support in their drive for political power, by fostering support in establishing a dictatorial state, in providing the rationale and impetus for war, and in the creation of a climate of indifference to the persecution and mass murder of the Jews of Europe and other so-called undesirables—have remained with observers long after the Nazis passed from the world scene. The Nazi assumption of power in Germany in January 1933 and the political reality that followed became the fulfillment of Hitler's blueprint.

Print media would not compete with the fiery rhetoric emanating from Nazi podiums across the country in the late 1920s. Nazi propagandists, carefully trained in specially designed schools of persuasion, canvassed the country, fomenting discontent among the populace. These rallles, carefully staged and choreographed, employed music and fiery rhetoric, building to a crescendo at the end of each rally.

Even before their takeover of power, the National Socialists learned how to repeat the simplest ideas, thousands of times, to spread their political message. Nazi messaging sought to enforce conformity, stress unity, and emphasize the value of the collective over the individual. One of the more famous propaganda messages of the day was the slogan "Ein Volk, ein Reich, ein Führer" ("one people, one empire, one leader"). One of the most provocative sporting images from the Nazi period that illustrates this misperception are the thousands of spectators at the opening of the 1936 Berlin Olympics raising their arms in the Hitler salute.

Propaganda would also trumpet the economic improvements under the Nazis, which stood out in stark contrast to the economic pain, hyperinflation, and record unemployment of the Weimar Republic. Nazi propaganda was a progressively influential and dangerous weapon as the regime moved to stifle democratic freedoms and exercise control over perceived threats through the coercive and often violent actions of the police-state authority.

In the new Germany, the exercise of propaganda and terror were closely linked; the security apparatus loomed large over opponents as paramilitary thugs roughed up opponents at rallies and engaged in street battles with the paramilitary organizations of rival socialist and communist parties. Nazi propaganda was particularly notorious for employing cryptic euphemisms such as "protective custody" (the arrest of political prisoners), "police action" (e.g., the invasion of Poland on September 1, 1939), or "special treatment" (deportations and executions). Once the propaganda apparatus was firmly established, the Nazis turned their attention to sport. They had to look no further than to their new ally on the Italian Peninsula, Benito Mussolini, and his National Fascist Party for a highly effective model of how to impose ideology on the whole realm of society.

"A TRULY TERRIBLE WEAPON"

Inspired by Mussolini's fascist movement in the early 1920s, a political and cultural force that also lent itself to the corruption of sport, the National Socialists moved quickly to consolidate their power and bring all elements of German cultural life under the control of the regime. Enemies were quickly purged from almost every independent media source, resulting in the "Aryanization" of newspapers, businesses, and other media outlets. This forced coordination, better known by the term *Gleichschaltung*, meant that all elements of German society would be brought "in line" with Nazi policy and ideology.

All levels of sport, from youth programs to the highest international competitions, fell under Reich control. Nowhere was this more evident than in the newly created Ministry of Propaganda and Public Enlightenment. Headed by Joseph Goebbels, the ministry, with 1,300 staff at his disposal, worked in harmony with party ideologues to set the agenda for the nation.[4] The public face of Nazi messaging, Goebbels was fiercely loyal to Adolf Hitler and realized his greatest successes in organizing the electoral campaigns of 1930 and 1932, including the pioneering "Hitler over Germany" technique, a barnstorming-style tour of Germany in an airplane, a striking innovation for the day. Though the propaganda minister himself had little personal interest in athletics, it did not take him long to realize that sport, especially the popular obsession of football, could be used to his advantage.

Among the many tools at his disposal, Propaganda Minister Goebbels used radio as the primary means for carrying official propaganda. Many of the most important sporting contests of the day were broadcast by radio: football, boxing, and the 1936 Olympic Games held in Berlin. News emanating from the "wireless" was often seamlessly blended with entertainment programming featuring well-known celebrities and singers. One memorable propaganda poster of the era read, "All Germany hears their Führer with the people's receiver."[5]

With radio poised to give the Nazi dictatorship access to nearly every living room in Germany, Aryan ideals of struggle, superiority, and supremacy would now be opportunistically extended to sport. A warrior mindset, instilled in Germany's football program, had not yet produced results. The warrior sport most admired by Adolf Hitler and the Nazi elite was boxing, but it was football that had captured the public imagination. But football in the late Weimar years mirrored the malaise in the country at that time. Such an unrefined style was in stark contrast to the technical beauty of other continental players from Austria and Hungary, ascendant at the time. Football would have to wait.

THE TRIUMPH OF PROPAGANDA

Totalitarian propaganda found its greatest aesthetic power through the cinema, where the Nazi command could offer the most authentic-looking images and thereby most persuasively misrepresent lies as the truth.[6] The Nazis were particularly enthralled with the use of film as an aid to the complete restructuring of German society. Motion picture would later prove to be a visually stunning medium for capturing the athletic excellence of Olympic competitors as well. Goebbels mastered the burgeoning film industry in Germany, using motion pictures and newsreels to document party rallies, speeches, and other events.

The eager volunteers in Hitler's cultural redesign were numerous artists, writers, filmmakers, and musicians who all benefited from the patronage of the regime. And no singular artist from this era was more well known than filmmaker Leni Riefenstahl. Hitler saw in Riefenstahl a gifted filmmaker who could capture his vision of German beauty and the projection of political and military power. Once she was promised full creative license and an unlimited budget, Leni Riefenstahl set out to produce a documentary film that would forever link her with National Socialism.

The 1935 film, titled *Triumph des Willens* (*Triumph of the Will*), captured vividly the proceedings of the 1934 Nazi Party rally at Nuremberg, the spiritual home of the Nazis and the grandest stage for the pageantry for which the dictatorship became infamous. The film remains a remarkable cinematic achievement, one of the most acclaimed documentary films ever created and an exemplar of classic nationalistic triumphalism. The design of the rally grounds, notable for an elevated stage and grandstands done in a monumental classical form, was envisioned by Hitler's official architect, Dr. Albert Speer.

Scenes of Aryan beauty are woven throughout the film, embodied in handsome young men exercising vigorously and preparing to become soldiers for the German people, all under the watchful eye of Adolf Hitler, dressed in full military uniform.[7] Sport does not feature directly in the film, but early in the film we see training exercises meant to resemble gymnastics and track and field events. The most intriguing of these quasi-sporting events required a twenty-kilometer walk and the completion of a two-hundred-meter obstacle course, both attempted as these exemplars of Aryan strength and vitality carried a ten-kilogram military pack. Two other events featured in the film, the final events of a type of militaristic biathlon: recruits shooting from two positions— prone and standing—and the hurling of a batonlike club resembling a grenade already in use by the German military.

Triumph was a box office success, but of more immediate use was the propaganda tool provided to the National Socialists to promote Nazi policy domestically and on an increasingly unstable world stage in the years to come. In this new age of motion pictures, German audiences flocked to the theater, more often to be entertained than lectured. Because movie audiences were attuned to escapist entertainment, propaganda films often appeared too heavy-handed.[8] Consequently, films about sport and other cultural endeavors proved highly popular. The Nazis would seize the grandest sporting stage of all in these days, the Olympic Games, and Leni Reifenstahl was there to document it in her inimitable artistic style.

FOOTBALL AND FASCISM ALLIED

As forerunners to the fascists in Germany and Spain, the Italians "perfected authoritarian football."[9] After seizing power in their "March on Rome" in October 1922, Mussolini and his Fascist Party moved rapidly to solidify their power, and sport rapidly became an affair of state. The athlete in fascist Italy was seen as a soldier-citizen safeguarding the physical health of the nation. The Italian fascists invested heavily in sporting infrastructure, bringing cohesion, purposeful direction, and a robustness to Italian sport.

The bravado and political successes of the fascist state carried over to Italian football. Fascism embodied a masculine identity, and the national game, better known by the Italian name, *calcio*, came to embody "virility, violence, combat, and struggle." The government undertook a massive reorganization of Italian first division football, which led to state control of the national team, a realignment of domestic leagues, the creation of a transfer market, and the invention of Serie A, the highest Italian league, which continues to this day. The regime transformed Sunday-afternoon football matches into rituals of unity, passion, and national identity.[10] These modernizations signified the rebirth of Italy and signaled to the world that the fascists were a rising force in both political and athletic spheres. Amid this assertion of newfound power and influence, Italian football would host the world's best footballers in the 1934 World Cup, only the second-ever international tournament devoted solely to football and the first requiring qualification.

MUSSOLINI'S *MONDIALE*

Italy hosting the 1934 World Cup would be equal to the Berlin Olympics in showcasing fascism's achievements and enhancing national unity behind football. The fascists attended to many details in organizing the tournament. Visiting fans, especially from the established and successful footballing nations of Holland, France, and Switzerland, were offered travel subsidies of 70 percent to come to Italy, and local travel was further subsidized. Publicity in the buildup to the tournament included eye-catching modernist posters and saturation marketing. Italian promotion and propaganda were so effective that FIFA president Jules Rimet wryly commented that during the tournament it felt like Mussolini himself was the president of FIFA.[11]

Italian team trainer Vittorio Pozzo came to football from track and field, and he soon became one of the most powerful figures in European football before World War II, favoring the direct English style of play. In his nearly thirty-year career managing the *Azzurri*, Pozzo dominated the Italian game as an authoritarian father figure and war hero who possessed a soldierly vision of his players. Practice sessions were like military training exercises, and Pozzo was notorious for using war cemeteries as reminders to his players of the sacrifice and obligations owed to their forefathers.

Benito Mussolini attended many of the Italian matches in the 1934 World Cup, and the passion for the home team was so intense on match day that the crowd could be easily mistaken for those attending a fascist rally. In an act of pure hubris, Mussolini had an additional trophy commissioned—the *Coppa del Duce*—whose dimensions dwarfed the FIFA trophy by six times. Not content with having home-field advantage, Mussolini also involved himself in the selection of referees for many of the key matches.

After beating Spain in the quarterfinals, Italy played pretournament favorite Austria in the semifinals. This would be the same Austrian team that was victorious against Italy just two years earlier in the 1932 Olympics and who were known for their stylish play and individual brilliance. On the day of the semifinal, on a rain-soaked pitch at the San Siro stadium in Milan, the Austrians not only had to contend with a sodden field, but they also were up against a young Swedish official named Ivan Eklind who had been personally chosen by Il Duce.

Neutrals suspected Eklind had been bribed, and it was later verified that he and Mussolini had dined together the night before the match to "talk tactics." Many remember that during the match the referee intercepted a pass by an Austrian player and headed the ball back to the Italians. Despite such controversy, the Italians and Austrians battled to extra time scoreless, and the Italians went through on a goal by the recently naturalized Argentine Enrique Guaita, a goal many still hold to be illegitimate as the Swedish referee denied an obvious offside call.

Their confidence growing after the 1–0 victory over the Austrians, Italy moved on to the final, set for the Stadio Nazionale PNF in Rome. On June 10, 1934, the entire nation of Italy paused to watch the *Azzurri* take on a young and talented but inexperienced Czechoslovakian side. Astoundingly, Eklind was again chosen to officiate the final match. Italy adopted an aggressive style of play that largely went unpunished, and after the Czechs had taken a late lead on a goal in the seventy-first minute, the Italians pushed for the equalizer, which came ten minutes later, scored by Argentine-born Raimundo Orsi. At the end of ninety minutes, with the score level at 1–1, the Italians managed the winning goal just five minutes into extra time. It was scored by Angelo Schiavo on a cross by Guaita, and Mussolini rose from his seat to applaud his champions.

The first World Cup trophy in the country's history was earned. The victory of the *Azzurri* in Rome solidified the popularity of Mussolini, and the national press exploited the victory by the host Italians. In an article titled "Soldati dello sport" (Soldiers of Sport), journalist Bruno Roghi reflected on the blend of sport and politics in the 1934 World Cup:

> They are rare, the rarest matches in which you see the metamorphosis of the players, no longer little coloured boys who go about their work, with the ball at their feet, but little, gallant soldiers that fight for an idea that is greater than them but who work for the divine unknown, that is the genius of the soldier on the charge. They are the matches, in other words, where not one squad of eleven men but a race shows itself with its feelings and instincts, its anger and its ecstasy, its character and attitude. The game that the Italians won at the stadium was this type of match. [12]

THE 1938 WORLD CUP:
ITALY REPEATS AS *CAMPIONI DEL MONDO*

Political tensions intensified in Europe as the *Azzurri* departed Italy to defend their World Cup title in France in 1938. The Italians fielded a nearly completely different side from their World Cup–winning team of four years earlier (only four players remained, with Giuseppe Meazza the best known) but with the same manager at the helm, Vittorio Pozzo. In their opening match against Norway, Pozzo's side was met by an estimated ten thousand political exiles and antifascist demonstrators (many of whom had fled their country after Mussolini's takeover) raining down a furious protest from the terraces. Police wielding batons restrained the protesters, but Pozzo met the abuse by ordering his players to raise their arms in the fascist salute, responding to his command, "Team, be ready, salute!" The players repeated the gesture, defiantly, as the abuse continued. Italy would go on to win the match 2–1 in extra time.

Italy defeated France and Brazil to make it to the finals, where a supremely confident Hungarian team was waiting for them after their 5–1 demolition of Sweden in the semifinal. Italy took a 3–1 lead into halftime, and Hungary never mounted a sustained comeback as Italy finished off the game as 4–2 winners. The win helped diminish lingering resentments of the alleged corruption that came with the Italians' hosting of the 1934 tournament. The World Cup would not be played again for another sixteen years as World War II would break out just a few months after the final.

In the years before Europe plunged into a world war, international matches like these from the World Cup took on added significance. Football's emergence as the national game in an ever-increasing number of European countries was reinforced by the growth of cross-border contacts, as domestic cups and competitions were supplemented by international fixtures and tournaments. As the Nazi regime looked outside of its borders for legitimization of its government and its football, Italy was an enticing and supremely successful model of how to seize political victory on the field of play.

FAIR PLAY? THE FIRST PROPAGANDA VICTORY FOR NAZI FOOTBALL

World War I adversary England, the acknowledged "masters of the game" and the nation against which all other national sides measured themselves, offered Nazi Germany the sternest test of their development as a footballing nation. Rivals on the battlefield and now rivals on the football pitch, England and Germany's friendly matches in the 1930s would become a type of proxy battle in a contest for international stature. Fixtures featuring these teams were matches of power, prestige, and influence. Footballers were seen as emissaries in the national kit, sporting diplomats of a sort. And any match between Great Britain and Germany or Italy was interpreted as an epic struggle between fascism and liberal democracy.

Britain saw an equal opportunity to challenge fascism in clear and certain terms. British footballers were perfect messengers of British cultural values, foremost among them the celebrated ideal of "fair play." Prominent officials in the British footballing establishment also believed that football could be a mechanism for peace. Sir Stanley Rous, the FA secretary for twenty-seven years, starting before World War II and serving through to 1961, famously claimed that football gives the world a much-needed international language. In Great Britain, isolationism and pacifism were subtly underneath such claims that international matches would be influential in securing peace and friendship among adversarial nations.

To the Nazis, though, sport was just another expression of the greater struggle. In both politics and sporting competition, the regime strived to glorify martial values, hardness, and self-discipline. Loyalty was especially prized in athletes. The government sought to inspire people, especially the youth, to join more forcefully in the creation of a new Germany. Sport naturally worked as a unifying force and as a subtle form of indoctrination, and when teamwork, camaraderie, and physical fitness were all glorified, the regime achieved its aims. In essence, athletes served as soldiers of sport. It was in this politically charged climate that the British FA extended an invitation to the German national team for a friendly match to be played in London on December 4, 1935. The match would be only the second meeting between the nations.

In England there was public outrage when the match with Germany was announced. The government policy in Britain was of détente with Nazi Germany, yet the government was unaware of the scheduling of the match until the English FA announced it publicly. Resisting the calls to cancel the planned match, the British government sought to stabilize their diplomatic relationship with Germany. British leaders were stridently opposed to using sport as a political weapon, standing by a long tradition of the independence of athletics from the geopolitical sphere. But one could not ignore the political implications of the match.

The highly touted game was played at White Hart Lane in North London, the home ground of Tottenham Hotspur, a club that historically has enjoyed strong support from Jewish residents in the immediate neighborhood. Some ten thousand German supporters were expected on match day, and worries were great that these supporters would be met with violent clashes. Police and British government officials envisioned racist, chanting, swastika-festooned Brownshirts marching through the capital. After arriving in London for the match, German manager Otto Nerz worked hard to distance the team from the government, claiming boldly that the DFB (the German football association) was a private association having nothing to do with the Nazi government. Straining credibility, the managing secretary of the DFB further claimed that the team was there to compete in London as ambassadors of sport. The German footballers were under strict instructions to respond "Keine politische Fragen"[13] (no political questions) to reporters' questions about the political undertones of the match.

When you watch newsreel accounts of the match and the preparations, there is a steady, cold rain falling on the thousands of German sightseers as they move their way across London. Shuttled by dozens of buses, the visiting German fans stopped traffic in the West End by sheer force of numbers, and even the steady rain could not dampen their enthusiasm. The number of police assigned to the match was tripled, and the German media devoted considerable attention to the game. In the end, fears of violence by the visiting fans proved unfounded. British authorities met the logistical challenge for transporting the German fans to the match. In an ironic turn, many of the German-speaking tour guides were provided by Jewish organizations in London. There is a good probability that many of these translators had earlier fled to London as the persecutions in Germany intensified after 1933.

With the most prominent members of the German Olympic planning delegation in attendance with Reichssportführer Tschammer und Osten, there could be no doubt about the political importance of the match to the German government. Arriving well ahead of kickoff, the crowd was orderly, and the home supporters were provided with a rousing rendition of the "Horst Wessel Lied," the Nazi anthem typically sung at annual Nazi party celebrations. The swastika flew over the stadium that day, though at half mast in respect for Princess Victoria, who had died the day before. Yet the provocations expected by match organizers never materialized. Outside of White Hart Lane, protests by Jewish groups and trade unionists proved little distraction to those gathered for the game. That almost one-third of the supporters who usually gathered on Saturday afternoons to watch Tottenham Hotspur were Jewish also mattered little to the singing crowd. Captains for the match were Eddie Hapgood for England and Fritz Szepan for Germany. England wore their new blue kits while Germany donned white shirts.

The German players gave the Nazi salute during the playing of the national anthems, but no Nazi insignia appeared on the German match kits, as a concession to the hosts. The rain stopped in time for kickoff, but the pitch, unable to shed the water, became a muddy bog. Surviving film clips show the German goalkeeper, in baggy, knee-length shorts, punching a ball from his goalmouth, barely able to jump because of heavy, muddied boots. Conditions likely affected the Germans more as they played in a defensive, tentative style. In a match celebrated by both sides as the epitome of "fair play," the visiting German squad was beaten soundly, losing 3–0 in front of fifty-four thousand spectators and a much larger audience listening at home on radio. Middlesborough's George Camsell tallied a brace, while Arsenal player Cliff Bastin, the London club's all-time top scorer until 1997, added the third goal. The "Übermensch" had been comprehensively beaten.

The mutual admiration of both teams served primarily to bolster the image of the Third Reich in Britain. At the celebration banquet that followed the game, Reichssportführer Tschammer und Osten spoke of the "blue sky of friendship between the two Nordic countries."[14] The British government later came under harsh scrutiny for suggesting violence would attend the match. At the same dinner, a spokesman for an Anglo-German advocacy group, Lord Mount Temple, rebuffed fears that Nazified football represented anything other than a sporting affair when he claimed, "The Germans have always been our good friends. They always fought fair in the war, and I hope we did the same. If another war comes . . . well, I hope the partners will be changed."[15]

What was expected to be a "grudge match" turned into a diplomatic coup as both teams exchanged gifts and pleasantries afterward. The trade unionists who had protested the match for months were roundly condemned for "bringing politics" into the sporting contest. Ultimately, though, the protestors would be proved right as the persecution was unrelenting back in Germany and the Nazi state moved closer and closer to initiating war in Europe. The British government's hesitation to challenge the blatant manipulations of the Nazis, paired with passivity in the face of rising German military strength, seemingly emboldened the Germans in the diplomatic sphere to carry on through with the infamous 1938 Munich Accords, when Neville Chamberlain acquiesced to German demands for the Sudetenland in Czechoslovakia. This match between England and Germany is often explained in historical accounts as yet another example of appeasement of the Nazi regime. Whatever propaganda victory was achieved in the match by the

Nazi state was dwarfed by the 1936 Berlin Olympics, the quadrennial festival of sport and the first monumental example of political theater and ideological manipulation on the international sporting stage.

CITIUS, ALTIUS, FORTIUS: THE NAZI GAMES AND CORRUPTION OF THE OLYMPIC IDEAL

Events inside Germany in the lead-up to the 1936 Summer Games forced a response from the international community. Beginning in the spring of 1933, mere weeks after the Nazis had seized power, thousands of Jewish athletes were banned from competing and thrown out of their courts, pools, tracks, and training centers. Elite athletes, especially those training for the upcoming Olympic Games, were most devastated. As the Nazis consolidated their power, the *Sturmabteilung* ("storm troopers," the SA), the foot soldiers of the Nazi Party, enforced boycotts of Jewish-owned shops and businesses while concentration camps were built at a rapid pace to hold political prisoners and gypsies. Jewish books were thrown onto raging pyres, and intermarriage was banned. These persecutions became widely known outside Germany, and the purges of Jewish athletes were in clear violation of Olympic rules. But calls for a boycott, a significant and definite threat to the Nazis, fell to the wayside under cynical Nazi promises of peace and harmony.

On the first day of August 1936, the Berlin games opened with the arrival of the Olympic flame, carried by a blond-haired runner who was carefully selected to embody the Aryan ideal. Hitler and his entourage, including Dr. Theodor Lewald, president of Germany's Olympic Committee, and Carl Diem, secretary general of the Organizing Committee of the Berlin Olympic Games, accompanied by members of the International Olympic Committee (IOC), walked into the Olympic Stadium amid a chorus of three thousand Germans singing the national anthem, "Deutschland Über Alles," immediately followed by the Nazi anthem, the "Horst Wessel Lied." Over the course of the next seventeen days, the world watched with amazement the athletic excellence of international competition intertwined with political manipulation. The five Olympic rings representing global cooperation and peace were now brazenly linked with the Nazi swastika, the symbol of Aryan superiority and racial domination. After Adolf Hitler opened the games with a short speech, chants of "Sieg heil!" filled the Olympic Stadium, and only the triumphs of a few African American track and field athletes a few days later would sidetrack the Nazi propaganda machine.

The 1936 Summer Olympic Games served as a vehicle to promote an image of the new Germany as a strong, robust nation brimming with Aryan ideals, while simultaneously boosting the esteem of German citizens. The games also gave legitimacy to the new regime both at home and abroad. An impressive Olympic village was created as part of the twenty million Reichsmarks (eight million dollars U.S. in 1936) invested by the government. The Nazis, desperate for an infusion of money, expected that the huge influx of tourists for the games would bring much-needed foreign currency into Germany.

By the start of the games, the Nazi government spent over forty million Reichsmarks building a state-of-the-art, 325-acre Olympics sports complex located in the western suburbs of Berlin. The centerpiece of the Reichssportsfeld was the massive Olympic Stadium, built of natural stone and seating 110,000 spectators. The impressive neoclassical structure included a special seating platform built for Hitler and other top Nazi officials. For the Nazis, international sport would be another weapon in the German arsenal. The Olympic motto, *Citius, Altius, Fortius* (Faster, Higher, Stronger), was now easily mistaken for the mobilization of the political machinery of the Nazi state.

Visitors, both athlete and tourist alike, were impressed with the modern facilities and the organization of the games. The games were a tool of Nazi "soft power" and sport as a means to win the hearts of the German people and the thousands of international visitors in attendance over the nearly three-week competition. A significant innovation of these games was the live radio broadcasts of the competitions, which were a perfect fit for the expertise the Nazi propaganda apparatus now enjoyed, and estimates are that three hundred million global listeners were tuned in to the broadcasts from Berlin. Broadcast of the Berlin Olympics included start-to-finish coverage of the events, with human-interest feature stories on individual athletes and an hour-long highlights show every evening at eight o'clock. On street corners in Berlin and other major German cities, people could listen to the competitions on loudspeakers. So compelling were the events that traffic slowed to a dead stop in some areas of Berlin.

Germany drew the largest assembled cadre of print journalists and photographers to date, including 800 reporters and 125 photojournalists from 59 countries, all of whom were carefully vetted by the Propaganda Ministry, which sought to control all flow of information. These "guests" of the Third Reich were provided comfortable, even generous accommodations and amenities. Foreign correspondents were given tours of the "successes" of the regime, which touted the economic and cultural rise of the Reich. True to form, a significant number of journalists, especially from the more isolationist-minded United States, often filed stories minimizing or negating early reports of mistreatment and violence against the Jews.

During the summer festival of sport, the security apparatus of the regime receded to the background as the SS, the SA, and the Hitler Youth were kept from public view and overt displays of militarism and racism were kept to a minimum. In an effort to minimize attention to German's rearmament program, the military barracks used by the Wehrmacht and located in the northern section of the Olympic village were relabeled and refurbished as athlete housing. Even though machine-gun training by Wehrmacht storm troopers rattled the Olympic grounds at times, few would link the rising militarism of the Nazi state to these games.

Organizers also toned down the racist messaging. At the Winter Games, hosted a few months before in Garmisch-Partenkirchen, visitors found signs affixed to toilets warning, "Dogs and Jews not allowed." Such indignities were not tolerated, though, and these barriers were soon lifted after IOC chief Baillet-Latour objected: "It is Olympia and we are masters there."[16] Quickly learning from this episode, and at the direction of Goebbels, anti-Semitic signage was removed from well-traveled roadways and gathering points across Germany ahead of the Summer Games. Two days into the competitions, the Propaganda Ministry's press office also instructed German newspapers to tone down any racial language on reporting the results of the Berlin games, decreeing, "The racial point of view should not in any form be part of the discussion of athletic results. Special care should be exercised not to offend Negro athletes."[17]

Intent on seizing on the ceremony and ritual already deeply ingrained in the Olympic Games, the Nazi state did what it did best: it conjured up a tradition seemingly originating in antiquity. An innovation of the "Nazi Games" that continues to this day is the torch relay, the emblematic start to every Olympic Games since 1936. This reimagined (some say reinvented) tradition was orchestrated by German Olympic official Carl Diem, who first proposed it to the Propaganda Ministry some weeks earlier as an advertisement for the new Germany across southeast and central Europe. Diem envisioned the torch relay as an ancient symbol of purity, a "reawakening of the mythic cult surrounding Prometheus whose theft of fire from the gods for the betterment of mortals had been honored in antiquity by torchlight parades."[18] In a curious side note, Diem mistakenly selected as his avatar an image from a relief, purportedly representing torchbearers crossing the finish line in an ancient competition, in the Palazzo Colonna in Rome, an ornate thirteenth-century residence that once hosted the poet Dante. But instead of runners, the figures are in fact *putti*, erotic lovers symbolizing something rather different.

Originating in the northern Peloponnesus, the torch relay created by the Nazis passed through seven countries on its nearly 3,100-kilometer journey to Germany. Each of the countries featured on the relay route would one day be occupied by German forces. In fact, maps produced for the event audaciously show the Sudetenland region of Czechoslovakia as part of the German nation. This disputed territory would feature prominently in the political sphere just two years after the close of the games as European powers negotiated to avoid another war.

With the world gathered in Berlin for the start of the games, the final two runners of the relay, tasked with bringing the torch through the streets of central Berlin, were carefully chosen by an aesthetics committee of the regime. The first was Siegfried Eifrig, a tall, blond, and blue-eyed sprinter who nearly qualified for the German Olympic squad and who took hold of the torch at the beginning of the Unter den Linden, Berlin's main boulevard. Eifrig passed by the Brandenburg Gate and some three hundred thousand people on the torch route. At the stadium grounds, Eifrig lit two urns that burned until the end of the Summer Games. From the urns, the flame was then transferred to Fritz Schilgen, who carried the torch on its final leg into the stadium. As the embodiment of the Aryan ideal, Schilgen also possessed a beautiful and graceful running style. Ascending the final flight of stairs, he lit the Olympic cauldron situated high above the grandstands in the Olympiastadion.[19] Schilgen's lighting of the cauldron is dramatically captured in the film *Olympia*. The games were officially underway. While American sprinter Jesse Owens would become the undisputed hero of these Olympics, the football being played was almost equal to the drama witnessed on the track. And once again, nationalist sentiment, fascist politics, and sport all came together in a passionate, sometimes violent, and decidedly unexpected way.

FOOTBALL AT THE BERLIN OLYMPICS

With the return of football to the 1936 Berlin Olympics, the fledgling Hitlerian regime was poised to take full advantage of the mass appeal of the game to the thousands of spectators who would fill stadia in and around Berlin in August. Omitted from the 1932 Olympics under suspicion that amateur status was a mere pretense for most of the elite European players of the day, the more likely reason for the eight-year hiatus in Olympic soccer is that the inaugural World Cup had been staged in 1930 and the world governing body, FIFA, wanted to assert the preeminence of the new tournament over all other competitions. Before the start of the Berlin games, sixteen teams agreed to participate, with Great Britain and host nation Germany seeded as joint favorites. But neither team would advance past the second round in a tournament marked by controversy, political manipulation, and fascist pageantry.

Britain had not competed in the Olympics since a devastating early round 3–1 loss to unheralded Norway in the Antwerp games of 1920. Thereafter, the British decided to sit out all of the Olympic football competitions until Berlin, upholding the virtue of "pure amateurism." Germany, unheralded in European football in the decade immediately after the Great War, witnessed a surge of success under the guidance of manager Dr. Otto Nerz. Under the supervision of the Nazi movement, the reorganization of the club system in Germany included abolishment of worker- and church-run clubs and the removal of Jewish and gypsy athletes from all sports clubs. These purges would not officially take place until the close of the Berlin Olympics, a move that was meant to placate those calling for a boycott of the games earlier.

The fierce nationalistic passion of these Berlin games, embodied by fans and players alike, was on full display in the opening match between the United States and Italy. The Americans had sent a competitive team to Berlin, unlike in previous Olympics, and they were met by an Italian team primed for battle. Increasingly frustrated by the stalwart Americans in the first half of the match, the Italians resorted to increasingly violent tactics in the second, with numerous reports of punching, kicking, and shoving of their American opponents. In fact, the play was so rough that two Americans were taken from the field, unable to continue. One had been kicked in the stomach and the other suffered a torn ligament after a particularly vicious push out of bounds.

Toward the end of the match, the German referee ordered Italian striker Achille Piccini to leave the pitch after he punched an American player. Piccini refused to leave, and when the referee moved to enforce his decision the other Italian players immediately surrounded him, held his arms to his side, and covered his mouth and eyes with their hands.[20] Astonishingly, the referee let play continue, and Piccini remained in the game. Though the Americans protested, the Italians' final result of 1–0 stood up after an American appeal was denied. Undaunted, the Italian Olympic side, amateurs to a man, lived up to the observation later made by Winston Churchill: "Italians lose wars as if they were games of football and lose games of football as if they were wars."[21]

Expectations were also high in 1936 for the German side after their third-place finish over the highly regarded Austrians in the 1934 World Cup. Thus Germany's debut in the Olympic tournament resulted in a 9–0 thrashing of Luxembourg a day after the contentious Italy-USA match. Impressed by such dominance, Adolf Hitler would be in attendance for the next German contest, a second-round encounter with Norway. Hitler was encouraged to attend his first football match by Albert Forster, a *Gauleiter* from Danzig (now Gdańsk, Poland, on the Baltic Sea), one of several regional administrators created after the Nazi takeover in 1933. The gathered crowd awaited what they thought would be another convincing German win.

Sitting with Hitler in the führer's box was Propaganda Minister Joseph Goebbels, German air force chief Hermann Göring, and Hitler's secretary, Rudolph Hess, the man to whom he dictated much of his manifesto *Mein Kampf* while in prison in 1925. Anticipation running wild, Goebbels later wrote in his diary: "The Führer is very excited. I can barely contain myself. A real bath of nerves. The crowd rages. A battle like never before. The game as mass suggestion."[22] The excitement would not last long. Before a home crowd of some fifty-five thousand spectators, Hitler and Goebbels watched Norway hand the hosts a shocking 2–0 defeat. Norway scored only six minutes into the match, and again six minutes from the end. Hitler left the match furious and well before the final whistle had sounded. By most accounts, this was the last match Hitler ever attended. Goebbels remarked in his diary, morosely, "100,000 left the stadium in a depressed state."[23] Hyperbole aside, Goebbels would return to football as a means of mass persuasion, albeit two years after the close of the games when Germany would once again take on the British on the eve of World War II.

The upsets on the Olympic football fields continued the following day as Great Britain was also bounced from the tournament, losing to Poland 5–4. The result was even more remarkable as the Poles played without their best player, Ernst Willimowski, left off of the Polish squad because he was unwilling to give up his binge-drinking habit. Remarkably, the British made the match close only after the Poles had surged ahead 5–1, coming back with three goals in the first nineteen minutes after the halftime interval.

Great Britain had labored in its opening match against China, a 2–0 win; before the second-round loss to Poland, the distractions could not have been greater for the team. Between matches, the unbreakable bond between the German state and sport was fully evident to the British squad. Called to a meeting some four hundred miles from Berlin, where most of the football matches were contested, the British footballers met the führer himself.

Taken to Hitler's mountaintop retreat at Berchtesgaden, high in the Bavarian Alps and overlooking Salzburg, the squad was accompanied by Hitler's personal bodyguard, the black-shirted unit of elite SS guards who were fiercely loyal to the dictator. Remaining photographs of the meeting reveal yet another propaganda victory for the Germans as each British footballer had to shake the hand of the dictator in front of the gathered press corps. Initially unaware of the damage that had been done, team officials shrugged off the meeting as an exercise in diplomacy on behalf of their country.

Even before play began in Berlin, the British players had refused to give the Nazi salute before any of their Olympic matches. This refusal may partially explain the handshake photo-op, but apparently there were limits to such requests. This "disobedience" was soon followed by a severe reaction from German diplomats, which set the stage for a capitulation to German demands in an act of appeasement that is still discussed to this day; the infamous Nazi salute offered by the British team before a friendly match staged in Berlin in May 1938. This match served as the last sporting contact between England and Germany, the two main protagonists on the world stage, before the outbreak of war in Europe.

The Olympic football tournament continued amid the political maneuverings of the Nazi regime. The play intensified, and the provocations and disagreements of the earlier USA–Italy match were mere skirmishes compared to what occurred in the second-round match between Peru and Austria. Coached by the English manager Jimmy Hogan, the Austrians faced a South American side that had demolished Finland 7–3. Just as the opening match against the United States had tested the Italians, the Austrians faced a similarly tough foe in Peru. In this quarterfinal match that brought with it international implications, Peru and Austria fought to a 2–2 draw at the end of full time after Austria had led 2–0 at the half.

After an initial fifteen-minute overtime in which neither team scored, tension built to an intense level. Likely enraged by the decision of the Italian referee to disallow three goals in the overtime session, a dozen or more Peruvian spectators poured onto the field, a number of them brandishing weapons, attacking the referee and a few of the Austrian players. The pitch invasion resulted in a leg injury to an Austrian player, and the match was abandoned in the second overtime, after the Peruvians had scored two late goals for a 4–2 victory.

What followed was an international dispute that continued well into the early twenty-first century. After hearing the result broadcast over international radio, locals in Lima, Peru, celebrated in sheer ecstasy. But at the same time the Peruvians were celebrating, the Austrians successfully filed an official protest with Olympic officials and with FIFA, who both conceded that the match needed to be replayed. In fact, to guarantee the safety of the players and an unbiased result, Olympic officials ordered that the rematch should be played in an empty stadium. In protest, the entire Olympic contingent from Peru left Germany on orders from the Peruvian president, Óscar Benavides, and they were joined in their protest by the Colombian Olympic team. The response in Lima was equally volatile, and angry mobs stormed the

German consulate and pulled down Olympic flags wherever they were found in the Peruvian capital. The protests even affected commerce in Peru, where Peruvian dockworkers refused to load goods onto German ships. Newspapers in Peru claimed that replaying the match was a betrayal by the colonialist powers who reigned over the international game. In their eyes, all of South America had endured a great insult by the European powers that ran the Olympic Games.

Tensions further escalated when five other South American countries threatened to leave the Berlin games. Joseph Goebbels's press office quickly made it known that the German government and the Berlin Olympic organizers had no influence over FIFA, the governing body that made the official decision to replay the match. In the end, Peru was a no-show for the rematch (rescheduled twice, ultimately), and the Austrians were declared the winners. In the semifinal match against Poland, the Austrians beat the Poles 3–1, setting up the final match against Italy, set for August 15.

In another match violently contested and featuring rough play, Italy emerged triumphant 2–1 over Austria, the final major tournament in which the Austrian nation would compete before their annexation by the Nazis in 1938. Scoreless at the half, the Italians managed to score late in the second, only to be pulled back eleven minutes later by the Austrians, who scored in the ninetieth minute to force extra time. After only two minutes of play in the extra period, the Italians scored the winning goal in front of a sellout crowd of more than ninety thousand fans. The celebrating players, with laurels on their heads, can be seen waving to jubilant Italian fans among thousands of spectators offering the Nazi salute at the awards ceremony. Even Italian dictator Benito Mussolini seized the moment to exorcise his long-held resentment against the Austrians for their influence in northern Italy by personally congratulating each of the Italian players on the team's return to Rome. With football the most popular spectator sport at these Berlin Games, the Nazi regime did not miss the chance to capture the happenings on film. They turned once again to Leni Riefenstahl, a filmmaker they knew they could trust, to infuse the games with a Nazi aesthetic.

THE AESTHETIC BEAUTY OF SPORT IN *OLYMPIA* AND FOOTBALL MISINTERPRETED

Among Leni Riefenstahl's numerous directorial achievements is her sport film *Olympia*, a two-part chronicle of the Berlin Summer Olympic Games. *Olympia* stands out as Riefenstahl's true masterpiece of groundbreaking filmmaking. She pioneered the use of many innovative techniques, the most notable being the use of rail-mounted and underwater cameras. Thirty-three camera operators shot nearly a million feet of footage, and over the course of eighteen months, Riefenstahl would painstakingly edit down the material to fit her artistic vision. The film, released in 1938, captured the resurgence of the new Germany, a country then on the march in Austria and Czechoslovakia, seeking territorial acquisition and the reversal of the punitive consequences of the Treaty of Versailles.

Olympia was a dynamic blend of sport, aesthetics, and propaganda that created a bridge from antiquity to the Nazified present. The prologue of the film is ethereal as ancient ruins emerge from a fog-enshrouded past and real athletes materialize from Greek sculptures. Whether intended or not, Riefenstahl's tribute to the body beautiful aligned with National Socialism's glorification of strength, purity of health, and physical perfection.[24] Part one of the film concentrates on track and field sports, and Jesse Owens stars. In the second part of the film, titled "Fest der Schönheit" (Festival of Beauty), many of the other team sports are presented in a highly stylized ballet of athletes moving through time and space, ending as daylight fades on the Olympic scene. The director briefly highlights gymnastics, yachting, boxing, distance running, field hockey, and aquatic events, all in rapid succession. Football also receives a stylized interpretation.

Yet in Riefenstahl's three-and-a-half-hour film, only three minutes and ten seconds are dedicated to football, and only the final between Italy and Austria made the cut. Much of the time, her camera crews were too close to the play, and the editing is abrupt. The only field view the audience is offered is taken at ground level. Riefenstahl's cameras focus almost exclusively on the movement of the ball, which by the nature of the game is unpredictable and dynamic.

Modern audiences likely find this section of the black-and-white documentary disorienting to watch. Tactics and team strategy seem unimportant to the filmmaker, and team play captured on film never reflects the players' movements away from the ball. The only view of the spectators attending the final comes when we are shown cutaway shots after goals are scored. The viewer is later treated to a promising and unconventional view from behind the goal, but in this position the viewer cannot keep up with the play, especially in the goalmouth, where we see the Austrian keeper spill a ball that leads to Italy's winning goal. Narration of the final match offers no information about the actual course of the tournament nor the final match, aside from the goals scored. In the service to her aesthetic aims, Riefenstahl isolates individual movements of the player and ball without giving a sense of the buildup of play. She also avoids the use of slow-motion photography, so effectively utilized in her dramatization of other sports during the Berlin games. One critic of Riefenstahl's coverage of the 1936 Olympic soccer final realized, "There is no place for slow motion in presenting soccer because, for Riefenstahl, the ball's roundness—the unpredictability of the game—violates the very idea of beauty, her ideology and aesthetic. If she had her way, the ball would have been as square and cubic as could be."[25]

In the end, the lasting record of the football matches in Berlin was sacrificed to aesthetics. Clearly, Riefenstahl lacked an understanding of soccer as a team (verses individual) effort, which was rather reflective of the larger German attitude toward soccer at the time. German football, especially at the international level, was known for having disciplined players who played with a robust individuality; the difficulty came in translating that individual talent into team wins.[26] So brief is the section on football in the film, that the other qualities of *Olympia* leave a much greater impression.

In the final scene of the film, the viewer witnesses an empty Olympiastadion and an accompanying bell tower from high above, as pillars of light are cast upward into the sky, ringing the stadium. There is a closing close-up of the Olympic flame in the cauldron and laurels placed on the international banners of the participating countries. Then the Olympic flame is extinguished, and the calm and tranquility of the moment lingers, a brief respite for the international community before the calamity that would soon come.

While there is general agreement that the Berlin games were a masterstroke of propaganda for the Nazis because of the magnificent organization of the games, the debate continues about the role Riefenstahl's *Olympia* might have played in advancing Nazi aims. *Olympia* has always stood in the very dark shadow of *Triumph of the Will*, which magnified the charisma of Adolf Hitler.

In *Olympia*, the blend of art and propaganda continued almost seamlessly. Riefenstahl never escaped the criticism that her work elevates fascism. Until her dying day, she denied any political aim to *Olympia*. Across Germany, Riefenstahl was celebrated, and the film was honored internationally with gold medals at major film festivals in Venice and Paris. Riefenstahl's film would also earn special recognition from the International Olympic Committee for documenting the beauty and delight of sport. *Olympia*, celebrated enthusiastically as art, did what it set out to do: glorify athletic prowess through the interpretation of the beauty of the human form in competition. The debate continues on whether that aesthetic vision was forever corrupted.

WAR BETWEEN THE TOUCHLINES: ENGLAND VISITS BERLIN

Germany averaged fewer than four international matches a year in the quarter century before Hitler took power, but in the first nine years of his dictatorship they doubled as the regime saw Germany's positive standing in the world increase. In 1935 alone, the national team contested seventeen matches, driven by the Nazis' demand that domestic clubs and employers release their players for the national team. A 6–0 loss to neighboring Austria in 1931 showed how far the Germans needed to go before being consistently competitive. Clearly hampered by playing teams of professional players, Germany would rapidly ascend the pecking order of world football through dogged determination; the rise of the domestic game, which fed creative and innovative players to the national team; and a foreign policy that aggressively sought appeasement from the widely admired "masters of the game," the English.

The Germans had long admired English football. Club teams touring Germany (at the same time the national side took on England in May 1938) drew record crowds of well over one hundred thousand. Because of their history as adversaries, a shared love for the game, and this one-sided admiration, no other international matchup compared to

England versus Germany in the 1930s. In these tumultuous times, football ceased being just a game. Choosing Nazi Germany as an opponent gave implied support to an increasingly aggressive regime. And on May 14, 1938, the most politicized match ever played between the two nations produced probably the most infamous event in the history of English football.

The Germany–England match came at a crucial point in world politics. England, well aware of the implications of antagonizing the bellicose German regime, instead sought a "quiet and restrained" response, seeing the fixture as effective cultural propaganda that might possess a greater utility than more overt means, the kind on full display in Berlin.[27] Thus the upcoming match was interpreted by the British government, the FA, and the British media as vitally important. But skepticism remained about sport's power to foster peace. Such skepticism did not escape the future prime minister of England either. With the 1936 Olympics as proof, Winston Churchill later observed, "sport, when it enters the international field in Olympic Games and other contests between countries, may breed ill-will rather than draw nations together."[28]

Few Germans, officially or otherwise, spoke openly about beating England, a team made up of experienced professionals. Germany came into the match brimming with confidence. Since Hitler's ascension to power, the national side had finished third in the 1934 World Cup and had won twenty-three while losing only three matches with three draws. Later in 1937, under the direction of new Reichstrainer Sepp Herberger, *Die Mannschaft* enjoyed a strong run of matches, with ten wins and a draw in their eleven matches that year, and they entered the England match on a sixteen-game unbeaten streak.

At political rallies and international sporting competitions, the Nazis wanted to project a picture of physical superiority, and against their old adversary, the battle was rejoined anew. German media were transfixed by the possibility that the host Germans would win this highly charged game. Interest from the public matched the media fervor; over 400,000 applicants sought the 110,000 tickets on offer.

After the *Anschluss*, the fabled Austrian Wunderteam, which had beaten England in 1936, had been absorbed into the German side. On the surface, the addition of the talented Austrians looked to create an unbeatable German side, but in competition the *Anschluss*-created team never really played in harmony, likely because of long-held animosities between the players, who just weeks earlier were heated rivals on the pitch. As was the case so often under German domination, resistance took hold.

Well aware of the importance of the match beyond the final score, England's players were tasked with a serious dilemma a few minutes before kickoff. Under pressure from British diplomatic officials, the FA instructed the English players to offer the Nazi salute when greeting the gathered crowd. English star winger Stanley Matthews, the first winner of the Ballon d'Or as the European footballer of the year (at age forty-one) and the only player to be knighted while still playing, initially recalled, "The dressing room erupted. There was bedlam. All the England players were livid and totally opposed to this, myself included. Everyone was shouting at once. Eddie Hapgood, normally a respectful and devoted captain, wagged his finger at the official and told him what he could do with the Nazi salute, which involved putting it where the sun doesn't shine."[29]

Recollections of this prematch discussion have conflicted. Some players were indifferent to the request, while others claimed to be sickened by it. While there was clear resentment about the last-minute nature of the demand, many players feared they would never be selected for any future England matches if they refused.

Every sports team playing Germany in this era faced the same diplomatic dilemma. British football officials and diplomats alike rightly assumed that, as was the custom of the day, England would return the "three cheers" salute the German team offered as visitors to England a few years earlier. Going into the match, tensions ran dangerously high between the governments of Germany and England. Though not in attendance that day, Hitler was represented by his top leadership, who all occupied the führer's box seats, including Propaganda Minister Goebbels, Reichsmarschall Göring, Hitler's personal secretary Rudolf Hess, and Foreign Minister Ribbentrop. Reichssportsführer Tschammer und Osten and the British diplomat, Sir Neville Henderson, were also present.

For this high-stakes match, the English FA had demanded that no Austrian player should appear; in reality, one player did suit up—the SK Rapid Vienna striker Hans Presser—who ended up scoring in the match for the pan-German team. Conditions for the match were stifling as the weather in Berlin was unseasonably warm for the month of May. Kickoff was set for midafternoon, and as the teams readied themselves for battle, they were met by a blistering hot afternoon sun. Taking the match ball in hand, the Belgian referee, accompanied by linesmen from each of the competing countries, was ready for play, and the teams lined up for the introductions. In a gesture still shrouded in shame and controversy, moments before the opening whistle, the English players obliged the Nazi request and stood at attention with right arms raised in the Nazi salute. The salute was met with a raucous roar from the home crowd. English diplomatic officials were satisfied, stating that England footballers had done "good work" for crown and country. That the English players would repeat the fascist salute in Milan in a 1939 match against the world champion Italians rarely gets mentioned in historical accounts of football in this period.

Yet memory can be an elusive servant. Collective British recollection of "the salute" has been tainted by postwar understanding of the excesses and crimes of Nazism. England captain and Arsenal standout Eddie Hapgood would recall in his 2009 autobiography:

> I've played for England before 100,000 screaming, yelling, heiling Germans at the Berlin Olympic Stadium, the day we humbled the prize of Nazidom on the world's most luxurious ground. I've kicked a football into Mussolini's lap in Rome, and experienced the worst refereeing of my life at Milan; I've been to Switzerland, Rumania, Hungary, Czecho-Slovakia, Holland, Austria, Belgium, Finland, France, Norway, Denmark, Sweden and Yugoslavia. . . . I've been in a shipwreck, a train crash, and inches short of a plane accident . . . but the worst moment of my life, and one I would not willingly go through again, was giving the Nazi salute in Berlin.[30]

But on the Monday following the match, the *Times* of London acknowledged, "[the] English team immediately made a good impression by raising their arms in the German salute." Other mainstream newspapers also unvaryingly failed to comment critically on the gesture at the time, though the picture of the infamous salute appeared in print across the world. Other testimonies of the England players after the war tended to exaggerate the reluctance of the team. One other match featuring the English draws comparisons here. Italy, not yet formally allied with Germany, continued to play amid the rising political tensions in Europe, and the scheduled match between the *Azzurri* and England (a competitive 2–2 draw) set for the magnificent new San Siro Stadium in Milan in May 1939 saw the English salute to all four corners of the ground, again in the fascist style and to little controversy.

On the day, observers reported that the Germans looked rested and ready after careful preparations. In contrast, the English players looked a bit haggard, having just completed a long and arduous club season. Appearances would be deceptive because in the end the match proved to be disappointing for the Germans. Though the hosts managed to equalize after the first English goal by Arsenal left winger Cliff Bastin, they would never mount a comeback.

Players and home spectators alike were conciliatory, and the match itself was one-sided, in keeping with the relative strengths of each national team at that time. The highlight of the match was a goal scored by Len Goulden of then second-division West Ham United, a goal that Stanley Matthews described as the greatest he ever saw in football. Goulden scored with a left-footed volley from twenty-five yards out that apparently ripped the net from the crossbar. As he trotted back to midfield, arms raised in the air, he reportedly shouted, "Let 'em salute that one!"[31] The Germans would not overcome a sixteen-minute span in which England surged ahead with three quick goals. After the halftime interval, the teams traded goals, and at the final whistle the English had claimed a convincing 6–3 win. The home crowd of 105,000 left the Olympiastadion in Berlin with no doubt about who was the superior side.

The propaganda coup that was the May 1938 match against England further emboldened the Nazi regime. Goebbels thereafter became actively involved in scheduling matches and publicizing them to a watching world. But once again, sport would not be so easily manipulated. On the football pitch, a complete reversal of sporting fortune followed for Germany's national soccer team. By the end of 1938, the blended German team posted no wins, losing five of seven matches with a negative twenty-two goal differential in that span.

PRELUDE TO WAR

> "Serious sport has nothing to do with fair play. It is bound up with hatred, jealousy, boastfulness, disregard for all rules and sadistic pleasure in witnessing violence: In other words, it is war minus the shooting."—George Orwell, December 1945[32]

Football continued in the intervening war years, amid hardships, deprivations, and barbarism. During the decade of the dictators, the infusion of politics and propaganda allowed the Italians to reach the zenith of the game as world and Olympic champions while Germany and Spain struggled to convert a totalitarian mindset into consistently winning football. Across Europe, domestic leagues soldiered on, often as pale imitations of the national sport before the war. And international matches remained highly politicized affairs, though nations matched as enemy combatants on the battlefields of Europe and North Africa would not play each other directly until long after the war.

The corruption of sport in the 1930s would only intensify once the violence began in war-torn Europe. Football became embroiled in the life-and-death struggles faced by those who would dare stand in the way of Nazi aggression. As Hitler's armies swept eastward on June 22, 1941, in Operation Barbarossa, rapidly conquering parts of the Soviet Union, the Ukrainian capital of Kiev held out as war raged on. Among the besieged city's defenders were players from the 1939 Dynamo Kiev club side, among the very best in Europe at the dawn of the war. Following months of violent occupation in desperate living conditions, football began to be played again in war-torn Kiev in 1942. Led by a charismatic goalkeeper named Trusevich, a new team called FC Start was formed amid the rubble of occupied Kiev, and the squad dominated a series of matches against other makeshift Ukrainian and Nazi-allied teams. Undefeated, FC Start soon caught the attention of Nazi officials, who set up a pivotal final match against an elite team made up of well-trained German air force soldiers. Myth and reality came together in a "Match of Death" as these brave Ukrainian footballers became legends to football fans both past and present.

3

THE MATCH OF DEATH

"For the Nazis, too, soccer was a matter of state. A monument in the Ukraine commemorates the players of the 1942 Dynamo Kiev team. During the German occupation they committed the insane act of defeating Hitler's squad in the local stadium. Having been warned, 'If you win, you die,' they started out resigned to losing, trembling with fear and hunger, but in the end they could not contain their yearning for dignity. When the match was over, all eleven were shot with their club shirts on at the edge of a cliff."—Eduardo Galeano, Latin American writer and football fanatic [1]

Distinguished Uruguayan author Eduardo Galeano, in his lyrical book on the history of soccer, *Soccer in Sun and Shadow*, relates this famous battle, the "Match of Death" between the formidable Dynamo Kiev team and the best footballers from the Nazi military in occupied Ukraine. Galeano glories in the humble but heroic Dynamo players who summoned their dignity and strength to beat the Nazi select side in convincing fashion. He laments when the Ukrainian players are summarily executed on the edge of a gorge called Babi Yar outside of Kiev. His adoring prose describes the tragic end of the Dynamo Kiev players as a monumental act of resistance in the face of guaranteed death. The only problem is that Galeano's account is simply not true. In his impassioned reporting, Galeano unwittingly perpetuates the mythic version of the match advanced by Soviet propagandists some fifty years earlier. But the meaning of the match was unmistakable.

   Legend often has an irresistible hold on the imagination. When the captivating story of a football match to the death emerged from the ruins of war-ravaged Ukraine, truth gave way to a compelling and heroic fiction. The well-known power of propaganda and sport to command attention during the monumental struggle between Bolshevism and Nazism during World War II was on full display in Kiev during the momentous year of 1942. This apocryphal football match is the story of an elite team of Nazi soldiers matched against a ragtag band of players cobbled together from the survivors of the brutal invasion of Kiev as the Nazi empire spread across Europe with alarming speed. Unable to avoid being caught by the German invaders, these brave footballers from the famed club Dynamo Kiev, with an unbreakable camaraderie and love for the game, played whenever and wherever they could under the yoke of German oppression.

   The inspirational tale of defeating the Nazis on a football pitch resonated onward for many years after the war. But which story would have permanence? Soviet army and intelligence services were the first to arrive in the Ukrainian capital of Kiev after liberation, and the former Dynamo Kiev footballers were among the very first survivors to be interviewed. A period of desperate uncertainty followed for the players: would people believe they were not collaborators, a charge that almost always brought with it execution? As recollections and testimonies were collected by the Soviet intelligence services, it became clear that the more potent of the emerging stories was the one reinforcing Soviet-style heroism, the tale that had taken hold in the collective consciousness of those who had survived occupation.

   The person singularly responsible for withholding the true version was the minister for the interior in the Ukraine, Timofei Strokach, who knew of the heroics of the former Dynamo players during the siege and occupation of Kiev since he had fought alongside them. Rather than complicating the story that had quickly captivated the public imagination, a decision was made to suppress the true version of events. The familiarity of the story to Strokach meant that he could also protect the players while advancing the myth. By protecting this oral tradition for the first decade after the war, the legend of the "death match" was born, and with it a compelling piece of propaganda. Strokach further prevented publication of any account that varied from the simplified legend that Ukrainian pride had triumphed over Nazi savagery.

The enduring nature of the myth speaks to the power of sport to inspire. It is under this fog of war that the true story of football in Nazi-occupied Ukraine is told. During their occupation of Kiev, the Nazis used football as an extension of their domination, much like Mussolini's fascists in Italy had done in winning the 1934 and 1938 World Cups, forever linking football with the glory of the fatherland. And the pursuit of these glories began with a declaration of war.

With the initiation of Operation Barbarossa on June 22, 1941, the armies of Adolf Hitler attacked the Soviet Union with breathtaking speed, and one country in particular, Ukraine suffered extensively under the horrors of Blitzkrieg warfare. The three-million-man-strong assault on the Soviet Union covered a vast swath of territory from the Baltic Sea in the north to the Crimea region of Ukraine in the south. Facing another half million auxiliary troops from nations allied with Germany, the USSR endured the full brunt of what the Nazis called a "war of annihilation." Ukraine, as a prized jewel in the holdings of the Soviet empire, offered robust industrial capacity and verdant farmland ripe for the taking. Eastern Europe offered Hitler the ideal territory to fulfill his ideological mission of returning the Germanic peoples, wherever they may be found, to a rural, agrarian existence. These fertile lands provided *lebensraum* (living space) for the Nazi empire to replenish itself and further expand. Throughout this process, the native populations would just disappear.

Unexpectedly, the arrival of the National Socialists represented new possibilities, foremost among them the hope for self-determination. But once the battle for the capital city, Kiev, commenced, it became abundantly clear that the Ukrainians were simply trading one brutal regime for another. Kiev, a city set on hills overlooking the river Dnieper, was encircled and laid siege to in unrelenting fashion. Among the thousands of defenders were members of the Dynamo Kiev football team, considered by many in the prewar years to be among Europe's best. One player in particular embodied the changing fortunes of war in occupied Kiev. Nikolai Trusevich, or "Kolya" to his close friends, was described as tall and supple, and he became the goalkeeper for Dynamo. Trusevich was a charismatic figure, often the life of the party, liking to joke with teammates in serious moments. His style was to play with his feet whenever he could, racing off his goal line to play the ball like an extra fullback.

Another player, Alexei Klimenko, was a skilled defender who joined Dynamo at about the same time. Klimenko was the youngest brother of a well-known circus family in Kiev. Eight of the Dynamo Kiev players ended up being the bulk of the Ukrainian national team in the mid- to late 1930s. Another favored player was Ivan Kuzmenko, better known to his teammates as "Vanya," a prolific goal scorer and a broad-shouldered man who had a shot as powerful and accurate as any seen in the top Russian league. These Dynamo players, who all served as soldiers in the defense of Kiev, fled the final onslaught on the capital, taking barges down the Dnieper and bringing club trophies and mementos along for the ride.

Kiev finally fell on September 19, 1941, and the city was set afire by both the Germans and the retreating Russians. Stalin had given a "scorched earth" order, intending to leave no usable building or industry to the conquering Germans. At the end of the battle, some 665,000 prisoners were taken from Kiev, the most acquired in a single action in history.[2] This number represented over 90 percent of all Red Army combatants at the start of the Battle of Kiev. The catastrophic scale of the defeat for the Russians meant that the gallant footballers who fought in battle were taken as prisoners of war. Of the civilians who remained, many were deported as slaves or expired from starvation. Just ten days after the fall of Kiev, the shock of the Nazi occupation would intensify with mass killings at a steep canyon on the northwestern part of the city, well known to the locals as "grandmother ravine," but in time, better known to the world as Babi Yar.

With the advent of this war of annihilation, the Nazi killing machine singled out all Jews in the occupied Soviet territories. German killing squads, known as the *Einsatzgruppen*, were charged with the elimination of all racial and political enemies. These mobile killing units followed the Wehrmacht into the Soviet Union and within hours claimed their first victims, usually by bullet. Nazi policy, enforced by these roving bands of killers, employed the most brutal means available, in which women and children were not spared. The mass killings at Babi Yar represent one of the single most devastating episodes of genocide in all of World War II. In apparent retaliation for a partisan attack on buildings used by the Wehrmacht, the German authorities ordered all Jews in Kiev to report to the occupying government for "resettlement." This term, a common euphemism for murder, meant that the collected Jews were marched to Babi Yar in huge columns under the guise of relocation.

The mile-long ravine is located about six miles from the city center of Kiev, and over the course of two days, victims were stripped of all of their possessions and forced to disrobe. Made to walk a gauntlet of soldiers wielding batons, the surviving individuals were then marched to the ravine. Between the religious holidays celebrating Rosh Hashanah, the Jewish New Year, and Yom Kippur, the Day of Atonement, 33,771 Jews were killed by divisions of the *Einsatzgruppen* with assistance from two Ukrainian police regiments. The reason this figure is so exact is that the men tasked with the murders kept meticulous records of their deeds. One eyewitness to the massacre was Kurt Werner, an actual participant in the mass killings:

> As soon as I arrived at the execution area I was sent down to the bottom of the ravine with some of the other men. It was not long before the first Jews were brought to us over the side of the ravine. The Jews had to lie face down on the earth by the ravine walls. There were three groups of marksmen down at the bottom of the ravine, each made up of about twelve men. Groups of Jews were sent down to each of these execution squads simultaneously. Each successive group of Jews had to lie down on top of the bodies of those that had already been shot. The marksmen stood behind the Jews and killed them with a shot in the neck. I still recall today the complete terror of the Jews when they first caught sight of the bodies as they reached the top edge of the ravine. Many Jews cried out in terror. It's almost impossible to imagine what nerves of steel it took to carry out that dirty work down there. It was horrible. . . . I had to spend the whole morning down in the ravine. For some of the time I had to shoot continuously. Then I was given the job of loading submachine-gun magazines with ammunition. While I was doing that, other comrades were assigned to shooting duty. . . . The shooting that day must have lasted until . . . 1700 or 1800 hours. Afterwards we were taken back to our quarters. That evening we were given alcohol [schnapps] again.[3]

As the occupation lasted another two years, more reprisal killings followed the original massacre at Babi Yar. Ultimately, 150,000 perished at the gorge.[4] Among the murdered were Soviet partisans, prisoners of war, and Roma (gypsies). But by the end of Nazi occupation, well over half of the victims were Jews, a fact completely unrecognized in Soviet memorialization of the genocide after the war.

FOOTBALL IN TIME OF WAR

The occupation of Kiev turned out to be complicated as the invaders were first welcomed, especially by nationalists who loathed the Stalinists. Several Dynamo Kiev players were listed as members of the NKVD (the Soviet secret police) in official team documents, and while this status afforded important privileges, it became a lethal danger in the new Nazi order. Many of the Dynamo players worked as nominal policemen, and a few had sustained involvement at communist party functions. But their political associations marked them for arrest at a minimum, or worse, interrogation by the Gestapo. Once captured, the Dynamo Kiev players were required to give an oath of loyalty to the new regime, particularly the enlisted men. Three players in particular fell into this latter group: Trusevich, Klimenko, and Kuzmenko. Also the ardent Stalinist Nikolai Makhinya was included in this initial sweep, and all four players soon offered loyalty pledges, thereby freeing themselves from the detention camps.

The Germans wanted to restore industrial infrastructure and get the bakeries working to feed both the army and the occupied residents of Kiev. Bakery no. 3 on Degtyarevskaya Street was the first to reopen. These are not the quaint bakeries one might find in a Parisian neighborhood but rather industrial complexes designed to bake bread for thousands. The search for workers for this massive bread factory was quickly undertaken. One of the best places to find workers was the center of Kiev, where cafés and shops started to gradually reopen. Sitting at a café one day, bakery manager Iosef Kordik noticed a man he thought looked very similar to Nikolai Trusevich. But the man before him was thin and gaunt, not the elegant man he once knew patrolling the penalty box for Dynamo. "Koyla" Trusevich had sustained a leg injury during the battle for Kiev, and Kordik looked long enough to realize that this familiar man walking with a limp was indeed Trusevich. The giveaway was a long scar on his right cheek.

Like the other exiles in their own land, residents of Kiev were forced to survive on three hundred grams of bread per day.[5] Bringing this haggard survivor something to eat, it didn't take Iosef Kordik long to realize he had the power to save this man, who in all likelihood would be picked up by the Germans sometime soon. Because Trusevich also had a Jewish wife and a daughter to provide for, the prospect of immediate work would be enticing. Kordik offered him a job at Bakery no. 3, and not long after the arrival of the former goalkeeper of Dynamo, the director of the bakery, a passionate fan, had an idea—"Let's have a football team." Kordik took the next step by searching for other teammates of Trusevich scattered throughout the ruined capital, hiding from the occupying forces. Searching the city in the spring of 1942, he found Makar Goncharenko, who had kept his kit and boots with the hope that he might play football again. He agreed to join in, and this diminutive winger proved to be a vitally important player to the team that was forming in the bakery. Not many Dynamo Kiev players remained, though. Some had died of starvation; others met their demise in the detention camps, in battle, or by summary execution.

In winter 1942, hunger was the more deadly enemy as the Ukrainians acclimated to the occupation, now six months old. The *Reichskommissariat* was the designation for the Ukrainian territories where extreme ethnic cleansing and looting occurred. The ruthless starvation of the local population was meant to depopulate Ukraine and to feed the advancing Nazi armies, as they would "live off the land."[6] Thousands died from starvation across Ukraine, and even more were deported as slave labor to Germany. The figure initially crucial to the survival of the Dynamo Kiev players was the bakery foreman Iosef Kordik, an ethnic German, or *Volksdeutsch*, who was afforded special status in the new hierarchy. A network of contacts provided a few more Dynamo teammates, and rival teams' players also wanted to join the bakery once word got out. From the crosstown squad Lokomotiv Kiev came Mikhail Melnik, Vasily Sukharev, and Vladimir Balakin. It was easy to persuade these players because daily existence was a fierce struggle. Most survivors lacked adequate food, shelter, and basic security. These men in the bakery became a maintenance squad, sweeping, loading, and unloading sacks of flour and bread trays. Sports celebrities from the ranks of boxing, gymnastics, and swimming were also evident in the food factory's labor force.

Over the course of several weeks in the early spring of 1942, Kordik assembled the players several times during the week, creating space for the workers to play football. As many of the Dynamo Kiev players were ex–Red Army soldiers, each had to keep a low profile, training in the bakery courtyard. Barred from using the team name *Dynamo* because of its Soviet heritage, a new team was created, calling itself FC Start, a name nearly identical in translation to English from the Ukrainian. Matches were played in Zenit Stadium, which is now part of a public park in Kiev where football is still played, usually at the amateur, Sunday-league level. By the end of the summer exhibition season, FC Start had played seven, won seven, and tallied forty-seven goals for—with a mere eight goals against.

THE GAMES BEGIN

Sport was used ostensibly in occupied Kiev to win the hearts and minds of the civilians; in reality, the football that summer served a darker purpose. The Nazis allowed the matches to pacify the local population, and the games also bought time for the full implementation of the policies of deportation and extermination. When the new national stadium was completed (left unfinished at invasion), a nationalist team called Rukh would play an all-German team to inaugurate the new pitch. From its inception, Rukh (which means "movement" in Ukrainian) was a club based more on political affiliation than talent on the pitch; these players proved to be a team of nationalist collaborators in the end. The player-manager of Rukh was Georgi Shvetsov, a former footballer and an ambitious anti-Semite. Shvetsov was almost singularly responsible for reintroducing the game to occupied Kiev.[7] But Shvetsov was thwarted numerous times in his recruitment of Dynamo players. His Ukrainian nationalism made him a highly likely candidate to collaborate with the Nazis, who shared his hatred for the communists. This divide is most responsible for the reluctance of the former Dynamo players to join Rukh.

As the leader of the Dynamo team, Trusevich was an inspiration, and he resisted recruitment to Rukh because he so staunchly opposed the Germans. Loyal to their goalkeeper were the other FC Start players. In the defense, there was Alexei Klimenko, the youthful but fierce defender, who was athletic and exceptionally fast but slight of build; the de facto coach and fullback Mikhail Sviridovsky, a member of the 1932

Dynamo team and older than the other players; and Fyodor Tyutchev, a defender who found an ally in Trusevich and his opposition to the Germans. In the midfield, there was Nikolai Korotkykh, once a fringe player who was loyal to the departed Russians but now an attacking midfielder given a chance to compete. The three players from Lokomotiv, Melnik, Sukharev, and Balakin, equally as famous as the Dynamo players,[8] all rotated positions across the middle of the park as well.

Leading the attack were forwards Nikolai Makhinya and Pavel Komarov, Dynamo's top scorer before the war. Komarov was a natural striker but hesitant going into "50–50 balls," those moments in a game where possession of the ball is there for the taking. Komarov's lack of physical presence was offset by a classic center forward named Ivan Kuzmenko, a man who cut a large, imposing figure. "Vanya" Kuzmenko had devastating power in his shot, and he was a tireless worker for his teammates. Conscientious in his training, one story has it that Kuzmenko took three deflated footballs and collapsed them into one another, creating a new ball with three times the weight of a regulation football.[9] This modification allowed him to strengthen his shot, an advantage that would later prove to be the difference in one close but vitally important match.

Alongside the hulking, powerful Kuzmenko was the flair player for FC Start, a gifted winger with a low center of gravity and such great balance that he could not be pushed off the ball: Makar Goncharenko, the player who had carried the dream of once again playing football when hostilities ended and had saved his football boots. Possessing a precise shot with superior vision for the game and deft on the dribble, Goncharenko became a crowd favorite. He could anticipate the movements of teammates, moving freely and avoiding the scything tackles of less-skilled defenders. His Dynamo Kiev teammates were so used to his scoring exploits that when he would go through on the keeper, they would start to walk back to their half of the field before the referee would signal for the goal.[10] The other players from Lokomotiv brought with them strong football reputations on par with the players from Dynamo Kiev, and they blended in rather seamlessly to this new Ukrainian side.

While the new team name, FC Start, represented a new beginning, it also meant more to those who wanted to eschew political alliances and any cooperation with the occupying enemy. With the announce-

ment by the Germans that a new season of football would begin on
Sunday, June 7, 1942, the FC Start squad was matched up against the
Ukrainian nationalist side Rukh. Arranged as a doubleheader, a match
between a Luftwaffe headquarters team and an air force supply services
team was scheduled at 1400, and the Rukh–FC Start match was slated
for 1730.

The three-year hiatus in top-level play meant that some semblance
of normalcy was returning to the Ukrainian capital. It also meant that,
lacking a proper number of teams, six squads representing the nearby
German garrisons would also compete in a series of exhibition matches
that fateful summer of 1942. These games represented the most notable diversion in many months. Free admission ensured a good turnout
as well. Posters were plastered on walls all over the city, and soon the
match featuring the Ukrainian teams was discussed excitedly by the
downtrodden residents of Kiev. Players for FC Start carefully considered the decision to play. Would it be seen as collaboration? Or would
their playing serve to boost morale among Kiev's inhabitants, who had
witnessed such profound deprivations and suffering that it beggared the
imagination just to remember them?

The esprit de corps was strong among the team members as they
had endured extraordinary events in the previous twelve months.
Though not in the Dynamo team colors of blue and white, the new
blended team played in red wool shirts found in a nearby warehouse
after the chaotic evacuation of the city, and game shorts were cut from
trousers. Workboots, casual shoes, and canvas footwear were the best
available football boots. Only the striker Goncharenko had proper
cleats. Better outfitted and better fed, the Rukh team also enjoyed
youth and greater fitness from the onset. But it took very little time to
figure out who was the more technically gifted team. A Romanian referee oversaw the first match, and with the kickoff, the familiarity of the
Start players canceled out the physical superiority of the nationalist
side. The final score was 7–2.

Vengefully, the organizer of Rukh arranged for FC Start to be
banned from training in the new national stadium. The only field available to them would be the Bakery no. 3 yard. But Iosef Kordik countered. He skillfully negotiated the use of another pitch. Without this
option, Start risked having to drop out of the exhibition matches altogether. This new pitch was the small neoclassical Zenit Stadium, which

today is located in the middle of Kiev, next to a regularly used public park and set in a hollow amid an expansive housing development.

Two weeks after the inaugural fixture, Start played two more matches, the first against a team of Hungarian soldiers whom they bested 6–2 and the second against a Romanian garrison team whom they beat resoundingly 11–0. With their reputation on the rise, the bakery team soon gained the affections of many residents of the Left Bank of Kiev. With the German authorities uninterested in meddling in the affairs of the organizers, the late afternoon games, now requiring an admission fee of five rubles, were must-see entertainment. The main local newspaper, *Nova Ukrainski Slovo*, published match reports from the beginning of the season but had conspicuously ignored the Start team. With the demolition of the German military team called PGS 6–0 on July 17, the local collaborationist newspaper could no longer ignore the bakery team.

One advantage enjoyed by the Start team was that the Zenit field was smaller than usual. The playing surface was rough, and the notion that a groundskeeper would tend the field was absurd in those days of scarcity. A running track around the stadium formed an oval, and the only seating ran the length of one touchline. The grandstand was located in the middle of the seating area and had a simple metal roof supported by pillars. Rudimentary terraces flanked the grandstands and offered bench seating on a raised embankment. Yet the parklike grounds offered enjoyment of sporting events and picnics for the local community.

As the more technically advanced team, FC Start could possess the ball longer on this smaller pitch and thus avoid being exposed for pace on the wings by their often younger, more fit opponents. Fans rallied around the team. Among their opponents, the Romanian auxiliaries most favored the Start players, who remembered these soldiers regularly appearing in the dressing room before some of the Start matches to share good wishes and to distribute smuggled food.[11] Late in July, the match with a well-regarded and recently bolstered Hungarian garrison team called MSG Wal resulted in yet another comprehensive triumph by the Start team, 5–1. Even with a revamped lineup that featured former professional footballers, the Hungarian allies to the Nazis were easily defeated, in part because they went down to ten men due to injury. Consistent with the rules of the day, substitutions could not be made, even for injuries. Shortly after the match, MSG demanded a rematch and German authorities obliged, prolonging the season, which should have ended on this match day. Set for one week later, the revenge match, the best attended of any of the matches featuring Start, was played in sweltering heat. Undefeated up to this point, FC Start players, already fatigued from a twelve-hour shift at the bakery, contended with a rested and fiercely competitive opponent in MSG Wal. At halftime, Start surged to a 3–0 lead on goals by Kuzmenko, Komarov, and Goncharenko.

The pressure from MSG mounted in the second half, and after conceding an early penalty that was successfully converted, the Start team allowed a second goal in quick succession. Observers at the match remembered that goalkeeper Trusevich was the only reason FC Start held on for a 3–2 victory. Despite near complete exhaustion, both teams embraced after the game, sharing laughter and soaking in the raucous cheers of the gathered crowd. Because Start carried the hopes of many Ukrainians, especially in communist circles, the Nazi authorities recognized an increased threat in the undefeated Start side. Intolerant of dissent and violent in reaction to perceived and real rebellion, the Nazis would not allow FC Start to become folk heroes. This presumed final match against the Hungarians served as a pretext to the much better known contest: the match against the best German football team in Ukraine, a team called Flakelf.

Historians have questioned the air of invincibility associated with the Flakelf squad.[12] Though elite Luftwaffe pilots were part of the team, the majority of the players were pulled from the antiaircraft batteries in and around Kiev. Routinely beating the Ukrainian national side Rukh, the Flakelf (the Flak Eleven) squad was undefeated up to this point. By calling on Flakelf, the Nazis set out to stifle any further inspiration FC Start could offer. The rapid and thorough defeat of Bolshevism in greater Ukraine needed to be matched on the football pitch. The match was set for August 6.

Despite being on a weekday that saw a diminished crowd, this match drew a large number of German spectators. These fans, fully expecting a reassertion of Aryan superiority and domination, left the Zenit Stadium late that Thursday afternoon in profound disbelief as the best of the German club teams in Ukraine lost convincingly 5–1. In a brutally played game with punishing tackles, the Romanian referee disregarded persistent fouling by the Germans. Ignored in the local propaganda newspaper and missing from any official reports, the win by FC Start further galvanized the citizens of Kiev. But the formal response by the Nazis to the positive public perception across the city was immediate. Posters and handbills appeared all over the city the very next day announcing a rematch on Sunday, August 9, only three days later, at Zenit Stadium. Published in both Ukrainian and German, the posters appeared on fences and lampposts and were plastered on building walls and shop windows all across the city. By using the word *revenge* on the poster, the "unofficial" result was acknowledged in a most public way. With the football season extended by yet another match, the expectations were exceptionally clear: the Germans were designated to win. Eliminating any reasonable time for recovery, the mere seventy-two hours between matches meant that the odds were stacked against the Ukrainians. As the invincibility of Hitler's armies was being tested in the stalled assaults on Moscow and Stalingrad at about the same time, the Nazis demanded capitulation in Kiev.

THE MATCH OF DEATH

Under this climate of uncertainty for the Germans, their best football team in occupied Ukraine found a most determined foe in FC Start, a team half starved and made up of *Untermenschen* supposedly destined to be vanquished by Aryan supremacy. It was a battle of fascism against Bolshevism. Curiously, the poster announcing the game listed fourteen Start players, including a Rukh player who only featured once in the first game when the bakery team was short on numbers. FC Start never played with such a full roster, and they often had trouble fielding a team with eleven men. More importantly, omitted from the poster was one of the best-loved and most charismatic players, "Vanya" Kuzmenko.

Rumors abounded that Flakelf was reinforcing their squad with established international footballers from across Europe. In the tense moments before kickoff, spectators sat in nervous anxiety, unsure what another Start victory would bring. The late summer heat added an edge to the match. German soldiers, armed with field rifles and leading a squad of Ukrainian policeman wielding pickax handles, were stationed all along the route leading into the stadium. A natural amphitheater, the stadium grounds were also patrolled by dogs for crowd control, which added an imposing danger. These were the same Alsatians used in the early days of conquest by the Wehrmacht the year prior.[13]

Relegated to the grassy ridges surrounding the field, the Ukrainian spectators formed a ring around it, sitting as close to the touchline as possible. The Germans and their associates, unsurprisingly, claimed all of the seats in the terraces, separated from the crowd by a small, waist-high metal fence. Children attended the match in large numbers, and several of the young boys, clamoring to be noticed by the match organizers, hoped to be chosen as ball boys. Lacking nets on the goals or fencing on the ends of the stadium, these boys would be needed. Ukrainian folk songs radiated from the stands before kickoff, albeit more subdued than they would otherwise be. Well aware of the importance this game had taken on, the players in the FC Start dressing room had to contend with an even greater sense of uncertainty and tension. These feelings heightened when suddenly the team was paid a visit by a tall, bald SS man speaking impeccable Russian. Many years after the war, Makar Goncharenko remembered the exchange: "I am the referee of today's game. I know you are a very good team. Please follow all the rules, do not break any of the rules, and before the game, greet your opponents in our fashion."[14] Though accounts differ on this prematch visit even occurring, there was a distinctive apprehension among the players about playing this "revenge" match. The sinister tone and intent of the message in the dressing room was clear as day. Concede defeat and salute in the Nazi manner before the game. The debate that ensued after the SS officer left consumed all of the players in the dressing room. Should they comply or resist? In the waning moments before the match kicked off, a steady stream of visitors continued into the locker room bringing food, well wishes, and words of caution as well. Over the course of nine weeks, in this most improbable of seasons, the players on FC Start were more unified and cohesive than ever. The team emerged from the dressing room and walked out, courageously determined to face their fate.

Crossing the cinder track of the infield as the crowd rose and surged forward, the players of FC Start walked toward the pitch for the introductions. Any who had watched the team before would notice that the tired and worn-out jerseys Start had worn throughout the summer had been replaced. Through donations from the local community, red socks and white shorts were added to complete the kit. Many speculated for years after the match that the new uniform looked like the kit worn by the prewar USSR teams. But Goncharenko admitted years after that it was mere coincidence that the team looked the way it did.[15] The Flakelf players wore their customary white kit, and with goalkeeper Trusevich donning his now-familiar black keeper shirt with red trim, there was the convincing air of a genuine international match.

In the moments before the referee's whistle to start the match, the German players snapped to attention and extended their right arms for the Hitler salute. Roars of approval from the German crowd followed the "Heil Hitler!" shouted in unison by Flakelf. A moment of dread and uncertainty overcame the Ukrainian supporters: would FC Start follow in kind? In a brief moment of silence, which must have seemed like an eternity, the Start players lowered their heads and slowly elevated their arms. What at first looked like capitulation to German demands quickly changed as the raised arms of the Ukrainian footballers snapped back to their chests, with each man shouting a familiar Soviet sportsman's chant of the day: "FitzCultHura!" or "Long live sport!"[16] Interestingly, this chant worked as an affirmation of goodwill and, more importantly, as an acknowledgment of the significance of the rematch.

Faced with an SS man as an official, Start players knew they would not be able to protest the anticipated rough play of Flakelf, nor could they match the brutal tactics of the Germans. They had to play within the rules and aim to win against a clearly reinforced Flakelf team. The starting players looked over to the substitute bench for Flakelf to find another full squad, while on their own bench they had only the team trainer. The match seemed to begin badly for FC Start, and the players seemed distracted. The harsh treatment they had expected began almost immediately. In the opening moments of the match, goalkeeper Trusevich took the brunt of the physical play. When he came out from his goal to intercept a crossed ball, he was knocked to the ground, and the referee ignored the foul. Ten minutes into the game, Trusevich attempted to claim a ball at the feet of a German player. The Flakelf forward made no attempt to stop his run, and he ran through unchecked, hitting Trusevich in the head. Knocked unconscious and without a substitute, Trusevich eventually soldiered on, though his focus was noticeably hampered. The Germans took the lead on their next attack into the penalty area.

The rough play continued well into the first half, with Flakelf players making tackles well after the ball had left the foot of the Start player. Often made in the "studs up" manner, this vicious Flakelf tactic left its mark on their legs of several Start players. On set pieces, Ukrainian players were often pushed out of the way, and on corner kicks jerseys were held to prevent them from jumping for the ball. But once again it was Kuzmenko who offered a lifeline to the struggling Start team. Because he had trained earlier with a weighted ball, Kuzmenko took a pass from Goncharenko inside the center circle and after only a few strides let fly with a shot from over thirty yards out before a defender could bring him down. The ball blasted in past the Flakelf keeper and the game was level.

FC Start played more defensively and managed to avoid the late tackles they knew would come. Again, in the face of youth and strength from the Germans, the technical superiority of FC Start remained. The perseverance of the Ukrainians produced results later in the half when the ball came out to Goncharenko on the wing and he drifted inside, beating several defenders and ultimately scoring the second goal. And before the half would conclude, Kuzmenko sent a long ball through to Goncharenko, who was at the shoulder of the last defender. Anticipating an offside call, he stepped back so that he could volley the first-time ball. His brilliance stunned the Flakelf keeper, and FC Start went into halftime with a 3–1 lead. The tenacity of Start inspired the Ukrainian crowd, and the rapturous joy of the spectators built to a crescendo. Some of the crowd headed for the terraces where they could taunt the German officers and dignitaries. In response, the German officers called in the dogs to control the crowd. In other areas of the football ground, fighting broke out between rival fans, many of whom were soldiers on leave and well lubricated from a full day of drinking. Ukrainian police and German guards maintained order, but it was the fans of FC Start who would endure the worst of the beatings.

The euphoria in the Start dressing room was soon dampened with the arrival of more visitors. First it was Georgi Shvetsov, the player-manager of Rukh and an opportunist who had much to lose with a Start victory. He struck a conciliatory tone, surprising since he despised the Dynamo team. He advised caution and that the Start players needed to protect themselves and the gathered spectators, who were in danger of Nazi reprisal.[17] Shvetsov's warning proved to be prescient with the appearance of a second SS officer, who politely reminded the Start players that even though they had played well in the first half, they should consider carefully the consequences of a victory.[18]

The second half began much as the first half ended, with players from both teams struggling to find a rhythm. In fact, because the crowd had become so strident, the physical play of the Germans seemed to wane as Flakelf appeared to be fearful of the Kiev fans watching, in the same way the Start players feared the assembled German soldiers. Start maintained their dominance, and with both teams scoring in the second half, the chance that Flakelf would mount a comeback seemed more and more remote. One ten-year-old boy in the stands that day remembered the match particularly well. Vladimir Mayevsky was brought to the game by his father, and he would later go on to play for Dynamo Kiev with some notoriety. Mayevsky recalled, "I remember that the whole of the central part of the stadium was taken up by Germans. There were Hungarian troops standing on the hill on one side and the rest of the audience were standing along the perimeter of the stadium. I remember our team scored a lot. Our best players were Goncharenko and Klimenko." Mayevsky was particularly impressed by Klimenko, who brazenly humiliated the Germans: "I remember he side-stepped all of the German defenders, including the goal keeper. Then he ran to the goal line, but instead of putting it into the goal he stopped it on the line. Then he ran into the goal, turned, and kicked the ball back up the field and into play."[19] Observers noted that almost immediately after this display, the SS referee blew the whistle to end the match at 4–2 despite the fact that ninety minutes had not been played.

DEADLY AFTERMATH

The mood after the match was subdued and somber. Unsure of the consequences to come, the FC Start players left the field quickly after the customary handshakes. The excited, triumphant crowd lingered in the stadium, savoring the victory and pushing the limits of what would be tolerated by the German guards as they mobbed the grandstand where the occupation officials sat. Exhaustion far surpassed any jubilation in the players' minds and bodies. In the days that followed the match, the Start players feared the worst given the history of brutal reprisals from their Nazi overlords since the occupation started.

Instead, they all returned to work at Bakery no. 3. Training also continued, and when Iosef Kordik announced that another Sunday fixture would be played the following week, the anxiety seemed to lessen. The German authorities, likely incensed by the insolence shown by the fans in their jeering during the match, also had to deal with a second embarrassment on the soccer pitch in three days. The humiliation the German masters experienced was further deepened by the newly bolstered pride felt by the residents of Kiev. August 16 was the date set for another rematch, this time against Rukh. A repeat of the opening fixture of the season, Rukh came into the match on a wave of momentum, having accumulated a number of victories, including a win against an up-and-coming local team called Sport. Showing no ill effects from the recent grueling schedule, FC Start improved on their original 7–2 score line against Rukh with a comprehensive 8–0 thrashing of the Ukrainian nationalist squad. Though this final match was much more disciplined than any of the other games that summer, the Start players could not anticipate the storm that was coming.

Working in the shadows was Georgi Shvetsov, the manager for Rukh, who could not abide another humiliating defeat to FC Start. Lobbying the German authorities for a response to the rebelliousness embodied by the victorious Start players, he found a receptive audience among some in the occupying government. Shvetsov's nationalism was in direct opposition to the presumed communism of the Start players. Claiming that FC Start challenged the authority of military rule and that a propaganda victory had been handed to the communists, Shvetsov apparently persuaded the Nazis to arrest the Start team.[20] With the handbill from the final game against Flakelf in hand, Gestapo agents appeared at the bakery and called players individually into Kordik's office. Because some names like Kuzmenko (who did not originally appear on the advertising poster) and Gundarev (who was actually a Rukh player) did not appear on the arrest list, it was clear that Shvetsov played some collaborative role in the arrests.

As each player made his way to the bakery office, the presence of the Gestapo was immediately alarming. The subsequent one-by-one disappearance of each footballer into a waiting car left no more doubts. One player not at the factory was the last to be arrested. The player-coach

Mikhail Sviridovsky was spotted refereeing a local match as part of his secret training for one of the local teams, a violation of occupation rules requiring all labor to be registered. He was taken to the Gestapo head-quarters with the rest of his Start teammates. Prisoners were placed in separate cells facing each other and able to see one another. Gestapo interrogators individually tortured and questioned the players. One player was singled out during the arrest, a former Soviet commissar, Nickolai Korotkykh, the only professional NKVD officer on the FC Start team. Korotkykh was from a rural industrial town in Russia and served in the Soviet secret police for two years before the war.[21] It is unlikely that his teammates knew about his link to Stalin's terror organization. Though all of the Start players were loosely affiliated with the NKVD, it was Korotkykh who had actually served as an officer responsible for enforcing Stalinist policies.

With a standing order to shoot any Soviet political officials, the exposure of this player was a shock to the other Start players. Speculation was that their midfielder teammate Korotkykh had been betrayed by his own sister, looking to save her family and herself from reprisal. But it is even more likely that the Germans already knew about Korotkykh's membership in the NKVD as he was immediately singled out upon arriving at the Gestapo prison. The others were interrogated three times daily for three weeks under an intense bright light that hung in each cell, with physical punishment alternating with intense questioning. Bizarrely, many of the prisoners had endured similar treatment for years during Soviet-era inquisitions. Torture, savage beatings, and sleep deprivation quickly took their toll. The Gestapo wanted any sort of forced confession, for any crime—petty theft, sabotage, or conspiracy. Strikingly, none of the players caved under the cruel pressure. But, eventually, Korotkykh succumbed to twenty straight days of interrogation, dying in a Gestapo prison cell, separated from the others. The remaining prisoners were taken to the Syrets concentration camp located at Babi Yar.

UNITED TO THE END

Imprisonment at Syrets reflected an exceptionally inhumane reality, even when compared to other Nazi concentration camps where the primary mission was to exterminate. Syrets was already notorious to the residents of Kiev, who knew it to be a place where the NKVD buried "enemies of the homeland." Divided in two by residential quarters and a working section, the living conditions in the camp were dangerous, unsanitary, and usually lethal. One dreadful feature of Syrets was unique: dugout barracks, hewn from the earth. These underground bunkers with corrugated metal roofs offered the barest of shelter and were quite simply unfit for human habitation. They contained bunk beds too small for a grown adult to lie down on. Starvation, the primary tool of murder, consisted of coarse bread and watery soup. Drinking water had to be carried by the prisoners from a nearby river, and the latrine was no more than a hole in the ground. In such conditions, disease ran rampant.

Syrets was established by the Nazis in 1942 as a subcamp of the Sachsenhausen concentration camp near Berlin. It was a few hundred meters from the Babi Yar ravine in the northwest suburbs of Kiev. The primitive open-air camp had a capacity of three thousand prisoners at any given time, but countless prisoners, or *häftlinge*, were shot or killed with gas vans, the same vans employed in the earliest death camps in Poland that same year. Rough estimates hold that twenty-five thousand people were killed in *Konzentrationslager* Syrets. Communists, Soviet POWs, and Ukrainian partisans all perished there, regardless of gender. One of the few successful revolts in the camp occurred in September 1943, a few weeks before the camp was liberated. Fifteen prisoners escaped, and one of these provided rare testimony of the death and inhumanity that occurred at Syrets and Babi Yar during the postwar Nuremberg Trials.

As no one was expected to survive Syrets, the camp effectively served as a killing center much like the Polish death camps of Sobibór and Auschwitz. Yet, upon arrival at Syrets, the ten FC Start players had an advantage—they were in much better physical condition than the typical prisoner. Quickly, the footballers were introduced to the camp guards and the commandant, SS-Sturmbannführer Paul von Radomsky. Radomsky was infamous among the inmates of Syrets for his sadistic cruelty. Responsible for the unending savagery in the camp, the commandant often terrorized prisoners by releasing his dog, a large German shepherd, to enforce his will. Guards under his leadership were given rewards for innovations in torturing and for killing their captives.

These severe punishments were typically meted out in the center of the camp. In one horrific example, prisoners were strapped to a table, with their arms and legs spread apart and tied down, and beaten by whip, sometimes until death.

The daily routine inside the camp was grueling. Days began with a predawn roll call lasting for hours. Any missing prisoners were accounted for, and the dead were identified and taken away for disposal. Harsh physical exercises often followed humiliation rituals. Prisoners did not wear uniforms; they wore what they brought on their bodies into the camp. After the roll call, prisoners marched out of the camp for hard physical labor, which involved cutting lumber, digging ditches, building roads, and repairing war damage. The workday ended some fourteen hours later with prisoners returning to the camp at 1800.

All of the prisoners, especially the well-known footballers of FC Start, lived under the constant threat of imminent death. Executions were scheduled twice a week on Fridays and Saturdays, especially for prisoners caught escaping. Commandant Radomsky was always present at these executions, and typically, twenty-five randomly chosen prisoners were executed. The once-healthy Start teammates began to look more and more haggard as their well-worn clothes became tattered rags covering skeletal frames. Most prisoners walked the grounds barefoot and half naked. Emaciated, the captives grew more pitiful in appearance with each passing day. The daily regime in the camp was so sadistically cruel that even if you survived the beatings, starvation, and random selections for murder, you still might fall prey to an obscenely arbitrary rule unknown to all but the person choosing to enforce it.

The ever-increasing savagery of Syrets challenged the survival capacities of the Start players, particularly when the fortunes of war changed for the Germans in late 1942 and prison guards accelerated their efforts at extermination. Goalkeeper Nikolai Trusevich, ever the encouragement to his fellow prisoners, passed on messages when he could, boosting morale much as he had done as a team leader on the field just a few months earlier. Acts of sabotage increased, and an arson attack on German administration buildings in Kiev at the end of February 1943 provoked the rage of Commandant Radomsky. When word of the attack reached the prisoners, they expected the worst. The alarm for roll call was sounded on the morning of February 23 and the captives scrambled into formation. Guards then walked behind each line, delivering random blows to the backs of select prisoners. At these random intervals, another guard followed behind and delivered a bullet to the back of the head of the stunned man. In retaliation for the partisan attacks in Kiev, Radomsky had decreed that every third man would be executed in this manner.

The silence that followed the sound of boots walking the frozen ground was the ultimate terror for these prisoners. If a man turned to look, he too was shot. As several men lay dead or dying, this is how death came to the once imposing FC Start striker Ivan Kuzmenko. A shadow of his former self, it was said that it took several blows of a rifle butt to bring the staggered Vanya to his knees. The bullet behind his ear quickly ended his suffering. On down the execution line, Klimenko and Trusevich also met their end. Trusevich died in his trademark black jersey with red trim, which he had worn for the final match he played in six months earlier. The bodies of the three murdered players were later unceremoniously dumped in the ravine at Babi Yar, buried like thousands of others before them.

THE LEGEND AND LEGACY OF FC START

That the surviving Start players had lost the three most charismatic, stalwart players on the team all at once was too much to bear. Expecting the same end for themselves, the prisoners struggled to find reasons to live. When news of the escape of Makar Goncharenko from a work detail at a boot-mending workshop outside of the camp reached the surviving group members, their spirits soared. Liberation finally came to Kiev in the early morning hours of November 6, 1943. As prisoners stumbled out of the Syrets concentration camp, they emerged into a city that had been completely devastated and set aflame by the retreating German army.

Within days of reclaiming the Ukrainian capital, Soviet authorities began to collect information on what had taken place during the occupation. Among countless stories of death at Babi Yar and of heroism on the urban battlefield, there were these accounts of survival through sport. FC Start had inspired locals to small acts of heroism: hidden artwork was revealed, icons restored to churches, remaining Jews hidden, and smuggled survivors returned to the light of day. When the war was over, the footballers from Kiev faced intense scrutiny for their activities during the war. In the eyes of many Soviet citizens, any actions other than armed confrontation during the war years were tantamount to cooperation. In turn, the surviving Start players were soon arrested and interrogated by local communist leaders and the new version of the Soviet secret police. Hastily formed tribunals initially regarded the footballers as collaborators ("servants of the occupants"),[22] but in return for their cooperation and silence, they were cleared of these charges, which would have brought execution or deportation to a Siberian gulag.

Soviet ideologues developed a comprehensive mythology of what had happened in occupied Ukraine. Government officials ensured that all narratives related to the football played during the summer of 1942 fit the Stalinist message. The new, official story emphasized the immediate and supposedly glorious death of all the FC Start players at the hands of the Nazi invaders. Censorship of the actual events continued well into the 1960s, when fragments of the true story were smuggled out of Ukraine. To this day, there are considerable variations in the telling of the events surrounding the Match of Death, with conspicuous gaps in the tale. Recognition finally came to most of the players of FC Start at the same time that the broader story became popularly understood. Posthumous medals were awarded to the four murdered players, and the rest were given medals for military valor.[23] In 1971, the footballers of FC Start were canonized as Soviet heroes with a granite memorial to the four slain players near the entrance gates of the modern Dynamo Kiev stadium. Sculpted from a single block of granite nearly ten feet tall, the rough-hewn monument features the martyred men, standing four across with square jaws, locking arms and looking tall and strong. The faces of the heroes surface from a recess in the face of the stone. The unnamed men, presumably Kuzmenko, Trusevich, Klimenko, and Korotkykh, are wearing their football shirts, muscles clearly defining them as they once were before the ravages of war. One figure on the far left looks down, almost regretfully.[24] Modern club anthologies for Dynamo Kiev make frequent reference to these heroic events of the "Great Patriotic War."

Another statue in the Ukrainian capital commemorates poignantly the Match of Death. It stands on the walkway leading into the old FC Start stadium, now part of a public park. Atop a fluted classical column rests a muscular, valiant figure kicking a football across the prone body of a vanquished eagle, representing the Third Reich. Both the monument and the myth of the death match once served the propaganda aims of the victorious Soviet system. FC Start winger Makar Goncharenko, who died in 1998 at age eighty-six, placed the deaths of his footballing comrades in the proper context. In his eyes, the war was

> a desperate fight for survival which ended badly for four players. Unfortunately they did not die because they were great football players, or great Dynamo players, and not even because Korotkykh was working for the NKVD. They died like many other Soviet people because the two totalitarian systems were fighting each other and they were destined to become victims of that grand scale massacre. The death of the Dynamo players is not so very different from many other deaths. . . . In those days, people were shot randomly; anyone could be shot, partisans, commissars, Jews, gypsies, saboteurs, thieves. At the beginning of 1943, when the situation at the front changed and resistance in Kiev started going up, executions became more common and basically anyone who was not serving the occupants could be executed or sent to Germany for work.[25]

These footballers became surrogates for the catastrophic losses endured across Ukraine. No single country lost more lives in World War II than Ukraine, and other than Poland no nation lost more Jewish lives, 1.5 million all told.[26] Remarkably, amid such commonplace agony and death, most of the FC Start players managed to survive. Without football, their survival to the end of the war was scarcely better than chance. The four men who died at the hands of the Nazis and their collaborators did so having played the game they loved in the worst conditions imaginable. These inspirations of the past, built on profound sacrifice and team unity, show once again that football has the power to inspire and to conquer oppression.

4

THE BEAUTIFUL GAME IN THE KZ

"The experiences of camp life show that man does have a choice of action. . . . Man can preserve a vestige of spiritual freedom, of independence of mind, even in such terrible conditions of psychic and physical stress. . . . There were always choices to make. . . . Fundamentally, therefore, any man can, even under such circumstances, decide what shall become of him. He many retain his human dignity even in a concentration camp."—Viktor E. Frankl, Vienna-born psychiatrist and survivor of Theresienstadt and Auschwitz[1]

Well before the armies of the Third Reich tore through Ukraine and the rest of Eastern Europe, conquering and murdering millions, the Nazi movement progressed gradually and steadily forward with a program of intimidation and persecution that one day would lead to the near-complete elimination of a people who had inhabited and thrived in Europe for more than a thousand years. In the chaotic years following World War I, Jews became a primary target of the National Socialist Party once it formed in Munich. The Nazis found their foothold by creating so-called internal enemies within Germany itself.

The Nazi revolution came to be an everyday part of the lives of ordinary Germans within weeks of Adolf Hitler taking power in January 1933. The party used the full backing of the government to legalize persecution and normalize terror. First, the Nazis cultivated allies by moving against an old foe, the communists. Inside Germany, the communists were both well organized and widely feared and had been an ideological rival of the Nazis during the party's first ten years of existence.

In rapid succession, trade unionists and social democrats were targeted along with a number of other vulnerable groups within German society. German Jews, homosexuals, Jehovah's Witnesses, the physically and mentally handicapped, and so-called mixed races were subjected to violent intimidation and legal edicts designed to marginalize their existence and, one day, set into motion the elimination of millions of lives.

A crucial step in the creation of the terror state in Nazi Germany was establishing the concentration camp system. Within weeks of assuming power, the SS set up these camps (in German, *Konzentrationslager*, abbreviated as KZ) as reeducation centers where enemies of the regime would be held in "protective custody for the restoration of law and order." But in reality these were destinations that echoed the radical ideological aims of the Third Reich. Concentration camps in the Nazi worldview were a microcosm of the Darwinian struggle inherent in life in the outside world: the fight of the superior to subdue the inferior.

Typically imprisoned without trial, internees endured the full weight of the state and the institutions fashioned to advance the "cleansing of the Volk." In legal terms and following the Nuremberg Laws of 1935, people were locked away for having committed *Rassenschande*—"crimes against the blood." From their very inception, Nazi concentration camps were brutal places where deprivation, starvation, torture, and systematic beatings quickly became the daily norm. Staffed by the SS and the German police, camps also drafted common guards from the general population once the war started; ethnic Germans were enlisted along with enthusiastic recruits from Ukraine, Latvia, Romania, and Croatia.

The largest of the camps also functioned as administrative headquarters for vast networks of satellite camps divided by region within the ever-expanding Reich. The first of these were Dachau, situated to the northwest of Munich, and Sachsenhausen, built to the north of Berlin. In quick succession, others followed. Buchenwald, established just outside of the historic German city of Weimar, joined these first camps, which soon became important instruments of the Nazi terror state.

Popular understanding of the concentration camps system in Nazi Germany is today clouded by confusion regarding the functions of various camps. The earliest camps were fundamentally different than death camps like Sobibór and Treblinka, which were not in existence until the middle of the war. The complex evolution of the camps at Auschwitz further confounds this common understanding. Auschwitz would evolve into both a concentration camp and a killing center. The significance of this distinction is vitally important to understanding how Germans rationalized and accepted the creation of the early camps at Dachau, Sachsenhausen, and Buchenwald. German conquests brought more and more people into mass detention, ultimately from almost every nation in Europe. From within these diverse groups of people came a seemingly endless supply of renewable slave labor, a resource that came to be even more important as the war progressed and able-bodied men were needed to fight.

Responses by prisoners (or *Häftlinge*) in these camps were as varied as the camps themselves. As one of the forms of cultural life that appeared in the camps, sport was a pursuit laden with the most ambiguity. In many memoir accounts, "sport" was often associated with harassment and torment by SS captors, who used compulsory exercise to persecute the old and infirm. The main function of this so-called sport was hazing the inmates and tormenting them, often to the point of utter exhaustion. The cruelty of such punitive exercise contrasted with the competitive sport pursued by privileged prisoners. Though not particularly widespread across the expansive universe of camps within the Nazi sphere, sport and competition offered human contact, solidarity, and, most importantly, a means of survival. Football was the most frequently organized sport in the long-standing camps that are still today known by their infamous names: Dachau, Neuengamme, Gross-Rosen, and Mauthausen, among many others.

The model every major concentration camp followed was KZ Dachau, established on March 22, 1933, just a few weeks after Adolf Hitler assumed power as Germany's chancellor. The camp quickly became a highly public symbol of the new regime. The Nazi-controlled press reported the opening of the camp with great fanfare, and coupled with the blindingly fast arrest of political opponents of the regime, the fear and intimidation of Dachau was cemented in the public mind. The earliest inmates, political prisoners from communist, social democratic, and other left-leaning groups, were arrested by the hundreds and often in the most public manner to produce the most public effect.

In short time, camps like Dachau became the destination for foreign political prisoners and prisoners of war. The number of Jewish prisoners at Dachau increased considerably following *Kristallnacht* on November 9–10, 1938. More than ten thousand Jewish men were deported to Dachau after waves of violence engulfed Germany and Austria, much of it orchestrated by the government. Most of these inmates were soon released after promising to leave the Reich immediately.

Dachau served as a training facility for hundreds of SS guards who were later deployed to other camps throughout the Nazi system. Under the camp's second commandant, SS general Theodore Eicke, regulations were instituted that drastically intensified the harsh conditions endured by prisoners. Eicke was elevated to inspector-general of all the Reich camps in 1934, and his system of punishment set out to humiliate, dehumanize, and deprive of all individuality the "enemies of the state."

Criminals were often installed as camp enforcers (*kapos*) and barracks guards (*blockälteste*) to keep order and discipline. The SS brought in violent career offenders to brutalize inmates and enforce rules. Named for the designation symbol on the chest of their prison uniforms, the "green triangles" were feared almost as much as the SS. The methods proved so effective at Dachau that they soon became the standard for all current and future camps. The cynical spirit of the camps welcomed each arrival to Dachau with the infamous inscription on the entrance to the camp's main gate, "Arbeit Macht Frei" ("Work makes you free"). Put up by Obergruppenführer Eicke, the slogan was used at several other camps in Germany and at the first camp at Auschwitz. Like many of the so-called innovations of the Nazis, the slogan predated the regime, appearing first with the Weimar government in the 1920s to promote public works programs.[2]

The core principles of the SS men who ran these camps were apparent from the beginning. One was to have an unquestioning loyalty to the cause and a hardness of the heart. Servants to the Nazi cause were protecting the Reich from an internal enemy. This mission was pursued with a religious zeal that, in turn, produced a powerful esprit de corps to perform their murderous work. Repeated almost everywhere in the Nazi network of detention, labor, and extermination camps, the methods of psychological torment were quickly perfected:

> The carefully conceived regime at Dachau . . . was not just brutal; it
> was designed to break the will of the inmate. . . . Dachau is infamous
> for the physical sadism practiced there: whippings and other beatings
> were commonplace. Prisoners could be murdered and their deaths
> dismissed as "killed whilst attempting an escape"—and a significant
> number of those sent to Dachau did die there. The real power of the
> regime at Dachau, however, lay less in physical abuse—terrible as it
> undoubtedly was—and more in mental torture.[3]

Sports in Dachau appeared quickly during the first few months of the
camp's operation. The staged events provided Nazi propagandists an
opportunity to highlight the supposed good conditions within the walls.
The archives of the memorial museum at Dachau contain six photos
from June 1933 published in a Munich magazine that capture prisoners
in the detention camp playing football in a common area. Heads shaven
and playing barefoot, the prisoners do not yet show signs of starvation.
Onlookers on the sidelines, wearing the same striped uniforms as the
ersatz players, seem eager to join the action.

Beyond such staged propaganda, prisoner-organized football was
played in Dachau as early as 1936, usually on Sunday afternoons, the
only time forced labor was limited. In fact, football was played so frequently that the camp command believed prisoners, mostly German
nationals at that time, might be entitled to the "state sports badge,"
signifying recognition for athletic achievement by the same government
that identified these prisoners as a threat to German society.[4] The irony
cannot be missed.

Football matches at Dachau were discontinued until 1941 (for reasons unknown), and when play resumed, competitive teams formed
around nationalities and labor groups. Prisoners from Poland, Yugoslavia, Czechoslovakia, Austria, and Italy formed the teams, drawing
players from their fellow countrymen. Polish and German priests even
played.

Though little is known about the games themselves, another artifact
from the camp archives at Dachau tells a story. A wooden cup, fashioned on a prison lathe by a carpenter, carries the inscription "Sieger im
Fussball, Dachau 1944" (Winner in football, Dachau 1944). Clearly, the
matches meant enough to the prisoners that a champion was crowned
that year, just before chaos, disease, and overcrowding rendered the
camp mortally dangerous even to the most able-bodied prisoners.

Matches in Dachau were played on the parade ground, the same square where the *Häftlinge* stood at attention, sometimes for hours, as attendance was checked against the previous roll call. Any discrepancy in numbers meant death if an inmate escaped overnight or from a work detachment outside of the camp. Even though the square lacked grass, makeshift goals were set up. Formal invitations were even sent by camp command to individual players (by name and prisoner number) known by their style of play. Prisoners who played also remembered the smell of the camp crematorium, from the burning bodies of prisoners who had been gassed or died by other means, wafting over the field. The roll-call square also witnessed acts of final desperation as some torment-ed prisoners ran from their columns and threw themselves onto the electric fence, bringing their misery mercifully to an end.

A handful of prisoners remembered one SS man, otherwise unre-markable, who was keenly interested in football. KZ Dachau guard Michael Redwitz, who served for eighteen months there as an SS offi-cer, after starting his career in Mauthausen, Austria, promoted these matches with enthusiasm. Redwitz charged the block elders from Bar-racks 2 with the organization of the camp competition.[5] Others testified after the war that inmates would bring stools from the barracks to the roll-call square to watch. Hauptsturmführer Redwitz was known to pull up a stool himself and join the prisoners for particularly interesting matches. This same man who deported untold numbers of men to their deaths at Auschwitz and who ordered the most barbaric punishments for minor offenses, taking part in some of the beatings himself, sat among the inmates as an enthusiastic supporter.[6] Despite his interest in the leisure activities of some of the prisoners, Michael Redwitz would eventually be held accountable for his crimes at Dachau and later Bu-chenwald. Captured by American troops in February 1945, Redwitz was charged with war crimes for supervising prisoner executions at Dachau and eventually hanged in 1946.

One remarkably powerful testimony of a Dachau survivor comes from an Austrian prisoner named Ferdinand Hackl. Hackl was a com-munist prisoner from Austria who fought against the fascists in the Spanish Civil War and ended up in the grasp of the Gestapo in 1940 following a failed attempt to flee to the south of France after the Nazi invasion. He remembers the hard ground of the *Appelplatz* and the primitive shoes and clothing the prisoners played in. Yet, despite enduring hunger and twelve-hour workdays, players and spectators alike drew pleasure from the games. Hackl reported you could forget about sorrow and hunger for a few hours and ignore the stench of death that hung over the camp. Games continued on Sundays until the days before liberation, when a deadly outbreak of typhus stopped football altogether. Dachau remained in operation until the final weeks of the war, as a final destination for thousands of death camp marchers. It was, by far, the longest serving concentration camp in Nazi Germany.

RAPID EXPANSION OF THE NAZI TERROR STATE

The political success and popular acceptance of the Dachau concentration camp convinced the regime to establish other camps near major German cities. Built early in 1936 in the Berlin suburb of Oranienburg, the "preventive detention" camp of Sachsenhausen imitated the geography and practices of Dachau and, in typical Nazi fashion, offered innovations in the incarceration and torment of prisoners. Built to coincide with the 1936 Olympic Games in Berlin, the main camp of Sachsenhausen was the remodeled version of a camp already in place at Oranienburg. It was built on a radiating pivot surrounded by eight-foot stone walls and outfitted with the most primitive of sanitary systems. Sachsenhausen also served as a model camp and training facility for SS guards who later worked at camps in Austria and Poland. Infamous Auschwitz commandant Rudolf Höss trained for over three years at Dachau and Sachsenhausen before his assignment to the death camp. In the end, more than two hundred thousand individuals were imprisoned at Sachsenhausen and more than a third of those perished.

By the summer of 1938, KZ Sachsenhausen was already overcrowded. Many survivors of the German camps echoed this reality: mental anguish was the greatest threat to survival; whatever the body might endure in deprivation or physical pain, the mind would not persist amid the demoralizing effects of the permanent uncertainty of imprisonment. Sport met the propaganda interests of the Nazis, and the model camp of Sachsenhausen worked as yet another component in an elaborate system of torture and degradation. Inmates remembered their arrival at the camp, having to pass through a "reception line" of guards and *kapos* wielding rubber batons, bullwhips, and rifle butts.

The daily ritual of roll call on the assembly square destroyed the morale of prisoners, terrorizing and exhausting the gathered throngs. A particularly insidious form of "sport" involved the "gymnastic exercises" required by the SS. Prisoners were forced to frog jump, duck walk, crawl, and repeatedly roll over in the mud and sand of the *Appelplatz*. For many survivors of these camps, the word *sport* conjured memories of sadistic punishment and torture and not of pure athletic expression.[7]

Many memoirs provide vivid accounts of such sport, whereas others, from the more privileged, remember organized sport as a diversion for camp staff and the fortunate prisoner-functionaries near the top of the camp hierarchy. In Sachsenhausen, direct witnesses to football within camp were scarce. So few records remain of these activities, in part because such sport was likely seen as a trivial pursuit in comparison to the life-and-death struggle within the camp. The prisoners' efforts to create an alternate reality by playing is bolstered in testimonies from a handful of inmates used in criminal proceedings against SS members in the postwar era. One report from 1979 from Sachsenhausen inmate Karl Graf outlines the development of football, growing from a clandestine activity to one actually sanctioned by the camp:

> From 1943 on . . . a football match between Polish and German inmates took place on the parade ground. In 1944, about 400 of the camp's inmates could participate in the aircraft factories [outpost Heinkel plants]. We received new drill clothes for that. The march from the camp to Heinkel got a lot of attention. We were chosen inmates, in front of us the camp marching band.[8]

These prisoners, an indisputable presence in the cities and towns that surrounded camps like Sachsenhausen, belie the postwar claims from so many Germans that "no one knew what was happening" in the concentration camps.

Relevant to cultural and sporting pursuits inside the camps, a system of privileges was introduced to reward increased productivity among laborers. Rewards ranged from small acts like replacing the prisoners' ubiquitous wooden clogs with leather shoes and being allowed to grow one's hair out to visits to the camp brothel. Those granted privileges became known as the *Prominenten*, and the system of patronage that followed reinforced existing power structures within the camp.

Boxing tournaments, musical and theatrical events, and football tournaments were the most common pursuits. In Sachsenhausen, the parade ground was measured anew and in one corner a makeshift soccer pitch appeared, complete with temporary goalposts and sidelines marked with chalk. Former inmate Arthur von Lankisch-Hörnitz remembers, "One should not picture something like a playing field in the conventional sense. . . . [The] football field was built voluntarily by the inmates, outside their regular work shifts."[9] The greater challenge often was in securing proper gear. Prisoners would "organize" (smuggle) all manner of personal materials, and kits and footballs were no exception. Another inmate, Franz Orzyschek, remembers the process well: "Money had to be acquired to buy football shirts. The organization needed to smuggle leather out of the concentration camp Sachsenhausen [shoe factory], at the peril of their lives. Even the acquisition of a tire pump, football bladders, and a bodkin [thick sewing needle] was not an easy task."[10] That such gear was secured in secretive fashion, yet with official approval of football matches in the camp, reflects the arbitrary and capricious nature of camp administration. Increased productivity and improved motivation may have served the war effort, but to the prisoners, specifically the fit and privileged ones, these pursuits were enriching and life sustaining.

Few other details about football at Sachsenhausen survive. Survivors sometimes disagreed about where in the camp games were actually played, and no records have ever been found on the composition of teams (aside from national allegiances), notable players, or match results. One of the first complete accounts of life in a Nazi concentration camp, published immediately following the war, was by Norwegian Odd Nansen, who kept a detailed diary of his experiences as a prisoner at Sachsenhausen. Nansen, an architect and the son of Nobel laureate and polar explorer Fridtjof Nansen, was imprisoned by the Nazis for his work with the nascent resistance movement in Norway. Before deportation to Germany, Nansen created a Jewish relief agency in Prague in the wake of the Nazi occupation of Czechoslovakia in 1938.

A non-Jew, Odd Nansen responded early and vigorously to the plight of Jewish refugees. His arrest by the Gestapo in the late evening hours of January 13, 1942, along with his expectant wife and their three adolescent daughters, brought the Norwegian to Sachsenhausen at a particularly brutal and chaotic time. Written on toilet paper and smuggled out on breadboards, Nansen's diary, published in 1947, chronicled in moving and poignant detail many aspects of life in the camp. On April 17, 1944, he observed that a camp football match between prisoners representing his home country and Germany teetered on the edge of violence. Early on, Norway stormed out to a 3–1 lead and tensions mounted. The dire consequences of ignoring camp politics were not lost on the Norwegians, and by the final whistle the German team ran out as 5–3 winners.

Few would risk pursuing victory at any cost in these places; your competitor on the pitch could later kill you in your barracks. The normalization of premature death in camps like Sachsenhausen is seen in one bizarre yet brief vignette from Nansen's diary. With a particularly exciting match captivating the attention of many of the prisoners gathered on the roll-call square, two orderlies carrying a corpse on a stretcher stopped to light a cigarette and watch the contest. Minutes passed, and when the action died down the two inmates resumed their work, continuing on to the morgue while loudspeakers in the camp played an operetta.[11]

Across the rapidly expanding Nazi terror state, greater numbers of people were ensnared, and soon men of different nationalities who had strived together for victory on the soccer field as teammates became adversaries. As members of the title-winning sides of 1923 and 1928 for Hamburg SV (HSV), Asbjørn Halvorsen and Otto "Tull" Harder formed the axis of the team for nine seasons at center midfield and striker, respectively. Both men would find themselves as enemies in KZ Neuengamme near Hamburg in northern Germany. Before the war, Halvorsen coached Norway in the 1936 Olympics, the celebrated match that saw his home country defeat the Germans 2–0 as Adolf Hitler looked on. Eventual bronze medalists in the tournament, Norway went on to play in the 1938 World Cup under Halvorsen, by that time a legend in Norwegian football.

When World War II began, Halvorsen joined sides with those resisting the Nazi vassal Vidkun Quisling and the collaborationist government installed during the war. As general secretary of the Norwegian FA, Halvorsen refused to cooperate in staging propaganda matches and took the extraordinarily risky move of leading the nationwide strike against the Nazi takeover of football. For his efforts, Halvorsen was arrested and detained in a camp near Oslo for almost a year before being sent on July 23, 1943, to the only concentration camp on French soil, Natzweiler-Struthof, sited in the Vosges Mountains near Strasbourg. Halvorsen kept up his defiance, refusing to beat another inmate as instructed, and he was tortured before being transferred to the camp located in his adopted home of Hamburg.

Awaiting him there was his old teammate, Tull Harder, now a hardened guard who had already served for four years in two separate Nazi camps. Arriving at Neuengamme as early as November 1939, Tull Harder enjoyed power and influence as a famous football player and as a corporal in the Waffen SS (the combat arm of the SS). Harder joined the National Socialist Party in September 1932, five months before the Nazis seized power, and in May 1933 he became a member of the SS. Such was his ardent nationalist pride that Harder often turned out for important football matches in his *Schutzstaffel* uniform.[12] As a player, Harder was the prototypical center forward: tall, strong, and imposing. Halvorsen, team captain and vocal leader, was a midfield general with a deft touch. In a photo of the 1923 championship team, Halvorsen and Harder are joined together with a victory wreath around their necks in celebration. Harder offers a wry smile as Halvorsen and the other HSV teammates pose stone-faced and serious.

By the time Halvorsen arrived at Tull Harder's camp, he weighed only forty kilograms (eighty-eight pounds). It is highly unlikely the Norwegian met Harder in the camp as the former HSV striker moved on to become camp commandant at a subcamp near Hannover a short while later. Asbjørn Halvorsen would miraculously survive Neuengamme, a camp with a 45 percent mortality rate. He returned to Norway and worked to reestablish organized football in the country. The two men would meet again ahead of a World Cup qualifying match in 1953, set for the new Volksparkstadion in Hamburg. Halvorsen expressed joy at the occasion and showed grace toward Harder when asked about the reunion. Yet questions remain about this generosity of spirit; was Halvorsen offering genuine forgiveness, or was the former Nazi captive unaware of Tull Harder's role in the war?

After the war, Harder was released from prison after serving only four and a half years of a fifteen-year sentence handed down in 1947 by a British court. At his war crimes trial, several inmates testified that Commandant Harder supervised abhorrent living conditions, including exposure, insufficient food and clothing, and physical abuse resulting in the deaths of 230 prisoners. Harder avoided the death penalty, in part because of testimony from former Hamburg SV fans; two of Harder's subordinates at the Hannover camp did not receive such testimony and were sentenced to death and later executed.

Three years after that Hamburg reunion, both men would be dead. Asbjørn Halverson died at age fifty-six, likely the result of his inhumane treatment in Harder's Nazi Germany. Otto "Tull" Harder died the year following. When Harder was buried in 1956, the HSV club banner was laid on his coffin and a club honor guard offered a remembrance as members of the Hamburg SV youth team carried his casket.

Such was the ambiguity of loyalties in the process of de-Nazification following the war that when the 1974 World Cup came to Germany, Hamburg was a host city. Promotional brochures produced by the German FA for the massive event listed HSV legends Uwe Seller, Jupp Posipal, . . . and Tull Harder. The inclusion of the former SS officer was only discovered the day before distribution, and the page featuring Harder had to be abruptly removed from one hundred thousand copies.

For the thousands interned at Neuengamme and its subcamps, Tull Harder was but one of dozens of SS guards to be avoided. But of the details that emerged during Harder's trials, one of the most confounding involved the HSV striker's claim of beneficence toward the prisoners. It is known that football was played by the inmates at Neuengamme from 1943 on. A camp clerk and former player with two obscure German clubs, Borussia Halle and TuRa Leipzig, Herbert Schemmel played on one of the teams featuring the hated block *kapos*. Most inmates estimated that no more than sixty games involving only four teams were ever played in Neuengamme. But Schimmel remembered vividly that Tull Harder "stuck in his memory in a very unpleasant way."[13] Harder claimed at his trial that he routinely welcomed prisoners upon their arrival in a friendly and kind manner. A local resident supported Harder's claim that he treated prisoners fairly and that he was the one responsible for setting up a football pitch in the camp. But such claims were grossly inconsistent with the demands placed on SS guards for hardness, discipline, and obedience. In his own defense, Harder added this bizarre claim about the high death rate in the camp he worked in: "The reason why so many people died in the concentration camp Ahlem [subcamp of Neuengamme] was because the prisoners' inner organs had been weakened by malnutrition while in the Jewish ghetto, and so they could not tolerate the healthy and generous amounts of food in the concentration camp."[14] Prisoners, naturally, recall things very differently. In fact, life for the incarcerated in Neuengamme was as desperate as at any camp in the Nazi system. Harder's claim of creating football in Neuengamme is refuted in vivid detail by those forced to actually survive in the camp. Collected reports from prisoners after the war contradict the former commandant and reveal the resourcefulness of the inmates, who would not accept their fate so passively: Leather workers in the camp fashioned balls out of scraps of leather, and football shirts were made from the remnant material from the camp dressmaker's shop. Carpenters built two goalposts, and each was installed by laborers who rammed the posts into the concrete of the roll-call plaza with iron pegs. Inmates struggled to find the rubber bladders for the footballs, and Harder showed his true nature when he demanded three hundred quality cigarettes and the full purchase price of 9.60 Reichsmarks for the three pieces.[15]

PERSECUTION IN GERMANY'S LITERARY GARDEN

The human resilience and motivation for survival displayed in Neuengamme was further tested in thousands more prisoners as the concentration camp universe continued to expand in Germany. In July 1937, in a clearing in a forest in central Germany, the largest of the concentration camps in the German Reich was established to contain the ever-rising number of prisoners designated as a threat to the German people. Buchenwald spread out across the idyllic landscape once traveled by the likes of Goethe, Schiller, Luther, and Bach. Just a few miles outside Weimar, the literary soul of classical Germany, Buchenwald eventually came to represent all the evils of the Nazi camp structure.

The front gate at Buchenwald greeted new arrivals with "Jedem das Seine" ("Everyone gets what he deserves"). KZ Buchenwald received the first prisoners taken from groups of political opponents—communist and antifascists, recidivist criminals, and targeted social groups such as Jehovah's Witnesses and the Roma and Sinti people. Political inmates became important to the prisoner infrastructure at Buchenwald, which saw a strong resistance movement emerge inside the camp. This movement also formed the basis of the sporting pursuits in the camp.

The camp served as an important source of forced labor for the dictatorship, with about half of all inmates working in nearby lumberyards,
armament production centers, and munitions factories. Before the war
came to a close, nearly 250,000 people were imprisoned in Buchenwald
and its 136 affiliated subcamps.

Buchenwald contained a wide range of cultural, musical, and sporting activities. The camp band before 1938 was made up of gypsy musicians. There was a cabaret, a string quartet, a camp cinema, a prisoners'
library, and performances of a number of plays, most famously the
Shakespearean comedy *As You Like It*. Buchenwald even had a zoo
outside of the camp fence with a bear pit that was home to a pair of
cubs.

Because almost every major camp had organized sport, it's important to emphasize the unique role sport played inside Buchenwald.
Younger captives were the most keen to play, and soccer dominated
their interest. In the camp's first year of operation, prisoners lacked
equipment and a field, but owing to the ingenuity of those with some
amount of influence, a proper ball soon appeared and the initial space
for play was secured. As was typical, the pitch was located in the square
near the camp canteen. Other sports, including handball, volleyball, and
rounders (a baseball-like game), were also recalled by survivors.

Organized sport met with opposition at first but was later welcomed
by the prisoners as a diversion from harsh living conditions. Competitive matches involved twelve teams, including (briefly) an all-Jewish
squad, and began as early as 1939. Camp commandant Karl Koch
granted permission for these contests, and soon overcrowding pushed
the games to an area called the "Little Camp," a quarantine section and
the site of the greatest suffering endured by prisoners in Buchenwald.
Though Koch was removed from his position in 1941 for corruption,
soccer in Buchenwald had strong momentum. In time, matches sprang
up in the subcamps as well. Members of the camp resistance in subcamp Dora-Mittelbau used soccer for relaxation and as a way to develop
international contacts. "Dora" housed a massive industrial complex in
central Germany tasked with creating so-called retaliatory weapons;
huge tunnels sheltered slave workers constructing V-2 rockets. Dora-
Mittelbau had one of the highest mortality rates in the Nazi camp
scheme due to the deplorable subterranean living conditions.

In Buchenwald, a second soccer pitch existed in the area of the infamous Little Camp. In the more than two years the field existed, prisoners organized championships, scrounged proper soccer boots, and somehow secured "flawless" kits created from the stolen uniforms of the Yugoslavian royal guard.[16] SS guards were regular spectators of matches between political prisoners and teams of inmates from what one prisoner called the "professional criminal class."[17] Cigarettes were awarded to winning teams.

In the frenzied weeks after unification with Germany, Austrian Nazis deported thousands of Jews to Dachau, Sachsenhausen, and Buchenwald. One of those caught up in the persecution was young Fritz König, who arrived in Buchenwald in 1938 and was assigned to the camp laundry because of his status as a youth player for SC Red Star Vienna. In a newspaper interview in 2008, König remembers the SS taking the lead role in creating the soccer teams. Initially, Austrian Jews played against German inmates likely from the "criminal pool." Remarkably, Fritz König was released from Buchenwald in July 1939, whereupon he made his way to the south of France. König found a game or two until, like so many refugees, he left Marseille to make the passage to Casablanca in 1940. His soccer odyssey continued when he joined up with Racing Club Morocco as a fleet-footed winger, and there he would keep company with future French national team star Just Fontaine. Fontaine was the leading scorer in the 1958 World Cup in Sweden, when he scored thirteen goals in six games and world football witnessed the debut of a seventeen-year-old Pelé for eventual champions Brazil.

As a survivor of Buchenwald, Fritz König enjoyed an escape from the efficient Nazi killing system that can only be described as fortuitous. So few others would claim such luck. Overcrowding intensified at Buchenwald in December 1942 (one in three would die during the year) as POWs swelled the population of the camp. This is also the time when the Little Camp was most deadly; the windowless horse stables with mud floors and a solitary latrine became the barracks for the new prisoners. Death and disease were rampant there, and the fortunate few to survived this place owed their fate to protection and privilege granted by the prisoner-functionaries who chose players for the soccer matches.

Another prisoner, Willi Seifert, a communist from the Plauen, near Weimar, offered his testimony immediately after the liberation of Buchenwald. Though brief, much of what is known about organized soccer in the camp comes from his report. Lost for forty years after the war until a faded carbon copy was discovered in an archive, Seifert's testimony is one of more than two dozen eyewitness accounts gathered by German-speaking U.S. Army intelligence officers. Many of the depositions, including Seifert's, were collected when the survivors were still behind barbed wire. Willi Seifert was highly active in the camp resistance movement and a *Prominenten* responsible for organizing the forced labor unit:

> Although the conditions for pursuing sports at Buchenwald were not exactly rosy (work days were long and hard), some people, particularly the younger ones, felt the need to play sports. Sports facilities, equipment, etc., were not available at all. Nevertheless, in a short while there was not only a ball but also a field, if one could call it that. Soccer dominated the field. Soon the square by the canteen was too small, so another playing field was created and in the very spot where the Little Camp stands today. . . . When the camp became overcrowded, the sports field had to make way for new barracks. Nevertheless, still another push was made for a new sport field, which was created in the forest near the gardening area. Sports were still played there for a while, then the gardening detail took over the field, sowed it, and harvested little—but we had been allowed to enjoy the sport field for a time.[18]

Once the soccer pitch was pushed further into the forest, all organized games in the camp stopped. Evident in his testimony are his antifascist sentiments; Seifert often framed the responses of his fellow sporting inmates in light of their value to the resistance movement in the camp. This is also the likely reason that, among the handful of testimonies available, so few details emerge about the competitions, notable players, or any rivalries. After the war, Seifert, a mason by training, stayed loyal to his communist leanings, becoming a lieutenant general in the East German police and supervising the construction of the Berlin Wall in 1961.

No reports or testimonies exist about soccer after 1942, when conditions in Buchenwald deteriorated rapidly and the only remaining soccer field was taken over by primitive barracks. It is commonly accepted that any propaganda or diversionary value soccer could provide the camp administrators was lost. With massive numbers of inmates arriving at Buchenwald in the spring of 1944, the camp descended into a hellish chaos in the final year of the war. Thousands arrived from the battle-front as POWs, and thousands more would make their way back into Germany as evacuees arriving on death marches from the Polish exter-mination camps. By the time the American liberators arrived at the camp at 3:15 in the afternoon on April 11, 1945, sport and any sort of cultural expression in the camp had long since ceased. More than fifty thousand people lost their lives in Buchenwald. General Dwight Eisen-hower, supreme commander of the Allied forces, toured the camp and wrote, "Nothing has ever shocked me as much as that sight."

HITLER RETURNS HOME

With the rapid expansion of the Nazi terror state in Germany and the Nazification of soccer from the club level to the national team, Hitler's regime expected to see success on the soccer pitch. But the game of football would not be controlled so easily. As the prisoners in the Nazi concentration camps showed, soccer was often an ally to the perse-cuted, offering meaning to imprisonment and a pathway of survival for many. At precisely the same moment that Hitler turned his attention to unifying his homeland of Austria with the German Reich, the national teams of Europe's best footballing nations were preparing for the up-coming 1938 World Cup, to be held in France. The highly regarded Austrians still enjoyed the legacy of *Das Wunderteam*, the legendary, even mythical side that dominated European soccer in the early 1930s. The prospect of a combined team to represent a unified Reich at the World Cup was tantalizing to German soccer officials.

When German troops marched into Austria on March 12, 1938, hundreds of thousands of Austrians lined country highways and city streets offering a rapturous welcome to columns of soldiers and to the motorcade carrying their new führer. Known to history as the *Ansch-luss*, the annexation of Austria was preceded by a political crisis secretly fomented by the Nazis. Cheering crowds of onlookers showered Ger-man soldiers with flowers, swishing their swastika pennants in joyous approval of the new political reality. Hitler's triumphal march into Vien-na would set in motion the Holocaust in Austria.

Though not all of Austria welcomed their German neighbors, the enthusiasm for this forced unification astounded onlookers and neutral observers. With the arrival of the Nazis came a lightning-fast persecution that alarmed even the Nazis themselves, who were well experienced in persecution and violence against Jews and other political enemies. One such bewildered observer was German-born writer and playwright Carl Zuckmayer, who had fled the Nazis in 1936. In the days after the annexation of Austria, Zuckmayer mourned Vienna with a voice of terror and disbelief as he witnessed the eruption of a ferocious nationalism that spared few of Vienna's Jews:

> That night hell broke loose. The underworld opened its gates and vomited forth the lowest, filthiest, most horrible demons it contained. The city was transformed into a nightmare painting by Hieronymus Bosch: phantoms and devils seemed to have crawled out of sewers and swamps. The air was filled with an incessant screeching, horrible, piercing, hysterical cries from the throats of men and women who continued screaming day and night. People's faces vanished, were replaced by contorted masks, some of fear, some of cunning, some of wild, hate-filled triumph. . . . What was unleashed upon Vienna had nothing to do with seizure of power in Germany . . . [it] was a torrent of envy, jealousy, bitterness, blind, malignant craving for revenge.

Vienna in 1938 was home to more than two hundred thousand Jews, and the famed Jewish soccer club Hakoah Vienna, with its Zionist loyalties, had the most to fear after the *Anschluss*. Nazi fascism eventually destroyed Vienna's celebrated café-society football, but much more importantly, the Austrian version of Nazism produced the deadliest of all the Nazi German *Arbeitslagers* (labor concentration camps), KZ Mauthausen, built in the heart of the picturesque countryside of upper Austria. Mauthausen witnessed abject cruelty and torturous labor, yet counter to the designs of the SS administration, organized soccer once again emerged. Privilege met with heroic resistance as football became a truly life-saving pursuit that kept many from the deadly granite quarries attached to the camp where the life spans of new arrivals were measured in days and weeks, not months. Austria was now the new Nazi battlefield, and territorial expansion offered wondrous possibilities for empire and for the nation's football. What followed is a fascinating blend of rebellion and survival, played out in a distinctly Austrian manner.

5

GENIUS ON THE DANUBE

Requiem for Vienna's "Decadent" Football

"Flectere si nequeo superos, Acheronta movebo" ("If I cannot bend the higher powers, I shall stir up hell," from Virgil's *Aeneid*, book VII, line 312).—Sigmund Freud's epigraph to *The Interpretation of Dreams*, foreshadowing the fearsome aggression of the Nazi era in Austria[1]

While Nazi Germany built concentration camps to lock away its own people, Germany's neighbor to the south, Austria, was thriving as a football nation, albeit amid serious political and economic turmoil that threatened to give rise to civil war. Benefiting from the establishment of a professional league more than fifteen years earlier, football in Austria captivated a wide swath of society, especially in the capital, Vienna. All across central Europe, in cities such as Budapest and Prague, fans turned out by the tens of thousands for league and international matches featuring some of the best players on the continent.

Football was largely an urban phenomenon, and the players who rose to the top of the game in these cities of the old Habsburg Empire learned the game on the streets and in the dusty open spaces of the suburbs. With Vienna as the heart of the game in central Europe, a generation of players grew up in the *Vorstädte*, the vast unplanned and unregulated industrial zones on the outer edges of Vienna. High-density housing, looming factories, and a patchwork of open spaces and agricultural common areas provided the destinations for pickup games and socializing, both with minimal interference. The *Vorstädte* also supported organized football clubs that would compose the best of the top league in Vienna, hailing from the working-class neighborhoods of Favoriten, Simmering, Hütteldorf, and Meidling.

Matching the passions and influence of the proletarian clubs were the supporters, players, and clubs celebrated by Vienna's intelligentsia in the most Viennese of locales: the coffeehouse. Legend has it that in the late seventeenth century, as the Ottoman Empire was repelled at the city gates, the retreating Turkish army left behind sacks of coffee beans, and this accidental gift became the eventual focal point through which the Viennese would later gather to discuss, argue, and coalesce around important ideas of the day.

The coffeehouse thrived at the end of the Habsburg dynasty and quickly became a public salon with a distinctly Bohemian feel. Vienna possessed a sophisticated football culture that overlapped the liberal bourgeoisie, the professional and working classes, and the city's burgeoning Jewish intellectuals. By the mid-1930s, specific cafés catered to particular clienteles and certainly held allegiances to specific football clubs. Players, club officials, fans, and sportswriters would gather at the local café, much like the pub in Great Britain. Passionate fans analyzed match results and team tactics, and debated late into the night the relative superiority of favored players. Not as straightforward as the sport's working-class associations in Britain, football in central Europe followed a more complicated path, having been introduced by the Anglophile middle class before being adopted by the rapidly expanding middle classes of Vienna, Prague, and Budapest.[2]

Vienna's two greatest rival clubs each had their own loyal coffeehouses. Supporters of Rapid Vienna, soon to be celebrated as champions of the new pan-German Gauliga, met in the Café Holub, and fans of Austria Vienna, the favorite club of the city's Jewish bourgeoisie, gathered at the Café Parsifal in Josefstadt, the Eighth District of Vienna. In the outer districts, the Café Resch welcomed players and fans from SC Wacker, the team from Meidling and a powerhouse in the 1940s.

But the coffeehouse laying claim to the title of unofficial center of the Viennese footballing scene was the Ring Café, once the home to Anglophile cricketers. The Ring Café was described in the newspaper *Welt am Montag* as "a kind of revolutionary parliament of the friends and fanatics of football." Fans would have to check their allegiances at the door, for "one-sided club interest could not prevail because just about every Viennese club was present."[3] The Ring Café was an essential part of a footballing revolution whose echoes would carry forward beyond another revolution now dominating Austria, the Nazi revolution poised along Austria's border.

The central figure in this golden age of Austrian football was Hugo Meisl, the coach and mastermind behind the team that dominated much of international football in the early 1930s, a team dubbed by the Viennese press *Das Wunderteam*. Meisl was a Bohemian Jew who emigrated from Czechoslovakia in his youth, relocating with his family to Vienna. Ambitious and innovative, despite his natural conservatism, Hugo Meisl advanced from the secretary position in the Austrian FA to the head trainer spot for the national team in 1912, a position he would only relinquish upon his sudden death in 1937. Meisl is credited with creating the world's first international club competition, called the Mitropa Cup, and for devising Europe's first tournament for national teams, the Dr. Gero Cup, a thirty-month-long league competition begun in 1927 and featuring European powers Czechoslovakia, Hungary, Switzerland, Italy, and Austria.

Meisl's style of football, called the Danubian style, eschewed the manner of play employed by teams from Britain and Italy; instead of the brute force of hard, physical tackling, leaving the scoring to a strong center forward, Meisl's teams instead played with finesse, guile, and an emphasis on individual creativity and "keeping it on the carpet." In a wonderfully complicated and Germanic phrase, this style of play was called the *Scheiberlgspiel*, and it rewarded enjoyment for the game built on constant movement of players who possessed cunning and exquisite technical ability. This was the style of the streets, where boys honed their footballing talents in the rough neighborhoods of working-class Vienna.

One pioneering player emerged from these dusty environs, a footballer who dominated the first decade of professional football in 1920s Vienna. Like so many before him, Josef Uridil, center forward for Rapid Vienna, arrived in the imperial capital as an immigrant, taking quickly to soccer as a youth. Uridil developed a bruising style of play that exemplified the proletarian origins of his home club. As the most popular Austrian footballer of the post–World War I years, the hulking Uridil became a hero of the coffeehouse and the dance hall. One contemporary observer described him this way: "Others scored goals before him, but not one of them had his enormous momentum, the irresistible force with which he powered across the football field. Woe betide the opponent who dared cross the path of this racing machine. He was knocked over, almost crushed and decomposed into his chemical constituents."[4]

Uridil remained with Rapid Vienna until the close of the decade. As Uridil's talent faded, another son of a Moravian immigrant family would surpass the striker, both in talent and public admiration. Matthias Sindelar, a supremely gifted center forward and a child of Favoriten, represented a new breed of player in Austria. Sindelar was delicate and smart, able to evade tacklers with balance and intelligence. Christened by sportswriters *Der Papierene* (the Paper Man), Sindelar had the deft ability to slip through opposing defenses as if he was "wafer thin," the literal meaning of his moniker. Sindelar shared the same ethnic heritage as Uridil, and both men enjoyed endorsement deals that supplemented their footballing incomes. But beyond the fame and wealth, the two players could not have been more different.

As Hugo Meisl crafted together his Wunderteam, selecting from a large pool of professional players, he had not yet included Sindelar in his national team on a regular basis, despite giving him his debut in 1926 as a twenty-three-year-old. The fans and writers who regularly convened at the Ring Café, dissatisfied with the play of the national team, clamored for more. Sindelar apparently fell out of favor with the disciplinarian Meisl, who favored physically imposing strikers. Others remained captivated with the popular "Sindi": Manchester United tried to buy Sindelar for the then astronomical sum of forty thousand pounds from Austria Vienna. It wasn't until 1931, when cornered in the coffeehouse by Vienna's most prominent football writers, that Meisl relented and brought back Sindelar. What followed was legendary.

What Meisl already had in his team was discipline, industriousness, and organization; he lacked a creative spark, and that is exactly what Matthias Sindelar offered. He was a playmaker with imagination who beat opponents with both spontaneous and well-planned moves. One of Vienna's foremost authors and a coffeehouse mainstay, Friedrich Torberg, described Sindelar as "endowed with such an unbelievable wealth of variations and ideas that one could never really be sure which manner of play was to be expected. He had no system, to say nothing of a set pattern. He just had . . . genius."[5] Looking back with the aid of a half century of perspective, esteemed football writer and keen observer of the contemporary game David Goldblatt describes Sindelar as the player who personified Vienna's obsession with football: "Viennese café society at last had a player and a game in their own image: cultured, intellectual, even cerebral, athletic but balletic at the same time."[6]

With Matthias Sindelar leading the attack, the Wunderteam usually lined up in a 2–3–5 formation, an attacking formation featuring a set of unorthodox forwards who moved all over the pitch, dragging defenders along with them. Between April 1931 and June 1934, on the eve of the second World Cup, the Austrians would lose only three of thirty-one matches, scoring 101 goals. This team is widely credited with inventing the modern way of playing the game, a highly fluid style that was popularly known as the "Danubian Whirl," and an aesthetic that was born in the coffeehouses of Vienna. Meisl's team chose passing over power and thinking over passion. It was widely imitated across Europe, an elegance likened to a kind of poetry on the pitch.

Hugo Meisl's squad began the decade by trouncing Scotland 5–0 in May 1931 and Germany twice; once away 6–0 and again in Austria's new national stadium 5–0, all part of an eighteen-game unbeaten run. The test would come in December 1932 when the Wunderteam matched up against England at Stamford Bridge in London. In the run-up to the match, Austria had dispatched all of the best European teams; the Swedes, French, Italians, Hungarians, and Czechs all lost to the Austrians. England was not the best team in the world at the time, declining to participate in the first two World Cup competitions, but their place as undisputed "masters of the game" was unchallenged. On home soil, England was unbeaten against foreign opposition. The English influence on the development of football around the world earned them honor and deference.

In the 1932 match in London, *Das Wunderteam* struggled in the first half, giving away two goals to the English in the opening half hour. The game would be broadcast back in Vienna to massive crowds in the Heldenplatz. As loudspeakers carried the live commentary, the Austrian faithful would have to wait until the second half for a comeback. Six minutes into the second half, Austria pulled a goal back, but a deflected free kick off of an Austrian defender bounded past the keeper, giving England a 3–1 lead. Sindelar answered with a wondergoal, a solo dribbling effort started at the halfway line and coolly finished with a backheel and a shot into the net.

A long-range blast by England widened the lead, but by now Austria was dominating possession, mesmerizing the English defense with an intricate web of passes and the ever-fluid movement of the attackers. But there was not time to catch up; England would finish 4–3 winners, despite an Austrian goal with five minutes left to play. The British press was delighted with the imagination of the Wunderteam, calling them a "revelation" and declaring the English team lucky to win. England, "splendid in isolation," gave Austria its greatest triumph in defeat. More than a moral victory, a marker had been laid down, and in May 1936 Austria would finally defeat England 2–1 at the Praterstadion in Vienna. Seemingly a bright harbinger of things to come, the match showed the Danubian School of football was now triumphant, becoming the reference point for European club and national teams alike in the decades that followed. But in less than two years' time, Austrian football would face a challenge that would destroy not only a beautiful football culture but also an entire civilization.

In Hitler's Germany, domestic and foreign policy intertwined. As the regime pursued "race and living space" (*lebensraum*) in both spheres, Europe waited anxiously as assurances that Germany would not violate Austrian independence fell to the wayside. Austrian football changed forever with the annexation of the country on March 12, 1938, as German tanks and troops rolled across the border. Attempts to assert Austrian independence in the weeks prior were undermined repeatedly by the Nazi government and their allies in the Austrian fascist movement. Contrary to popular perception, the union of these German-speaking nations was enthusiastically received. A retroactive, manipulated election in April 1938 sealed Austria's fate: more than 99 percent of the Austrian people who voted chose to join with Germany.

Photos from the era show adults and children waving pennants adorned with swastikas and shouting jubilantly when the Nazis rode into Vienna. Immediately, the violence and persecution intensified. Waves of anti-Semitic actions against Austria's Jews began, the scope and intensity of which shocked many. Austrian Jews who had the day before been coworkers, neighbors, and friends bore the brunt of their compatriots' aggression. These vicious displays, some prompted by Germans but often initiated by Austrians themselves, saw Jews attacked and beaten. Mass arrests and expulsions from universities and businesses followed. The Gestapo, accompanied by Austrian Nazis and right-wing sympathizers, seized Jewish businesses and property, looted homes, and humiliated people on the streets. Crowds gathered to watch the ritualized degradation where artists, professors, journalists, and wealthy Jews dressed in their finest clothing were forced to scrub sidewalks with toothbrushes. At times, the water provided the persecuted was laced with acid.

Within months, the same discriminatory measures introduced in Germany over a period of five years were rushed through the Ostmark. The other major European powers did nothing to stop the hysterical violence and oppression. In an age of appeasement, with Hitler now poised to claim the ethnic German Sudetenland in Czechoslovakia, almost every aspect of Austrian economic, political, social, and cultural life was radicalized. Football did not escape the Nazi revolution. The Austrian FA, among the oldest in the world, was abolished, the top division in Austria was reassigned to the seventeenth *Gau* of the Third Reich (a political-geographic boundary), and purges of the top football clubs began immediately. Two days after Nazi troops were welcomed into Austria, there was a mass emigration of managers and players, along with Jewish sport journalists. After the spring 1938 season, the Nazis also moved to abolish professional football, which they saw as rife with Jews and an affront to pure sport. Jewish sports clubs such as the famed Hakoah Wien (Vienna) were shut down, their assets absorbed by the government. The purge extended to the record books: Hakoah's football match results were expunged, and opponents who had already played against the club were awarded 3–0 victories.

JEWISH VIENNA RESPONDS TO THE "LONGEST HATRED"

Well before the orgy of violence that attended the *Anschluss*, anti-Semitism festered and thrived in Vienna and throughout most of central and eastern Europe. In response to the rising anti-Semitism, a small movement of Jewish intellectuals enthusiastically embraced calls for Jewish self-defense through a strengthening of body and character. By the early 1920s, the Jewish inhabitants of Vienna swelled to 10 percent of the city's total population of two million. Sport, and in particular football, was the perfect vehicle for training up a generation of gifted and self-determined athletes in the Austrian capital. SC Hakoah Wien was one of the earliest embodiments of what the polemicist and founding father of the Zionist movement Max Nordau called *Muskeljudentum*, or "muscular Judaism." This doctrine was an ideological commitment to destroy the anti-Semitic myths of a weak-bodied and effeminate Jewry only interested in making money off of sport rather than playing it.

Hakoah Wien, formed in 1909, advanced the Zionist cause by wearing the Star of David proudly on the chest of their blue-and-white kit, the traditional colors of Israel. Jewish football clubs like Hakoah were usually funded by conservative Jews seeking social mobility and acceptance. The name *Hakoah*, meaning "the strength" in Hebrew, was a nationalist declaration in line with other club names, such as Hagibor ("the hero"), Sampson, and Bar Kochba (named for the heroic Jewish fighter who led a revolt against Roman rule in second-century Palestine). Defensive sports like boxing, fencing, and judo were especially popular in the early years in these clubs, but soccer soon outpaced them all, both in participation and popularity.

SC Hakoah Wien rapidly moved up the divisions of Austrian football, gathering an ardent following. Jews of all political and philosophical persuasions, once wary of the proud and self-identified Jewish football club, attended Hakoah matches in droves, often filling the club's new eighteen-thousand-seat home stadium in the Leopoldstadt, Vienna's second district. The best players from Budapest and Prague were drawn to Vienna by higher wages and stronger competition. Czech writer Franz Kafka was rumored to be a supporter. But anti-Semitism reigned in Vienna in the first two decades of the new century. Favorite epithets raining down on the Hakoah players from the terraces included "Judensau" (Jew pig) and "Drecksjude" (Dirty Jew).

The pinnacle of Hakoah's success on the pitch came in 1925, when they claimed their one and only Austrian club football championship in dramatic fashion. With two games yet remaining in the season, Hakoah's goalkeeper, Alexander Fabian, broke his arm after a collision with an opposing player. At that time, no substitutes were allowed, and it looked bleak for Hakoah. Badly injured and his arm in a sling, Fabian quickly returned to the game, swapping positions with a teammate.

Fabian took a position on the right wing, and with only nine minutes remaining he joined in a decisive counterattack and ultimately scored the winning goal, securing the title for Hakoah.

SC Hakoah Wien, in a pioneering move, capitalized on their domestic successes by touring Europe, the Middle East, and America. Tens of thousands turned out for Hakoah matches in Chicago, Philadelphia, Providence, and St. Louis. The fast-paced, elegant passing game of the Viennese club was celebrated by fans and journalists, who swarmed the players wherever they went on the tour.

One match on May 1, 1926, versus a Select XI at New York City's Polo Grounds drew forty-six thousand spectators. Hakoah Wien's six-week, eleven-match tour drew major controversy, though, amid the rapturous reception. Four of the games were played on Saturday afternoons. Unyielding, Hakoah pressed on with "Sabbath soccer," combating the nativism evident in the United States that Jews posed a threat to the "New America" now striving for economic and cultural greatness. Many Hakoah players marveled at the lifestyle and the lack of endemic anti-Semitism in places like New York City, so much so that nine of the best Hakoah players emigrated together.[7]

Never again would Hakoah Vienna reach such lofty heights, and the club languished in the lower ranks of Austrian football until dissolved by the Nazis in 1938. One player from the title-winning team was especially drawn to America, the famed Hungarian coach Béla Guttmann. A center midfielder for Budapest powerhouse and Jewish club MTK, Guttmann later played for Hakoah Wien until his own immigration to America in 1926. The brash and charismatic Guttmann survived World War II, but several of his Hakoah teammates would not survive Hitler. Team captain Max Scheuer fled to France and briefly played for Olympique Marseille along with another Hakoah teammate who would later join the French Resistance. Scheuer was caught trying to reach Switzerland and summarily executed. At least five other Hakoah players also died in the Holocaust, bringing to a tragic end some of the best of the Jewish cultural renaissance that enriched fin de siècle central Europe.

THE NAZIFICATION OF AUSTRIAN FOOTBALL

Nazi sport policy, consolidated and thoroughly radicalized after the 1936 Berlin Olympics, moved next against the fertile youth sport movement in Austria. Club sports were reined in and all major sport activities were transferred to party-affiliated organizations like the SS, the Hitler Youth, and the Nazi labor movement. The effects were immediate and drastic. Training in race consciousness expanded, military qualities in sport were promoted, and school sport was expanded significantly. At the top level of Austrian football, clubs like First Vienna and FK Austria saw prominent board members and club officials with Jewish backgrounds sacked.

Attention then turned to the Austrian national team. Conventional thinking in the Nazi leadership was that the infusion of Austrian talent into a new Reich national team would make the squad invincible. But the animosity between the best footballers of each nation grew by the day. Despite the ecstatic reception given to the Nazis in the spring of 1938 and the widespread acceptance of the *Anschluss* within the football establishment, deep divisions remained. Many in Germany viewed the Viennese with suspicion and uncertainty, and the doubts were reciprocated. Well before the "union," many Austrians viewed the Germans as *Piefkes*, dour and unimaginative pessimists who could not shake their austere Prussian heritage. In kind, many Germans, particularly those from Berlin, viewed Austrians as *Ösis*, uncultured mountain people or, specific to the once-proud Austrian capital of Vienna, an arrogant collection of intellectuals morbidly fascinated with decadence and decay.

Three weeks after the *Anschluss*, the Nazis scheduled a reconciliation match on April 3 that was stage propaganda masquerading as genuine competition. The Praterstadion in Vienna was adorned with swastikas, and prominent Nazi party members were in attendance. Rumors had it that the game was supposed to end in a satisfying but unprovocative 1–1 draw. Matthias Sindelar requested his Austrian teammates play in their patriotic red-white-red kit. Boundary lines were quickly drawn; this would be no "friendly match."

From the start, the Ostmark XI dominated the game but failed to score on several early chances. Sindelar was said to have missed a handful of shots with such controlled precision that it appeared to be defiant gamesmanship on his part. Grainy newsreel footage shows Sindelar moving effortlessly across the pitch, the ball seemingly tied to his boot by a string. It is probably the only film of Sindelar playing. Myth and facts blur together in the retelling of this match, but at the seventy-minute mark, Sindelar latched onto a rebound from the German goal-keeper and buried the ball in the bottom right corner for the first goal of the match. The crowd erupted, and a few minutes later his friend Karl Sesta of FK Austria Vienna netted the second goal, a cheeky free kick from forty-five yards that Sesta lobbed over the German keeper. As chants of "Österreich, Österreich!" rang out across the grounds, legend holds that after the second goal, Sindelar sprinted over to the directors' box where the Nazi elite watched, arms raised and dancing joyfully.

Whether such an outburst led to serious consequences for Sindelar and his mates remains a point of contention to this day. Exactly one week after the match, Sindelar once again found himself at the mercy of the new Nazi masters as his image appeared in the Viennese edition of the party newspaper, the *Völkischer Beobachter*, on election day as Austrians "voted" on unification with Germany. Purportedly offered in his own handwriting, paired with a picture of the Viennese idol, Sindelar endorsed the *Anschluss*: "We football players thank our Führer from the bottom of our hearts and vote yes!"[8]

Just a few months after the radical takeover of Austria, Matthias Sindelar would retire from football and settle into a life as a café owner in his childhood neighborhood of Favoriten. Sindelar purchased the café from Leopold Drill, a Jew forced to sell under the policy of Aryan-ization, the legalized theft of Jewish businesses, institutions, and dwell-ings in the greater German Reich. But by most accounts, Sindelar paid a fair price of twenty thousand marks. The Austrian star, who never hid his Social Democratic loyalties, chose to stay in Vienna rather than seek a safe, lucrative payday in England. Sindelar also continued to steadfast-ly refuse head trainer Sepp Herberger's pleas to join the new unified national squad. "Sindi" played his final match for Austria Vienna the day after Christmas in 1938. True to form, he scored the last goal of a legendary career in a 2–2 draw with Hertha Berlin SC. Less than a month later, the hero of the Wunderteam would be found dead in his apartment under mysterious circumstances.

With the "reconciliation match" behind them, DFB officials in Ger-many seized upon the political changes in Austria. DFB director Felix

Linnemann, working on instructions from above, gave the order to build a squad to represent the expanded Reich, stressing harmony and Teutonic brotherhood. Linnemann, a German nationalist if not an ardent Nazi, stated at the time, "In our sphere as well as in others, a visible expression of our solidarity with the Austrians who have come back to the Reich has to be presented. The Führer demands a 6:5 or 5:6 ratio. History expects this of us!"[9]

While Sepp Herberger had been instructed to field a blended team evenly stocked with footballers from the Ostmark and the "Old Reich," he knew the folly of the plan, realizing that in recent matches against the Austrians, acrimony ran high. Herberger, a simple and apolitical man, was even less convinced of this mission upon seeing the deep divisions within his new team. Practice matches often resulted in humiliation for the Austrian players (9–1 in one early game). Tensions boiled over as the two groups dressed in the locker room one day in the spring of 1938 as the team prepared for the upcoming World Cup in France. As the players stared at each other, a Viennese player named Josef "Pepi" Stroh of FK Austria Wien started juggling a ball to the ecstatic though exaggerated applause of his Austrian teammates. Pepi stopped and, self-satisfied with his impressive display, handed the ball to Fritz Szepan, who had risen from the bench at the bidding of his German teammates. Matching Pepi touch for touch, Szepan was exact in imitating the technical brilliance of the Austrian. As he finished, he volleyed the ball against the wall behind the seated Austrian players, mere inches above their heads. Unsure if a fight was going to break out, Szepan broke the silence when he whispered, "You arseholes." Distracted and fractured, the German national team, united under the swastika, went out of the 1938 World Cup in the first round, losing a replay to lowly Switzerland.

When war finally came to Austria, domestic club football compensated for the deprivations and served as distraction. Spectators flooded stadiums, especially when German teams came to town. In the popular mind, the Germans played a strong, athletic style, not terribly creative but blindly obedient. The Viennese style depended on cunning, scoring through complicated moves and impulse. The rivalry contrasted the German march against the Viennese waltz.[10]

Contemporary reports noted that fans in Vienna had become more radicalized, with fighting erupting in the terraces on a regular basis.

Especially in Vienna, Austrian football experienced a boom, and crowds surged at important matches even when players were called away for war service. Kurt Neubauer was a kid in Vienna when Nazism took hold in the years after the war had begun. The future newspaperman remembered that there were only two diversions for an adolescent in that time—you could go to the movies or go to a soccer match:

> I was at the Stadium when *Admira* played *Schalke 04* and yelled my head off at the *Piefkes*. Soccer gave you a chance to protest. I was at the last international match, Germany vs. Switzerland, in 1942. Little Switzerland beat the Germans 3 to 2 and when they played the Deutschland hymn nobody sang it. The newspapers were furious. They said losing didn't matter, but of course it did, and the way people behaved when they played the German national anthem was unacceptable, and of course it was.[11]

One match stands out, not only in the memory of at least one Austrian teenager but also in press reports from November 1940: Admira versus Schalke 04, the dominant club from the Ruhr region of western Germany. Fifty-two thousand fans gathered to watch another so-called reconciliation match. In the first eighteen months after the annexation, Viennese teams excelled against German clubs. Austria Vienna beat Schalke 2–0, and Rapid Vienna trounced reigning German champion Hannover 96 11–1. Football was one of the few pursuits where Vienna once again enjoyed dominance and glory, a brief return to preeminence as a European capital.

Austrian glory against German teams took some time to achieve. In June 1939, Admira first faced Schalke 04 in Berlin for the final of the Gauliga championship. In the Nazi period, Schalke 04 played for nine of the ten championships contested, winning six of them. With hundreds of thousands listening on the radio back home, Schalke 04 thrashed the best of the Austrian league 9–0, leading to an escalation in animosities between supporters of teams from the Reich and Vienna.

The stage was now set for the 1940 match between Admira and Schalke. The crowd, unruly and primed for battle, responded to every hard tackle made by the visitors with venom and rage. Anticipating trouble, officials ordered a massive display of uniformed and plainclothes officers. Schalke played a physical style of football, and the excessively partisan crowd fed off of it. It didn't help that the referee from the June 1939 match, a German, had taken charge of the match in Vienna. After waving off two early goals by Admira, inciting the crowd further, the referee disallowed the go-ahead goal, a header by an Admira forward. The contest ended a 1–1 draw and the violence spilled over. Police, called in to quell the rioting, could not contain the Viennese fans, who destroyed stadium seats, broke windows, and attacked the gathered security forces. Anti-German anger, replete with anti-Nazi epithets, resulted in the destruction of Gauleiter Baldur von Schirach's limousine, his tires slashed and windows smashed.

Such violence was reciprocated in the *Altreich*, but spectators in Vienna gained a reputation in the Nazi security state as a threat. A problem for the Gestapo for the rest of the war, soccer in Vienna remained very popular despite the decline of the league as the Reich struggled to fight the war. Though the top domestic club championships continued until March 1945, football in Austria would never again reach the pinnacle attained by domestic clubs and the renowned Wunderteam.

Several months after the Admira–Schalke 04 debacle, Rapid Vienna earned a measure of revenge in a comeback win against their old rival Schalke in the 1941 German club championships. The greatest Austrian club victory of the era saw Rapid welcomed back as champions by tens of thousands of soccer-mad fans at Vienna's Westbahnhof train station. Trailing 3–0 at halftime, Rapid Vienna stormed back for an improbable 4–3 victory. But the victory did not make the front page back home as newspapers in Vienna carried the news that on the very same day German tanks stormed into Russia. Within a few short weeks, almost every player from the victorious Rapid Vienna squad was ordered to the front.

At the very same moment Hitler's new national team crashed out of the 1938 World Cup and the rivalries between the best domestic clubs in Germany and Austria reached a fever pitch, Nazi Germany readied for war and a new concentration camp was being constructed on the banks of the Danube. The famous river coursing through the heart of Austria that inspired luxurious waltzes and had come to symbolize the best footballers in Europe would now bear witness to many of the greatest atrocities committed during the Nazi era.

AUSTRIA'S AUSCHWITZ:
FOOTBALL IN KZ MAUTHAUSEN

Perched atop a hill overlooking the pastoral splendor of the Austrian countryside, the Mauthausen concentration camp became a site of horrific torture and punishment for thousands of prisoners in the Third Reich's maniacal quest for empire and racial purity. Stretching for miles in each direction from this hilltop are vistas of the nearby rugged Alps and verdant forests abounding with wild game. Down below, the namesake picturesque Austrian village sits on the northern shore of the Danube, peacefully welcoming visitors seeking refuge and solace in the parks and hiking trails that crisscross the countryside. The beauty of this upper Austrian landscape was forever scarred with the opening of Mauthausen on August 1938.

KZ Mauthausen, established in the first six months after Nazi Germany's annexation of neighboring Austria, stands alone in the architecture of death devised by the Nazis. Extermination through labor was the destiny of men and women deemed incorrigible or unfit for rehabilitation (or "reeducation") as criminals, political opponents, and enemy combatants. Mauthausen was carefully chosen by Reichsführer-SS Heinrich Himmler and his cadre of economic and security state advisers for its proximity to nearby stoneworks and central rail lines and waterways. The granite quarries at Mauthausen had long provided the hard, durable stones for the magnificent buildings, bridges, and streets in Vienna, Budapest, and countless lesser cities across the old Habsburg Empire.

These stones would build another empire. Hitler's grandiose building plans for Berlin included a massive new Reich chancellery, and in his boyhood home of Linz, only fourteen miles upriver from Mauthausen, he envisioned a one-hundred-thousand-seat athletic stadium, an art museum to house the world's greatest (looted) collection, and a mausoleum complex with a crypt to hold his mortal remains. Vast quantities of granite were required for such plans.

As one of six major camps established in an expanding Reich before the start of World War II, Mauthausen and subcamp Gusen were classified as Category III camps, the only camps given that status by SS general Reinhard Heydrich, chief of the Reich Main Security Office and the mastermind behind the first of the death camps established in

Poland to implement the Final Solution. Mauthausen and Gusen were "camps of no return" and the deadliest camps in the Reich proper. The quarry, with three-hundred-foot-high walls and a winding staircase with 186 steps known as the *Todestiege* (the "stairs of death"), required grueling and dangerous manual labor as prisoners blasted, hammered, and picked at the stone walls until the granite gave way. Hauling blocks of stone up the stairs was life sapping, and countless men buckled under the weight of fifty- to eighty-pound blocks. [12]

The first prisoners to arrive at Mauthausen were three hundred criminals from Dachau, and soon thereafter transfers arrived from Sachsenhausen. Former Mauthausen inmate Joseph Hertzler recalled the start of the day in the labor camp:

> The inmates were usually awoken at 4:30 a.m. with beatings. After the torture of washing themselves, there was a watery soup and then there was the roll call, standing still for hours and, at 7 a.m., the departure for work. On the way, as long as the road was flat, the *kapos* would shout: "Who is our misfortune?" and we had to answer: "The Jews." If an inmate was seen not to answer, he was beaten. And so it went on. We were employed mainly with the building of the Russian camp and the sports ground. When we came to the sloping sides of the site, the *kapos* would kick the Jews in the last rows and give them a push so that some would fall down the slope. [13]

This pathway down to the quarries was where SS guards shouted out a mock warning—"Achtung, parachutist!"—before pushing weary prisoners to their deaths below. Cruelty abounded. New arrivals were often encouraged by camp guards to join in "raspberry-picking details" by approaching the electrified boundary fence, where they would be shot "while trying to escape," the common euphemism for summary executions in the camp.

Daily life at Mauthausen was also one of monotony and boredom. After the roll-call bell to start the day, prisoners scrambled to the *Appelplatz* as quickly as possible to join the ranks. The captives fell into rows of twenty by barracks, awaiting assignments to work units usually outside of the camp. Prisoners marched everywhere under the close watch of SS guards and block *kapos*. Return to Mauthausen after a workday of eight to eleven hours meant another roll call, and any deaths or escapes during the day meant hours of waiting in formation.

Mauthausen was an imposing place: with 462 yards of eight-foot-high granite walls, stone watchtowers, and electrified barbed-wire fencing, it resembled a castle-turned-prison. Unlike other camps in the Nazi system, which gave glimpses of normalcy and freedom, Mauthausen was completely sealed off from the world of the living.

Along with recently established labor camps near the quarries at Flossenbürg (near Nuremberg), Natzweiler-Struthof (in the French Alsatian Alps), and Gross-Rosen (in Polish Silesia), Mauthausen was poised to enrich the regime while standing as a very visible threat to any who would oppose. In the Nazi mindset, it was especially fitting that the opponents of the regime would work slavishly to build it. Hitler's architect, Albert Speer, was once overheard saying, "After all the Jews were already making bricks under the Pharaohs."[14]

Responding to overcrowding in the main camp, the satellite camp of Gusen I was established in December 1939 closer to the Danube River, where shipments of granite made their way ninety miles east to Vienna and points beyond. The other subcamp that contained large numbers of prisoners was Ebensee, located in the mountains in the resort region of the Salzkammergut. A short drive from Salzburg and Mauthausen, Ebensee became well known to Americans as the war came to a close when Allied troops stumbled across the camp and army photographers documented thousands of emaciated and diseased captives awaiting liberation in one of the most beautiful locations in all of Austria. Next to alpine meadows and crystal-clear streams were the typhus-infested concentration camps at Ebensee, overflowing with the piled corpses of the dead and the desperate, vacant stares of prisoners clinging to life inside barbed-wire gates.

Yet amid the degradation, starvation, and cruelty, football persisted. A handful of memoirs emerged from the Mauthausen camps remembering with pride the soccer played on the *Appellplatz* at the main camp. The earliest reports record Spanish prisoners, the unfortunate lot who fled to France as anti-Franco Republicans only to be deported to Austria by the collaborationist Vichy government in 1940, as the first to arrange soccer matches in the winter of 1940–1941. Playing at first with a ball made of rags against teams cobbled together from other nationalities, the games drew increasing attention from prisoners and guards alike. Teams of Spaniards, Poles, Germans, and Yugoslavs later gathered uniforms, proper football boots, and a ball.

Many prisoners likened the soccer matches and other pursuits in the camp, such as plays, circus performances, and live music, to a subtle rebellion against their Nazi captors. While many *kapos* were violent and forbidding to their assigned prisoners, others showed a more humane side. *Kapo* Stefan Krukowski remembered the importance of these activities at Mauthausen in his chronicle, a rare testimony for someone directly implicated in the crimes: "These sporting events had in addition to the element of sport also something at the theater about them—they meant a great deal. They made one forget the everyday tragedy, sometimes made one laugh, sometimes aroused emotions, and they certainly helped. Help like all attempts to raise the spirits of the prisoners."[15]

The activities of another Mauthausen *kapo* illustrate a darker, more sinister perspective. Franz Unek, a criminal brought to Mauthausen in one of the very first transfers from Dachau in August 1938, acted as benefactor and hanging judge according to some. A block leader, Unek, remembered by witnesses as a capricious murderer, was hanged in July 1945 at Mauthausen. His typed confession, taken after the war, was both a mea culpa and an evasive denial of his crimes.

Franz Unek played an important role in offering hope to the prisoners. One prisoner under his watch, Oskar Schlaf, recalled:

> This man [Unek] was the camp executioner, and he organized the inmate football matches between 1943 and 1945. Some inmates were allowed to play football on Sunday mornings in the roll call area. Unek was the initiator and had wooden cups made for the winners. I found two of these wooden cups [probably made in Mauthausen by unknown inmates] and two leather football casings owned by Unek in May 1945 in Block 7 and took them with me to Vienna.[16]

The wooden cup found by Schlaf currently resides in the artifacts section of the Mauthausen Memorial Museum.

With prisoners working from dawn to dusk, Saturday at noon was the formal end of the workweek and Sundays became game day. Besides the roll-call square, another field complete with goalposts and level ground was constructed to meet the requirements of the SS team, which played in a regional league nearby. Ebensee also featured an SS team. Interest in football in the camps was high because SS guards often had time slots in their schedules dedicated to sport. The soccer pitch, located to the west and adjacent to the main camp entrance road, was later replaced by an infirmary camp (a hospital in name only; prisoners went there to die). The playing area was better known to survivors as the Russian Camp as it held Soviet POWs for much of the war. One rare archival photo taken immediately after liberation shows local Austrians burying the dead in a mass grave that took the place of the soccer pitch. In the background can be see one of the goals still in place, just below the stone walls of the main camp.

The only detailed records of specific matches at Mauthausen that survived the Nazi destruction of camp records shortly before the liberation on May 5, 1945, show the final three months of competition in the prison camp league. These rare summaries of three matches from the spring of 1945 speak of the camp competition at its peak, in a time when overcrowding, disease, and arbitrary murder were rampant:

> March 20, 1945: "The last game between select XI teams, Vienna and Spain. Vienna wins 5–2, the strikers forceful in attack, runners working selflessly on defense. The Vienna goalie was tested by the dangerous Spanish attack."

> March 25, 1945: (Two games on this Sunday) "Traditional encounter between the Spanish and the *Unnekleuten* [the Vienna side, apparently taking the name of block *kapo* Unek]—and the first game between the Spanish B team and a combination team of Germans, Czechs, and Yugoslavs. . . . Vienna takes 1–0 lead but match ended 1–1. The second match must be stopped. An air attack [by Allied bombers] forces the referee to abandon the match fifteen minutes before the end of normal time."

> Easter Sunday, 1945: "The two teams from the Mauthausen camp. This time Spain defeats the Vienna XI 5–4."[17]

From early 1943 until late spring 1945, boxing and these football matches entertained and sustained the prisoners in Mauthausen. Matches were also reported in subcamps Gusen, Ebensee, and Loibl-Pass. Established in June 1943, Loibl-Pass (south) was one of thousands of SS *Arbeitlagers* in the Nazi sphere. Prisoners from Mauthausen slaved to bore a mile-long tunnel in the southern Austrian Alps linking the country to Slovenia. Traces of football in the high mountain camp included a seventy-meter field behind the bunkhouses, carved into the hillside like steppes, where up to fourteen prisoners competed on Sunday afternoons and before early snows ended the summer contests. Though prisoner accounts in these camps are often incomplete or missing, a clear picture nonetheless emerges. Amid the diversions of football, grim reality was never far away. One prisoner lamented, "A strange world indeed, because even on those late sporting afternoons, our jailers were present, and we were in their clutches; the Bunker 200 meters away from the ring; Block 20 further away, and in the sky above the camp the smoke of the crematorium, all that was enough to bring us back to earth, to the hellish world of the camp."[18]

Only those who survived Mauthausen leave us their harrowing stories. So many others were lost to the horrors of the Holocaust. In later years, one name emerged from an untold history, a largely unknown Italian prisoner and a one-time player for the AC Milan side of the mid-1940s that featured the legendary Giuseppe Meazza. The prisoner, Ferdinando Valletti, was a defensive midfielder who worked his way up to Milan from lower-division sides Helles Verona and Seregno before suffering season-ending injuries in his second season with AC Milan, opting to work as an engineer at the nearby Alfa Romeo automobile factory.

Ferdinando Valletti's life changed forever one night in March 1944 when a knock at his door led to arrest and eventual transport to Mauthausen. Betrayed by a coworker who denounced him as a leader of a strike at the factory, Valletti left his family and his pregnant wife for an unknown fate. As a laborer, Valletti walked a fine line in the quarries at Mauthausen until his transfer to a labor detail constructing underground tunnels at nearby Gusen. Luck shined on the young footballer one day when an SS guard received word of Valletti's sporting background. An officer followed up and asked if he could play well enough to join a team full of camp guards. Already weakened and malnourished, Valletti took the risk and said, "Yes, I played for Milan." The officer replied sardonically, "Okay, let's give it a go; if you told the truth, fine, and if you are lying, we will kill you straightaway."[19]

Ferdinando Valletti passed the life-and-death test, playing barefoot, wearing his ragged trousers during his tryout, and using every ounce of energy he could muster. Valletti became a reserve player for the SS team, and privileges followed as he was transferred to the camp kitchens, greatly improving his chance for survival. Valletti had left Italy weighing seventy kilograms (154 pounds), and when released from the Gusen concentration camp in 1945, he weighed just thirty-five kilograms (85 pounds). The promising young player, robbed of his prime years as an athlete, escaped death and the life-draining work in the stone quarry because of his talent as a footballer. The capacity to play never returned to Valletti, but he remained connected to the game, managing a few Serie C sides (the Italian third division), holding onto the unshakable optimism that had kept him alive during the war.[20]

The best complete account of the inmate experience in Mauthausen comes from camp clerk and onetime chairman of the Mauthausen Memorial Committee Hans Maršálek. Born to a Czech family in Vienna, Maršálek fled the National Socialists in 1938, joining the resistance in Prague. He managed to survive for over three years, evading capture by the Gestapo until 1942, when he was arrested as a communist and deported to Mauthausen. Maršálek passed through several difficult work detachments until he was reassigned to the camp clerks' office in 1943. From this relatively secure position, he worked to save vulnerable prisoners while occupying a central role in the active resistance movement within the camp.

An important chronicler of life in the camp, Maršálek recalled later in an interview after liberation that inmates used Sunday afternoons to rest and store up reserves for another week of grueling labor. Some would mend clothing, cut hair, or get a shave. Diversions included inmate chapel services, concerts performed by the camp band, and football matches. Maršálek, likely responsible for assigning some of these privileged prisoners to preferred work details that provided meaningful food and freedom to play, also remembered the nature of the entire camp system; you were forced to contribute to your own destruction:

> As a clerk, you get to hear about all sorts of things . . . you're in the clerks' office, with a roof over you. At that point, at the beginning, and for a long time afterwards, I didn't understand that of course I had also become part of this death factory. I only understood this later, when I saw how the Jews, the Russians were playing the balalaika [guitar-like, triangle-shaped string instruments] and dancing. . . . Then the Russians were taken away, and the next day I crossed them out in the daily record. Dead. They went to the gas

chamber. . . . But you have to do more than just be a wheel, or a cog,
in the death factory.[21]

Privileged prisoner-functionaries like Hans Maršálek existed in what
Holocaust survivor Primo Levi calls the "gray zone" of the camps, an
existence steeped in moral ambiguity. In every camp, there existed a
hierarchy, a system of patronage and privilege. Because the history of
the camps is told by the survivors, the delicate matter of listening to
these histories necessitates an understanding of the moral ambiguity of
living within these gray zones. The prisoner-functionary acquired privilege, sometimes through blind luck, as in the case of Valletti, the former
AC Milan player, but much more often through an astute understanding of camp or *Lager* hierarchy.

Atop the camp structure were the Nazi masters, but below was a
complicated, ambiguous leadership comprising *kapos*, labor squad
chiefs, barracks leaders, clerks, camp laborers, and others. These destinations of retribution and death were designed to reduce and eliminate
the capacity to resist. Arrival in the *Lager* was a terrible shock, indeci-
pherable. To most, the enemy was all around. For the new arrival, there
was not yet a solidarity among companions. Kicks, punches to the face,
and an outburst of orders screamed with true or simulated rage greeted
the new prisoner. Stripped naked, shaved of hair, and dressed in rags,
prisoners endured an entry ritual that began the process of dehumanization. One would immediately become subservient to camp authority;
the first blows came not from SS guards but from fellow prisoners.
Each new inmate was seen as an adversary, a competitor for survival.

Sport in the concentration camp often served this aristocracy. Privilege was found among a small minority of the *Lager* population, who
are a majority of the survivors we rely on to tell the story of football in
the Nazi system. In exchange for privilege, the *Prominenten* kept order.
For the individual prisoner, body reserves were consumed in weeks.
Hunger begat disease, which in turn begat an early death. The only way
to secure food was to secure privilege. And football provided access to
that privilege.

Primo Levi, a leading voice among survivors of the Nazi camps,
cautions that our penchant to simplify the history of the camps is a
Manichaean tendency; we seek clean distinctions between winners and
losers, Nazis and prisoners. On the surface, a captive who seeks privi-

lege seemingly contributes to the Nazi killing machinery, but we should resist this tendency toward oversimplification. Levi writes: "the network of human relationships inside the Lagers was not simple; it could not be reduced to the two blocks of victims and persecutors."[22] As an inmate at Auschwitz, Primo Levi was an intimate witness to the consequences of this system of patronage in the camps, as some prolonged their lives while others, outside of the hierarchy, died often abruptly and anonymously. Relating this caution to the existence of competitive sport in concentration camps, Levi acknowledges the moral calculation:

> This is certainly the reason for the enormous popularity of spectator sports, such as soccer, baseball and boxing: the contenders are two teams or two individuals, clearly distinct and identifiable, and at the end of the match there are vanquished and victors. If the result is a draw, the spectator feels defrauded and disappointed. At the more unconscious level, he wanted winners and losers, which he identified with the good guys and the bad guys, respectively, because the good must prevail, otherwise the world would be subverted.[23]

Soccer in places like Mauthausen takes on profound meaning as a means for survival, certainly, but also as an attempt by individuals to reestablish order and restore some moral authority to one's limited choices within the camp.

While the war intensified as the allied armies fought more resiliently against the Nazi aggressors all across Europe, concentration camps proliferated. By summer 1942, the first of the extermination centers in Poland were operational. Shockingly, in two of those death camps, Auschwitz and Majdanek, in eastern Poland near Lublin, football and boxing entertained. At Majdanek in July 1943, one team composed of Slovak cooks competed against other camps. In Stutthof, near Gdansk on the Baltic coast of Poland, only privileged Norwegian prisoners played. Stutthof was the very last camp to be liberated, on May 9, 1945, a day after German capitulation.

The labor camps at Gross-Rosen (in western Poland) and Flossenbürg (in eastern Germany, near the Czech border), both infamous as stone-quarry labor sites, also saw matches organized by nationalities. The Polish team in the camp at Gross-Rosen stimulated great patriotic passion, often winning against an all-German squad. In both labor camps, teams were afforded the customary benefits of playing: better rations and improved working conditions.

Aside from the camp complex at Auschwitz-Birkenau, no other major concentration camps in the German Reich or eastern territories witnessed competitive football after 1943. Of the other major camps in the Third Reich, Ravensbrück—the camp north of Berlin created in 1939 for women that included sterilization experiments—and Natzweiler-Struthof—the perversely beautiful camp in the French Alsatian Alps, opened in 1941 to punish Jews and resistance fighters in its pink granite quarries—little evidence has been found regarding competitive or recreational sport.

ELEGY FOR VIENNA'S BELOVED CAFÉ SOCIETY HEROES

The rise of fascism in Germany and Austria forever altered the face of Europe. Football was the most popular sport in the interwar period, and when war came again to the continent, the game was both a proxy for fighting and a means by which those caught up in the conflict could survive. As the Nazis sought to build an empire and wage a war of annihilation against their enemies, football persisted. This game of the masses, first played in the streets, between the curbs and lampposts of dozens of Europe's capital cities, was now played in the most unlikely of places: in concentration camps, at transit centers, and in the darkest corners of Nazi-dominated Europe, the ghettos and extermination centers. In these places of indescribable despair, football came to represent hope, survival, inspiration, and, to the demagogues and dictators, manipulation and domination.

The Holocaust would intensify across the Nazi-occupied territories, and with the death of café football in Vienna, the heroes of the Wunderteam faded into memory. The brightest of the Viennese football stars, Matthias Sindelar, came to symbolize the wasted potential of a lost generation in the Nazi era. His untimely death at thirty-five left his reputation unsullied, even elevated as a romanticized martyr during a time of barbarism. In Vienna's Zentralfriedhof Cemetery, not far from the final resting places of Beethoven and Schubert, the grave of Matthias Sindelar preserves the iconic hero of the coffeehouse as if he had just stepped off the football pitch. A bronze football rests on a marble slab below the likeness of Sindelar, his receding hairline and kindly face looking outward. He wears his vintage kit with the floppy collar and stitched-up neck. Now in verdigris, streaks of rain have etched lines that look like beads of sweat dripping down his face. The Nazis called him the "best known soldier of Viennese football," emphasizing the martial qualities, the *Kampf*, of the Austrian striker. But the fifteen thousand Viennese who attended the funeral of their beloved "Sindi" remembered the artistry of the striker who had defiantly refused to bow to the Nazis. In an obituary penned two days after Sindelar's death on January 23, 1939, the literary critic and habitué of Vienna's café scene Alfred Polgar remembered Matthias Sindelar this way:

> He would play football as a grandmaster played chess: with a broad mental conception, calculating moves and countermoves in advance, always choosing the most promising of all possibilities. He was an unequalled trapper of the ball and stager of surprise counterattacks, inexhaustibly devising tactical faints. . . . Sindelar's shot hit the back of the net like a punch line, the ending that made it possible to understand and appreciate the perfect composition of the story, the crowning of which it represented.[24]

The death of Matthias Sindelar was shrouded in controversy. Almost immediately, friends and admirers suggested suicide. Sindelar had been found by a close friend following a night of heavy drinking, unconscious and lying naked next to his girlfriend of ten days Camilla Castignola, also unresponsive. Police initially ruled their deaths an accident, but the public prosecutor delayed the final ruling for six months until Nazi authorities ordered the case closed. The "romantic liberal mind" in Vienna could not let the athlete-artist die a mundane death; rumors of his Jewish heritage leading to a Gestapo-ordered murder persisted.[25]

The best evidence points most clearly to carbon monoxide poisoning resulting from a blocked chimney flue in Sindelar's apartment block. Matthias Sindelar was not gassed by the Nazis nor was he Jewish, but he clearly distanced himself from the eruption of fascism in Austrian life. The darker, more profound reality is that his Austrian compatriots would play a significant, outsized role in the conduct of the Nazi war. Austrians would also feature centrally in the perpetration of the genocide against the Jews. Key leaders in the extermination designs of the Third Reich (Hitler, Adolf Eichmann, SS security chief Ernst Kaltenbrunner, and the commandant of Sobibór and Treblinka, Franz Stangl) were Austrian. In the death camps, Austrians comprised 75 percent of SS commanders and 40 percent of the staff. Mauthausen survivor and famed Nazi hunter Simon Wiesenthal estimates that Austrians were directly responsible for the deaths of three million Jews and Roma-Sinti people during the Holocaust.[26]

After the Nazis secured Austria and Czechoslovakia, by intimidation and duplicitous diplomacy, they invaded Poland on September 1, 1939. For the next six years, Poland would endure the most brutal occupation imaginable, worsened by the devastating and simultaneous aggression of the Soviet Union following the Molotov-Ribbentrop Pact, signed in secret a month earlier, which divided Eastern Europe between Hitler and Stalin. In less than a year, the extermination camp at Auschwitz, which would come to represent the totality of the Final Solution in the minds of the public, would open for business.

With the first arrival of prisoners on June 14, 1940, a new phase of the Nazis' war against the Poles, Slavic civilization, and the Jews was formalized at Auschwitz. Alongside the inscrutable histories of the millions sent to die in Poland, we once again encounter sport. The immense importance of the games played in these Polish camps is reflected in the memoirs and postwar testimonies of those who survived in the eastern colonies. These stories naturally follow from the experiences of the captives in the Reich camps, as countless thousands who began their detention in Germany were shipped off to the occupied territories of Poland and Eastern Europe, where they were crammed into ghettos, corralled as slave laborers, or, in the ultimate tragedy, selected for extermination. The arrival depot in Auschwitz, in the small, otherwise forgettable town of Oświęcim in southern Poland, is where these stories of sport and survival in the Polish killing fields begin.

Architect of the BreslauElf and wartime partner Sepp Herberger, who joined the Nazi Party in 1933 but eschewed politics in managing *Die Mannschaft* for over two decades, 1937. Schirner-Ullstein Bild/The Granger Collection.

Der Papierene: genius Austrian footballer Matthias Sindelar, 1932. Lothar Ruebelt-Ullstein Bild/The Granger Collection.

A mutually beneficial relationship. Schalke 04 captain Fritz Szepan meeting *Der Führer* at the Reich Chancellery in Berlin, October 1937. Heinrich Hoffman-Ullstein Bild/The Granger Collection.

Reichssportführer Hans von Tschammer und Osten lecturing Germany's first-ever national team coach Otto Nerz and Fritz Szepan at Berlin's Olympic Stadium, 1936. The Granger Collection, New York.

Le jeu a commencé!
Das Spiel hat begonnen!

'The play has started'

N°60

Cartoon postcard from the 1930s featuring a stereotypical Jewish Russian exile as a football being booted from the world. United States Holocaust Memorial Museum, courtesy of Wiener Library.

Future German national team trainer of the 1974 World Cup champions and international player Helmut Schön in a friendly match against Denmark, a 1–0 win in Hamburg, November 17, 1940. The Granger Collection, New York.

The best of his generation: Fritz Walter, wearing the German shirt in the final year of international play under the Nazis (1942), would outlast Hitler, going on to captain a resurrected German national side at the Miracle of Berne in 1954. The Granger Collection, New York.

Polish pariah: *Volksdeutscher* Ernst Willimowski, Silesian-born star for Polish club and national teams, chooses football and identity with the German national team, 1942. The Granger Collection, New York.

The salute. England defeats Nazi Germany 6–3 in Berlin in front of 110,000 people on May 14, 1938. The Granger Collection, New York.

Fritz Szepan of FC Schalke 04 scoring the first goal in a 2–0 win against First Vienna FC to claim the 1942 German domestic championship. The Granger Collection, New York.

Nazi propaganda photos of beleaguered prisoners playing at KZ Dachau, June 10, 1933. Bundesarchiv, Bild 152-03-13 (top) and Bild 152-03-10 (bottom), photos by Friedrich Franz Bauer.

Soccer match in the Poniatowa (Poland) labor camp, circa 1941–1944. Nearly every prisoner in the camp was eventually murdered. Ghetto Fighters' House Museum, Israel.

Handshakes at the start of the Nazi propaganda film *Liga Terezín* of the September 1, 1944, match featuring *Jugendfürsorge* (youth welfare) and *Kleiderkammer* (used clothing) squads. Chronos Media, Germany.

Play during *Liga Terezín*, September 1, 1944. Chronos Media, Germany.

Corner kick leading to a goal in *Liga Terezín*, September 1, 1944. Chronos Media, Germany.

Terezin ghetto favorite and former professional Czech goalkeeper Jirka Taussig in *Liga Terezín*, September 1, 1944. Taussig survived Theresienstadt and later Auschwitz. Chronos Media, Germany.

Souvenir poster from Terezín for team Aeskulap, signed by prisoners. Original color watercolor by W. Thalheimer, 1943–1944. Památník Terezín, copyright Zuzana Dvořáková.

Survivor of the Russian front Herbert Pohl dons the red shirt and black shorts of Dresdner SC in a 4–0 victory over LSV (Luftwaffe) Hamburg in Berlin's Olympic Stadium, June 18, 1944. The Granger Collection, New York.

Austrian civilians conscripted to offer a proper burial to the murdered on the former SS soccer field in the Mauthausen (Austria) concentration camp, May 10, 1945. USHMM, courtesy of Ray Buch.

Matches featuring survivors captivate throngs of fans in Munich after the war. Ghetto Fighters' House Museum, Israel; photo by Isak Sutin.

Matches were a popular diversion at the Zeilsheim DP camp (near Frankfurt), circa 1946–1947. Yad Vashem.

Jewish refugee Aaron Elster, hidden for two years in an attic in Poland, posing in the uniform of his youth team in the Neu Freimann DP camp near Munich, 1946. USHMM.

The rescued making the save for team Hatikvah (The Hope) in the Bergen-Belsen DP camp, the largest in Germany. Yad Vashem.

Inside the fence where a soccer pitch once stood. On the other side, the unloading ramp and the path to death. Auschwitz-Birkenau today, 2015. Courtesy of the author.

6

FOOTBALL IN THE
POLISH KILLING FIELDS

Eyewitnesses to Nazi Terror

Then, after he has placed his hand in mine
with cheerful face, whence I was comforted,
he led me in among the hidden things.
There sighs and wails and piercing cries of woe
reverberated through the starless air;
hence I, at first, shed tears of sympathy.
Strange languages, and frightful forms of speech,
words caused by pain, accents of anger, voices
both loud and faint, and smiting hands withal,
a mighty tumult made . . .
—Dante Alighieri, from Canto III of *The Divine Comedy: Inferno* (vv. 19–28)[1]

ARRIVAL

The train arriving at the Birkenau death camp followed the same path as dozens of trains before it. Passing underneath the unmistakable arched gateway and watchtower and continuing on into the camp, it stopped at a ramp platform. The ramp, later remembered as a place of infamy, was the site of a *Selektion* made by the arbiters of death where every deportee was chosen to work or designated for the walk to the gas chambers. Fourteen-year-old Georg Koves, taken from his home in a

Jewish section of Budapest, arrived with thousands of others. There was a great commotion with many people moving about outside of the stopped train, the banging and clattering sounds of the doors being opened on the cattle cars. Suitcases and baggage were to be left on the platform, with disinfection awaiting a select few. The deportees caught their first glimpse of the workers, who had the appearance of convicts, with their shaved heads and skullcaps atop and wearing the striped duds of criminals. The sunken eyes and emaciated features of the workers were immediately alarming to those disembarking from the train. The workers implored the youngest arrivals to claim sixteen years as their age and to be enthusiastic about working when asked. The *Selektion* involved first separating the elderly, women, and children from the men, and with it came increasingly frantic and desperate goodbyes. The maelstrom of confusion, fear, and uncertainty only increased as the new arrivals were marched for a medical inspection. To be sent "Links!"— left—meant death, but if you were told "Rechts!"—right—it meant a stay of execution and assignment to some sort of labor detail. The superficial decision took all of two or three seconds. A flood of people, the so-called unfit, moved left and forward like an unbroken stream. The young George Koves, selected as fit, moved with the others to the sauna area, which was set between the four main gas chambers and crematory at Birkenau. Koves described the scene unfolding before his eyes:

> The road led through a gate of woven barbed wire to somewhere farther inside the area behind the fence where, it appeared, the bathhouse must be: we set off along it in slack clusters, not hurrying but chatting and looking around, with the soldier, not saying a single word, listlessly bringing up the rear. Under our feet there was again a broad, immaculately white, metaled road, while in front of us was the whole rather tiring prospect of flat terrain in air that all around was by now shimmering and undulating in heat. . . . From what I saw of the area on this short walk, on the whole it too won my approval. A football pitch, on a big clearing immediately to the right of the road, was particularly welcome. Green turf, the requisite white goalposts, the chalk lines of the field of play—it was all there, inviting, fresh, pristine, in perfect order. This was latched onto straightaway by the boys as well: Look here! A place for us to play soccer after work.[2]

The remembrances of Georg Koves are actually the creation of Terezín and Birkenau survivor Imre Kertész. The 2002 Nobel Laureate in Literature, Kertész fictionalizes his personal experiences as one of the youngest survivors of the death camp at Auschwitz (or Oświęcim in Polish) in the acclaimed book *Fatelessness*, from which this passage comes. Through Koves's voice, we also learn that vile deception was crucial in convincing new arrivals to cooperate with the mechanisms of murder:

> All along, I hear, everyone is very civil toward them swaddling them with solicitude and loving-kindness, and the children play football and sing, while the place where they are suffocated to death lies in a very picturesque area, with lawns, groves of trees, and flower-beds. . . . Adding to this . . . was the crafty way in which . . . they had induced me to change clothes, simply with the ruse of the hook and the number on it.[3]

These scenes of arrival, deception, and death are further replayed many times in the actual testimonies of those who played soccer and survived in Auschwitz-Birkenau. From the earliest days of the camp at Auschwitz I to the satellite labor camps and the extermination center at Birkenau, the game of soccer persisted.

PRIVILEGE AND SOCCER IN AUSCHWITZ-BIRKENAU

In the beginning, the concentration camp at Auschwitz did not look like most of the other concentration camps in the Third Reich. Created originally as a barracks for the Austrian cavalry before the Great War, it was converted by the newly independent nation of Poland into an army base in the years between the world wars. Auschwitz I was first a detention center for Russian prisoners of war once the former Axis allies had declared war on each other after Operation Barbarossa, the Nazi invasion of Russia, began on June 22, 1941. Conversion of the Austro-Hungarian-era barracks began in earnest once the Germans acquired prisoners faster than they could dispense with them. Within a few months, the SS leadership in the camp launched plans for another camp, much larger in scale and with deadly ambition. Located two miles west, the Auschwitz-Birkenau camp is what most people envision

when they think about the Holocaust. It has taken on iconic status as
the representation of the evils of National Socialism in Europe. This
was the site of industrialized murder on a scale scarcely imaginable
before the war. It is a vast expanse of land where row after row of
wooden barracks housed those who managed to escape the initial selection for death on the infamous railway ramps, only to later face the trials
of slave labor within the camp complex. It is also the site of the four
largest gas chambers and attached crematoria found in the Nazi camp
system.

Among the very first prisoners brought to the Auschwitz I camp in
1940 was the eighteen-year-old Kazimierz Albin, prisoner number 118.
Among his earliest recollections of the camp was the realization that
those with privileges were afforded unusual leisure activities. One Sunday afternoon, Albin and his barracks mates noticed a group of *kapos*
playing soccer. Several of the players showed real talent. When the
concentration camp at Auschwitz began, the men selected to oversee
the barracks and the work details for in and around the camp typically
were German criminals. These were men who often surpassed the SS in
their cruelty toward prisoners. In exchange for their service, they were
afforded extra privileges—one of which was the chance to play soccer in
their leisure time. Albin realized that "these Kapos wanted to amuse
themselves. They played football amongst themselves, but taking on
players of a different nationality brought an extra edge . . . and for us,
being on the team meant getting extra food rations and being given
lighter forced labor, so it was a chance to survive."[4]

In keeping with the wartime demands of a nation suffering significant losses in armament production back home in Germany, slave laborers from Poland clung to life in the Nazi camp system. A few records
exist of prisoner soccer played in the transit camp at Trawniki, the
training center for many of the guards who went on to work in ghetto
deportation squads, as escorts for transport trains, and as guards in the
killing centers. Trawniki is notorious in the history of the Holocaust for
providing guard units for the Operation Reinhard killing centers at
Sobibór, Belzec, and Treblinka. Soviet prisoners of war and conscripted
civilians (most often young Ukrainians) made up the vast majority of
these units. Trawniki men also watched over dozens of forced-labor
camps for Jews, including Auschwitz and the desolate and pitiless camp

at Poniatowa, near Lublin, another camp where soccer briefly appeared.

Such privileges as those seen in Auschwitz reflected the ever-evolving nature of relationships between the Germans, their collaborators, and favored prisoners, who were most often Polish. A working relationship between a prisoner and a "superior" Aryan, defined in unequal terms with this inferior "Slavic" captive, often proved to be the deciding factor in whether or not one survived these camps. Because football was a prominent benefit afforded prisoners, it quickly created favored status among the prisoners. Become useful to a specific German, and you provided yourself a means for survival in places that were extremely capricious and random in their lethal consequences. Rather than a genuine affection, the loss of a useful prisoner represented a major inconvenience for the German, and a new prisoner had to be trained as a replacement.[5] Consistent with the struggle for life that played out in all aspects of these camps, the rivalry for prestige and privilege continued on the soccer pitch. A camp aristocracy emerged quickly in almost every camp, and in the Auschwitz camp system, there were several camp orchestras, and sporting competitions were on frequent offer. Boxing and soccer were the two most prominent examples. In fact, boxing acted as a proxy revenge for prisoners against their functionary masters, most of whom were German criminals.[6]

Despite being targets for brutality, many captive Poles enjoyed watching the impromptu soccer games of the intermittent league created by the privileged. Erick Gronke, a camp *kapo* at Auschwitz I and a soccer player himself, was in charge of one particular *kapo* team. Polish prisoners were enthusiastic in their assembling of their team, and in their search for players they were able to find some genuine stars of prewar Polish soccer. The central midfielder of one team was Sylwester Nowakowski, the man who led the fourteen-time Polish champion Ruch Chorzów to the league championship five times in the 1930s. Another was midfielder Antoni Łyko, who famously scored for Wisła Kraków, one of Poland's oldest and most successful clubs, in a 1–0 friendly win against Chelsea in May 1936. Łyko was selected for the 1938 World Cup in France (though he did not travel). He was well known among the prisoners from Kraków, and his lightning-quick play on the right wing was complemented by a striker from Warta Poznan, Wawszyniec Staliski, who prior to the war had scored eleven goals for the Polish national team. Mixed in among the team were other professional players from various Polish first and second division clubs. Because the Poles were only allowed to wear wooden shoes in the camp, a type of clog, the German *kapo* Gronke took the extraordinary effort of "organizing" eleven pairs of tied shoes for the Polish team. This probably meant acquiring the shoes from recent arrivals in the camp, who in all likelihood had already been murdered immediately upon arrival.

The Germans so desperately wanted a competitive match that they arranged for additional food rations for the starving prisoners chosen to play. The promise of cigarettes, valuable as barter currency, earned loyalty from other players. On a beautiful Sunday afternoon at the close of the summer of 1941, the first Germany–Poland game was played on the roll-call field at Auschwitz I, and both teams faced each other wearing the ubiquitous long striped pants. Almost all the other prisoners stood around watching in awe as the Polish team was winning 3–1. Soon other games became the focus of attention in the camp, despite the loss of players to human-made famine or exhaustion. Few were spared in these early, brutal days of the first camp. In July 1941, Antoni Łyko, who played one final match on the eve of his death, was marched barefoot to gravel pits located just outside of the fence. There he was executed alongside another footballer from the popular Polish club Cracovia. Their murder was supervised by one of the camp doctors, and executions like these were often attended by other SS officers and their wives. Other players died from exhaustion or were murdered. And just as rapidly, new players replaced those lost. One player was Jozef Korbas, an extraordinary but diminutive striker who scored three goals in his Polish national team debut against Bulgaria in 1937, and who before the war played in sixty-nine games for Cracovia, scoring fifty-four goals. Before the end of his captivity in Auschwitz-Birkenau, Kazimierz Albin helped create another team called Poland B, and in their first game they played against the second *kapo* team and won 7–0. Albin recalled their successes: "Skinny and small against big and fat opponents, we dominated in speed and technique. Playing against them was like playing against children. The audience would laugh out loud sometimes, including German prisoner functionaries and SS men. Our opponents would react with fury."[7] Unlike so many others, Albin escaped the camp in 1943, and he immediately went into hiding in Kraków, joining up with the clandestine Polish home army and fighting until the Nazi retreat from Poland in early 1945.

The year 1944 proved to be pivotal in the operations of the affiliated camps at Auschwitz. As the final groups of deported Jews left the ghetto camp of Terezín in northern Czechoslovakia, the influx of prisoners from across Europe to Birkenau was reaching its zenith. The arrival of tens of thousands of Jews from Hungary and the camps to the east, which were being pressured by the advancing Russian army, meant that the killing machinery was also accelerating. Yet, for a lucky few, arrival at Birkenau meant the extension of life. Jirka Taussig (later known as George Tesar, a rejection of the town name *Taussig* from the German) was one such prisoner sent to Auschwitz-Birkenau in 1944. When word quickly spread among the German functionaries of the camp of Taussig's exploits as a goalkeeper in the "Liga Terezín," he was transferred to a section (or block) where prisoners played under the watch of the SS. He was also awarded a job that did not jeopardize his health; he unloaded cargo. Taussig recalled, "My name was well known then, and when they needed a good goalie they found me in the camp. . . . Transports arrived from Hungary, bringing several soccer players. They organized two or three teams to play against each other. No snow was falling. It was almost like a regular game with grass and goalposts."[8]

One match, between members of the SS and a team composed of prisoners from the Czech family camp (B2b), was played in February 1944. A teammate of Taussig, René Edgar Tressler, played as a left forward, and the two expected to continue their success from the soccer league from Terezín. Fiercely competitive, Tressler describes the initial match in his Czech-language autobiography, *Escaping Destiny*. With great pride and determination, the recently arrived Czech players thwarted every attempt on goal. Taussig, with "hands like fly paper," denied the SS until it was made clear to him by spectators and more seasoned prisoners that if he wanted to live, he would concede. Fearing the consequences of a win over their SS masters, Taussig recognized the threat and let in two quick goals, handing victory to the SS team.

René Tressler, later a star with the Czech first division team Sparta Prague, was among the youngest players in the camp. At the end of the war, and hanging on to life in the same camp as Elie Wiesel (KZ Buchenwald), Tressler joyously hugged his rescuer, an African American man who jumped down from his tank on April 11, 1945. Not yet eighteen, exhausted, and starving, Tressler had endured the very worst the Nazis had demanded. For Taussig, the games in Auschwitz only lasted a short while until he was sent to the Sachsenhausen outside of Berlin, after which he was transferred to another camp in Bavaria. By this time, he was no longer allowed to play goalie, and after being caught smuggling bread, he was forced to demonstrate his athleticism—but this time, in a life-threatening game of punishment: "I received the punishment of running on all fours up and down a hill—back and forth on my hands and knees. . . . [Unlike the vast majority of prisoners at the end of the war] I was in such good shape, I did it well. My fingers were bleeding, but I didn't give in. Everyone was impressed by the way I carried out the punishment. Even the Nazis watching me got so excited they decided to stop me."[9] Both young Czech players survived death marches into Germany and found liberation by American soldiers.

Czechoslovakian teenager William Schick, bewildered and confused, arrived at Birkenau and was abruptly tattooed with the number 170938 on his left forearm. This indignity was a permanent reminder that he was no longer seen as a human being by his captors. Like Taussig and Tressler before him, Schick was deported from the transit camp of Terezín and arrived at Auschwitz in the now-familiar cattle car, part of a transport that numbered three thousand. People were told that they were going east on a "work detail," and many died on the journey. Their arrival in the southern Poland death camp of Auschwitz-Birkenau was at once disorienting and chaotic. Blinding floodlights greeted the Jews as they poured out of the cattle cars. SS guards and their prisoner conscripts shouted orders at the new arrivals: "Raus, raus! [Get out!] Schnell, schnell! [Quickly, faster!]" Those who survived the journey were immediately corralled. Schick recollects: "We arrived at Auschwitz in the evening. When they opened the door of our cattle car, there were German soldiers with guns and German shepherd dogs. Prisoners in blue and white striped uniforms, who worked for the Germans, called 'Kapos,' were also waiting for us. They beat the hell out of us with sticks they carried."[10] Soon Schick was marched to Camp B2b, the only family camp in Birkenau. There he met the *kapo* of his block, who wore the black triangle assigned to criminals. Schick soon learned that the man was a German who had committed a murder before the war.

After a period of time in which Schick and the others in his barracks acclimated to the increasingly grim conditions of the camp, a surprise request was made by the *kapo*: "He came into our camp one day and asked if any of us played soccer. I was a soccer player. . . . I raised my hand because I had been part of a semi-pro soccer team in Prague before the war." Schick remembers what happened after one match against another camp within Birkenau: "After we won the match he gave each one of the members of our team a six-inch piece of salami. We had to be careful with the salami. If you ate all of it at one time you could die. Our stomachs were not use[d] to such rich food."[11]

Such stories of survival, of resistance, and more often, of death present conflicting questions of morality and propriety in the choices made by the imprisoned. Primo Levi, the famous Auschwitz survivor, critiques the ethics of playing soccer at Auschwitz in his book *The Drowned and the Saved*. Even in his own circumstances, he acknowledges that he survived because of a combination of blind chance paired with a fortuitous work assignment in a subsidiary chemical laboratory. Levi also carries the irreconcilable burden of having witnessed the drama of the survivors firsthand. When analyzing the ethical circumstances of these soccer matches, Levi acknowledges that the prisoners who were most likely to survive Birkenau were the prisoners from what he called "the grey zone."[12] For Levi, this "grey zone" was part of the inverted moral universe that epitomized the death camp of Auschwitz. In it were special squads of Jews, called *Sonderkommandos* (or SK), selected to empty the gas chambers and transport the murdered to the crematoria ovens. Levi called the creation of these squads National Socialism's "most demonic crime."[13] But he goes on to say that, like those who survived by playing sport, no one ought to judge these individuals. To do otherwise would mean that the guilt would be shifted away from those truly responsible: the Nazis and their collaborators. Within these places of great terror and suffering, there was a network of complicity, collusion in mass murder set up by design from the very beginnings of these camps across Europe, where perpetrator and victim were joined in the institution of death, in the work of extermination.

One of the few eyewitness accounts we have of any football matches between prisoners and SS guards at Auschwitz comes from a Hungarian physician named Miklós Nyiszli. He served as an assistant and specialist in forensic medicine to the infamous Dr. Josef Mengele. Assigned to work alongside the *Sonderkommando* in Crematorium II, in a specially designed operating theater and pathology office, Nyiszli conducted autopsies and provided consultation to Mengele in his "research" on twins within the camp. In his 1960 memoir, a landmark testimony of the events in this highly secretive part of the camp, he tells of the juxtaposition of two completely inconceivable and incompatible events. The first event centers on the horrific sounds of an execution of seventy women by individual gunshots that occurred just outside of his office. Dumbstruck with the realization that some of the victims had survived, Nyiszli escapes the dreadful scene by retreating outside. As he takes a short walk in the early evening hours down the same gravel path described by the writer Imre Kertész, a walkway that divided the well-kept lawns of the crematorium courtyard. Nyiszli glances across the camp grounds to see the chimneys of the crematoria operating as usual. And a short while later, he takes in a second, most peculiar scene:

> It was too early for dinner. The Sonderkommando brought out a football. The teams lined up on the field. "SS versus SK." On one side of the field the crematorium's SS guards; on the other, the Sonderkommando. They put the ball into play. Sonorous laughter filled the courtyard. The spectators became excited and shouted encouragement at the players, as if this were the playing field of some peaceful town. Stupefied, I made that mental note as well. [14]

The yard referred to by Miklós Nyiszli in his memoir is located behind Crematorium II, and on the east side of Crematorium III, in the camp known as "B2f," where there was a sports ground that enabled the *kapos* and the *Vorarbeiter* (labor foremen) to pass the time and, to some observers, work off the excess calories they had confiscated from the thousands of people attempting to survive by the slimmest of margins within the killing center. [15] As information about the camps around Auschwitz gradually seeped into the world's consciousness, Allied planes began to target the industrial sites adjacent to Birkenau. A number of the aerial photographs taken of the Birkenau death camp reveal the staggering size of the camp, but none of these reveals any sports fields. Yet it is not likely that such areas would have needed to be more than simple flat spaces for "sports" events to take place. Probably the best aerial picture, taken by the Allies on August 25, 1944, shows the yards behind Crematorium II and the east side of Crematorium III, the site of the most widely discussed football matches at Auschwitz. Adam Cyra, historian at the Auschwitz-Birkenau Memorial and Museum, said this main football pitch was intentionally set up to the right of the Birkenau train ramp: "For people who were about to die, the vision of prisoners playing football against the Kapos was meant to be reassuring."[16]

Primo Levi further is widely acknowledged as having popularized this account of the SK versus SS match from Nyiszli's memoir, and he doubts that such a match ever took place with any class of prisoner as this would violate the racial codes of the camp. But from testimonies of the few who played there, we know such matches did take place. Levi also believes that only these "crematorium ravens"[17] could enter the field of play as near equals of the SS men. Despite their seemingly shared complicity in the killing at Birkenau, these football matches at the doorstep of death, at least for a fleeting moment, reduced the distance between perpetrator and victim.

Yet the very existence of the *Sonderkommando* meant that, in the Nazi worldview, the Jewish workers of the *Sonderkommando* were "dirtied with their own blood" and, like the biblical Cain, had killed their own brothers.[18] But closer scrutiny, benefiting from subsequent revelations about soccer in Auschwitz, exposes the truth that such competitions were yet another means by which the Nazi elite expressed their utter contempt for the prisoners. Because there were several other football matches in Auschwitz-Birkenau pitting the SS against different Jewish prisoner groups (e.g., Terezín transfers, new Hungarian arrivals, and gypsy teams), none of which would have been a part of this "grey zone," these matches meant perpetuation of the racial domination built into the very structure of the operations of the camps. And because the SS were always victorious, the illusion of racial superiority was maintained. More than mere entertainment, the soccer matches at Auschwitz existed as sacraments of degradation and domination for the SS.

INCONCEIVABLE SOCCER: SS GUARDS VERSUS THE GYPSY CAMP

Though Jewish and Polish political prisoners overwhelmingly bore the brunt of Nazi persecution in World War II, other groups suffered immeasurably as well. The Nazi genocide of the Romani and Sinti, much like the systematic murder of the Jews, was racially motivated. The murder of the Romani was methodical and intended to definitively exterminate these people throughout German-occupied territories. But the persecution of these ethnic groups did not begin with the National Socialists. The term *Zigeuner* (meaning "untouchable," from the Greek, referring to the position of the Roma in the Indian caste system), used for centuries by German-speaking populations across Europe, continues to be used to this day, though it is now held as stigmatizing and pejorative. Historically, numerous antigypsy laws were on the books across Europe and within Germany, particularly Bavaria, the birthplace of the Nazi movement, and the registration of all gypsies over the age of six began in 1899. Photographs, fingerprints, genealogical data, and information related to movement and property were all collected by government officials. Information related to "criminality" was of particular interest to these officials, guided by the racist idea that gypsies possessed a genetic tendency toward criminal behavior. In this eugenic age, concerns about mixing the German gene pool with such "work-shy" vagabonds intensified in the national conversation.

Within German academic circles, the argument that some lives were more worthy than others was also gaining traction. The odious term *Ballastexistenzen*[19] was introduced by eugenicists, claiming that those whose lives were merely ballast (or dead weight) within humanity should be removed from society. Thus perceived criminality among the gypsies, transmitted genetically, posed an imminent threat to Germany. And when the July 14, 1933, Law to Prevent Heredity Diseases was passed in the first six months of Nazi rule, it wasn't long until imprisonment, sterilization, and euthanasia were employed to control such threats among Roma and Sinti populations. The legal restrictions intensified in September 1935 with the passage of the Nuremberg Race Laws, which further prevented intermarriage, defining Jews and Roma/Sinti as distinct racial categories. This "racial hygiene," first promoted widely in the United States decades before World War II, acquired a murderous form when the Roma and Sinti peoples of Europe were systematically killed. Beginning in summer 1941, Sinti and Roma were routinely shot by the German Wehrmacht, the SS Einsatzgruppen (mobile killing squads), and Order Police units working behind the Eastern Front and throughout Poland, Ukraine, Belarus, and the Baltic States. No distinction was made between Jews and gypsies. Many others were deported from their homes across Europe to the killing centers in Poland, particularly Auschwitz-Birkenau. At the end of the war, estimates of the number of Roma and Sinti murdered by military units and in concentration camps reached half a million. Of the forty thousand German and Austrian Sinti and Roma registered in the Third Reich, more than twenty-five thousand perished.[20]

The intersection of sporting life and the experiences of the Roma and Sinti people parallel those of Jewish and Polish groups. For example, in July 1936, during the run-up to the Berlin Olympics, hundreds of Roma and Sinti were interned at the Marzahn camp outside Berlin, just as was done in other cities across Germany. June 1938 saw hundreds more deported to other camps, such as Dachau, Sachsenhausen, Buchenwald, and Mauthausen in Upper Austria. Among the many thousands caught up in the escalating Nazi genocide was a German citizen named Walter Winter. In his 2004 autobiography, *Winter Time: Memoirs of a German Sinto Who Survived Auschwitz*, we learn of the importance of sport in surviving these camps. Walter Winter enjoyed football from a young age, playing street soccer and joining the local football club in his small town in northern Germany when he was ten or eleven. Winter's older brother, Erich, worked his way into a league football team, VfL Oldenburg, at age seventeen, a remarkable feat for a player so young and from a persecuted ethnic group.

Regarded as an outsider in his own country, Winter joined the Kriegsmarine (German navy) in December 1940 and was conscripted to serve in an antiaircraft battery, a position from which he was never promoted because of his Sinti heritage. Discharged as non-Aryan, Winter was soon arrested and deported, along with two family members, to Auschwitz I and then marched to Birkenau. Under the euphemistic guise of being "evacuated to the east" and under the promise of land to cultivate upon arrival, Winter instead was branded with a camp number (Z3105, "Z" for *Zigeuner*) and assigned to a work unit outside of the camp. Isolated by assignment to the "gypsy camp" (labeled B2e on the camp's master map), Winter claimed his spot on a three-tiered wooden bunk, with ten men assigned to a bunk and only straw for a mattress, all under a wooden barracks originally designed as horse stables.

During his time in the death camp, Walter Winter contracted typhus and witnessed numerous crimes and cruel murders. One of his responsibilities was as roll-call clerk for his block, and he even served one day in Crematorium III as a laborer who fed wood for the ovens, a highly unusual assignment given that anyone who worked in the epicenter of the killing operations in Birkenau was routinely executed within three months, making way for another group of *Sonderkommandos*. Yet, amid such great anguish, he bravely challenged his tormenters, once beating up an SS guard and brazenly confronting the notorious Dr. Josef Mengele when he requested extra rations to feed the Sinti children in his care who were starving. Early in August 1944, the "liquidation" of the gypsy camp was completed by the SS at Birkenau. The remaining 2,900 survivors, mostly women, children, and the elderly, were murdered on the night of August 3. In advance of this "liquidation," about three thousand gypsy prisoners had been sent on trains to work as slave labor for Reich armament industries. Winter was sent to Ravensbrück and then Sachsenhausen. Both his brother, Erich, six years his senior, and his new bride were also imprisoned in Ravensbrück. Perversely, his brother was sterilized and his wife died in the camp on Christmas Eve 1944, just three days after losing their child at birth. Before the nightmare would end, Walter Winter was pulled from Sachsenhausen to fight the advancing Russians, who were rapidly closing in on Berlin. In the last weeks of the war, Winter suffered a shoulder wound, requiring an operation performed without anesthesia by an SS doctor. When the war was finally over, Winter navigated his way back to Germany, hopping trains first to Berlin and then to Hannover and Bremen, as he worked his way back home to northwest Germany. On his travels, his group passed themselves off as sleeping American soldiers, covering themselves in blankets. Soon thereafter, he was reunited with his parents, who also miraculously survived the war.

During his time in Auschwitz, Winter remembers one day in late spring or early summer 1944 when a new roll-call leader named Hartmann,[21] an SS man, arrived in the gypsy camp. He asked the block seniors and the roll-call clerks (of whom Walter Winter was one) to identify who the footballers were among the prisoners. Many prisoners, including Winter's brother, Erich, expressed an interest and, once designated as trainer, Winter selected eleven to twelve players. Hartmann provided gear and provisions that had likely been "organized" by theft from new arrivals to the camp. After a brief period of training and the additional recruitment of a Jewish player from an adjacent block, the gypsy team was ready for a competitive match. With the SS guards crowded around the field as spectators, watching intently as many had bet on the outcome of the matches, Winter describes the excitement and the uncertainty of playing against the Germans:

> The first match was arranged: Auschwitz Main Camp v. Gypsies. There were six Polish national players in the Main Camp team. Kick off. Only a reduced SS presence remained in the camp, all the other SS men were at the sports field. SS lined the field on all sides as no prisoners were allowed to watch. Our camp lay directly adjacent to this sports field so we were able to watch. The electric current was switched off on the perimeter fence on the sports-field side. Everyone ran to the fence—the entire Gypsy Camp stood at the fence as spectators, with kith and kin, as the saying goes, or on the roofs of the blocks. The match began. We attacked from the start and scored the first goal after ten minutes. I thought, "Now all hell will break loose!" Normally the SS men from the Main Camp were rivals of those from Birkenau but at this moment they were sportsmen. As we scored, our SS, the Birkenau SS, began to fire off their revolvers, like fireworks going off. So now, on, on! In the second half, we scored again. All hell did break loose! I thought, "Lad, if only you survive this!" The two SS factions began to abuse one another and were close to hitting each other. Shortly before the end we conceded a goal. We won 2–1. That eased things.[22]

Soon after the first match, the gypsy team played a return match, which they lost 2–1, likely restoring balance to the perception of Nazi dominion over the "subhuman species" that inhabited the camp. For a time, the SS man Hartmann made sure additional rations were provided the prisoners, but when the field, created from open space immediately to the west of the gypsy camp, was reclaimed for a new male prisoners' infirmary, the matches ended. Winter speculates that another reason the games ended is that Hartmann had received word that he had lost two sons to the war, and from that time on he lost interest in the diversion of football in Auschwitz. Though the team was disbanded, the prisoners played among themselves, and at great risk, between the barracks, but only when the SS guards had cleared off for the day.

Another prisoner, a Hungarian named Sandor Schwarcz, was also selected for slave labor in Birkenau in early July 1944, and soon after, as he sat in a different barracks (Block 9), the overcrowded bunkhouse that he shared with hundreds of other prisoners, he was approached by men searching for soccer players to add to a gypsy team. Agreeing to play, in part to alleviate his boredom, Schwarcz joined a team made up primarily of these same German gypsies and two Jewish footballers. Playing under the watchful eye of the SS, his team beat all comers, including a match contested under gunpoint. But the result was drastically different when they played the SS, a well-fed and organized side: his ragtag gypsy team lost 8–0. With the "liquidation" of the gypsy camp in August 1944, these matches ended and the SS murdered nearly all of the gypsy players. Miraculously, Schwarcz survived this deadly selection, and he even escaped the gas chambers on October 24, 1944.[23] Like Winter, Sandor Schwarcz had been transferred to other camps in the Nazi sphere, moving through Gross-Rosen, Dachau, and finally Mühldorf, where he survived the war.

Others remember well the football matches. Former prisoner Bronisław Cynkar (number 183) played as a goalkeeper in the Auschwitz I camp in the early days:

> I was a part of soccer games played on the roll call field during the winter 1940–1941. As a goalie I was very valuable. Whenever I'd play goalie, high bets were placed in favor of the Polish team winning. On Saturdays there were so-called small games, played among the Poles. The big games were very famous and were played between national teams on Sundays. These games were very festive. When the teams entered the field, the camp orchestra would play. The games were treated very seriously. In order to strengthen their team, Germans would bring players from Dachau. The games were very popular among the prisoners as well as the SS men. A lot of SS men would give up their Sunday pass and stay in the camp instead to be able to watch the game. Sometimes the games would take a long time—two or two and a half hours. As a goalie for the Polish team I was pretty famous among the prisoners and they all liked me.[24]

Soldiers from the German army also found themselves trapped in the camps. From the testimony of Kurt Hacker (prisoner 130029) collected by the Auschwitz State Museum, these soccer matches enabled prisoners a measure of camaraderie. Hacker, incarcerated at Auschwitz for his activities in the resistance movement, remembers football in the main camp and his conversations with another prisoner: "I personally knew, quite well, the striker of the Polish national team [a man named] Bartor, who played at that time on the left wing. . . . I talked with him a long time about the football."[25] Hacker was originally a young Wehrmacht soldier from Vienna but was arrested for resistance activities, driven by his communist sympathies. After a short stint in a Reich prison, he was transferred to Auschwitz, where he spent two and a half years until liberation. Hiding in the camp in the final days in order to avoid the death marches, Hacker later served as the director of the Mauthausen (Austria) memorial and, in the years before his passing, as the chair of the International Auschwitz Committee, a survivor-outreach position he was appointed to by the Polish prime minister.

Former prisoner Mieczysław Pietrzak recognized in the soccer games opportunities for resistance:

> The second source of new information about life outside of the camp was prisoners brought from General Government [the Nazi term for occupied Poland] and beyond. At first they were very quiet and closed off. After a month of camp experiences they would get used to the conditions and slowly open up to relate to others. It helped to have the Sunday soccer games played between block prisoners and German *kapo* against the team made up of SS men. Prisoners were the audience. During these games, prisoners were able to talk to each other freely and even share confidential information.[26]

The randomness of surviving in a place like Auschwitz is vividly illustrated in the life of one Leo Goldstein, a Polish-born Jew caught up in the maelstrom of the war. Managing to survive in the death camp of Auschwitz up until 1944, Goldstein was queuing up with other condemned prisoners destined to be gassed when he was suddenly pulled from the line by an SS guard named Otto who was purported to be a German international footballer. Ordered to return to his barracks, Goldstein remembers weeks earlier having a conversation with the same guard, who had entered his barracks to ask if any of the prisoners were familiar with the rules of the game. No one answered immediately, and after a long delay Goldstein finally murmured, "I once read the rule book." This Otto arranged matches between guards from Auschwitz and soldiers and guards from other nearby camps. Later chosen to referee, Goldstein had to show the greatest tact, knowing he could not run afoul of any of the players on the field. Despite having no formal training as a match official, Goldstein managed to survive the death camp and went on to become an Israeli citizen who settled in New York

in the postwar years. Saved because he officiated in the camp, Goldstein also remarkably continued his refereeing career, serving as a linesman in a particularly violent and brutal Group 2 match between host
Chile and an Italian team reduced to nine men in the 1962 World Cup
that witnessed a caution twelve seconds into the match and near aban-
donment of the game by officials. But as difficult as that afternoon in
Santiago must have been, it was mere distraction compared to his officiating experiences in Birkenau.[27]

Another resistance fighter active in and around Kraków, a man
named John (Jan) Komski, recalled his imprisonment at the Auschwitz
extermination camp after his capture in Czechoslovakia, where he was
hoping to serve in the Free Polish Army being formed in France. In
mid-June 1940, Komski was among the very first group of prisoners
assigned to Auschwitz on the day it opened. As were so many others
who would follow him, he was marked with a red triangle, designating
political prisoners, and his forearm was tattooed with a number: 564.
Moved around to three other camps after being caught following an
escape from Auschwitz in 1942, Komski was liberated by the U.S. Army
from Dachau in southern Germany in April 1945. Many years after the
war, when he was asked by an interviewer for the U.S. Holocaust Memorial Museum, "What choices could one make in the camp that would
help you survive?," Komski recognized that those with special talents
had a greater chance for survival: "Sports people, you know, those who
could play a soccer game, had a time, good time for survival. . . . The SS
would get tired of this camp routine, and they would say, 'Oh, let's play
a game.' So they would play a game. In camp Gross-Rosen, where I was
sent later on in 1944, the commandant of the camp was a sportsman,
and a soccer player himself, so we had 27 teams [to play in the]
game[s]."[28] He added that in Auschwitz, a painter, a musician, and a
cook could all earn a little more food by being useful to the SS. But if
you were from the educated classes, like lawyers, academics, and scien-
tists, your chances for survival were slim.

Acclaimed Czech Jewish novelist and playwright Arnošt Lustig, a
survivor of Terezín, Auschwitz, and Buchenwald, writes about football
in Auschwitz in his 2006 book *Fire on Water*. Lustig, a goalkeeper who
actually won a Nazi-equivalent of an MVP award in the camps, offers an
unsentimental portrayal of the Shoah, often writing about minute acts
of heroism in desperate circumstances. Lustig witnessed his own father

being sent to the gas chambers and his mother stripped nude and paraded before a crowd in the camp. Reflecting on his experience in Birkenau, Lustig confronted those who might doubt his experiences given the fact that soccer was on offer in a place of such deep suffering:

> There was no way to tell him that we also learned something in the camps. Once I told him [a doubter] that we played soccer there, and I saw the thought go through his mind: see now, you got to play soccer. So it couldn't have been all that bad. How could I have explained to him in that same moment that the SS bet on our games as if they were at dog or horse races or cockfights? How many people were cremated in between? Or that anybody who injured another player on the field in Auschwitz-Birkenau went straight to the ovens? The player who fouled another—Nazi-like—went up the flue like the rest?[29]

In a conversation long after the war with an interviewer, Lustig added

> I was sentenced to death three times. I spent one month in quarantine, waiting to be gassed. We played soccer in the quarantine because you cannot wait for your death. It would be too depressing. Plus, at 17, you simply do not believe that they are going to kill you. If they kill you, fine. And I mean, fine, "quote, unquote." We will see. This is your attitude. So I cannot say that I didn't learn anything. I learned a lot.[30]

Whether one was waiting for death or another chance to secure nourishment for another day, sport in the camps also brought great uncertainty. Used as a punishment, sport had the capacity to kill. From the archives of the Auschwitz State Museum, former prisoner Władysław Plaskura relates the trepidation of sport as punishment: "Speaking of the camp sports we really have to distinguish between another sport used by SS men. Penalty exercises that were also called 'sport,' prisoners were greatly afraid of. Camp's leadership would use these kinds of punishments often for even minor offences."[31] Though organized soccer is not mentioned in prisoner testimonies of this sort, the historical record is replete with examples where concentration camp victims ultimately succumbed to these wicked consequences.

A DIFFERENT SORT OF BATTLEFIELD

Persecuted groups were not the only captives in the Auschwitz concentration camp system. Prisoners of war and forced laborers from all
across the Third Reich were brought to the Auschwitz III camp. Located four miles from the main camp of Auschwitz I, this slave labor site,
called Monowitz E715, became operational in October 1942. The SS
oversaw the construction of the Monowitz-Buna camp and all other
forced labor subcamps encompassing the Auschwitz sphere. Ultimately,
there were twenty-eight Auschwitz subcamps located throughout
Upper Silesia, all situated close to industrial facilities.[32] Armaments,
cement works, power plants, and the massive camp at Monowitz were
all designed to service the IG Farben Buna plant. Concentration camps
existed as a lucrative commercial enterprise, supplying the Reich military industry with slave labor and a system of patronage. Initially, there
were about ten thousand Auschwitz prisoners based at Monowitz-Buna,
with a peak of more than forty thousand inmates in all of the associated
slave labor facilities in the Auschwitz orbit.[33] Conditions in these satellite camps often mirrored those at the main camp or Birkenau. Probably the most notorious subcamp was Fürstengrube, located near a coal
mine. If you were sent to this camp, it was equivalent to receiving a
death sentence. Life expectancy in these conditions was measured in
weeks and not months. At the Monowitz camp, living conditions were
so severe that by the late winter of 1943, the wasting away of the
inmates was obvious enough to provoke an investigation by the supervising company IG Farben, Germany's largest chemical company at the
time. The result was the first systematic *Selektion* at Monowitz by the
SS. Of the nearly 3,500 prisoners, half were forced to make the return
journey to Birkenau, where they met their fate in the killing center.

Following such selections, able-bodied Jews were brought from
Auschwitz-Birkenau, and the diabolical pattern was repeated. Those
who managed to survive the slave labor were boarded three to a bed in
stifling and vermin-infested barracks. Laborers were provided minimal
food and the barest of clothing supplements to their standard camp
uniforms. These prisoners were also subjected to the humiliation of roll
calls in the predawn hours regardless of weather, and they were put to
work on eleven-hour shifts carrying heavy loads, often while on a forced
trot march. It only took three to four months of such grueling labor for

prisoners to break down, reducing them to walking skeletons. Routine selections continued, and those deemed unfit for work were reclaimed by the SS and taken to Birkenau for immediate death in the gas chambers. Even with higher food allowances, prisoners were not expected to live more than four to six weeks as the war came to a close. Even as the death toll rose and the Russians closed in on the Auschwitz camp system during late 1944, the neighboring Buna plant was never completely finished and prisoners were soon deported or forced on death marches back into Germany.

Built alongside the massive IG Farben factory in southern Poland, Monowitz also held the political and military enemies of the Third Reich. Captured British soldiers worked alongside Jewish concentration camp inmates in an enormous factory complex responsible for the conversion of coal into synthetic petrol and rubber. One Allied combatant, a Welsh soldier named Ron Jones, was taken prisoner in North Africa in January 1942 while fighting against the Afrika Korps forces of the "Desert Fox," Field Marshall Erwin Rommel. The lance corporal spent three and a half years in Nazi captivity, surviving three camps and an eventual death march back into Germany. Upon capture, Jones was kept in Lansdorf POW camp alongside the distinguished British actor Denholm Elliott, who would later find fame as cinema hero Indiana Jones's sidekick Dr. Marcus Brody. Elliott was a wireless operator for the RAF when, in late September 1942, he was shot down on a mission raiding U-boat pens in northern Germany. In October 1943, Jones was shipped off to Monowitz E715. There he and his fellow POWs worked six days a week, twelve hours a day with only random Sundays off. A typical day would start with a six a.m. roll call on the main camp square. He usually worked with a gang of nine men who were supervised by a German engineer, a man they called "Meister."

Jones recalls witnessing the savagery of the *kapos* assigned to the Jewish work details. Though they were forbidden from talking with the Jewish prisoners, they would surreptitiously share their Red Cross food parcels with the emaciated prisoners. Documents reveal that the British prisoners regularly witnessed the beating and murder of Jewish inmates at the IG Farben factory. They also observed hangings and the putrid smell of the smoke pouring from the crematoria at Birkenau just a few miles away. In one part of the factory, at the top of the tall filtration towers, Jones remembers seeing trains arriving at Birkenau off in the distance, particularly in the summer of 1944 when mass deportations from Hungary began.

By comparison, conditions were more bearable in the POW camps as more food was available and a greater number of diversions were made possible. The diversion that stayed the longest in his memory was football. As at the ghetto-camp Theresienstadt, the Red Cross visited many camps during the war, and when the message reached the aid agency that football was being played on Sundays in the Auschwitz POW camp, they provided the prisoners with boots, shorts, and four sets of shirts, one each for the English, Welsh, Scots, and Irish players. Ron Jones played goalkeeper in the red shirt of the Welsh team, which was embroidered by a fellow inmate with the crest of the Prince of Wales. The field allotted to the POWs was passable but lacking crossbars; the goalposts consisted of only thin white posts stuck in the ground. Camp guards would come out to watch along with other POWs and locals from the factories. Unlike in many of other camps, especially the labor camps, the Germans declined the competition, largely because most guards were over fifty years of age or were rendered invalid from service on the Eastern Front.

Most matches were played in the summer of 1944, and once the snow came in October, the games ceased altogether. Four teams were selected from hundreds of prisoners, and probably no more than six or seven matches were played, with games of six-a-side football. One aspect of these matches is that they served as a way to relieve tension from the increasingly frequent Allied bombing raids in the area. In one raid in August 1944, as the air campaign intensified considerably over Germany, the IG Farben factories were hit by Allied bombers, resulting in the deaths of thirty-eight British POWs. Jones, active as a footballer before the war in Newport, Wales, recalls, "The chance of a game had been hard to turn down, right or wrong, I enjoyed it enormously, [but] looking back, we were perhaps naïve. We were lined up for team photos afterwards, and we can all be seen smiling into the lens."[34] The concern here, more obvious from the distance of time, is that this football likely served as an elaborate propaganda exercise. By demonstrating the supposedly humane conditions in the POW camps, the Nazis helped put some distance between the Wehrmacht, which controlled the prisoner-of-war camps, and the SS, which inflicted the most barbaric methods on their Jewish captives.

Of the few permitted forms of recreation in Monowitz, the most popular were the football matches. At the direction of the warehouse chief for the used clothing department, SS-Rottenführer Josef Stahorski, these matches were played on the roll-call square between privileged groups of workers. This was a familiar pattern in the Auschwitz-affiliated camps. Teams built around the food warehouse staff were matched against the used clothes warehouse staff or the kitchen and hospital staffs. The more popular matches involved teams made up of nationally identified players and mixed professionals. Oftentimes, prisoners would volunteer to play these matches, hoping to be noticed by more prominent inmates who held a modicum of power in the camp. Usually, the reward for a good performance on the pitch was an extra portion of soup or a loaf of bread. Such matches could be life extending. One prisoner, Józef Tabaczyński, managed to get himself transferred into the kitchen unit, and his vivid description of a match one late autumn day continues to inspire decades later:

> With envy I would watch these prisoners, who on Sundays would play soccer on the camp's roll-call field. I have to admit that it wasn't the desire to play that caused my jealousy but the opportunity to get an additional food portion that the players would receive from the camp's kitchen. I saw that one of the organizers of the games was a Polish prisoner, Paweł Stolecki, who was a part of the *kapo* in *Bekleidungskammer* [the used clothing warehouse]. I tried to draw his attention to myself a few times, but since I didn't know him well, it was hard to do this. It was late fall, maybe November. I was losing my strength when fate smiled on me. One Sunday during *Lauseappel* [roll call], I was called by my barrack leader [barrack number 21]. He asked me if I had any items to exchange because Stolecki wanted to see me. Thinking that he may want to talk about playing soccer, I ran to him. I was right. Stolecki asked me to play in the game that was about to start. I was given a soccer outfit, and full of joy I joined the team on the field. This time the Polish team was playing against the Germans. The excitement among the prisoners was obvious. I realized that I didn't have enough strength to play sacrificially. I didn't even like the position I was assigned [left wing], but the game itself was very familiar to me, since I used to play for a team from Zaglebie [Lublin, Poland]. I decided to at least play technically correct. I was succeeding, since I was able to kick the ball to my teammates every time I got a chance. I listened to the cheering crowds' comments

with pleasure. I remember one of them, saying: "You just give him food and he'll play." At one point there was a corner kick announced. It was by the German goal line. The players took positions and waited for the kick. The player kicked it too high and none of the Polish players who were expecting it were able to reach it. Nobody was watching me at the moment when I realized that the ball was heading directly toward me. I didn't even think when I kicked it toward the enemy's net. This sudden well-directed kick completely surprised the German goalie. The audience went crazy! No surprise there. This was the first and the only goal of this game. The Polish team won. After I scored this famous goal, I let myself only pretend to play. I don't think anybody blamed me for that.[35]

Particularly compelling were matches when a Polish side would play a team of German *kapos*. There was enthusiastic support from the inmates gathered on the sidelines whenever the Poles scored, and such outbursts eventually forced SS supervisors to stop organizing these matches altogether.

FOOTBALLERS IN STRIPES: KZ GROSS-ROSEN AND SATELLITE CAMP HIRSCHBERG

A satellite camp of the Sachsenhausen concentration camp system, the Polish labor camp known as Gross-Rosen was created in 1940. Located near the present-day city of Rogoźnica in the province of Lower Silesia in western Poland, in 1941 KZ Gross-Rosen was designated an autonomous labor and concentration camp. The majority of the early arrivals labored in brutal conditions in a nearby granite quarry, with other business enterprises added over time. One of the best-known subcamps of Gross-Rosen is Brünnlitz, the destination of the Jewish workers protected by Oskar Schindler after the closure of the labor camp at Płaszów outside Kraków. Eleven hundred Jewish prisoners were transported for labor at Brünnlitz. This camp, established in an empty textiles factory, was the last stop for the *Schindlerjuden*, where they were able to survive the war upon liberation by Soviet forces advancing to the west.

Famous Nazi hunter Simon Wiesenthal was an inmate at Gross-Rosen. Wiesenthal was sent to Płaszów, and in October 1944 inmates were also then moved to the Gross-Rosen camp. In January 1945, when the advancing Russians forced yet another evacuation, Wiesenthal was in the group taken in open freight cars to Buchenwald and then only a few days later by truck to Mauthausen, arriving in mid-February 1945. Fewer than half of the prisoners survived the journey, and Wiesenthal was placed in a warehouse sort of barracks for those deemed mortally ill, where he managed to survive on two hundred calories a day until he was liberated by Americans on May 5, 1945.[36]

Prisoners at Gross-Rosen worked primarily as forced laborers in the building of the camp and in the nearby SS-owned granite quarry. The average life span of quarry worker at Gross-Rosen rarely exceeded five weeks, with prisoners typically forced to work twelve hours a day on starvation rations and then also forced to build prison barracks in the evenings in the early stages of the camp. Subsequently, the connection of Gross-Rosen to the German armaments industry resulted in a rapid expansion of this satellite camp system. The epicenter of an industrial complex and administrative network of at least ninety-seven subcamps, Gross-Rosen also contained one of the largest groupings of female prisoners in all of the Nazi concentration camp system.

The inmates at Gross-Rosen were predominantly German and Polish political prisoners, but fifty-seven thousand Jews were transferred to the camp from October 1943 to January 1945.[37] Most of these came from Hungary and other parts of Western Europe with the initial evacuation of Auschwitz-Birkenau in the fall of 1944. This last mass influx of inmates was also the result of the final liquidation of the Polish ghettos and the mass deportations of Hungarian Jewry in 1944. The main camp at Gross-Rosen was liberated on February 13, 1945, and of the estimated 120,000 prisoners held captive throughout the Gross-Rosen system, about one-third died either in the camp or during the evacuation and the subsequent death marches that followed.[38] This final tally excludes the countless Russian prisoners of war who were typically executed upon arrival. Gross-Rosen was an evil place of arbitrary violence and the full expression of the policy of "extermination through work" practiced so pervasively in the concentration camp system.

Very little of the camp remains today aside from the granite gatehouse, constructed by inmates in 1944, a replacement of the wooden original, and a few remnants of the camp canteen, and the foundations for barracks and various administration buildings. To the right of the main reception building is the *Appelplatz*, where prisoners remember football being played. Like many camps in the Nazi torture system, Gross-Rosen was infamous for inhumane living conditions, a general lack of even rudimentary medical care, starvation diets, and the brutality of the SS guards and their associated functionaries.

Seventy years after the war, the quarry walls reach forty meters high and water now covers the bottom of the pit, which hides another ten meters of excavated quarry underneath it.

Exceptional in its brutality, the camp at Gross-Rosen witnessed moments of respite from the violence and death. The soccer games in Gross-Rosen created special relations between the victims and their tormentors. Right next to the soccer pitch was a special recreational lodge where every Sunday the camp commandant reclined with his staff and their wives and children. Taking in these Sunday games, the SS showed their approval of exceptional play by throwing cigarettes on the field. Players were given additional rations, and their workload was often reduced with free evenings opened for practice. Surprisingly, prisoners on the sidelines who were spectators did not seem to mind the special privileges given to these footballers.

The memorial and museum that now stands on the grounds of the former Nazi concentration camp is charged with the preservation of artifacts and conducting ongoing research on the camp. One recent exhibition tells the story of the sporting activities in the ruthless labor camp, most notably the brief boxing and soccer competitions. The Heroes in Striped Uniforms exhibition presents to the world little-known testimonies from the most improbable football league imaginable.[39] This story begins as the war was clearly going against the Third Reich and many commandants in the labor camp system were recognizing the tenuous nature of their assignments. In the summer of 1943, Lagerführer Walter Ernstberg decided to allow soccer games in Gross-Rosen, and privileged German prisoners were given responsibility for selecting players, organizing teams, and arranging matches. Such an allowance served Nazi ideology well as prisoners were pitted against one another in a battle for continued existence. And in one exceptional case, prisoners were matched against a group of SS guards.

The football matches at Gross-Rosen were played on a field created from the parade grounds, covered with sharp gravel more suitable for parking cars. Portable goals were set up, and the touchlines were outlined in ground-up limestone. Along the main camp road, the Hauptla-gerstrasse, box stands were set up for the SS, and the roof and windows of the camp kitchen substituted for terraces. Against camp rules, and at great risk to their own lives, camp tailors made shirts and shorts for the teams while cobblers made leather boots in secret. Matches were played on a relatively fair basis with players on equal status, to ensure matches would bring more satisfaction. These games had no signifi-cance in the daily life of the camp because, in fact, the field on which the matches were played was really a place of punishment, humiliation, and the daily reassertion of camp rules. The functionaries of the camp were the masters of life and death. Prisoners had to contend with daily suicides, but these were unremarkable to the prisoners who had been here for a time. Yet others fought on, seeking the privilege to play and hopefully survive.

All the miseries of daily life faded into the background in anticipa-tion of the main match between Germany and Poland. For weeks the camp buzzed with excitement. There were no training sessions because prisoners usually worked half-day shifts at the massive quarry, unearth-ing the extremely hard black-and-white Silesian granite. The quarry was close to the Project Riese (German for "giant"), an unfinished network of bunkers and tunnels purported to protect the führer, with granite taken from the site slated to be used in this massive building project. Among the prisoners, there was little cohesion or mutual support. Filth covered every barrack, workshop, and item of clothing as little running water was available. The chaos of the camp meant organizing food and other rations was much more difficult. All of these conditions made the emergence of the soccer games even more unfathomable.

Initially, teams were organized by the German prisoner functionar-ies according to work division. Quarry workers were represented by team Steinbruch (quarry workers), builders were represented by the team Bauleitung (the "board of construction"), and prominent workers were represented by the team name Helden (heroes). In April 1943, a bulletin board in the camp called the "Das Gross-Rosener Sport Echo" announced the formation of teams, and soon thereafter games took place every Sunday afternoon on the roll-call field. The German *kapos* created a team called Deutsche I, and a Polish committee selected the Polish representation, forming the team Polen I. One of the prisoners at Gross-Rosen, Kazimierz Burkacki, remembers these preparations well:

"I received real soccer shoes and a sweater. I was overwhelmed by fear. I noticed that next to the goal nets was a huge pile of shoes. I realized right away that these shoes belonged to my fellow prisoners burned in the crematorium."[40]

After the initial novelty wore off and it was apparent that the play was mediocre, camp inmates demanded higher quality. With the permission of Commandant Ernstberg, teams were arranged according to nationality, ensuring that the best players would turn out. Organizers visited every new trainload of prisoners and found soccer players who had played professionally before the war. They would make sure that these players were not sent to the quarry but instead were given light workloads and additional food portions.

Among the most famous of the footballers at Gross-Rosen were the Gadaj brothers, five keen footballers and patriots who resisted the German occupiers. All five brothers fought in a partisan unit led by celebrated Polish war hero Major Henryk Dobrzański, the first Polish partisan commander to emerge after the defeat of the Polish regular army. The postwar sporting achievements of the Gadaj brothers have been commemorated by the Gross-Rosen Memorial Museum, and the town stadium where the brothers learned the game of soccer is named after them. Imprisoned at Gross-Rosen between 1943 and 1945, Władysław, Marian, and Mieczysław Gadaj played for the quarry laborers' team, and, except for Mieczysław, all of these brothers survived the war. One of the brothers, Marian, arrived at Gross-Rosen in June of 1943 and remembers well that first day: "They welcomed us with bats. One by one, each person would step through the gate occupied by two Gestapo . . . in the meantime I noticed the soccer field and felt a little hope. I thought that if you can play soccer here, then maybe you can live here."[41] Soon after his arrival, team organizers sought him out from the new prisoners, and he eventually played left back for his camp team. Similarly, a player for the well-known Polish team Pogon Lwow, Czeslaw Skoraczynski, was found in a cell with a number of other prisoners brought from the death camp of Majdanek who were waiting out quarantine because of typhoid. Soon after recovering, Skoraczynski joined his new teammates and played well. As a reward, he received the sustenance that would ensure his survival for another day: a bowl of soup with a slice of bread.

Before the first official games ever kicked off, chance favored the Poles. In harmony with camp rules, organizers allowed the Poles to have their team kits sewn in their country's colors. The white and green of the German team (ironically colored the same as the criminals in the camp) was matched against the red and white of the Polish team, the colors of political prisoners in the camp, all marked with the red triangle of their ratty camp uniforms. These colors of the Polish national team inspired pride and offered the briefest of encouragement to the players. Prisoner Arnold Mostowicz recalls:

> Two teams run out onto the field. The prisoners are in stripes; SS men are wearing white T-shirts and green breeches from their uniforms. The game was fierce. The prisoners, who loved the sport, felt that there was something deeper and more important hiding behind those games. It was as if, thanks to the players who were representing them, they could taste the illusion of revenge, or feel the false triumph over their oppressors. [42]

The peak of the soccer league at KZ Gross-Rosen came in the spring of 1944, when numerous teams involving more than one hundred players competed. [43] In the final game of the season, Polen I played against Deutsche I. This is the most frequently recollected match in Gross-Rosen. Polish survivor Tadeusz Sliwinski remembers:

> The game was passionate, but fair (the referee made sure of that) and it drove the fans crazy. Even Muslims [or "musselmen," the walking skeletons on the verge of death by starvation] would stop looking for food and would wake up for two hours from their obtuseness. Fan reactions to different plays and goals were identical to the ones prewar during games on the club fields of Kraków's most favored clubs, Cracovia and Wisla. Shouts would rise up to the sky. [44]

On the day of the big game, during the early morning hours of work, prisoner Zdzisław Lewandowski produced a well-crafted wooden trophy in one of the camp workshops. Later, his friends in the forge added a thin metal plate to it for an inscription of the winning team's name. Minutes before the match, Lewandowski smuggled the trophy from the workshop to the camp, at great personal risk, and handed it to the captain of the German team. This gesture gave rise to a storm of applause from the audience.

Players competed with such passion that they ignored the poor playing conditions and the physical play, bordering on violence, of the German players they were matched against. Some players left the field with
skin missing from their legs, and many required care in the camp infirmary after games. One onlooker and a member of the Polish resistance,
Czeslaw Skoraczynski, still recalls the passion and bravery shown on the
field that day as the Poles took on the Germans: "[The] physical
strength and the nerve of our German opponents were met with our
unheard-of ambition, peace, and technique." The Poles won the game
1–0 thanks to a goal scored by Lewandowski. But the camp's commander and SS men were not amused. In the evening that followed, the
Polish players were resting in Block 20 when a group of German soldiers barged in. They quickly barricaded the door, and after all routes of
escape were blocked, more soldiers came in with bats. They commenced beating anyone they could find. With the end of the beating
came the realization that the consequences of victory against the Germans, whether imprisoned captives or guards, almost always meant violence. Another prisoner named Jozef Trebarczyk admired the determination of the players:

> On one side you had eleven heartless criminals who were rested, well
> fed, and wearing leather shoes, and on the other side you had eleven
> Hungarians who were starving, looking gaunt, and wearing wooden
> shoes. The Hungarians were competing bravely. They were kicked
> and pushed, but they would get up and match the brutality and
> cruelty with their soccer abilities. Bruised and broken, they would
> leave the field. The Hungarians were able to tie the game, but at
> what cost?[45]

Aleksandra Wolska, director of development at the Gross-Rosen Museum, acknowledges that the commemoration of these games and of the
lives of these players "gives back humanity to the prisoners of Gross-
Rosen. They lived here in horrible conditions. They didn't even know if
they'd live to see another day. But they kept their humanity, that's what
gave them the need to play sports. . . . Today people are not able to
imagine how brave and strong these players had to be to show up to
play."[46] The possibility of playing these football matches on the edge of
death provided opportunity, if only for a fleeting moment, to forget the
hell that was the camp. The prisoners could think about something

other than hunger, barbed wire, and the *kapos*. The games didn't appreciably reduce the death rate, increase the food rations, or lengthen the hours of sleep, but they undoubtedly strengthened the will to live. Others doubted the decency of playing soccer in Gross-Rosen: "Playing soccer in the conditions we found ourselves in was unnatural, and it seemed like a desecration of the pain and death that surrounded us. You could not describe the emotions."[47]

Late in the war—and the result of the liquidation of other camps where competitive soccer had been played in the collapsing Nazi empire—a final set of matches was played in the Polish countryside at a camp called Hirschberg. Set at the foot of a picturesque mountain range in southwest Poland, now along the border with the Czech Republic in an area known as Lower Silesia, the surrounding region of the camp had long been a part of the German Empire, especially after Prussian-led unification in 1871. As a subcamp of KZ Gross-Rosen, Arbeitslager (AL) Hirschberg was one of two camps in Jelenia Gora specifically built in 1944 to receive Jewish men who had been "evacuated' from Auschwitz-Birkenau. Both camps in this ruggedly beautiful location provided laborers for a nearby coal mine and a cellulose wool fiber factory. In October 1944, seventy Jewish prisoners from Birkenau arrived, joining one thousand men already there. The camp population further swelled beyond capacity with the liquidation of Auschwitz-Birkenau and Gross-Rosen at the start of 1945.

The transport of prisoners to AL Hirschberg arrived in the warm autumn climes in 1944, and their newly issued uniforms, striped and made of artificial wool, offered some protection from the chill that accompanied the beginnings and ends of days in the camp. With Sundays free from arduous labor in the factories and mines, prisoners wandered about the camp, happening upon a strange site: groups of prisoners readying the *Lagerplatz*, the area where prisoners gathered daily for the often long and torturous roll-call procedure, for a soccer match. An area that measured some seventy to eighty meters long and thirty to forty meters wide was roped off. Chalked lines were being laid down, designating not only the field boundaries but the penalty areas. Two goalposts were fastened to the ground; these were authentic goalposts, but they were lacking nets.

Spectators soon gathered around as the preparations ended and two teams ran onto the field. Prisoners, in their striped uniforms, had been given leather boots to replace the standard wooden clogs, and they had cinched the legs of the prison pants with string before tucking them into their boots. The opposition also played in the green breeches of the standard SS uniform, with white undershirts as their jerseys. A quick count revealed eight players to a side, and the highest-ranking officer of the regular camp personnel, Oberscharführer Handtke (or Hanke), refereed the match. Of great shock to the four or five hundred prisoners surrounding the makeshift field was the prematch handshake between the team captains: an SS man and a prisoner. These weekly matches began earlier in the summer of 1944 with the regular arrival of Jews from Hungary. Across Europe at this time, it was well known that Hungary possessed many cultured footballers, and with eminent Hungarian teams such as Ferencváros, MTK, and Újpesti containing many elite Jewish prisoners, the SS sought to break up the monotony of guarding and escorting their Jewish captives by creating a sporting pastime. Perversely, such an endeavor violated Nazi racial law, but in the peculiar reality of the concentration camp universe, executioner and victim once again came together on the field of play.

Exhausted, starved, and beaten down, the prisoners' team, consisting mostly of Hungarian Jews, moved effectively through the field, stringing together numerous passes and efficiently building an attack against the more hapless SS team, who chased the ball from end to end. Strong technique and skills were evident among the prisoners. Polish resistance member, survivor of the Łódź ghetto, and Hirschberg camp doctor Arnold Mostowicz was a witness to this match. In his memoir, *With a Yellow Star and a Red Cross*, he writes:

> A fierce struggle was taking place on the field. The striped jackets flew in the air like the wings of some grotesque exotic birds. From time to time, the players of the prisoner team raced along the field as if those wings could lift them behind the barbed-wire fence, away from the Germans, to the freedom they longed for. They often showed off for the public, their public, soccer tricks that were all the more rash because they were performed in the boots that they were given for the duration of the match only. Besides, those boots must have been very uncomfortable for some—two Hungarians had changed them for their own primitive wooden clogs, which were now duly knocking on the hard surface of the Lagerplatz.[48]

Like at a football match in their own country of origin, the spectators cheered, whistled, and protested referees decisions, as if they enjoyed the same freedom of the terraces as they did during their civilian lives. This fleeting and momentary joy, this expression of anger toward one's captors, would typically result in severe punishment or immediate death. But this short break in their tragic circumstances seemed to represent a precious reclaiming of one's humanity for the enslaved. Such acts of humanity, evident in the organizing of football matches, were also contrasted by mindless brutality and murder. Mostowicz acknowledges that even though the SS had accepted the rules of play for the soccer matches, the daily reality of the camp soon reasserted itself. He even speculates that one reason the guards remained in their green uniform pants instead of shorts, which would have allowed much more freedom of movement, is that the remaining part of the uniform was a very clear reminder that not all of the camp rules had been abandoned. The prisoners' striped attire further reinforced this point. In this surreal suspension of reality in the labor camp, Mostowicz continues his description of the match:

> The SS men smiled indulgently as if to remind them [the prisoners] that this temporary interruption of the normal relationship between prisoners and guards would eventually come to an end. The smiles of the Jews were brought about by the joy that humiliated people feel when aware of their transient superiority. The SS men were joking the whole time, and when they lost the ball they laughed loudly and hid that way their momentary defeat. When one of the Jews lost the ball or played poorly, it was obvious that he exposed himself to the bitter reproaches of his colleagues and, of course, the spectators. For them, something much more important was behind the sport contest: something that allowed them through the intermediary of their representatives to taste illusory revenge, to win an imaginary victory.[49]

As the match moved toward the intermission, it was clear that the effects of forced starvation were beginning to show. The SS team pressed forward and the prisoners defended, often desperately. Keeping the score close was a young goalkeeper from a small town near Budapest named Ferenc Moros, the same man who served as captain at the start of the match. As the prisoners struggled to keep the SS team from scoring, Moros was stalwart in protecting his goal. The crowd took to chanting his name with each save. Unusually tall and graced with long arms, Moros charged out on breakaways and played balls out with miraculous foot saves. The Germans even recognized his heroics as he pulled shots back from the goal line.

With the score 1–0 at the half, a ten-minute interval allowed the lagging camp team to catch their collective breath. The SS enjoyed beer, and the kitchen *kapo* brought a makeshift rutabaga soup for the prisoners. Clearly, it was a battle between technique and physical strength and conditioning, the latter two attributes possessed by the guards. Mostowicz found it remarkable that in the second half the prisoners were able to summon reserves of endurance and purpose, so much so that they dominated the remainder of the match. But with a pair of dubious calls made late in the game by the SS official, the match hinged on an awarded penalty to the SS. Silence fell on the grounds, when just a few moments earlier, epithets, shouted in Polish and Hungarian, had rained down on the official. It was the last minute of the match and, with the highest drama, Moros saved the shot. Before the final whistle sounded, the spectators poured onto the field to celebrate with him. Observers described the whole spectacle as both surreal and tragicomic.[50] Though it ended in a win, this game was the final match in the Hirschberg camp as the prisoners began work on Sundays and the autumn rains began, turning the *Lagerplatz* into a small pond.

As a tragic coda to the final match, the sudden nature of death in these Nazi camps was evident when the heroic goalkeeper, Ferenc Moros, fell victim to a capricious fate. Shot while working in a lumberyard, Moros lingered in hospital until an operation was attempted to save his arm, which had been shot through, along with his leg, by a guard who was mistakenly instructed (by a vindictive *kapo*) that he was trying to escape. In truth, Moros had not complied with an order refusing his use of the latrine and had instead relieved himself behind a pile of logs, infuriating his foreman. The attempted amputation of the arm was unsuccessful, and Ferenc Moros soon perished. The next day, Moros's body made the same journey hundreds had made before as his remains were taken to the furnace room at the adjacent factory. Shortly after Moros's expiring, the man who refereed the match, Oberscharführer Handtke, was heard reflecting about Moros, "Der Bursch war ein wunderbarer Torwart" ("That chap was an extraordinary goalkeeper"). Such an unexpected eulogy was an acknowledgment that even in the morally inverted world of the Nazi camp structure, genuine football talent was celebrated.

DEPARTURE

One final account of soccer in the Polish killing fields reminds the modern-day football fan of the consequences of perpetuated indifference. In a powerfully rendered story, Tadeusz Borowski, a non-Jewish resistance fighter imprisoned at Auschwitz-Birkenau at the same time many of the Liga Terezín deportees arrived at the camp, recalls the utter depravity of the Nazi system. Widely hailed as a masterpiece of Holocaust literature, Borowski's story brings out the competing themes of victim and bystander as he describes the earthly departure of a group of Jewish victims just arrived during a soccer match near one of the crematoria at Birkenau. Once seen as apocryphal but now verified by eyewitness testimony, Borowski's story offers an unblinking glimpse into the utter depravity and systematic brutality and dehumanization of Birkenau. His story of football at Auschwitz one idyllic late spring evening is at once peaceful and horrific:

> A train had just arrived. People were emerging from the cattle cars and walking in the direction of the little wood. All I could see from where I stood were bright splashes of color. The women, it seems, were already wearing summer dresses; it was the first time that season. The men had taken off their coats, and their white shirts stood out sharply against the green of the trees. The procession moved along slowly, growing in size as more and more people poured from the freight cars. And then it stopped. The people sat down on the grass and gazed in our direction. I returned with the ball and kicked it back inside the field. It traveled from one foot to another and, in a wide arc, returned to the goal. I kicked it towards a corner. Again it rolled out into the grass. Once more I ran to retrieve it. But as I reached down, I stopped in amazement—the ramp was empty. Out of the whole colourful summer procession, not one person remained. The train too was gone. . . . Between two throw-ins in a soccer game, right behind my back, three thousand people had been put to death.[51]

7

THE CURIOUS STORY OF DUTCH SOCCER DURING NAZI OCCUPATION

"Football should be like the Olympics were in ancient Greece: when you took part in the games you moved into an area of peace. Bitter adversaries could compete without bloodshed. Even if they were at war, there was no fighting. Enemies could engage in sport with all hostilities suspended."—German-born rabbi Albert Friedlander, on the football-loving Dutch and rival Germany[1]

European football persisted under the direst of circumstances in the East. The eventual partition of Poland by colonial-minded Nazi Germany and the Soviet Union in 1939 shattered Polish football. The Nazis set out to destroy Polish civilization and eliminate the elite among Polish society—army officers, politicians, intellectuals, and cultural figures were marked for extermination. Auschwitz-Birkenau is the eternal reminder of these genocidal aims. Yet football continued in the relative calm of the Nazi occupation of Western Europe, albeit usually as a rare entertainment. The line between independence and collaboration became increasingly blurred. Of the countless stories of football in Europe during World War II, none are as peculiar and interesting as those of Dutch football under Nazi occupation.[2] For over a century, the Kingdom of the Netherlands prospered economically, enjoying the benefits of neutrality as Europe battled and burned. But over five days in May 1940, as Nazi soldiers poured across their borders, all sport in the Netherlands stopped. The games would return just as quickly as they had ceased, and soon Holland returned to the familiar.

Early on, the Nazis pressed many young Dutch men into forced labor in Germany while others went into hiding for fear of being deported to Poland. Yet the numbers of people caught up in the soccer boom soared. Football grew dramatically during the war as participation rates increased, club membership rose, and attendance skyrocketed. Amid the well-known stories of Dutch resistance during the war were more common stories of indifference, complicity, and collaboration as Holland's Jews were systematically removed from all levels of Dutch society, including Holland's football clubs. In the main deportation site in the Netherlands, the Westerbork transit camp (the same concentration camp through which Anne Frank and her family passed), we find a football league. When the story of football in occupied Holland is told, one can better understand that the current fanaticism for the game enjoyed by the Dutch actually began during the war era.

As in other European capitals, such as Vienna and Prague, the Jewish presence in Amsterdam before the war carried over to the wildly popular football scene. The popular Amsterdam club Ajax, whose De Meer home grounds was located near one of the main Jewish districts, enjoyed the most passionate support from the city's Jewish section. Jewish players and club directors at Ajax were especially beloved by supporters and generally safe from anti-Semitic reprisals outside of the club. Success on the pitch didn't hurt either.

Amsterdam had four other major Jewish clubs that drew increasingly large crowds as football became the most popular spectator sport all across Europe in the 1920s. These fanatical supporters had their favorite players, of course. An American-born right-winger for Ajax, a man named Eddy Hamel, was particularly adored. One section of the Ajax fans gathered in the terraces between the halfway line and the corner flag, on Hamel's side, to cheer him on, then switched to the opposite corner at halftime.[3] Eddy Hamel would soon find himself trapped in the tightening snare of Nazi occupation just a few years later. But we must rewind the clock a few hundred years to better understand why Amsterdam became a sanctuary city and a distinctly Jewish capital in Western Europe.

REMBRANDT'S NEIGHBORS AND THE END OF JEWISH AMSTERDAM

Before the conflagration of the Second World War, Amsterdam benefited from a long and prosperous relationship with the "People of the Book." Jews first lived in Amsterdam beginning in the early 1600s, landing there after fleeing expulsion from the Iberian Peninsula. Persecution in Catholic Spain and Portugal meant that the Netherlands would begin to earn its reputation for tolerance and freethinking. The material and intellectual wealth of the Dutch Republic in the seventeenth century brought even greater contact with the world, and Jewish Amsterdam featured prominently in the business and political communities of the city at that time.[4]

Pogroms in Eastern Europe in the nineteenth century would create yet another Jewish diaspora, bringing a new flood of Jewish refugees to Western Europe; many of these settled in Amsterdam and began the process of successful assimilation into all features of Dutch life. In the century that followed, Dutch Jews enjoyed a long period of peace and prosperity, much of it centralized in the largest Dutch city, Amsterdam. Interestingly, by 1939 half of all the Jews living in the country resided in Amsterdam, which made up 10 percent of the total population of the Netherlands.

The rich cultural history of Dutch Jews came close to being completely extinguished with the Nazi takeover of the Netherlands in May 1940. But shockingly, there was a delay in the implementation of the Nazi policies of isolation, persecution, and expulsion. Not until two years after occupation began would the Nazis move against the Jews. But once they did, the arrests and deportations were swift.

The main collection point for Amsterdam's Jews was the Hollandsche Schouwburg, a theater in the Jewish Quarter, cordoned off by barbed wire at the occupation. Most of the adults registered there would perish in Poland. These Jews, taken from their homes (in alphabetical order, a systematic and orderly process) and deposited in the theater, endured inhumane conditions—stifling heat, pitifully inadequate sanitary conditions—and little to no food or medical supplies. Terrified captives sat wherever they could: in the auditorium, on the stairs, and in the theater boxes and balconies. Many simply paced the aisles, nervously awaiting news of any kind. One arrival, Willy Alexander, described the barbarism in his wartime diary entry for March 25, 1943:

> There are at present 1,300 people in that little "Hollandsche Schouwburg." It gets so hot and oppressive (and of course smelly) that everyone just begs for drink after drink. Only the old women are permitted to sleep on mattresses—others just occasionally. For all these 1,300 people there are just two men's toilets and three women's toilets, and one or two washbasins. Inside the auditorium the people going to Westerbork are waiting and upstairs are those to be sent to Vught [labor camp]. But it all seems to be so haphazard that it depends on the mood of the gentlemen in power whether you go to Vught or Westerbork. On a couple of occasions something didn't quite suit a.d.F. [SS-Hauptsturmführer Ferdinand aus der Fünten, the head of the Central Office for Jewish Emigration in Amsterdam] and then just like that half the theatre-full was sent to Westerbork.[5]

Behind the neoclassical façade of the theater, on one of the busiest boulevards in the Amsterdam city center, the suffering was only beginning for Holland's Jews. Six months after slave laborers were sent to German and Austrian labor camps (Mauthausen, the worst among them), Amsterdam's tram drivers delivered their fellow citizens to the city's central train station under the careful supervision of the city's police force. The primary destination would be the Westerbork transit camp in Drenthe, a three-hour ride northeast of Amsterdam near the border with Germany.

In a tragic irony, Westerbork was created three years earlier to shelter Jewish refugees from neighboring Germany. Because the Netherlands had been the destination for thousands of German and Austrian Jews fleeing persecution in the first days of Nazi rule, it was a cruel fate to be caught up again in the Nazi web. Amsterdam had been the most secure, prosperous, and probably best assimilated Jewish community in Europe, offering a sense of security that would be shattered as the first deportations began in July 1942. Of the 140,000 Jews living in Holland in 1940, about 25,000 were émigrés from the Reich.[6] When the gas chambers in Poland were operational by 1942, Dutch Jews knew they were in for the worst of it. Word had traveled back west of mass murders behind the front in faraway killing fields in Poland and Russia. Now Westerbork would be a staging area and the first stop on the journey to Auschwitz, Sobibór, Mauthausen, and, in the final days of the camps, the Czech ghetto-camp of Terezín.

The first mass deportation of Dutch Jews included the dispatching of four hundred young Jewish men, first to Buchenwald, and then to Mauthausen in Austria. These Dutch Jews were from a group who had been arrested in the Jewish Quarter in a vicious reprisal for an incident in an Amsterdam tavern in which German soldiers were accidentally sprayed with ammonia. The prisoners arrived at Mauthausen on June 17, 1941, and immediately upon entry to the camp, fifty were killed when they were chased naked from the bathhouse to the electrified fence.

Dozens more were murdered in the granite quarry of the camp. According to witnesses, Jews were not allowed to use the stairs leading to the bottom of the quarry; instead, they would have to slide down the loose stones at the side, where many were severely injured or killed. At the bottom, survivors would then shoulder the heavy rocks, and when the prisoners were forced to run up the 186 steps, many rocks immediately fell downhill, crushing those below. Every Jew who lost his rock in this manner was brutally beaten and forced again to carry the stone to the top. Many were driven to such great despair in the first few days at Mauthausen that they committed suicide by jumping into the granite pits. So many died a gruesome death in the first few days that the new barracks were cleared of Jews not in six weeks but barely three. When asked by local officials how the Dutch Jews had adapted to the new camp and the hard work in the quarry, Commandant Franz Ziereis answered, "Ah, hardly a one is still alive."[7]

The arrests and terror faced by Jews were not part of the lives of the average Dutch citizen. Aside from isolated incidents of violent reprisals by the Nazis, there were actually two occupations in Holland: one for the average Dutch national, benign for the most part, and one devastating occupation for the Jews. The Germans viewed the Dutch as a "kindred race," fellow Germans who had strayed but who would be ultimately integrated back into the *Volksgemeinschaft*, the historic Nordic community.

Unlike the death and fearsome choices faced by conquered countries in Eastern Europe, the occupation of the Netherlands was, in the words of one Dutch historian, "limited to signs on the street, notices in the newspaper, stories and sounds on the radio."[8] This isn't to say that living conditions during the war weren't severe; the war began with the savage bombing of Rotterdam, and news coming through radio and newspapers could not be trusted. Watchful Gestapo agents and their local helpers in the NSB (the Dutch Nazi Party) enforced curfews, and food became scarce late in the war.

A disturbing reality of the Nazi occupation in Amsterdam, the least anti-Semitic city of many dismantled by the Holocaust, was the poor survival rate of the Jews living there. By comparison, Jews had a much greater chance of surviving the genocide if they were living in Berlin. Around 75 to 80 percent of Holland's Jews perished in the Holocaust.[9] The death rate for Jews in Holland was double that of those killed in Belgium, four times the proportion lost in France, and outpaced the percentage murdered in Germany, where persecution began much earlier.

Geography made escape difficult—Holland lacks the dense forests that preserved many in places like Belarus, home to the famous Bielski partisans who fought back and offered sanctuary to hundreds—and the ruthless efficiency of the Dutch administration ensured maximum cooperation with the Nazis' deadly plans. Yet the Netherlands is famous for hiding places, and two-thirds of those who went into hiding, assisted by the Dutch underground, did indeed survive, but eleven thousand were exposed and turned over to the Nazis.

Outside of the Reich proper, the Germans could not have deported so many Jews on their own. The occupiers always required willing accomplices. Denunciations were common in Holland as the Gestapo relied heavily on neighbors turning in neighbors. Civil servants in Amsterdam also played a significant role in the deportation of Dutch Jewry, providing the names and addresses of the victims. The city's police force, numbering more than 2,400, was then ordered to collect and detain the Jews. Police were sent in pairs to remove Jews from their places of residence. Opposition to the orders was rare, but the process often left a lasting impact of the dire predicament faced by the victims. Some officers encountered entire families of Jews already dead, suicides by gassing. Other victims jumped out of apartment windows when the police arrived. A few officers strongly objected to being involved in the arrests, but others were always readily available to take their places.

Cooperation of public servants was guaranteed through the *Ariërverklaring*, the "Aryan Declaration," whereby all civil servants in the Netherlands were forced to document whether or not they were Jewish. None of the Dutch civil administration or policemen in Amsterdam refused to sign the October 5, 1940, declaration. Any Jews who sought hiding places created "problems" for these prosecutors. Other departments within the Dutch police force had to be created, many of which were staffed by special detectives (under the Bureau of Jewish Affairs) who were anti-Semites, gleeful to hunt down the missing. Dutch historian Guus Meershoek explains why these roundups went so smoothly: "Because the police were known and trusted, because they came reluctantly [most police held serious doubts about arresting Jews], they persuaded their victims that resistance was pointless. . . . In this way they were the most efficient executioners."[10]

Another sad episode in March 1943 saw the Amsterdam fire brigade turn their hoses on local residents protesting the arrival of deportation trucks for children from a Jewish orphanage. Voicing outrage on behalf of these most helpless of victims, the crowd became unruly and Amsterdam's firemen stepped in to keep the peace, enforcing the will of the German occupiers. Whatever reluctance remained among government officials, Dutch submissiveness eventually turned the unwilling into complicit executioners.

The popular perception of the Dutch during World War II was one of heroic confrontation against Nazi occupiers. But the truth is more complicated. And damning. The persistence of this image is due in large part to the February 25, 1941, strike when many in Amsterdam rose together as one to protest the arrest and violent treatment of hundreds of Jewish men. Led by communist dockworkers, the strike saw factories shut down, public transportation come to an abrupt halt, and the city paralyzed. Lasting only a couple of days, the small-scale rebellion was met with extreme violence; the Nazis unleashed their guns and grenades in crushing the general strike. Such methods had become routine by this time.

Within a few months, a central office for emigration (the *Zentralstelle*), modeled after the offices established in Vienna in 1938 (under the direction of Adolf Eichmann) and in Berlin and Prague the following year, solidified the incremental measures now taken against the Jews. Such enmeshment and indifference to the plight of the oppressed would extend seamlessly to Dutch football.

"LIKE NOTHING HAD CHANGED": DUTCH FOOTBALL DURING OCCUPATION

Within the first year of Nazi occupation, the step-by-step persecution of Dutch Jews resulted in their removal from employment, sports clubs, schools, cafés, and public places. The elimination of Jewish influence in Dutch football actually began before the Nazis required such measures. In August 1941, the Dutch FA (the NVB, Nederlandsche Voetbal Bond) cooperated with local officials who banned Jewish referees, and a month later Jews were banned from Dutch sports altogether. The compulsory sign "Verboden voor Joden" (Forbidden for Jews) started appearing above entrances to football grounds across the Netherlands, and Amsterdam's five Jewish clubs pulled out of the city league. Protests were few and far between, though a handful of clubs refused to cooperate, at least initially. The purge of Jewish referees also created a crisis. The Dutch FA scrambled to fill the vacancies, often running matches shorthanded.

The amount of football played in war-torn Holland continued to surprise while the monumental struggle raged across Europe. The supposed "racial harmony" between Germany and Holland meant there was little interference in Dutch football. Purges dramatically changed the game in Holland, as Jewish players starred for almost all of the top clubs. But in time, they would not be missed. Footballers who continued on were required to carry a Dutch FA identity card at all times. Shortages also meant that three players often shared one pair of allotted football boots, shorts and shirts required textile vouchers, and inflated pigs' bladders from local butcher shops substituted for footballs. One junior member of Amsterdam club DWS, Jan Hobby, remembered sacrificing the essentials for a proper pair of football boots:

> I wanted to buy real football shoes with the shoes voucher. At the time, you still had those old-fashioned boots with steel noses. They had leather studs with three small nails. My parents didn't like it, but the cobbler still gave me those boots for the shoe voucher. This meant I couldn't buy normal shoes, but I didn't care. I'd wear clogs.[11]

Hardships and scarcity of material goods would not keep Dutch footballers on the sidelines.

One well-known figure from Dutch football epitomizes the danger faced by Jews living in Amsterdam after 1940. Fans of a certain age in wartime Holland fondly remembered Hartog "Han" Hollander as the voice of the Dutch national team. Hollander is credited with popularizing the game in the Netherlands, once a fringe pursuit. Dutch families in the 1930s gathered around their wireless radios in their living rooms, tuning in for Hollander and his imaginative, sometimes embellished accounts of the national side. The pioneering sport journalist was equally blessed as a keen observer of the game and as a master storyteller. And in tolerant Amsterdam, it didn't matter that he was of Jewish descent.

Hollander's boss, Willem Vogt, cofounder of AVRO (Algemene Vereniging Radio Omroep, or General Association of Radio Broadcasting) in the mid-1920s and one of the very first radio broadcasters in the Netherlands, remembered Hollander when they served together in World War I. Hollander had kept his army bunkmates captivated with his tales of football matches from his youth. He made his first live broadcast for an international match featuring Holland versus Belgium on March 11, 1928, and it wouldn't take long for Hollander to become a household name. A few years later, the Netherlands was the only country to buy broadcast rights to the World Cup in Italy in 1934, and Hollander was there. He also reported live from the 1936 Berlin Olympics, the "Nazi Games" infused with politics and propaganda. In return for his reportage in Berlin, Hollander was awarded a signed certificate by Adolf Hitler, an honor he would need to call upon just a few years later.

On the air, Vogt sat by his side as a "minder," reining in Hollander as needed. Vogt endeared himself to audiences by opening their broadcasts with the line, "Nice weather, Mr. Hollander." But in May 1940, Vogt sacked his longtime friend along with every other Jewish employee of AVRO. Vogt's decision came only six days after the Dutch capitulation to Germany and weeks before the first German measures against the Jews. In all likelihood, Vogt wasn't motivated by a deep, abiding anti-Semitism. In many ways, Hollander's fate was decided in much the same way as that of every other Jew in Holland; it was the Dutch way to quietly cooperate and to avoid provoking the Germans.[12]

SUNDAY AFTERNOONS ON THE TERRACES:
FOOTBALL AS SURVIVAL AND DIVERSION

The passion for football in the Netherlands during the occupation was so fervent that many Dutch considered loyalty to their local football club on equal standing with their national identity. As Holland is a small country, both in geography and population, club loyalties are spread among a small number of clubs, but undoubtedly the most popular clubs hail from the largest cities in the Netherlands: Amsterdam, Rotterdam, and Eindhoven.

Fans in the rural provinces often favored their local side, usually playing in the lower divisions, but come Sunday afternoon thousands turned out for matches featuring Ajax, Feyenoord, and PSV Eindhoven. The harbor city of Rotterdam also hosted one of the oldest and most beloved football clubs, Sparta Rotterdam, a club on the fringes of greatness, as the game was imported by the British to the Netherlands in the late 1800s, with clubs like Sparta, and later Ajax, adopting classical Greek names.

German soldiers followed the Dutch leagues, now a competition divided across five districts in a reorganized Dutch league. For many Wehrmacht soldiers, the tedium of guarding docile Holland made watching football an exciting prospect. At the home stadium of Feyenoord, soldiers were provided half-price tickets. Feyenoord would go on to win the first Dutch championship of the occupation (1939–1940) in a 2–0 victory over Heracles, and later finished runners-up twice to ADO den Haag. Other German soldiers stationed at the Ajax home grounds were often granted permission to use the Ajax pitch for pickup games. Special matches at the Olympic Stadium in Amsterdam also drew crowds in excess of fifty thousand.

Football may have stopped altogether in other parts of occupied Europe, but the Dutch simply would not give it up. Across all divisions of Dutch football, players scrambled to adjust to the "New Order" in their country. Bob Janse was one such player caught up in the tumult. Janse was part of the club Hermes/DVS of Schiedam, based in a western suburb of Rotterdam and one of the oldest football clubs in Holland. He confessed that not even a war would keep players off the pitch: "If there was ever any suggestion that we should stop playing as a sign of resistance, there would be immediate protests from the players. Football was the only diversion they had."[13]

The Nazis were delighted with the outburst of interest in competitive soccer in the Netherlands. Reichskommissar Arthur Seyss-Inquart once remarked, cynically, "He who plays sport does not sin." The Nazis understood well the need to pacify the local population, having subdued the Czechs, Poles, and Scandinavian countries in the previous two years. When German bombers unleashed their payloads over Rotterdam at lunchtime on Tuesday, May 14, 1940, the port city's stunned citizens scrambled for cover. Fires raced throughout the city center, and more than nine hundred people were killed. The shocking horror of the bombing raid led to Dutch capitulation the next day.

Sparta Rotterdam wasted little time in finding a path back to competition. While German soldiers bivouacked under Sparta's terraces and played on the club's home pitch, the club moved against its own members. Sparta likely had the greatest number of Jewish members of all the Rotterdam clubs, and unlike PSV, Ajax, and Feyenoord, Sparta's wartime archives are a unique treasure trove of material about club action and inaction related to the occupation. The revelations found in these archives were recently explored by British journalist Simon Kuper in his penetrating 2012 book, *Ajax, the Dutch, the War*. Published first in Dutch, Kuper's analysis shows a curiously indifferent Sparta board of directors as the occupation intensified.

Like AFC Ajax, Sparta Rotterdam imposed a ban on Jewish involvement a full month before the German edict. While Sparta demanded the resignation of its Jewish members, Dutch courtesy required the club to offer full refunds of the club fee. And when all of Holland protested the deportation of a large group of Jewish men in February 1941, Sparta's main concern seemed to be what to do with the player who may or may not have called a referee a *boerenlul* (literally, "farmer's penis") during a match.[14] The minutes of the disciplinary hearing show the board could not resolve the absurdly insignificant issue.

A later meeting of the Sparta board showed the depth of indifference shared by so many Dutchmen, footballers and citizens alike, as Sparta officials held another extensive debate on the exact size of the sign installed on the stadium grounds forbidding Jews. An emergency meeting was called, and the much-too-large sign was replaced with a more discrete one. By October 1941, all eighty Jewish members of

Sparta Rotterdam, many of whom had been lifelong members, had left. Remarkably, Sparta Rotterdam appears to be the only Dutch football club or sporting association whose board meeting records reflect upon the expulsion of the Jews from Holland. [15]

The Netherlands enjoys a reputation for heroic resistance during the war, owing in large part to the worldwide popularity of Anne Frank's story, though ultimately tragic in its conclusion. Yet rarely do we see any descriptions of the suffering endured by club members. Absent are reports of acts of rebellion or assistance to the persecuted in the records of Holland's major football clubs. No one would want to leave a record of any of this in the Nazi terror state. Yet Sparta Rotterdam would be made proud by the response of Reinder Boomsma, an outside-right for the club until 1908 and a Dutch colonel who became an expert in cryptography in the Great War. Boomsma was one of only two Sparta members to have actually served in the Dutch resistance. Boomsma fell into Gestapo hands after the clumsy handoff of British code messages by a Dutch airman. Implicated and arrested, the onetime Sparta player was sent to the concentration camp at Neuengamme near Hamburg.

A message later smuggled out of the camp in a matchbox by a released fellow Dutch prisoner reflected a hopeful, optimistic Boomsma, holding up well and in good spirits. The brief note even mentioned that the colonel had trimmed down to his playing weight when he patrolled the right flank as a winger for Sparta Rotterdam three decades earlier. His assignment to the camp kitchen, usually a lifeline, was short-lived though, and Reinder Boomsma died on the evening of May 26, 1943, having collapsed in the camp earlier in the day. [16] Survivor accounts from Neuengamme connected Boomsma to soccer matches in the camp. It is likely the resistance leader viewed these competitions as an opportunity to build contacts and pass on information, a resolution he would not see come to fruition at liberation.

Just a month earlier, Rotterdam was officially declared *Judenfrei*, or "cleansed of Jews," by the Nazis. Amid the exceptional stories of heroism, you are more likely to find mundane indifference or passive collaboration among average Dutch. Jaap van der Leck, the manager of the Dutch club De Volewijckers, well known for resisting the Nazis and their Dutch collaborators, acknowledged that few footballers took great risks in fighting back:

> There was no real organised resistance in the sports world. . . . In
> those days, you took refuge in sports, so to speak. You thought the
> war was bad, but didn't quite go as far as Gerben Wagenaar [one of
> two brothers on the team who resisted] and say: "I'm joining the
> underground movement." You were too afraid. In fact, you were
> sticking your head in the sand.[17]

De Volewijckers of Amsterdam-North came out of the war on the right
side of history as they were regularly recognized as a "resistance club"
by the fans of the Dutch league, and consequently drew the attention of
the Nazi security apparatus. Another Rotterdam club, Xerxes, celebrated the courageous work of Meijer Stad, one more mythic figure in the
Dutch wartime story, who played a minor role for his club but would
risk his life repeatedly for his country, surviving a Nazi execution squad
before working as a football scout in the postwar peace.

Few clubs publicly resisted the occupation government, and even
fewer formally aligned themselves with the occupiers. But it may be no
surprise to find the Dutch club from the Nazi occupation headquarters
of The Hague to be tarnished with the collaboration label. ADO den
Haag, repeat champions of the Dutch top division in 1942 and 1943,
had a strong association with the NSB, the Dutch Nazi Party. For many,
the singular and most visible reminder of the traitorous Dutch Nazi
movement at ADO (second only to the German strain of National Socialism in membership) was Gerrit Vreken.

Gifted as a footballer, the young and naïve Vreken joined the NSB at
a young age. As a member of the ADO first team, Vreken openly supported the NSB during the war, traveling to away matches in his uniform and black boots and drawing the ire of teammates and opponents
sympathetic to the resistance. Fans would turn out for matches featuring Vreken and ADO den Haag just to heckle the visiting side. Like
countless young men across the Netherlands, Gerrit Vreken was unemployed and called up for labor duty in Germany in 1940. German demands for laborers steadily increased as the fortunes of war shifted. By
most estimates, about half a million Dutch workers responded to the
call for *Arbeitseinsatz* (forced labor deployments), traveling east to the
Reich labor camps, factories, and farms.[18] An uncle who was a member
of the NSB suggested to his nephew, Vreken, that he would be better
off reporting for this *Arbeidsdienst* (labor service) to avoid having to
leave the Netherlands. Vreken was candid in his admission after the

war: "I was 18 and knew nothing about politics. It allowed me to stay in the Netherlands and continue to play football with ADO. . . . If you wanted to stay in the *Arbeidsdienst* after the first year, you had to join the NSB as a sympathiser. I thought about it for a long time. But I was in trouble, so what could I do? For me it was always an escape route."[19]

ADO den Haag was not the only Dutch side with NSB members. Though ADO had become known as an "NSB club," there were members of the Dutch Nazi Party playing at other clubs as well. Of all the clubs that make up Dutch football, three legendary clubs have long dominated the Eridivisie, the top division in the Netherlands, established formally in 1956: AFC Ajax of Amsterdam, Feyenoord of Rotterdam, and PSV Eindhoven from southern Holland. For each of these popular clubs, fragments of wartime history emerge to reveal yet another complicated set of circumstances and responses from players, spectators, and club officials. What is not surprising is that these top clubs would have members join the side of the enemy. It is surprising that so few gave so little thought to the consequences of their actions. For a club like Ajax, whose home grounds were not far from the Jewish Quarter in Amsterdam, the primary wartime mission seemed to be protection of the club and its interests. Nothing mattered more to Ajax loyalists than the preservation of the club.

Even with a strong Jewish fan base, Ajax was not immune to this reality. One player named Harry Pelser, who spent time in the Ajax first XI from 1939 to 1944, joined the NSB at the behest of his family. Before the war, Harry's father, Joop Pelser, also played for eight seasons at Ajax and was a member of the club's executive committee. Pelser, a center-half and part of the Dutch championship-winning teams of 1918 and 1919, was one of four brothers who played for the Ajax first team. During the war, Joop Pelser saw one son join the Waffen SS, and another make the Ajax first team. From 1942 on, Joop Pelser worked for the German bank Lippmann, Rosenthal, and Company, which was founded by the occupying Nazi authorities to plunder Jewish property. Bank accounts, artwork, and personal jewelry from Jewish holders were deposited in the bank as the owners were carefully and systematically detached from their property.

High-ranking Nazis could then select from the art holdings in the bank, and ultimately the bank financed the Westerbork transit camp, the destination for many of those stripped of their residences and belongings. A teammate once remembered the "accidental" collaborator Harry Pelser this way: "He was a member of the party and I saw him read the NSB newspaper *Volk en Vaderland* [Folk and Fatherland] . . . [but] Harry didn't betray people." Harry Pelser himself confessed that his family joining the NSB was a logical decision; his mother had signed him up. Many others in Holland, Austria, and Germany joined the National Socialist movement as ambitious opportunists. Few would see the consequences of their decisions. Onetime Ajax captain Joop Pelser was one of these opportunists; he served as a guard at the Hollandsche Schouwburg, the collection and registration point for nearly every Jewish adult in Amsterdam. The theater was a miserable place of suffering for Jews, as nearly every adult who entered this detention center would die in the Holocaust. A few children escaped, smuggled out of the building when public trams blocked the view of the theater entrance; a lucky few were smuggled out in rucksacks and potato bags.

Ajax had a better record than most Dutch clubs in offering assistance to desperate Jewish members because of the wealthier membership roll. Ajax was largely a Gentile club, and to the Jewish community, knowing these so-called outsiders increased the likelihood of survival. Prewar bonds among members were strong, and they relied on informal networks of association with the club. Of course, within this same network we also find plunderers, camp guards, and those willing to betray the hidden and be handsomely rewarded to do it. Some Ajax members played for German club teams and others for the reconstituted national side for Holland; a few even complied with the compulsory Hitler salute in these Nazi-sanctioned matches.

One compelling rescue story from club records involves the future club chairman Jaap van Praag, who spent almost the entirety of the war hiding above a photography shop. The shopkeeper was unaware of his presence throughout the two and a half years that van Praag lived there. Much like the Anne Frank family in the *Secret Annexe*, Jaap van Praag would sit motionless for hours in a chair, having relocated there after first hiding in the flat of former Ajax player Wim Schoevaart (who served well into his nineties as Ajax's club archivist). The rescued van Praag would preside over Ajax's "Golden Age" in the late 1960s. Jaap van Praag would hire Rinus Michels and develop a young Johan Cruyff, winning the European cup three successive times, from 1971 to 1973.

While Ajax had a complicated wartime history—many club members were protected and many collaborated while others were purged and rescued—in many ways, the efforts to protect the club's interests were similar to any other institution in Holland. The wartime choices faced by the top clubs in Dutch football represent an insular microcosm of Dutch society. But the same solidarity within the club that protected a few Jewish associates also protected those who collaborated. After the war, Ajax sanitized its past in official club records, replete with denials of collaboration. The official club history, published fifty years after the war, made the outrageous claim that there were no Jewish deaths at Ajax. But these members had been expelled (or resigned) by 1941 and murdered by the end of 1943, making the claim technically correct but morally repugnant. After the war, many clubs formed "purification [purge] committees" where punishments were meted out. But in the end, most who cooperated with the occupation forces were let go or stuck around the club and were tolerated. Most clubs were rife with collaborators; Ajax was no different.

The rest of Holland was not as forgiving after the war. If you were branded a collaborator, Dutch society shunned you. Some of the most indelible photographs of the liberation of Holland are of collaborator hangings and the head-shaving humiliation of Dutch women who provided "comfort" to Nazi soldiers. Retribution was severe, often extending down the generations. Grandchildren could expect to carry the mark of collaboration for the rest of their lives because of their family name. Yet the many who casually collaborated also resisted; many stories abound of Dutch guards and policemen warning Jewish friends of impending raids. Remarkably, the Ajax club patriarch Joop Pelser, forever tarnished by his collaboration with the Nazis, was one whose motives are not so discernable. In the same period that he assisted with the deportations, Pelser warned the Jewish friend of one of his sons of an impending raid, even going as far as hiding the friend in his house for four months.[20]

With ADO den Haag seen as a "collaborationist club," there naturally existed a counter on the side of opposition. That club was AVV De Volewijckers from Amsterdam-Noord (North), a club formed in the post–World War I excitement of the new Dutch league football. Two brothers playing for De Volewijckers, Gerben and Douwe Wagenaar, became celebrated in patriotic Dutch households as active members in the resistance. Gerben, a left midfielder and team captain, was constantly tracked by the Germans, and so he had to retire from football. But his brother Douwe, who was also club chairman, rallied the De Volewijckers players, and on August 3, 1943, in a match against VUC, De Volewijckers played in orange shirts, the proud colors of the Dutch national team before the war, instead of their traditional green-and-white club shirts.

Such a brazen act of defiance did not go unnoticed. Douwe Wagenaar told of his harrowing detention after the contest: "I was arrested immediately after the match. . . . After three days I was released again." Players were also protected by the club, ensuring that they would not have to work in Germany, as so many young Dutchmen were required to do. Douwe recalled how De Volewijckers players looked out for each other: "One of our members worked at the labour office. If one of our boys was under threat of being called up for forced labour, he would put their [ID] cards to the back of the box again." Matches featuring collaborationist and resistance clubs drew intense attention from both spectators and occupation authorities. De Volewijckers team manager Jaap van der Leck remembered how one young man walked into the changing room after a heated match against ADO den Haag in 1944: "There was a sudden raid and he was afraid he would be arrested. We got him to safety using the laundry basket."[21] The war years saw the club rise to the pinnacle of Dutch football. In 1941, De Volewijckers enjoyed a successful run, having been just promoted from the third tier to the first division. The club would replace rival ADO in the top spot, winning the league in 1944. More than a victory on the pitch, De Volewijckers provided war-weary Dutch fans with a tangible and exciting response, rich in symbolic meaning, to Nazi oppression.

HIDING IN PLAIN SIGHT

In the final full year of the war, famine and increasingly harsh living conditions imposed by the Nazis took their toll. Famine conditions shocked the country in the Hunger Winter of 1944–1945, when the Nazi occupiers cut off the food supply in retaliation for a railway strike. Responding to these food shortages throughout the country (and weakening body strength in the athletes), the NVB gave players permission to play with a smaller, lighter ball; size 4 balls replaced full-sized foot-balls. Strangely, the Dutch seemed reluctant to give up their football. Fans living in urban centers swapped match tickets with farmers in the countryside for cheese and vegetables.

If you lived outside Amsterdam, it was rather unlikely you were aware that Jews were being targeted for extermination. One telling wartime story holds that a Jew in the countryside seeking shelter from a roundup first had to explain to potential rescuers who the Jews were, and then why they were being persecuted by the Germans.[22]

Beyond the stories of the famous and privileged within Dutch foot-ball, there are a number of examples showing the common person struggling to endure the war. One great survival story from the time of occupation involves a seventeen-year-old Jewish boy named Herman Menco. In Rotterdam, between 1942 and 1943, a former Dutch inter-national player, Sjaak de Bruin, concealed Menco, who first came from Winterswijk, in eastern Holland on the German border; De Bruin often smuggled the young man into matches at De Kuip Stadium.[23] That Jews left their hiding places to attend football matches continues to astound.

As Europe anxiously awaited the Allied invasion that would liberate the continent, Dutch football fans of all stripes continued to support their home sides. Herman Menco, hiding in the home of the De Bruin family, bleached his hair to appear Aryan and would only leave the De Bruin house on match days. Usually, children didn't need ID cards and could easily blend into the crowds. To be Jewish at any match was courting disaster. Yet, on most Sunday afternoons, the De Bruin clan blended in with thousands of men who made the hour-long trek from Rotterdam south to the Feyenoord home grounds.

Herman Menco found great joy in attending football matches, and he may have been the only Jew in the Feyenoord grounds as the depor-tations had been running for months by that time. The football ended for the hidden Jewish boy in 1943 when German soldiers knocked on the door of the De Bruins. Menco was the one who spoke the best German, so he answered the door. He showed the soldiers around, and they liked what they saw. The soldiers requisitioned the De Bruin home, and Manco scrambled to find another hiding place, eventually relocating to a rest home run by the Dutch Reformed Church. Ulti-mately, Herman Menco was betrayed like so many other Jews in Holland. But his story would not end there: in 1944, by a miracle, Menco survived Auschwitz.[24]

Unlike the other major clubs in Holland that kept a low profile, PSV Eindhoven found itself directly entangled in the Holocaust in the final two years of the war. The city of Eindhoven is a provincial town in the south of Holland that suffered massive destruction of the city center toward the end of the war. During the occupation, the club played on, fielding a strong team that finished second in the 1940–1941 championship. Once the war turned against Germany, in its desperate struggle to resist the advance of the Allied armies following D-Day, life for the Dutch would become equally despairing.

PSV (Philips Sport Verenigung, or "sports union") Eindhoven was founded in 1913 and had not been relegated from the Dutch top division since earning promotion in 1926. The club would win the first of nearly two dozen national championships in 1929 as much of Europe rumbled toward authoritarianism. The city of Eindhoven and the Philips electrical company long enjoyed a close relationship, interwoven in commerce and sporting culture. Founded by the owners of Philips, PSV Eindhoven played in their distinctive red-and-white vertical striped kit, drawing support from much of southern Holland.

The close proximity of the only Nazi concentration camp in occupied northwestern Europe to Eindhoven brought both terror and opportunity. The Vught transit camp (Herzogenbusch to the Germans, located just fourteen miles north of Eindhoven) was only one of two concentration camps in Western Europe, outside of Germany, to be directly administered by the SS. The first commandant, transferred from the Gusen subcamp in Austria (part of the Mauthausen system), brought a brutality that made Vught unendurable. Vught was open for about sixteen months between June 1943 and September 1944, when deportations across Holland were at a peak. The camp confined more than thirty-one thousand prisoners, later shuttling most of these to other camps, especially Westerbork.

Vught held Jewish deportees and political prisoners from Holland and Belgium. Conditions were deplorable in the first few weeks of operation as internees suffered severe maltreatment at the hands of guards. Resistance fighters were routinely executed in nearby woods. Appropriate clothing was also in short supply. Food shortages quickly led to starvation, and polluted water worsened infectious diseases already running rampant in overcrowded barracks. Though fewer than eight hundred prisoners died in the camp, the starvation rations and viciousness of the guards, many of whom were members of the NSB, made Vught a place of infamy. After the war, the camp served as a prison for Dutch collaborators and captured Germans. But during wartime, an opportunity was presented to the chairman of Philips.

The Holocaust came to PSV Eindhoven when Frederik Jacques Philips, son of the cofounder of Philips, opened a factory inside Vught soon after the camp was established. Frederik Philips, determined to hold on to the company, had remained in Holland after most of his family had already fled to the United States. As the director of the electronics factory inside the labor camp at Vught, Philips walked a fine line between collaboration and resistance.

Philips's factory continued to support the German war industry but with decreasing effectiveness toward the close of the war. Philips would be imprisoned himself by the Nazis when his workers went on strike in the final year of the war, but in the end Philips saved the company and ensured the survival of 382 Jews in his employment, calling these workers "essential," much as Oskar Schindler did in occupied Poland. Philips was also a fanatical supporter of PSV Eindhoven for ninety-three of his one hundred years; he was particularly famous late in his life for watching matches from the terraces alongside his factory workers rather than in corporate luxury box seats.

With such cooperative relations with German occupying forces taking place, admittedly under the threat of violent force, one might mistake the occupation as nothing more than an inconvenience. But Dutch Jews who ended up in Westerbork understood fully the consequences of Nazi ideology. Contemporary observers noted that most of the Dutch didn't seem to be fleeing terror but rather escaping the tedium of living under an occupation that was largely peaceful, at least until the end of the war. Many soccer players during the war recognized their unique position. Feyenoord player Jan Bens, a member of the first XI during the war years, acknowledged as much: "We were privileged. We would always get a meal after the training, because Feyenoord took care of that. I didn't experience hunger during the war, while there were people dying of starvation. As Feyenoord players, we had an advantage. The baker and the butcher, who were Feyenoord fans, often gave us something extra."[25] Bens made his Feyenoord debut in 1940 at age seventeen and went on to net twenty-five goals in seventy-six appearances. Jan Bens also had the dubious distinction of being the first ever player to be red carded in *De Klassieker*, the heated rivalry match against Ajax. Bens was sent off for punching the Ajax goalkeeper.

KAMP WESTERBORK: FOOTBALL IN DEATH'S WAITING ROOM

Ignaz Feldmann settled into his seat on the train carrying a small band of inmates from Westerbork to Amsterdam, anticipating a hard day's work ahead. This group of men was designated for a work "kommando" set to clean out an abandoned factory. Feldmann was well known to almost everyone in the detention camp at Westerbork, situated at Drenthe in the far northeast corner of the Netherlands. The stocky, imposing man, a resident of the camp since November 1939, had been the captain and a star footballer for Hakoah Vienna, the Jewish club that claimed the 1926 league championship in Austria. In the camp, Feldmann was known as a strong, persuasive personality not afraid to speak his mind. Across the way, Ignaz Feldmann overheard a conversation that was quickly becoming heated. He rose from his seat, looking to restore the quiet before the prisoners had to disembark and begin their day. Fellow inmate Fred Schwarz, part of the same labor detail and a former football player himself, tells the story:

> It is Monday. We are sitting in the train from Beilen to Amsterdam. We have a compartment for eight; it is cramped but better than nothing. In the baggage net, Jaap finds the sport page from the *Telegraaf*. He reads and begins to complain horribly, "Look at that! They hauled Jack and me away on a damn evening when all the guys supported us and now I see that those jerks are just playing football like normal!" Feldmann listened to the agitated footballer and said, in his best Viennese, something that I translate simply as, "Well, let them burst, then we'll go ahead and play our own competition in Westerbork." From that moment until Amsterdam-Muiderpoort, we talked about nothing other than the organization of a future competition. [26]

Before Westerbork was converted to a transit or "gateway" camp in July 1942, Jewish refugees from Germany and Austria lived there from as early as October 1939. The Dutch government had created the site as a destination to house many of the prewar migrants leaving Nazi Germany. Located in one of Holland's more inhospitable areas, with heathland and sandy soil stretching for miles in every direction, the camp left those detained there with feelings of desolation. Dusty and infested with flies in the summer, Westerbork did not improve with the arrival of winter, which was bleak, wet, and windy, exposed to North Sea storms that blew in frequently.

Like other outposts in the Nazi concentration camp universe, Westerbork was converted to a detention facility that rewarded obedience. First arrivals in the camp became the ad hoc rulers. Privilege demanded cooperation, and soon prisoners were beholden to their Nazi benefactors. Jewish captives residing longest in Westerbork held important positions in the camp hierarchy, from which, ultimately, life and death decisions were made. The *Prominenten* decided who would be fed, protected, and entertained. They also decided who would be chosen to meet the transport quotas set by the Germans and their Dutch collaborators.

Prisoners were allowed some freedoms; men worked outside the camp in relatively good conditions. One guard was assigned to sixty laborers, suggesting a calm, trusting work consignment. Women could shop in nearby towns in support of their duties in camp. Hospital patients sought consultations from specialists drawn from academic centers of Groningen. Letters and parcels brought valuable correspondence into the camp along with vital supplies that reached needy captives. Inhabitants also made the most of the opportunity, coupling up and producing babies, many born in the camp. Conditions remained calm until deportation to Poland radically altered camp life.

These choices of the *Prominenten* encompassed the cultural activities in the camp, which were divided by privilege and nationality. Music, theater, and cabaret regularly took place beginning in 1940 with the production of Shakespeare's *A Midsummer Night's Dream*. The Jewish council also took responsibility for organizing a chamber music ensemble, a choir, and a symphony orchestra that included thirty to forty of Holland's most talented musicians. Westerbork became a site famous within the Nazi camp system for cabaret performances, presented in

German and for the entertainment of the SS only. But all cultural activities tapered off between October 1943 and March 1944 as a result of the constant deportations. By the start of August 1944, all cultural activities in the camp had stopped.

Many of the prisoners at Westerbork came first through Kamp Amersfoort, a converted Dutch army barracks that would eventually swell beyond capacity with thirty-five thousand prisoners. A penal work camp near Utrecht in central Holland, Amersfoort served as a deportation center to larger concentration camps at Buchenwald and Natzweiler-Stutthof (France), along with Westerbork and destinations in the east. By April 1943, almost all of the Jewish population in Amersfoort was transferred to Vught. Amersfoort was arguably the most sadistic of the three main camps established in the Netherlands, especially following the mass deportation of Holland's Jews to Poland.

The most popular leisure pursuit in Westerbork undoubtedly was organized football. Played regularly in the refugee camp on the sandy soil of the *Appellplatz*, matches often featured German teams against Austrian ones, but as the camp population swelled after the Nazi invasion of the Netherlands in May 1940, the games went away and the deadly serious struggle for survival began. The Westerbork detention camp existed in the early phase of the war as a holding facility for prisoners, mostly German Jews and others exempted from deportation who helped to expand and administer the camp as the Nazi grip on Western Europe tightened. The camp soon took on a double identity as most inmates sent to Westerbork after the summer of 1942 stayed for only short periods of time; the more permanent camp population of about two thousand people stayed indefinitely. For nearly two years, the camp remained under Dutch control until the deportations began all across Holland. The privileged prisoner class was composed of a Jewish council, camp employees, and other camp functionaries who were given considerable autonomy.

On July 1, 1942, the Nazi *Sicherheitspolizei* (state security police) took control of the camp, and within two weeks the systematic transfer of Holland's Jews began. Prisoners assisting in day-to-day operations of the camp enjoyed unusual freedoms compared to other camps in the Nazi system. Inmates developed apprentice-style workshops—leather goods, metalworks, and shoemaking—and a functional hospital, which, at its peak, had hundreds of beds and dozens of physicians. The camp even had its own currency. A school and a wide range of sports and cultural activities also occupied the time of longer-term prisoners. A Jewish police unit (*Ordendienst*, or OD) kept order and assisted with deportations. The OD men, mostly Germans and Dutch, were often recruited from the dregs of Jewish society. Unrefined, brutish, and lacking human compassion, these guards were loathed by the prisoners. The Jews in the camp referred to these collaborators as the "Jewish SS." In their green uniforms and jackboots, the OD modeled their behavior on the German guards, who freely used the fist and boot heel to inflict quick and decisive punishment.

Most of the liberties allowed by Nazi officials kept up the deception that Westerbork was merely a rest station on the way to labor camps in the East. New arrivals were pacified and cooperation guaranteed. As became the custom in Nazi-occupied Europe, deportees were forced to buy their own train tickets, financing their own journey to their deaths. A particularly effective lie was the signage appearing on trains leaving Westerbork, many marked as a round-trip return from Auschwitz. In Poland, a similar deception masked the secret Treblinka death camp as new arrivals were calmed by the sight of a freshly constructed arrival depot with an elevated train platform, a wooden clock, and fake rail terminal signs. These "innovations" to murder would convince many, especially the uninitiated at Westerbork, that they would survive.

The train carrying Ignaz Feldmann and his mates returned to Westerbork, and almost immediately their plan to create a football league inside the camp was set into motion. Gaining the approval of camp commandant SS-Obersturmführer Konrad Gemmeker was relatively easy. Gemmeker, who served as Westerbork commandant for nearly all of the Nazi control of the camp—October 1942 to April 1945—delegated operation to the German Jews, like Feldmann and his group, a collection of prominent Jews known as the *Alte Lagerinsasse* (old inmates). Footballs were ordered from the outside, old remnant crates in the camp were turned into football boots, and fabric from a local textile mill was made into colorful uniforms. Two collapsible goalposts were positioned in the central parade grounds (the *Appelplatz*), the assembly space where the competition would begin. In order to contact the widest number of players possible, announcements were placed at all the different work divisions in Westerbork. Louis de Wijze was one of the first to sign up:

I could play football fairly well. Before the war I played for Quick of Nijmegen in the first class [division], and that was enough to give me a chance. Football was an outlet for me. In the one-and-one-half-hour-long match, there existed for me, just as earlier, nothing else in the world except a leather ball and a goal. I summoned up courage and resilience. In addition to that, football gave me the chance to stay longer in Westerbork. Feldmann, who was the trainer, held some influence in the camp and could say, "Now, I want to keep my football players here for the time being." In this manner, one was elevated [literally, "preserved"] from the masses.[27]

Two memoirs written after the war provide much of what we know about football at Westerbork. Fred Schwarz, an Austrian immigrant from Vienna and a left-back for the "technical service" team, published his account of survival and soccer in his 1994 memoir *Treinen op Dood Spoor* (Trains on a Dead Track). Schwarz richly details his friendship with Ignaz Feldmann and the debt he owed the Hakoah Vienna footballer at Westerbork. The other memoir is the only widely available English-language account, the recent translation of Louis de Wijze's 1997 staccato-voiced memoir *Only My Life*. De Wijze's book is a concise yet vivid description of his tormented journey from the soccer field at Westerbork to Auschwitz and finally into the heart of Germany. The indefatigable Dutch footballer survived a death march and recapture by the Nazis only to escape one final time, fleeing with the wives and children of fugitive SS officers.

Players invested surprising amounts of time and energy in setting up their sporting pursuits. The soccer passion of these prisoners also inadvertently played into the hands of their captors. Routinely, Nazis and their collaborators would ask their captives: "Why would we allow all of these pursuits—the cabaret, music performances, and football—if we are planning to kill you in the east? Why would we set up a hospital, with a modern operating room, a cancer research facility, and a theater if you are destined to die?" With approval from the Nazi authorities and the enthusiasm of the players, the football league seemed to be a legitimate leisure pursuit. While some would see through the elaborate charade, most would not. Clearly, football at Westerbork was pursued for pleasure and diversion. While it seems at odds with what we know now, propaganda and persecution rarely enter into survivors' recollections of the league and its players. To blame the captives of Westerbork for joining in the deception is to blame the victim of a monumental crime.

By the summer of 1943, the football competition in Westerbork was well underway. Each Sunday held two matches played by teams (usually eleven versus eleven) chosen according to their work divisions. Matches started at 1500 followed by another match at 1700. Each team had a consistent roster and matching uniforms, and lineups for game day were determined by team captains. And Ignaz Feldmann stood as league commissioner, and also refereed and offered his services as masseur. Many rated Feldmann the best player in all of the camp competition. One player who benefited greatly from Feldmann and the camp league was Schwarz, the Austrian immigrant. But he was puzzled by rules laid down by the former SC Hakoah captain: "Feldmann thus held control [supervised] and gave good advice. His most important principle was that you 'restrain yourself' the evening/night before a competition. Alcohol only existed for the upper [class], and from what I hear even there only as an exception, so what did we have to restrain ourselves from?"[28]

The archives at the Westerbork Memorial also provide fragmentary evidence of match schedules and the organization of the league, set up by the working divisions called *Dienstleitung*. The fragments capture the moments when the football league at Westerbork was well known and spectators flocked to the matches, excitedly anticipating the Sunday-afternoon contests. One match schedule from September 24, 1943, lists team names, assigned game times, and names of trainers and captains. From these shreds of evidence, we can patch together a picture of what it must have been like to persist and even thrive in Westerbork.

The level of play in the camp league was decent but rather inconsistent. By the fall of 1943, ever greater numbers of people were being deported to extermination camps in Poland, and the pool of players grew smaller and smaller. Only the old inmates would have been in the camp the longest, and a few lucky ones with good connections to these prominent prisoners would stay behind.

In order to keep the league going, a new plan emerged: every Sunday available players would be gathered together and teams assembled accordingly. Established teams divided by *Dienstleitung* had disappeared in cattle cars. A series of photographs became famous after the war for documenting conditions in the camp during this late period.

Some of these images also capture one of the final matches. One poignant black-and-white photo shows hundreds of spectators surrounding the field boundaries. The trees are stripped of their leaves and a child with the yellow Star of David on his dark sweater faces the camera directly.

Another photo taken at the same time captures two competing teams after a match. Twenty-four players stand arm in arm, some kneeling in the front row, and the charismatic Ignaz Feldmann stands to the far right, stylishly sporting a full suit that is also marked with the Jewish star. Feldmann has the face of a boxer, likely the result of a combative style of play in his earlier years. His nose is offset and points violently to the left, projecting a pugnacious image. Both photos were taken at a time of hastened deportations to the killing centers in Poland. By the end of summer of 1944, all football competitions in Westerbork ended. Most camp residents would leave on the final transports in September 1944, bound for Theresienstadt in Czechoslovakia.

Before the final push to empty the camp, as the Allies planned the D-Day landings that would bring the war finally to Germany's borders, Nazi officials at Westerbork wanted to curry favor with leaders back in Berlin. In May 1944, Commandant Gemmeker commissioned a film by the Jewish prisoner Warner Breslauer to document with his 16-millimeter camera the activities in the transit camp. Breslauer was a refugee in the camp, like so many others. His film, now incomplete and showing the ravages of time, was discovered after liberation, and the footage contains some of the most disturbing and oft-reproduced images of the deportation of Jews during the Holocaust.

Powerful scenes on the train platform include Jews, Roma, and Sinti calmly boarding train cars as if it was a commuter train; SS officers standing nearby, with their German shepherds straining at the leash; German and Jewish functionaries smoking cigarettes and checking lists on clipboards; a solitary young girl, her head wrapped in a white scarf, standing peering out of the door of the cattle car just before it is closed; and a note thrown out of the window of the accelerating train. The film is not meant as propaganda, such as those films made in Theresienstadt (Terezín); Commandant Gemmeker wanted to promote his efficient and thorough leadership. A special point was made to briefly feature a soccer match in the film. The level of play is poor, and the game is disorganized because these are "leftover players," the remnants of all the transports that preceded them. But it did not matter that the football on display was not realistic or impressive. Most unsettling are deportation scenes in the film, in which more than 4,500 people in one transport are sent to their deaths: close-up images of train wheels slowly turning over, the locomotive hissing plumes of white steam into the air, and the camera panning back to show a long view of the train leaving the station in slow motion toward a barren landscape. When liberation finally came to Westerbork on April 12, 1945, by Canadian forces, only 876 inmates remained.

PRISONER HEROES: WESTERBORK LIVES REMEMBERED

The stories of soccer during the Holocaust in the Netherlands are best told through the lives of people who celebrated football and endured long years of Nazi occupation. Westerbork was usually the last stop for many who would not survive the war. Their last moments provide reason to remember individual stories of perseverance, however short-lived. Here is a brief roster of only a few of the people who sought joy and diversion in soccer as they passed through Kamp Westerbork, the antechamber to the killing fields to Auschwitz-Birkenau:

Juda de Vries

A goalkeeper before the war, Juda de Vries was quite gifted with his hands; the HFC Haarlem man played for his hometown club for several years before becoming a well-known tailor. A highly popular player, de Vries saw hundreds of supporters fill the great market in Haarlem for his wedding in 1938 in celebration. De Vries arrived at Westerbork sometime in 1942, where he was assigned to the sewing detail. The goalkeeper would write a letter to his wife while interned at Westerbork: "Jenny, please send my boots."[29] De Vries later expected to play on a factory team in Germany, but instead he was sent to Sobibór in May 1943, where he was murdered upon arrival.

Fred Goldstein

Probably one of the best footballers in Westerbork was the other popular goalkeeper, Fred Goldstein, who was born in 1906 in Germany. One day in 1938, as he worked as a car mechanic, he was abruptly arrested. Knowing the threat his Jewish identity posed, Goldstein fled to the Netherlands. As a refugee in Westerbork, Goldstein jumped back into his previous profession and served as the private chauffeur to the camp commandant. Goldstein also played as team captain from the beginning of the football competition at Westerbork. Goldstein and de Vries likely faced each other in camp matches. The chauffeur would spend the entire war in Westerbork, outlasting most of his fellow inmates.

Hans Dieter Blume

Blume was an *Alte Lagerinsasse* (old inmate) and one of the earliest arrivals at Westerbork in 1939. Blume became a member of the *Ordendienst* (Jewish camp police), which gave him much greater freedom of movement than most prisoners and allowed him to participate in the football league. Blume (born 1923) stayed in the camp for almost five years until the summer of 1944, which brought an end to his football career; during an attack by Allied airplanes, he sustained a bullet injury to his leg, and camp doctors could do no more than amputate the mangled limb. Blume was deported with most of the other Westerbork Jews in September 1944 to Theresienstadt and eventually Auschwitz. He did not survive the war.

Maupie Beetz

A player for the second team at Ajax, Maupie Beetz instead followed his heart and his friends in playing for the Amsterdam team VVA. In May 1940, Beetz was assigned to a satellite labor camp when he made the acquaintance of one of the SS officers at Westerbork. This connection and his enthusiasm for soccer got him a job with the camp police there in 1942. Playing football in the camp felt like a liberation to Beetz and certainly a distraction, given that the camp police assisted with the dirty work of deportation. Beetz was eventually freed from the camp at liberation as one of the few remaining soccer players from the heyday of the Westerbork league.

Erich Gottschalk

Erich Gottschalk rose up the ranks in German football, playing with a Jewish team from Bochum as early as 1933 before it was *verboten* to play on Aryan teams. Gottschalk (born 1906) played as a defender and contributed to the last championship in 1938 for his local team in lower-tier association football. Another old inmate, Gottschalk spent many years as a prisoner in the Drenthe camp until his wife and young daughter (who was born in Westerbork) were deported to Eastern Europe in September 1944. Gottschalk survived the war, but his wife and child were murdered.

Simon Hornman

Sparta Rotterdam had one of its own represent the club inside Westerbork. In September 1941, teenager Simon Hornman was purged from the club's membership, and just a few months later he was transferred to the camp from Hangar 24 (known locally as "Loods 24"), the first collection point for Jews called up or captured in Rotterdam and the islands of South Holland. Hornman worked at Westerbork as a messenger while playing league football on Sunday afternoons. The Sparta man twice avoided the transports, the first time miraculously by hiding inside the camp. The second escape required that he leave the camp altogether, hiding "underground" until his liberation day came in the spring of 1945.

Sam Stern

As a child growing up in an Orthodox Jewish family, Sam Stern (born 1919) skipped Jewish school lessons to play soccer with his mates. Growing up in Assen, just a few miles from the desolate wasteland that would become Kamp Westerbork, the youngster found work in the *Krankenhaus* (camp hospital) with the help of newly befriended German Jews shortly after his arrival on August 18, 1942. Stern soon joined the football competition, playing with his brother-in-law for the hospital team. A few months after his arrival, Stern's connections kept him from the transport that sent his parents and grandparents to the gas chambers at Birkenau. The popular young man also enjoyed some celebrity in the camp: a drawing by a prisoner dated March 5, 1945, shows cartoonlike scenes of Stern pushing a wheelbarrow, playing an accordion, and playing soccer "kitted out" in bright-colored shorts and proper football boots.[30] Often, artists in Westerbork created caricatures of the footballers in action. One picture drawn by Belgian artist and prisoner Leo Kok (who perished in Ebensee, Austria, six days after liberation) shows Louis de Wijze with a cigarette dangling from his lip as he balances a ball on his foot. In his postwar memoir, Sam Stern remembers climbing on the roof of a building in the camp and crying almost uncontrollably at the sight of Canadian tanks barreling down the road leading to Westerbork, bringing with them long-awaited liberation.

Louis de Wijze

The young nineteen-year-old Dutch Jew played in the Westerbork league soon after his arrival in November 1942. Louis de Wijze had made his top-flight debut with the first team of Quick Nijmegen two years earlier when the core of the team had been mobilized for war. One story goes that his first touch of the ball in his first game resulted in a goal, a free kick from twenty yards. Later, de Wijze took special delight in the memory of his last game against Arnhem, with a large group of the Nazi elite watching from the grandstands—he chuckled at the thought that, as he put it, "the krauts had been applauding a Jewish boy."[31] In Westerbork, de Wijze played right wing and striker for the "communications boys" team. Because of his youth and his reserves of strength, de Wijze survived transport to Auschwitz, earning selection to the labor camp at Auschwitz III, also known as Monowitz. There, de Wijze was ecstatic to play football again, and he enthusiastically related this story to his new *kapo*, a small man named Benno who had taken over supervision of de Wijze's work unit one Monday morning in 1944:

> Filled with pride, I had entered the field with my teammates. It had been a great feeling to substitute the squeaky-clean, colorful soccer attire and real leather shoes for the smelly prison clothes adorned

with the hated number [de Wijze was given number 175564 upon arrival at Auschwitz I]. For the first time in a long while I had not felt like a number, an animal in the herd. With complete dedication I threw myself into the match, and it felt like time had been turned back a few years.

Briefly, I had forgotten everything around me. It had been a fantastic match. We had been behind but came back every time. Bobby Prijs, our left wing [a footballer from ZFC Haarlem], had been playing like a real star. He had tied the score with a hard, diagonal shot, 1–1. In the second half, we once again fell behind, but Bobby gave me the golden opportunity, and I scored the tying point. Then, during the last minutes, I scored the winner with a long-distance shot. As we walked off the field and the applause engulfed us, I knew I was famous. I could not have wished for a better debut. Everybody congratulated me after the game.[32]

After the postmatch showers, the left-back assigned to defend Louis de Wijze (from the "Red Triangles" team, a communist squad) approached the teenager to offer his respect and to ask about the boy's prisoner status. Before de Wijze would go to bed that evening, he had been reassigned to a better unit, one that spared him grueling labor and enhanced his meager food rations. Yet hard labor, sickness, and exhaustion took their toll every day in the labor camps associated with Auschwitz. Those who survived to work the next day lived under the agonizing threat of being selected for extermination at Birkenau should they not perform to the satisfaction of their unit's *kapo* or his supervisor, often an ambitious and sadistic SS underling.

LEAVING WESTERBORK

By summer 1943, the deportations from Westerbork to the east would increase dramatically. At the same time, when the death camps in Poland were operating at peak efficiency, Dutch Jews were expelled by the thousands. Among the deportees was Han Hollander, sent along with his wife and daughter to the Westerbork transit camp on September 16, 1942. As a famous figure from the Dutch sports scene, Hollander figured he could wait out the war, protected in his mind by his fame and a signed certificate from Hitler. Other prominent Jews had been guaranteed safe passage to the so-called spa resort of Terezín. The Dutch FA had even requested that, if Hollander and other notable figures from Dutch football were to be deported, the authorities would send them to a protected country estate where hundreds of other conspicuous Dutch Jews were held. Nazi officials denied the motion.

At Westerbork, Hollander worked at the canteen and for a magazine inside the camp. His stay should have been temporary but for some sort of conflict. Maybe it was the fact that Hollander was a temperamental character, or maybe someone carried a grudge. One rumor held that his wife had made disparaging remarks about their Nazi captors. Perhaps he had boasted around the camp of his protected status. Whether or not he called upon his certificate with Hitler's signature is unclear. After eighteen months, Hollander found himself on a transport to the East and a bewildering trip across the continent, unsure of what lay next for him and his family. Powerless to affect his fate, Han Hollander, his wife, and their daughter were almost certainly killed immediately upon arrival at the Sobibór death camp along with all 2,416 passengers on their transport.

The constant presence of death in Westerbork threatened even the youngest of football fans. One surviving letter from the occupation, written by a young boy named Joop Levi who was taken from his home in the roundup of Dutch Jews, shows the depth of the Netherlands' obsession with wartime football. Young Levi sent a handful of letters to his uncle Jacob while he was held in the transit camp of Westerbork. On yellowed, lined paper and written in pencil, Joop's childish scrawl asks his uncle to provide an update on match results for the football clubs in his hometown of The Hague. Just four days after the famous Dutch soccer figure Han Hollander was killed, Joop Levi and his parents were murdered on July 13, 1943, at Sobibór.[33]

The Netherlands remained captive to Nazi Germany until the bitter end. When liberation finally came on May 5, 1945, almost immediately there were football matches again. This time they were against soldiers from a different kind of occupation force: the Allied liberators. Matches featuring local teams such as SC Heerenveen (from northwest Holland) competed against British teams made up of players from the Royal Navy, the RAF, and the Scottish Highlanders. The first international match after the war between the Netherlands and another English military side was set for June 1945 in De Kuip Stadium. More than sixty thousand spectators filled the grounds, and Feyenoord supporter Frans Appels was present that day and fondly remembers the inspirational national anthem, the "Wilhelmus," being sung proudly across the terraces: "Everyone stood and sang along. After all, it was the first time in five years that we could sing it without danger of punishment. I had tears in my eyes. Of course, nowadays, it is difficult to imagine that it was as important as it felt at the time."[34]

Shortages continued long after liberation. In a photo from May 1947, the first eleven of Ajax are dressed in old shirts donated by Arsenal FC of London. On the far left, seated, is Rinus Michels, the future Ajax manager and the architect of Total Football, which brought the Dutch to the pinnacle of the world's game in the 1970s.

Liberation brought attempts to render justice as well. Members of the NSB and any remaining German SS were pursued and, in some high-profile cases, punished by Dutch courts after the war. Many of these war criminals were detained in the Levantkade, the hastily constructed detention camp on an island in the old docks area near Centraal Station in Amsterdam.

When the Nazis were defeated and the accounting began, very few clubs emerged clean from the shadow of the war. Special "purification" committees judged the behavior of football players and club officials, many of whom were hurriedly ejected from their clubs. Others were suspended or voluntarily withdrew their memberships out of public pressure or shame. Ajax player Harry Pelser, along with many other NSB members, were detained at the Levantkade. The younger Pelser was forced to work a potato field for more than a year wearing only the clothes he had brought with him into the camp: a single sweater and trousers. Pelser remembered: "My right shoe was broken, I had to fix it with pieces of string. Other than that I was treated well. The guards never beat me up."[35]

Most others never suffered the indignity of imprisonment. ADO player Gerrit Vreken, he of the impressive Dutch Nazi regalia, was also detained after the war along with dozens of Dutch Nazis who served the occupation government in The Hague. After ten months of labor, Vreken convinced his judges that he had done no "lasting harm." But his old club ADO suspended him and revoked his voting rights (a consequence of some import) for ten years; Vreken assumed a normal life after the reckoning. Like many in these times, Vreken faced a precarious position. Collaboration was always the path of least resistance.

From the earliest days of the occupation, Jewish referees bore the brunt of the persecution, at least professionally. The most famous of the Dutch referees banned during the occupation was Leo Horn, a Jewish migrant from rural Holland who turned to officiating after his playing career was cut short by injury. Horn fought bravely in the Dutch resistance, adopting the alias "Dr. Van Dongen" and riding his bicycle with the serpent-entwined Staff of Asclepius symbol on the side. Horn worked to transport dozens of Jews into hiding, but he was better known for leading a ten-man resistance unit in spectacular raids on German munitions wagons.

Leo Horn continued to referee after the war, taking charge of the historic 1953 match at Wembley Stadium when the "Mighty Magyars" of Hungary humiliated the English 6–3. His fame grew in the 1962 World Cup in Chile as the center official in three group-stage games and as a linesman for the final. Horn was among the top officials in Europe, overseeing two Champions' Cup finals in the years that followed. A celebrated hero of the Dutch resistance movement in Amsterdam, Leo Horn was part of a generation of Jewish men who survived the Holocaust, built up business empires in Holland (becoming a textile magnate, he would survive his brother Edgar, who died in a Nazi camp) and invested their fortunes in the flourishing Dutch soccer scene in the 1960s, professionalized for the first time in 1954.

Scarcity of the material goods needed to put on soccer matches near the end of the war also reflected the accelerated and stark absence of Amsterdam's Jews. One letter from the final six months of the occupation, dated November 4, is addressed to the board of Amsterdam club Neerlandia from a concerned resident named J. Kleerekooper, who expresses his dismay at the local club:

> Honorable gentlemen,
>
> I am aware that in many areas there are great shortages, which on occasion force us to take all sorts of emergency measures. However, what I observed at your ground today seems to me somewhat to exceed the common term of "boundaries." The question to which I refer is the corner flags that mark your ground.
>
> These consist of parts of prayer clothing used by Israelites.

> Personally I regard myself as a freethinker yet I none the less find the solution that you have found at the least inappropriate, certainly when one considers where this clothing comes from and why it is no longer where it ought to be. [36]

The letter concludes with the author asking the club to return the prayer clothes (known in Orthodox Judaism as a *Tallit*) and apologizing, in a typically Dutch fashion, for "interfering" in the club's internal affairs. In response, the club pledged to return the *Tallit*. But to whom would the club make the return? Questions like this one would not be asked in the Netherlands for many decades after the war.

Journalist Simon Kuper, who spent much of his childhood in the Netherlands, recently conducted a number of interviews for his book *Ajax, the Dutch, the War*. Recording their experiences late in life, Kuper captures the powerful memories of now-aged survivors who were caught up in the Holocaust and the wartime soccer scene in the Netherlands. In London, Kuper tracked down a diminutive British Jew named Leon Greenman. Greenman knew Eddy Hamel after meeting the former Ajax outside right-back first in Westerbork and again in Auschwitz. Both Hamel and Greenman could not prove their Anglo identities and thus were deported with all of the other Dutch Jews. Greenman was one of the thousands deported from Hangar 24 in Rotterdam. Had either man been able to prove his nationality, one suspects, especially for Hamel, that he would have been sent to Terezín, the Czech ghetto-camp for "protected Jews" of Western Europe. Greenman recalled in his interview with Kuper:

> It's strange how things went. It could've been anybody, but it happened to be Eddy and myself. We shared the top bunk. There was more fresh air at the top, and if the *Kapo* passed, you were lying out of his sight. In the beginning there were eight of us lying on the planks of the top bunk. But more and more people were selected, and then there were only three of us left. Two had to lie with a leg over the edge. So it was hard to sleep. Eddy and I often rubbed our backs against each other. His body was very warm, you see. And we were very cold. [37]

After about three months, another big selection was ordered by the Nazi officials at Birkenau. Greenman added: "From early in the morning until late in the evening: just looking at your body. We had to take our clothes off and stand in the queue. Eddy Hamel was standing be-hind me—his name begins with an H and mine with the G. He said to me, 'Leon, what is going to happen to me? I have an abscess in my mouth.' It did look swollen."[38] The anger flared as Greenman continued with his recollection:

> We had to pass between two tables. There was an SS man sitting at each table. If you weren't fit you went to the left, and if you were fit you went to the right. When I passed between the tables they pointed to the right. And when Eddy passed, I looked round: he was sent to the left. That unfortunate moment. I thought he was going to the hospital. But I never saw him again. It took a few months before I realized that they really did gas people. It's not a lot that I know about Eddy. It was very cold in the camps. We only had a jacket and trousers. And his back was warm, you know?[39]

Because the Nazis kept such detailed records of their deeds in places like Auschwitz-Birkenau, we know that Leon Greenman's wife and in-fant toddler son, along with Eddy Hamel's wife and twin sons, were all murdered at Auschwitz on the first day of February 1943. Greenman learned after the war that of the seven hundred people expelled from Westerbork as part of the transport that included himself and Hamel, only he and a friend named Leon Borstrock survived.

AFTERMATH AND LIGA TEREZÍN

As Western Europe tried to rebuild following the war, the Netherlands quickly took to restoring its institutions, cleansing civil service agencies of Nazis and their collaborators, and going about the business of re-claiming sport, among a number of other cultural pursuits. The ques-tion of collaboration haunted the Netherlands. No other country out-side of Poland lost more of its native Jewish population. The perpetra-tors themselves acknowledged the ease with which this was accom-plished. At his war crimes trial in Jerusalem in 1961, Jewish emigration expert and central planner of the Final Solution Adolf Eichmann mar-veled at the efficiency of the Dutch collaboration in ridding Holland of its Jews: "The transports run so smoothly that it is a pleasure to see."[40]

Complicity in the deportations was largely forgotten by contemporaries. Like nothing had changed, football rolled on. Much as they had done during the war, the Dutch embraced the game wholeheartedly in the ensuing years. Club allegiances remained very strong after 1945.

Just as quickly, a national narrative emerged in the Netherlands that celebrated those renowned instances of resistance and rescue that captivated a world still trying to make sense of the horrific consequences of World War II. One commonly held view was that more people in Holland joined the resistance after the war than before it. The nation wanted to embrace a comforting past. And for some Dutch, giving false directions to the invading Germans constituted their greatest act of resistance for the entirety of the war (apparently, this is a practice that continues today for a few ornery Dutch who meet up with lost German tourists).

But the Holland of Anne Frank is a fiction constructed to soothe a guilty national conscience. The fact that the Franks and many of their fellow exiles were betrayed, usually by their countrymen, is often lost in the compelling tale of hope, youthful idealism, and a girl's coming of age in a time of war. The myth of heroic rescue in Holland persists today, despite the efforts of modern-day Dutch historians to correct the historical account. Yet these same myths have been rebuffed in Poland and France, which do not share the Dutch peculiarities of geographic and linguistic isolation. Soon, there will be no living witnesses to challenge the myth.

The Dutch response to the Holocaust is an echo of Auschwitz survivor Primo Levi's "gray zone," where complex and horrendously difficult moral choices were faced by both victim and bystander. The Nazis were so effective at creating what one writer called "choiceless choices" in the Nazi camps.[41] Westerbork stands as unique in the history of the camps because of the similarity of life there to that under occupation elsewhere in the country. Detainees who distanced themselves from the operations of the camp likely hastened their deportation to a near-certain death.

Those prisoners who chose to cooperate as functionaries typically did so in order to save their lives. Each faced an unbearable moral ambiguity. Nepotism was a nearly irresistible temptation when transport lists were drawn up. Playing in a camp orchestra or on a football team for the entertainment of the torturers gave rise to feelings of angst and uncertainty. Captives chose football as diversion and an escape, but more often than not, the games sustained life and offered a measure of resistance. In the end, this "choice" was enough for most: ensuring survival.

One can understand why a guilty country would bury the past as quickly as possible. Many lives were lost and countless people suffered the indignity of an occupation that turned violent and ruthless in the final days of the conflict. Dutch football clubs cleansed their membership rolls, and a new era of Dutch football was lying in wait. The brilliant players who would one day capture the imagination of the world with their sophisticated, skillful brand of play that rewarded risk and eschewed convention were born immediately after the war. The world would have to wait for this brilliance as the postwar generation (Johan Cruyff, Ruud Krol, Johan Neeskens) needed time to come of age while cities were rebuilt, Dutch football academies blossomed, and normal life was reclaimed. The revolution in the world's game would see the *Oranje* of the 1960s and 1970s build on the football fervor shown by players and spectators during the war, who played and watched when most of their European neighbors simply struggled to exist.

Another aspect of the postwar reckoning was the important duty to remember. One marvelous example of the cultural heritage left behind by Holland's Jews is the magnificent Portuguese Synagogue built in 1675, which stands today as a monument to Jewish influence and wealth in the city center of Amsterdam. Every May 4, a memorial service is held in front of the synagogue commemorating the war dead. Memorials have sprung up across Holland, though few tend to acknowledge the Jewish victims, instead choosing to emphasize the war and Nazi crimes.

One laudable exception is the memorial at Westerbork, designed by a survivor in 1970 and situated on the spot where the railroad tracks cut through the center of the camp. There, curled-up rails reach to the heavens and twin slabs of marble carry a passage from the Hebrew Bible, written more than two thousand years earlier. The passage is from Lamentations and is customarily read aloud by Orthodox Jews on the date commemorating the destruction of Solomon's Temple and the exile that followed at the hands of the ancient Babylonians. Fittingly, this verse now recalls the civilization destroyed by the Nazis:

They hunt our steps,

that we cannot go in our streets;
our end is near, our days are fulfilled;
for our end has come.
—Lamentations 4:18

Where football was once played on the assembly square now stand 102,000 stones, each representing a life that passed through Westerbork. The stones are arranged to make out a map of the Netherlands. There are no mass graves on the grounds, unlike nearly every other Nazi camp. Instead, the remembrances here are for the tens of thousands who stayed for a short while before being sent to their deaths.

One final story from the last days of Westerbork demands telling. The train carrying away Ignaz Feldmann, Fred Schwarz, and others to Terezín, Czechoslovakia, brought yet another surprising turn. Terezín, the ghetto-camp thirty miles north of Prague, also contained a great number of prominent and well-known Jewish deportees from all over Western Europe. In the new camp, Feldmann met an old SC Hakoah Vienna teammate, Ignaz Fischer, who happened to be one of the most popular players of a football league set up in Terezín. Feldmann arrived too late to be involved in the league, but he soon learned of the great meaning affixed to the league by the prisoner-players in Terezín.

By the end of September 1944, Terezín was emptied and the last remnants sent to various destinations in still-unconquered Germany. The Westerbork Jews were among the first deported as they were the last to arrive at Terezín, and Ignaz Feldmann found himself sent to the extermination camp at Auschwitz-Birkenau. He remained there for about a month, enjoying relative safety as a *kapo* because of his football fame. Feldmann was granted protected status by an SS guard who recognized his old adversary from the football pitch back in Vienna. Ordered to form two columns, the prisoners hurriedly lined up. The guard supervising labor assignments immediately recognized Feldmann's name on his list. His angry, threatening tone shifted in an instance to excitement. The two had played against each other, the guard for Austria Vienna and Feldmann for SC Hakoah Vienna. The SS man even remembered playing alongside Feldmann as part of the Austrian national selection team.

Ignaz Feldmann's stay in Auschwitz was brief, and by late 1944 he was deported to Sachsenhausen, near Berlin, as the death camp was now under pressure from advancing Soviet troops. Before Germany fell, he would be sent to Leipzig to work in a munitions factory, and it was in this southeast corner of Germany that Feldmann made his last stop as a prisoner of the Third Reich. Eventually, Ignaz Feldmann was liberated in April 1945 as a prisoner at the German camp of Ohrdruf near Buchenwald.

The charismatic and resourceful Feldmann managed to involve himself in the dramatic scenes of liberation at Ohrdruf. On April 11, 1945, newsreels capture the group of military brass and enlisted men touring the camp. Astoundingly, Ignaz Feldmann is seen escorting Supreme Commander of the Allied Expeditionary Force General Dwight D. Eisenhower around Ohrdruf. Emaciated men wander about the camp, and small fires still burn behind barbed-wire fences. Corpses are strewn across the grounds and other bodies still smolder on cremation pyres. Other images show generals Omar Bradley and George Patton, visibly shaken at the horrific sights, standing alongside the Jewish footballer.

Generations of Americans and Europeans would forever remember these pictures as prime evidence of the Nazis' crimes. But few know of the experiences of those held prisoner in one of the final stops made by the Westerbork Jews. Recall the months spent by the Dutch deportees in Terezín in the last year of the war. Because Terezín served a unique role in the Nazi propaganda effort to obscure their murderous deeds in Europe, football there took on much greater significance than the football played at Westerbork. Called Liga Terezín, the soccer league in the ghetto offered new arrivals a glimmer of hope in what became the final stop before Auschwitz. In the ghetto-camp at Terezín, we find the battle joined anew between Nazi oppressor and Jewish victim, in a citadel town built during the Austro-Hungarian Empire. And in the courtyard near one of the barracks of this ghetto-camp, a dusty soccer pitch was born.

8

GHETTO SOCCER IN LIGA TEREZÍN

For seven weeks I've been here,
Penned up inside this ghetto.
But I have found my people here.
The dandelions call to me
And the white chestnut branches in the yard.
Only I never saw another butterfly.
That butterfly was the last one.
Butterflies don't live here,
In the ghetto.
—from the poem "The Butterfly" by Pavel Friedmann,
who later perished in Auschwitz on September 29, 1944[1]

The Czech capital city of Prague was one of the great Jewish centers of culture and learning for centuries in Europe before the continent plunged into fascism at the start of the 1930s. Like many Jewish communities across Europe, Prague was vulnerable to the same risks and perils that plagued other major cities—discrimination, expulsions, and violent pogroms. But in the decades immediately before World War II, Prague was well known as a stable, welcoming, and thriving destination for Jews in central Europe. Though their presence was restricted to the traditional Jewish Quarter situated between the Staré Město (Old Town) and the Vltava River known as Josefov (named in tribute to the reformer Habsburg emperor Franz Joseph), by 1938 nearly half of all the Jews living in Bohemia and Moravia called Prague home.[2] These numbers swelled significantly with the flow of refugees seeking safety from Nazi Germany after 1933.

A year almost to the day that Austria was absorbed into the Third Reich and Vienna witnessed waves of violence against its Jewish population, the Nazis marched into Prague. The arrival of German soldiers on March 15, 1939, was not met with rapturous celebrations as were seen in the Austrian capital and the rural provinces. Czechoslovakia had been essentially sacrificed months earlier by the major European powers negotiating a peace during the Munich Crisis of 1938. But Hitler's appetite for territories and the war-feeding natural resources they provided would not be satiated. He had long targeted the German-speaking *Volksdeutsche*, the ethnic Germans living in the Sudeten region of Czechoslovakia, for integration back into the German Reich, and the peaceful acquisition of the country gave the Nazis time to build their war machine.

The occupied Czechs responded grimly to their new Nazi masters, but the rejection of the "New Order" would not slow down the implementation of policies meant to intimidate and subjugate. Propaganda campaigns worked in seamless harmony with the new office for emigration, the Zentralstelle, set up in July 1939 by Adolf Eichmann in Prague. With a swift ferocity, Eichmann and his small office of deputies set out to cleanse Prague of its Jews, using the city also as a transit center for outlying areas in all Czech territories, now identified as the Protectorate of Bohemia and Moravia on Nazi maps. Eichmann proclaimed he would "sweep the streets clean of Jews," threatening mass expulsions to Dachau if the Jewish community of Prague did not cooperate with self-deportation measures. Escalating restrictions were placed on the Jews of Prague, but these had a lessened effect with the outbreak of war in the fall of 1939 because the Jewish population of Czechoslovakia was spread across more than 450 villages and towns.

The first deportations from Prague began on October 16, 1941, with the first of five transports directed to the Polish city of Łódź, then the largest ghetto in German-dominated Europe.[3] Within a month, transports also began to a new Jewish internment center forty miles north of Prague, created from an old garrison town built during the eighteenth century in the reign of the Habsburg Empire.[4] The town was Theresienstadt (Terezín to the Czechs), and the ghetto-camp would become unique in the history of the Holocaust, offering a distorted lie of Nazi beneficence to a disinterested world.

Theresienstadt began as a citadel-style fortress, complete with ramparts and a moat that at occupation held several hundred German soldiers. The stronghold at Theresienstadt included a bastion called the "Small Fortress," a Gestapo-run prison (which once held the Bosnian Serb Gavrilo Princip, who sparked World War I by assassinating Austrian archduke Franz Ferdinand) that became infamous as a destination of punishment and death for Theresienstadt prisoners.

Terezín stands alone in the Nazi system as the only camp mentioned directly in the Nazi German planning for the Final Solution to the Jewish Question outlined in the Wannsee Conference in Berlin on January 20, 1942. The city and the region changed forever when Terezín became a ghetto, a concentration camp, and a Potemkin-style village that, at one time or another, held over 150,000 Jews, of which only 16,832 were still alive by the end of the war.[5]

At the end of 1941, Terezín received Jewish labor details sent to prepare the fortified city for its new role as a counterfeit "model camp" for Jewish internees. In time, two propaganda films would masterfully maintain the ruse that Theresienstadt was a "paradise" destination.[6] The first transports carrying around ten thousand Jews arrived in early January 1942, and immediately a Jewish council (*Ältestenrat*) was set up by the Nazis with a lead "elder" and a thirteen-member council to govern the camp. Believing that further deportations could be avoided through productive labor, the Council of Elders joined the SS command in administering the ghetto. The so-called model ghetto featured significantly in Nazi plans to deport well-known Jews from Germany, Austria, and later conquered territories in Western Europe.

Once built to house a civilian population of seven thousand, Theresienstadt soon reached a peak of 58,497 people as trains bringing thousands of aged and war-disabled Reich Jews arrived in the first six months, flooding the ghetto and presenting camp officials with unsolvable problems.[7] Initially, transports unloaded prisoners at a local train station three kilometers away, forcing new arrivals to walk the remaining distance with luggage (fifty kilograms were allowed) and children in tow. This changed in June 1943 when a railway spur was constructed to bring the cattle cars directly into the fortress.

The population of Theresienstadt swelled beyond imagining. Inevitably, the mortality rate in the ghetto-camp skyrocketed; in September 1942 alone, 3,900 people from a total population of nearly sixty thousand perished.[8] At about the same time in Warsaw, the waves of deportations of Aktion Reinhard (an operation named after SS general Reinhard Heydrich, the central architect of the Holocaust) to Bełżec, Sobibór, and Treblinka were subsiding, which meant that the gas chambers of these death camps could now take nearly twenty thousand new arrivals from Terezín.

In the decade before the war, there was no sport in Europe with a reception and public effect comparable to that of football.[9] Yet across the continent during the war, European domestic leagues went largely dormant as players were recruited for service to country or were engaged directly in combat. Long before the Nazi occupation, Czech soccer was among the best in the world. In fact, 1934 represented a high point for the Czechoslovak national side at the World Championships in Italy, with the Czech team making it all the way to the cup final only to lose to the host Italians 2–1.[10] Competitive soccer flourished in the most unimaginable place: a Nazi ghetto-camp named Liga Terezín. Soccer in Terezín was anchored in the larger Czech sport culture: some of the ghetto teams were named after famous Czech clubs like Sparta or Slavia, prominent clubs that carry on to this day.

Players comprised many nationalities from across Europe, most notably drawn from groups of Czech, German, Dutch, Danish, and Slovak deportees. Czechoslovakia had by far the largest number of young men in the premier division, especially among the few professional-level players drawn from top domestic club teams and national Olympic player pools. Teams in the Terezín leagues were most often organized by profession (e.g., cooks, technicians, ghetto police, or guards). Adding to the peculiar nature of this league was the reality that games were played throughout the ghetto almost entirely during the time of Nazi rule: the main premier league ran almost as long as the camp was open, from 1942 to 1944.

Amid severe overcrowding, compulsory labor, and never-ending food shortages, an astounding cultural life existed in the Theresienstadt ghetto. Almost unparalleled in the camps and ghettos across Nazi-dominated Europe, the captives in Terezín sought to reclaim their culture, on the verge of extermination by the Nazis. Auschwitz survivor Primo Levi said of the Jewish victims in the ghettos and camps, "the Nazis set out to destroy the soul before they killed the body." Creative expression flourished in this ghetto; the arts and humanities found expression in the sometimes mundane but regularly deadly experiences in the ghetto-camp. Nazi officials encouraged these cultural pursuits in service of their political deceptions. A lessened presence of the SS and sympathetic ghetto policemen drawn from Czech Jews allowed for much greater freedom than existed elsewhere. Prisoners could move about the town, sharing information and developing networks.

Because a significant number of artists and musicians came to Theresienstadt from Prague, music and the visual arts prospered. Cabaret groups, an opera, and operettas were staged, complete with printed handbills. Small classical orchestras existed alongside musical instruction and criticism. Many of these efforts, including new compositions that debuted in the ghetto, had to be completed in secret. Musicians and artists often used found materials, scraps of paper, and smuggled canvasses and paints to do their work.

Famous intellectuals from Germany, Austria, Holland, and nearby Prague became famous figures in the ghetto, giving more than 2,400 lectures on subjects ranging from literature and cinema to physics and art. The SS command took notice and soon conscripted artists in Terezín to paint pastoral scenes in support of the "embellishment" in spring 1944. Other artists captured the true face of the ghetto through drawings, watercolors, and paintings later smuggled out. Those who were caught depicting reality in the ghetto were taken to the Small Fortress, where they were tortured and usually executed. Only one painter is known to have survived this prison.

Hopeful, resilient acts of cultural and athletic expression gave meaning to the daily struggle to survive. Though privilege protected the most famous of the Theresienstadt artists, musicians, and sportsmen, ultimately almost everyone faced deportation. One graduate of the Prague Conservatory set out to reclaim a sense of humanity and challenged the Nazis using a monumental masterpiece of religious music from eighteenth century Italian romanticism. That graduate was composer and teacher Rafael Schächter. Using a smuggled score and a single reclaimed piano, Schächter brought together a 150-person choir for sixteen performances of Giuseppe Verdi's *Requiem Mass* between 1943 and 1944. His Terezín choir responded to the enveloping terror that surrounded them with an unyielding humanity. Schächter and his choir found temporary solace from their deprivations and hard labor. The endurance and strength required to memorize this difficult piece of music is all the more impressive when one realizes they were doing it under a Nazi-imposed famine.

Members of the Council of Elders in Terezín questioned why Jewish singers would perform a Catholic mass when there were suitable alternative works available, some by Jewish composers. Schächter's answer was clear and unequivocal: this would not be a meek submission to terror—the *Requiem* would confront the Nazis with Verdi's thunderous portrayals of the Day of Judgement. The risk was great. Schächter give his chorus a translation of the Latin words so they were fully aware of the meaning of their singing. Seen through the eyes of the prisoners, the mass became a defiant act of resistance.

When the Terezín choir performed their last concert, it was in front of gathered dignitaries on June 23, 1944, when the ghetto became a propaganda piece in the Nazi effort to deceive the International Red Cross and the world. Before the performance, Schächter had told the members of his choir, "We will sing to the Nazis what we cannot say to them."[11] Under duress, Rafael Schächter and the Terezín choir, now down to about sixty members, performed for the visiting delegates and the Nazi high command. Singing proudly the Latin words "nil inultum remanebit"—"nothing shall remain unavenged"—gave the prisoners the spirit and fortitude to persevere.[12]

On October 16, 1944, most of the members of Rafael Schächter's choir were deported to Auschwitz and murdered almost immediately upon their arrival. "Rafi," sent along with the group, survived Auschwitz, but his end came in the final weeks of the war. Most likely dying on a death march in April 1945, Schächter did not live to see the liberation of Terezín a month later.

With the power of art and music as an inspirational parallel, sport also gave hope and resilience to the thousands of prisoners held captive in Theresienstadt. No other sport or cultural activity reached as many captives, young and old, privileged and anonymous, as soccer.

The new arrival of thousands of deportees brought devastating consequences to every resident of the Czech ghetto. By the end of 1942, the most lethal year in the short history of the ghetto-camp, Nazi administrators began to heed international calls for inspections, most notably by the main world refugee organization, the International Red Cross (IRC). This period is also when organized soccer leagues first appeared in Terezín. While transports were regularly departing to the

Baltic States, Belarus, and the Polish camps of Treblinka and Auschwitz, the Germans presented the world with the image of Terezín as a
sanctuary for prominent Jews. Yet Theresienstadt suffered a death rate
equivalent to that in Reich concentration camps like Buchenwald and
Dachau. Among the famous faces of Terezín were some of central
Europe's most notable footballers, who soon realized they had an opportunity to lace up their boots once again. But each would be faced
with a moral dilemma: "If I play football, will I assist the Nazis with
their murderous deceptions? And if I don't play, will I surely starve to
death?" Their answers provided life-affirming inspiration for the captives waiting to learn their fate, a testament to the human spirit in the
darkest of places and, one day, an important witness to an immense
crime.

Events elsewhere in Europe would soon influence the prisoners at
Terezín in a profound way, creating the most infamous incident in the
history of the collection ghetto. In October 1943, nearly five hundred
Danish Jews were deported to Terezín, and at the urging of King Christian X, the Danish government immediately protested, offering a steady
and relentless diplomatic effort that resulted in significant international
pressure. After lengthy negotiations, which dragged on for months, the
Nazi regime relented and ordered officials at Theresienstadt to ready
the ghetto for a visit, scheduled for June 23, 1944.

To ready the camp for the IRC inspection, the SS ordered a major
beautification project to create the façade of a "model ghetto." A mass
deportation of 7,500 prisoners in May 1944 to Auschwitz emptied
crowded barracks. Jewish prisoners were recruited to clean streets and
sidewalks. Buildings were given fresh coats of paint, and park benches
and flower gardens suddenly appeared from nowhere in the large open
spaces of the ghetto. Newly created recreational facilities included a
children's playground and a music pavilion in the town center. A prayer
hall was added as well as a library stocked with hundreds of books.

Other buildings in the ghetto, long derelict in appearance, were
brightened. The Nazis left few details overlooked as their slave laborers
refurbished a town café and opened a ghetto bank, with camp money
printed to "pay" Jews for their labor in ghetto factories and workshops.
Streets were given familiar civilian names, replacing the military numbers and letters used before. Inmates transformed a local gymnasium to
look like a performance stage, and it was on this stage, and on the

makeshift soccer fields in the ghetto, that the most compelling acts of resistance by the prisoners occurred.[13]

Along with two representatives from the Danish Red Cross, who were tracking the Danish Jews deported to Theresienstadt, lead delegate Maurice Rossel (the Belgian envoy of the International Red Cross) was joined by Theresienstadt Commandant SS first lieutenant Karl Rahm and one of his deputies. For the June 23, 1944, visit, the SS laid out a carefully predetermined route for the IRC delegation to follow, with stops scheduled down to the minute. There would be no deviation from this route. Inmates rehearsed their jobs: deliveries of fresh vegetables passed by, bakers offered their freshly baked bread, and workers sang brightly along the walking tour. All of these stops were queued by messengers running ahead of the entourage.

Densely packed dormitories where up to four hundred people lived were opened up and furniture, drapes, and flower boxes added to the soiled rooms. Czech Jews wore civilian clothes instead of their striped prisoner uniforms. Decorative signs pointed to the café, bank, swimming pool, and ghetto post office. People gathered around café tables sipping what appeared to be coffee but was instead water dyed black. A jazz band, calling themselves the Ghetto Swingers, played in the music pavilion near the main square. The visitors were further captivated by cheering crowds at a soccer match held in the camp square. Fittingly for a scripted tour, as the IRC delegation passed by, a goal was scored. But a bruise under the eye of the town "mayor" Dr. Paul Eppstein, the main elder of the Terezín *Ältestenrat*, hinted at another truth.

Terezín survivor Vera Schiff later compiled her memories of the ghetto in her memoir, *The Theresienstadt Deception*. As a witness to this bizarre visit, she is convinced that if the Red Cross had wanted to see beyond this charade, they could have: "All they had to do was take a turn in a different direction than the accompanying SS suggested or ask a probing question."[14] Had the entourage opened a door or peered into an unapproved courtyard, the lethal truth would have been revealed. The visiting dignitaries were taken in by the deception, largely because they expected to see ghetto conditions like those in occupied Poland, where people were starving in the streets and armed policemen patrolled ghetto boundaries. The Red Cross inspection lasted six hours, half of which were spent at a lavish luncheon hosted by the Nazi command. The cultural events lasted another week.

Of the three individual reports filed after the visit, none uncovered the deception. In fact, Maurice Rossel ended up repeating some of the information provided by his Nazi guides. One scandalous passage stands out from his report: "[We were] extraordinarily amazed to find the ghetto town which lives almost a normal life." Later, the IRC would try to keep these testimonies secret because they did not fit with accumulated news from other ghettos and camps across Europe.

Why the IRC delegation did not demand to see Birkenau, where a "family camp" of ghetto Jews had been set up as a sham complement to Theresienstadt, remains a mystery. Thousands had been deported there in the weeks prior in order to create the impression that Terezín was not overcrowded and dangerous. Told by their Nazi hosts that the Czech ghetto was the "final camp," it stretches the imagination to think that Rossel and his team of visitors could not see that in June 1944 Theresienstadt was not a satisfactory answer to the question of where all the Jews of Europe had been deported. After the June visit, the lead representative from the International Red Cross, Rossel, sent a glowing letter of thanks to his counterpart in the German government, going so far as to enclose photos of the delegation's visit to the camp as mementos of the pleasant excursion. The Belgian concluded his letter by expressing his sincere gratitude: "The voyage to Prague will remain an excellent memory for us and it pleases us to assure you, once again, that the report about our visit in Theresienstadt will be reassuring for many, as the living conditions [in the camp] are satisfactory."[15] With only rare exceptions, every prisoner at the "family camp" was sent to the gas chambers at Birkenau a few weeks later when it was clear to Adolf Eichmann that the Red Cross commission would not ask to see Auschwitz.

Until the very end of Nazi rule in Czechoslovakia, the deceptions continued. On March 5, 1945, Adolf Eichmann visited Theresienstadt for another inspection with an eye on escaping justice. Realizing that he and the Nazi high command might use Terezín's Jews as bargaining chips in endgame negotiations, Eichmann sought to further hide the atrocities that occurred there. Such delusional thinking, that these Nazi criminals could simply bargain their way out of the hangman's noose, guided Eichmann to order a second beautification of the ghetto in advance of an April 1945 IRC visit. This time, the Nazis offered up their recently completed propaganda film as exonerating evidence. This final formal inspection of the ghetto-camp produced a less favorable reaction, though the film clearly helped to mask reality.

The SS had systematically eliminated all traces of what happened before 1945, including destruction of the highly incriminating RHSA (Reich Security Central Office) archives stored in the ghetto. The RHSA, as a division of the SS, possessed the most damning evidence of the genocidal crimes of the Third Reich. In the end, little evidence of mass death and starvation was found. Nonetheless, the IRC stationed a representative in Theresienstadt for the remainder of the war. A glimmer of justice came out of this last visit as the IRC successfully negotiated the release of all Danish Jews, leaving Terezín by Swedish Red Cross buses. Though the Red Cross saved thousands of lives with their care packages to prisoners during the long European war, this final report from the April 6, 1945, visit to Theresienstadt, published months after the liberation of Auschwitz, did little more than offer international validation of Nazi efforts to hide their crimes.

THE NAZI'S CZECH "SUMMER CAMP": THE PROPAGANDA FILMS

As part of a grand effort to perpetuate the myth of German civility in these times, Nazi officials ordered the production of two propaganda films to document life in the camp. One film, which turned out to be the second made in Terezín, was a feature-length production directed by a well-known German actor and director in the autumn of 1944. This film is better known to the public as a monumental hoax to portray Terezín as a leisure destination.[16]

Depicting the concentration camp of Theresienstadt as a paradise, the film presents the Jews of Europe as "guests" of the Third Reich and not "enemies of the state," as popularly understood in these times. The beautification program worked well to rid the ghetto of squalor and made possible the fabricated social and cultural events that featured prominently in the second propaganda film. The film has a number of sequences that depict workshops, allotment gardening, and all manner of entertainment and a seemingly endless number of leisure activities such as open-air cabaret, staged musicals, children's opera (e.g., audiences in Terezín saw more than fifty performances of *Brundibár*, a

Hansel and Gretel–themed story composed by Terezín prisoner Hans Krása), academic lectures, concerts, and relaxing gatherings around communal living spaces, as if the inhabitants are on a holiday at a resort. In the film, ghetto facilities are highlighted to give the impression that this bucolic town contained the same cultural and intellectual offerings of the cities of origin from which the inhabitants came: Prague, Vienna, and Berlin.

The initial organization of the propaganda film started as early as December 1943, at the beginning of the great beautification program, with actual filming beginning seven weeks after the IRC visit of June 23, 1944. In a cruel irony, the film was funded by the Jewish prisoners themselves, costing some 350,000 Czech crowns at the time, all of which had been confiscated from incoming Jewish prisoners. The twisted mockery is that Jews were not only forced to make a film designed to conceal their own destruction, but they were also forced to fund the film as well. To maintain the façade of normalcy, no transports were ordered during the summer of 1944 while filming was taking place. The work was completed in early September 1944 after eleven days of filming.[17]

Written and directed by prisoner Kurt Gerron, a famous German Jewish actor and cabaret star, the film was officially called *Theresienstadt: A Documentary Film from the Jewish Settlement Area*. But this is not the title history remembers. Survivor accounts and testimony given in the postwar trial of the SS camp commandant who supervised the creation of the film give it the ironic title *Hitler Gives the Jews a Town* (*Der Führer Schenkt den Juden Eine Stadt*), by which the film has been popularly known worldwide for nearly fifty years.[18]

The Prague newsreel company Aktualita was selected by Gestapo officials to complete the film, and after editing, which took five to six months, the final version was completed in March 1945. This delay prevented the work from being effective as mass propaganda. Produced predominately for foreign audiences, the film disappeared after the war after what was most likely a very limited screening to groups of high-ranking SS officers and, separately, to individual Swiss and Danish diplomats and delegates of the International Red Cross.[19] Twenty minutes of sporadic footage are all that remain of the original film.

All of the actors and inmates in the film are, of course, Jewish, and it is the will to survive that motivated the prisoners to appear in the film.

The most haunting scenes reveal a group of children gathered around outdoor tables awaiting an afternoon snack. The energy of youth shines fleetingly as buttered bread is passed around the tables. But the eager, happy faces of the smiling children hide a disquieting reality. Terezín survivors later reported that these scenes had to be filmed multiple times because the children, starved for weeks, ate the bread too quickly. All of the children were deported to Auschwitz after filming was completed. Kurt Gerron was put on the last transport from Terezín to Auschwitz as well and was gassed on arrival.

One of the final matches of the professional-level soccer competition called Liga Terezín dominates the second propaganda film. The Nazis directed Kurt Gerron to feature the September 1 match between the *Jugendfürsorge* (youth welfare unit) and *Kleiderkammer* (used clothing store) teams. Interestingly, more than a quarter of the running time for this main ghetto film consisted of the featured soccer match. During filming, hundreds of children are shown sitting as spectators and filling the arcades, rising three stories high above the courtyard pitch. Individual players are easily identified when both teams emerge from the tunnel for the warm-up, the prematch greetings, and the coin toss with the referee. The German narration of the film frames the soccer match as just another leisure option among many for the Jews in this "spa town":

> NARRATOR: "Use of free time is left to individuals. Often, workers flock to soccer games, Theresienstadt's major sports event." *The camera pans across the courtyard of the ghetto's old military barracks. Hardly a spot remains open in the balconies overlooking the dirt pitch. Two teams are seen dashing into the barracks. One team wears white jerseys with the Jewish star. The other team appears in a dark kit.*

> NARRATOR: "The teams each have only seven men, due to limited space." *Players warm up and shake hands with the referee.*

> NARRATOR: "Nevertheless, enthusiastic fans watch a spirited game from beginning to end." *The match begins, and immediately the skill of the players wearing the dark shirts shows. The play is determined and of a high quality as the competitors give a genuine effort. Quick passing and deft movement produce exciting give-and-go exchanges.*

Later, a corner kick is skillfully headed into the goal. Two minutes pass without narration until the film abruptly shifts to scenes of public bathing facilities. Highlighting the "immaculate" hygiene in the ghetto, a line of naked men process into the showers. [20]

Dutch historian Karel Margry has studied extensively the Nazis' Terezín propaganda films and in a recent interview noted, "The surprising thing is how long the football sequence is. It makes football in Theresienstadt look more important than it was, which is part of the propaganda idea behind it. The SS realized that football is something that not just the people in the ghetto, but people all over the world liked." [21] The SS realized the propaganda value of football, creating what some call the "summer camp effect." [22] Other sporting activities that appear in the film include a Czech high-diving champion, men's track and field, and women's handball. In its totality, the *Documentary Film from the Jewish Settlement Area* reinforces the myth that Jews had arrived in a resort town, complete with rich cultural offerings and wide-ranging leisure activities. Tragically, most of those appearing in the film, both as spectators and athletes, were murdered just weeks after the end of filming.

In addition to the main propaganda films from Terezín, there was also an earlier Terezín film done by Jewish inmate Irene Dodalova and filmed by German security police (SD) cameramen. Shot in 1942, this first film, more brief than its successors, is a prologue intended to reflect "normality" through realism. Numerous shots of the so-called Jewish self-administration (food distribution, youth welfare, and the work and economic departments) of the ghetto are interspersed with scenes of labor, leisure, and life in the barracks. The film also tells the story of an individual family from Prague arriving and settling into the camp. [23]

Football is shown briefly in this film too. In late October 1942, coinciding with the worst period in the ghetto when captives endured the most misery and the death rate was the highest, prisoners played soccer on embankments around the fortress. The games were played on a very cold, muddy field next to a newly constructed crematorium (shown briefly in the background) built to the south of the ghetto walls to handle the mass influx of bodies requiring disposal. Though this first film was not meant directly as propaganda, the realistic scenes likely inspired Nazi officials to move forward with their more sophisticated deception. One can view the Dodalova film as a test run for the later films.

Terezín survivors and historians have long assumed that the staged nature of the main, more well-known *Documentary Film from the Jewish Settlement Area*, detracted from its impact. But Dutch historian Karel Margry argues differently:

> The film's visual authenticity is much greater than most people think. Many of the things shown in it actually existed in Theresienstadt or formed part of the prisoners' daily life—and not just in 1944, but before as well. A number of scenes were filmed on locations that had not been "beautified." Even the narration—the main truth-distorting element in the film—contains elements of factual truth. In the final analysis, the film's blatant dishonesty turns on what it did *not* show: the hunger, the misery, the overcrowding, the slave work for the German war economy, the high death rate, and, most of all, the transports leaving for the east.[24]

One survivor in particular recalled the power of these deceptions many years after the war. Peter Erben, one of the star players of the Terezín top league, remembers the difficulty in relating his ghetto experiences to his post-Holocaust life: "We didn't try to explain, because nobody would understand us," he recalls. "I'm very lucky that in this film, I see myself playing football. [This means] that everything was true, not a story I was telling to somebody."[25]

Curiously, the dated black-and-white film remains a powerful piece of propaganda, incomplete as it is. At the time of completion, the most notorious of the propaganda films created by the Nazis did not reach a wide audience. Yet one can witness surviving film clips on websites, readily employed by Holocaust deniers in their grotesque perversion of historical fact for many years after the war. The films represent another attempt by the National Socialists to deceive those who one day would judge them. At the center of the more widely known of the propaganda films was the league football, employed as a means of mass persuasion for future observers of this place of indescribable suffering, the ghetto Terezín.

LIGA TEREZÍN

Prisoners in Theresienstadt responded to their harsh captivity in many ways. Music and art in the barracks and public spaces often reflected the moment and offered a glimpse of escapist wishes. Thousands also responded by using their tortured bodies in athletic competition. Though their Nazi captors attempted to corrupt their athleticism for their own propagandistic purposes, the inspiration that organized football brought into the ghetto seeped down deeply into the lives of thousands in Terezín. Whether it was afternoon "kickabouts" outside of the boys' homes or the regularly scheduled matches featuring former professional footballers, soccer enthralled many. These Sunday-afternoon matches came to be known as Liga Terezín, and many would owe their lives to their existence.

Liga Terezín consisted of three leagues: a main, professional-level league and leagues hosting amateur and youth players. The premier league played a regular schedule in spring and autumn seasons. Initially, the top division featured ten teams (expanding to twelve in the second season), and the second division held two groups of seven teams each. Two teams from the lower division earned promotion, with the bottom two teams of the top league relegated to the lower tier. Wins earned teams two points, and in the first spring league, the kitchen team (Köche) tallied a 60–18 goal differential, nearly twice that of eventual winners Kleiderkammer (clothing store). Köche would go on to claim the fall 1943 championship. Altogether, some 667 players chased the football in Terezín.[26] Summer 1943 saw the first league and division competitions, and a cup competition was added in the fall when the weather stayed unseasonably warm. All teams in Terezín played first-round matches until twelve teams remained. From there, group winners of three four-team pools played a round-robin playoff to determine the champion. Sparta outlasted all comers.

Tournaments were usually held in the fully enclosed courtyard of Block H5 (the Dresden *Kaserne*, or barracks), where spectators sat in the windows overlooking the square.[27] Matches usually involved seven players on a side, consisting of a keeper, two defenders, a back midfielder, and three strikers, with teams wearing uniforms with a yellow star on them. Halves typically lasted thirty to thirty-five minutes with a ten-minute extra period as needed. Games were high scoring (658 goals in ninety games in spring 1943), often mirroring the scores found in modern-day futsal (soccer variation with a smaller field and five players per side) matches.[28]

Match tickets quickly became a hot commodity in the ghetto. Women in the ghetto workshops created the football strips worn by the youth players. These primitive uniforms were sources of unity and provided a bond among teammates. At the highest level of play, teams traded flags before matches. One such rare artifact, an Electricians' team flag, which was exchanged in a game on August 13, 1944, now resides in the Beit Terezín archive in Israel.[29]

Other barracks hosted matches, usually in the open spaces of central courtyards. With women housed in the Dresden Barracks, the site of the most important matches in Terezín, the Hannover Barracks, home to many workmen, staged other matches. Even for a city converted to a Jewish ghetto, and the only one of its kind in Nazi Europe, the Hannover field was a poor substitute. With rocky pavement on each side, footballers were careful to avoid falls from the pitch. Games were interrupted with the arrival of delivery vehicles bringing mattresses, furniture, or other supplies. Plum trees lined one side of the field, and players remember playing on when the ball bounced off of the branches and back onto the field. One macabre event saw nurses on the second floor taking away a dead woman distracted by an ongoing match down below. Leaving their stretcher in the entry gate to the barracks, the nurses turned back to watch. Death had become so routine in the ghetto that residents of Hannover Barracks had to walk around the corpse as captivated fans watched on.[30]

The *Ältestenrat* explicitly supported Liga Terezín, with many of the most important matches opened by a delegate of the council. Interestingly, the Jewish self-administration office also set up a soccer commission, led first by a rabbi, and separate discipline and umpire commissions, often awarding prizes to the respective winners of each league.[31] One trophy, donated by another labor department in the ghetto, was an "elegantly carved" goalkeeper.

The soccer committee, made up of former professionals and high-status members of the Jewish community, supervised the umpire commission, and each took their duties very seriously. Out of necessity, the umpire commission (comprising former professional referees from Germany, Austria, and Czechoslovakia who had refereed in their re-

spective premier leagues) increased over time from about a dozen officials to twenty-four. These referees oversaw a seemingly exhausting
schedule of matches: more than 778 league and cup matches, 512 youth
games, and several exhibition matches. [32]

Former Terezín inmate Kurt Ladner, a player on the "youth welfare" team, remembered that only seven umpires managed the top
league matches but that they served the community admirably. The
remaining umpires carried on with dozens of other matches. Junior
umpires, coming from the soccer-mad boys' homes in the ghetto,
trained in practices and yearned to move up the ranks, but, in the view
of one unnamed survivor, "the junior umpires have not proven themselves enough in practice to bring relief to the current league umpires." [33]

Across Theresienstadt, captives avidly followed the games. Results
were posted publicly at the Magdeburg Barracks, the seat of the Council of Elders. Volunteers were recruited to secure and repair goals,
locate substitute benches, line the fields, and remove rocks and debris.
The soccer committee also assigned a doctor to each major match.
Sporting posters advertising the matches were drawn by Terezín artists.
Game results, league standings, and statistics appeared in the sports
pages of makeshift ghetto newspapers, published by the Jewish children
in the ghetto. Children also played in their own youth league, taking
team names from Jewish heroes and, in one instance, Arsenal, as many
Czech Jewish youth were fans of English teams.

Ivan Klíma arrived in Theresienstadt in 1941 along with his parents
as a confused and frightened ten-year-old. Klíma had no idea he was
Jewish until the Nazis occupied his hometown of Prague. Baptized as a
Protestant, Klíma lived in the ghetto from 1941 until the Russian liberation in May 1945. Like so many Czech boys, he was obsessed with
soccer, joining with the youth team Blau-Weiss (blue and white, the
colors of the Zionist youth movement in central Europe, which were
also the colors of the famed Hakoah Vienna). In the ghetto, Klíma
risked everything to find a proper pair of football boots:

> One day, I got into the warehouse where suitcases were stored and I
> found mountain climbing shoes in one of them. I took them and had
> no idea what punishment could follow if anyone found out. I tried
> them out in the [youth] match of Prague against Berlin that hap-
> pened on Bašta III [the south rampart lawn]. I played in them until

halftime, got through the opponents defense, and even scored the leading goal. But the shoes were scraping me, so I took them off at halftime and played barefoot as the goalie. I wasn't as good as the goalie. I got scored on half a dozen times, and we lost 1–6. When I wasn't playing, I went to watch the matches of the grownups. . . . I loved to play because it was an escape from a catastrophe. We did not think of the transports, not even about life in the ghetto or the stress that Terezín caused us.[34]

Blind fortune saved Ivan Klíma and his family; his father was an engineer in the ghetto, sparing the family from deportation. Klíma survived the occupation, going on to become an acclaimed novelist and playwright and writing about his experiences as a highly respected dissident voice in postwar Czech society. He outlasted two totalitarian regimes to see his once-blacklisted books translated into twenty-nine languages. Klíma was also honored with the Franz Kafka Prize for literature, an award given to Nobel laureates as well as his fellow countryman Václav Havel. But it was his experiences in the boys' homes of Terezín that forever shaped his life.

When Czech civilians were forced out of the town in summer 1942, Jewish leaders in Theresienstadt created special homes to shield and protect children from the deadly realities of the ghetto. Organized by building, many of the boys' homes (*heims*) promoted a communal spirit in keeping with Zionist ideals. Surreptitious schools were set up in the rustic barracks to fulfill the hope that Jewish children had a future. Students lacked paper, pencils, and schoolbooks, but their drive to learn was nurtured by caring teachers who taught using only their memories.

Sport fit perfectly in building and galvanizing a collective identity, and the boys of Terezín really took to it. The importance of the games to the children, as spectators and as players in the youth league, cannot be overstated. Terezín's young, aspiring sports journalists excitedly relayed news of the leagues to almost all of the ghetto's youngest captives. Soccer consumed much of their time outside of school and the camp duties assigned by parents and mentors. One teacher-mentor remembered fondly by survivors was František Maier, the organizer for the youth team Nesharim (Hebrew for "eagles") and goalkeeper for top-division side Jugendfürsorge. Maier led the group of boys from the famous L417 room in Theresienstadt. The Czech children's magazine *Rim, Rim, Rim* (Go, Go, Go) was secretly published in Terezín throughout 1944 and was the house magazine of the boys from home VII in ghetto building L417. An unnamed but earnest reporter offered this detailed account of a spring 1944 youth league match between Hagibor and Union to his restless readers:

> I arrived at the yard of the Dresden Barrack, which had turned into a football field. . . . At that moment, the umpire blows the whistle and Hagibor takes the field. It is exactly the third quarter. One can hear the people cheer and Union arrives. After kickoff, the game begins. It is the third quarter and two minutes. . . . Attack after attack. Sadlo, Hagibor's right wing, tears away and scores the first goal in the twelfth minute. After that everybody gathers in the center. Now the game is heating up. . . . Union's center forward gets the ball, passes to right wing Kovanitz, who pulls through and kicks. A brilliant goal. . . . Hagibor's players are obviously angry, attack and kick . . . and goal! Hagibor leads 3–1. The second half starts with fierce inter-action. . . . Hagibor is again successful, makes its fourth goal. The score is 4–1. Union's line of strikers attacks; the center forward hits a cannonball toward the goal. At this moment it happens; Hagibor's goalkeeper Parille lets the ball slip in. It was clearly his fault. . . . The game is getting uninteresting now. Both sides are exhausted. They are all saving their strength for the end. But all of a sudden here comes Kovanitz; he runs and shoots a goal. . . . The game is great again. . . . Strike after strike. In that moment, the left wing makes a beautiful shot: GOAL! 7–5. The umpire blows the whistle. The game is over and Hagibor wins. [35]

League soccer shows up frequently in the diaries and memoirs of these child prisoners and in their art from the ghetto, famously documented after the war. [36] The fact that children particularly loved to play reflects the true labor of childhood, the unbridled joy of playing. Street soccer was played all over the ghetto as kids used shoes, rags, and rocks for goals. The newspapers, drawings, collages, and journals kept by children in the ghetto also reveal an innocent fascination with this alternate reality. All around is suffering and death, but to focus on the joy of sport helped distance these impressionable young people from the worst of it.

The children of Terezín loved their football. Many remember the contributions of a German Jew named Alfred "Fredy" Hirsch, who landed in Prague in 1939 after fleeing Nazi persecution. Many give credit to Hirsch for establishing the rich educational and sporting programs for children in the transit camp. The confident and charismatic Hirsch arrived early at Terezín, part of the *Aufbaukommando* tasked with setting up the administration of the ghetto. Fredy was crucial in setting up the *heims*—the eleven children's houses in the ghetto where mentors and teachers carried on training the next generation. Hirsch organized sporting competitions (the 1943 "Maccabi Games" stand out) and theater productions for hundreds of children held captive in Terezín. Teamwork, responsibility, and physical fitness, wrapped in a Zionist message, inspired these youngest prisoners.

Pavel Weiner was a twelve-year-old boy in Terezín when he started to keep a diary of his experiences in one of these famous boys' homes, L417. The diary covers the final year of his three-year imprisonment in Theresienstadt, revealing in poignant detail his obsession with soccer, arguments with his parents, daily worries about hunger, fears of atrocities in the camp, and ongoing dread about deportation. Dozens of match results and hand-drawn sketches of players adorn his diary. Adolescent angst dominates his writing as he ruminates about cravings for freedom, food, and friendships. Pavel was committed to his schooling, and always preoccupied with the next soccer match. He appears to be a temperamental boy, often quarreling with his friends, teachers, and parents. As he tried to absorb the horrors of the camp, he also distanced himself by focusing on football.

For so many boys in Terezín, nothing could compare to playing and watching soccer. The men in the top league were heroes. One Sunday-afternoon cup final in 1944 was all the boys could talk about. Pavel Weiner returned from the library, where he had finished reading *The Merchant of Venice*, and as he tried to meet up with his father from another barrack, he worried that they would be late. Young Pavel picks it up from there:

> *Sunday, 13 August 1944:* I quickly eat supper and go straight to the match. The match between Rapid and Spedice [Spedition] for third and fourth place is not interesting and its score is 3–1. The Dresdner Barracks are overcrowded when the final begins. Both teams [Jugendfürsorge, or "Jufa." and Elektra] are greeted with applause. During the game, blue pieces of paper are thrown to the ground. The Jufa team is cheered on boisterously. At halftime, Jufa is ahead one to nothing. During the second half the goals start to pile up. Passer is playing very roughly, and when he kicks Franta, he is

thrown out of the rest of the game, which ends in a score of 5–1. Jufa wins the cup! On the way home we meet a boy who, as a result of a bet on the game, must walk around with a muzzle and a leash of a Great Dane.[37]

Soccer was an escape from a crushing and deadly reality. With so many captives playing football in nearly every open patch of grass and in the quads of the largest barracks, conversations inevitably turned to who the best players were and who could claim the honor of the most beautiful goal scored in Liga Terezín. Most famous among all the players, especially among the Czech population, was former Czechoslovak national team player Paul Mahrer, imprisoned at Terezín soon after the German occupation. Mahrer featured a half-dozen times for his country, starring in the 1924 Paris Olympics. Soon upon arrival, he joined up with Liga Terezín for the Butchers' team. Though Mahrer was over forty years of age when deported, he was wildly popular, particularly among the soccer-crazy boys of Terezín. Amid this popularity, Mahrer acknowledged in a sobering recollection, "Football was a kind of comfort in hell's waiting room."[38]

The account of one spectacular goal, scored in the final summer of organized play in Terezín, finds its place time and again in memoirs and in archival records of ghetto football. Even though so few early memoirs focused on football in Terezín, deeming it inconsequential to the prisoner experience, a goal by one of the great ghetto strikers stands out in recent recollections. A thirty-five-meter blast into the upper corner of the goal (slightly larger than a two-meter-high-by-three-meter-wide handball goal) by Egon Reach is mentioned by more survivors than any other. Reach, a member of the league commission and a player from the Kader team (second in the spring 1944 league), scored in a July 2, 1944, match. The goal gave Kader the lead, but on the day, rivals Elektra (the electricians' team) battled back to tie the game 2–2.[39] Memory can be unpredictable and malleable; these contemporary recollections suggest that the importance of football to lifting up the spirits of the prisoners was better appreciated with the passage of time.

In the summer of 1944, at the start of the final year of operation of the camp, there were between two and three thousand women and men who played soccer, primarily on the earthen walls of the ramparts on the southwestern outskirts of the ghetto or in the Dresden courtyard.[40] In the highest league in the ghetto, some teams were more dominant than others. In one notable instance, the youth welfare department team (Jugendfürsorge) beat Hagibor (the team named after a Jewish sport organization from Prague) 14–1 in the ninth round of the Terezín league in 1944. One-sided games were not unusual, and the youth care team in particular enjoyed success because of recruiting. Judging from the extant league tables, there were typically three to four teams vying for the league championship in a given season (out of twelve). And not surprisingly, the teams representing the butchers and the kitchen usually fared well.[41]

There were practical concerns in the administration of the Terezín league. Composition of the teams changed frequently as many were deported or died within the ghetto walls. Replacing deported players presented a real challenge for organizers, but the additional food rations given to players made this a highly desired leisure pursuit. Every Monday, from ten a.m. to two p.m., there was a transfer window during which teams replaced players who had been lost or deported. Typically, you needed excellent social connections to be allowed onto a team, and you often needed to have a respected position or job with a corresponding favorable allocation of food.[42] In order to play for an hour or more on end in the league games, you needed these food reserves. Survivors reported that the football, at every level, was not a consolation but an effort to reclaim their humanity.

The popularity of the best matches in Terezín translated into a demand for an added competition. In the very month that saw an acceleration of final deportations from the ghetto, a "SuperCup" competition was born. Played in the Hannover Barracks on September 1, 1944, the match brought together the winners of the spring 1944 league, SK Sparta, to play against cup winners Jugendfürsorge. A capacity crowd of 3,600 spectators saw SK Sparta unexpectedly crush Jufa 8–1.[43]

Players were adored by the fans, and artist "Honza" Burka, more famous in the camp as a prolific striker, remembers well the ghetto soccer in his book *To Paint, So as to Survive*.[44] Burka played for Jufa, and he fondly recalls Sunday game days when soccer provided a respite from the anguish: "The size of the square at Dresden barracks was 45 by 75 meters. Since there was not enough room for everybody, many crowded in the arcades of the barracks. . . . For many prisoners this was a special day, when they could forget their misery for a few hours."[45]

Preservation from the unremitting hunger in the ghetto was a privilege not afforded to those gathered in the arcades. Most players were well aware of their privileged status. By the very nature of the camp and ghetto system devised by the Nazis, prisoners had to fight among each other, often fiercely, to survive. But with fame came little need to quarrel. Interviewed many years after his time in the ghetto, Burka remembered well how he could expend so much energy in practices and matches without suffering from starvation. He recalled fondly the kindness of strangers in the daily struggle to eat:

> As a player, I wasn't hungry in Terezín, because I worked in the kitchen of the Dresden Barracks and that had one advantage for the physical state of the players of our team. Games were usually played on the weekends. In those days I would ask the head of the kitchen, Greta, a very nice woman, if I could give out the lunches. That was without problems. In front of the kitchen, in a long hallway, young girls stood to collect the meal vouchers from the prisoners. I sometimes gave them the signal to let my teammates through so they could be well taken care of. They sometimes came two or three times and they would carry away full tins of food, and that is how they had enough energy to play soccer.[46]

The footballers in Terezín were protected, especially the young men who made up the great majority of the teams. Naturally, when these players were given special access to quality food, it meant that someone else, with a voucher, was deprived. But the protests were few and the celebrated status of these men prolonged their lives.

As players in the ghetto competed under the daily threat of deportation and death, their popularity only grew. Among the spectators were SS officers who enjoyed special box seats reserved in the middle of the barracks courtyard. Each SS man had his favorite team, and betting on the matches entangled the officers with the prisoner-players. Acclaimed Czech author Arnošt Lustig, a fifteen-year-old Jew in Theresienstadt, wrote of his experiences at one of these soccer matches where a loss meant that lives hung in the balance:

> I would bet that the defense—the goalie, and who knows who else from the midfield—would very soon get a summons card for a transport east. Some officers inspect lists of transports from Prague so they can take off former players from Hagibor [an all-Jewish profes-

sional team]. . . . Soccer is a bridge from the past; we are privileged to watch individual players and make guesses as to what will befall them. For a number of people, soccer is worth the risk, which no one tries to hide, even though there's not much talk about it. After each serious injury, the affected player finds himself in a transport east, though a great many players would have been there long ago were it not for soccer.[47]

Lustig later survived Auschwitz and Buchenwald before making a harrowing escape in 1945 from a transport train headed to Dachau that had been bombed by an American fighter plane.

Burka also remembers people queuing up in the early morning hours waiting for the chance to enter the barracks to watch matches:

The center box at the first floor was kept for the SS and I am convinced that during the matches all the hate that existed between us was gone; the SS men applauded loudly and enthusiastically during the matches as if they were Jews. . . . My team won the title in the league of 1942, in the 1943 league the butchers won. Before the final match our trainer gave to each member of our team half a lemon. It remains a mystery, how he managed to put his hands on such a treasure.[48]

In his autobiography, *In My Own Footsteps*, Petr Erben writes extensively about his experiences playing fullback for the youth welfare department team. Deported late in the war to the ghetto at age twenty-one, Erben kept up his fitness with daily runs and regular involvement in athletic activities. He recalls: "I was young and worked at a job that did not cause me physical hardship. My view was that the food in the ghetto was good and the quantity reasonable. For old people who did not work it was not enough. I, on the other hand, received from time to time additional rations at work, here a piece of bread and there some cheese. Those who looked well and had no Jewish nose got more."[49] According to Erben, the matches had a competitive atmosphere and players would often insult each other before matches. "The playing was serious. . . . We played 'fair play' and did not hurt each other. We really felt to be sportsmen. There was a healthy envy. We won—you lost, but the friendship endured."[50] Though hardly representative of the typical experience for an inmate of Terezín, this privileged status undoubtedly helped Erben survive and later endure slave labor in the notorious labor camp of Mauthausen toward the end of the war.

Petr Erben also found himself entangled in Nazi propaganda. He was required to take part in Kurt Gerron's "record" of the ghetto, and he played the role of actor in several scenes, taking a coffee in the ghetto "coffeehouse," watching a dance competition, and competing in the final league match. For the match, Erben played defense, and he featured conspicuously, wearing a white bandana and shown in the film as running at full pace to catch up to a ball nearing the goal while under pressure from a defender. Though so much of the propaganda film was staged, when the cameras were focused on the Sunday league matches, no one needed to act. Their joy was authentic.[51]

The Terezín league sometimes included players from different national teams across central Europe. One player mentioned frequently in survivor accounts is Jirka Taussig, the onetime goalkeeper for the Czechoslovakia national team. Taussig was well known to the soccer players of Terezín even before his arrival in 1943. "They told me I was like a strip of flypaper," Taussig recalls.[52] Also a standout player in Czechoslovakia's youth system, Taussig was banned from playing after the Nazi takeover of his country and was sent via transport in June 1943 to Terezín.

Because he was already known to many of the captives at Terezín, there is the suggestion that there was active recruiting of players, possibly even before prisoners had deboarded the trains. Of his time playing for the Kleiderkammer team in Terezín, Taussig recalled in an interview:

> We were the stars of Terezín; every Sunday afternoon 3,500 fans came to watch the league matches. Youth saw us as a model to imitate, we gave them hope, and we represented life. In all the misery and suffering hope was a rare thing! We played for them, because we knew that shortly they would be sent east and we felt that we gave them a little spark of light before their death.[53]

The formal league competitions in Terezín ceased at the end of September when five thousand of the most able-bodied men were deported to prevent a rebellion. With the final departure of the transports on October 28, 1944, whatever soccer teams remaining were disbanded. After this final push, only about four hundred people (mostly women) remained in the ghetto. As in other camps in the colonial east, the scramble to cover up Nazi crimes raged on. In November 1944, the ashes of over twenty thousand inmates were dumped into the nearby Ohře River, a tributary of the Elbe.

These athletic performances at Terezín were a source of strength and personal pride, and they served as a symbol of resistance. By the time recording for the second propaganda film began, the Allied landings at Normandy were a well-known fact inside the camp. Later that summer of 1944, the Soviets liberated the death camp of Majdanek in eastern Poland, revealing to the world the full scope of the Nazi crimes. And from September 1944, Allied aircraft frequently appeared in the skies above Terezín. It was at this very moment in the history of Terezín that the soccer league reached its completion and the fateful destiny of the remaining prisoners of the ghetto Theresienstadt was made known.

THE LEGACY OF GHETTO THERESIENSTADT

In the final eight months of the war, chaos reigned in the Nazi empire. Allied forces were closing in on the Reich from all sides, and a desperate attempt to hold on to Jewish prisoners saw dreadful death marches commenced, first in Poland and later in other occupied territories. Terezín would bear the consequences of these forced migrations as more than fifteen thousand entered the ghetto-camp as haggard survivors of barbarous labor camps and extermination centers.[54] Most arrived at Terezín in open freight carriages, with many arriving on foot in the chaos of the final weeks of the war.

Among these prisoners were those who had left Theresienstadt just weeks earlier only to return to their misery. The new arrivals brought deadly typhus into the ghetto. The miserable, hungry, and sick masses needed the greatest care, and Terezín could not provide it. The ghetto-camp was liberated by the Russians on May 8, 1945, the same day of the German unconditional surrender ending the war in Europe. Twelve thousand inmates plus another five thousand evacuees from other camps lived to see freedom.

Justice was served for notorious camp commandant Karl Rahm, who was installed as senior SS officer in February 1944, just ahead of the beautification project and the final propaganda film. Rahm oversaw all of the mass deportations toward the end of the war, which resulted in the deaths of thousands in Birkenau's gas chambers. Soon after the evacuation of the ghetto, Commandant Rahm was captured by U.S. forces in his home country of Austria and was later extradited to Prague in 1947, where he was put on trial and hanged four hours after his guilty verdict.

Hundreds would succumb to diseases like typhus and malnutrition in the weeks following liberation despite the efforts of relief agencies and the Red Army. Once quarantine was lifted, thousands of survivors, representing twenty-nine nations, were finally saved and repatriated to their homes. Memorialization of the dead began almost immediately, beginning with the graveyard outside the Small Fortress, where Jewish and Russian victims of the typhus outbreak were buried.

In the four years that the ghetto-camp Theresienstadt was in operation, tens of thousands of people entered the walled town with the hope of extending their lives just a bit longer. Unbeknownst to many, Terezín was merely a holding pen for Auschwitz. In the end, thirty-five thousand died within the ghetto itself, with most of these victims coming from among the very young and the elderly. But the vast majority, nearly eighty-eight thousand people, was sent to the Polish extermination camps. Of those who were deported to Poland, just 3,097 survived.[55]

The first major memorials at Terezín appeared in 1955. As the decades passed, select buildings were restored, testimonies were gathered, and a documentation archive was established. Antifascist and anti-imperialist remembrances dominated the communist years, with Jewish victims ignored altogether. As late as 1989, no museum, monument, or plaque honored those who suffered in Theresienstadt. The memorials that did follow were scattered across the former ghetto: at the crematorium and the columbarium (the repository of cremated remains of victims), at the arrival depot and the boys' home of Building L417 (the main museum and start of the ghetto tour today), and at the Magdeburg Barracks, the seat of the Jewish "self-administration."

Efforts to preserve the deteriorating town have uncovered inspiring sites of survival that have become sites of remembrance. Modern restoration work recently revealed a hidden prayer room with Hebrew script and stars still colorfully visible on the walls, where prisoners held on to faith in the face of abject terror. The last signs of life were etched on the walls of the Poterne III, a dark tunnel gate that once held prisoners awaiting deportation to Auschwitz. Names, initials, dates, and a few pictures (a Chanukah menorah and portraits of ghetto police members) were inscribed on sandstone walls. Oft-repeated dates of 1942, 1943, and 1944 mark the final moments for many. Erosion and vandalism threaten to wipe away these records.

Collective memory of the incarceration and suffering at Terezín echo forward. Graphic and literary remnants, carefully preserved, fill the main ghetto museums. Among the youngest prisoners, art and diary keeping were precious records of personal experience. Children embraced their chance to draw and paint. These activities gave meaning to experience, especially for those unable to articulate what they were enduring. One Bauhaus-trained painter who supervised art instruction for the children of Terezín managed to hide five thousand of their humble drawings in a suitcase left behind with a friend before her deportation to Auschwitz in October 1944.[56]

The story of Liga Terezín would not be told formally and completely until the twenty-first century. These prisoner-players left a legacy, like their fellow captives, produced under the most inhumane conditions. Today, the modern day Dresden Barracks, where the most important Liga Terezín matches were once played, are derelict and in need of significant restoration. Visitors are kept away for their own safety. Yet playing the sport that continues to captivate the world today nourished the souls imprisoned in Terezín.

For those who clung to life through football, Liga Terezín was the best organized and most distinctive of the football leagues that emerged in the Nazi camps and ghettos. The league drew the biggest crowds and offered the highest quality of football owing to the collection of famous Jewish footballers. The commitment and enthusiasm for football was unmatched. In the most unique of all the destinations in Nazi Europe, football rejected the deceit and subterfuge of the Nazis. The most essential human right—the right to exist, to live—was celebrated on the courtyard soccer fields of Terezín.

In contemporary Prague, the Pinkas Synagogue, located in the heart of the historic Jewish Quarter, venerates the thousands of Czech Jews lost in the Holocaust. Inscribed on the walls of this once-active sixteenth-century synagogue are the names, birthdates, and dates of disappearance of 77,297 lost to Nazi aggression in occupied Czechoslovakia.

Recorded from transport papers, Nazi registration lists, and survivor testimonies, each victim has a name. Of the names collected by town of origin, one stands out, in the Brno section: Pavel Breda. This player from the league at Terezín is the second footballer seen running onto the courtyard field in the infamous propaganda film.

Sadly, these memorials sometimes do little to assuage the fears of those still alive to remember the Nazi menace. Such indifference to the past remains a serious concern to many as the scourge of racism and anti-Semitism remains. One modern witness who remembers vividly the horrors of this time is Dr. Toman Brod, a survivor of Terezín. Brod recalls, "Football was a matter of pleasure. We needed some pleasure in our desperate times, our desperate lives." Brod, today a Czech historian, was in his early teenage years a loyal Liga Terezín supporter. "Many things were crazy, but they were reality, and so it was very important not to lose our sense of human dignity."[57] In November 2011, for the first time since his return from Theresienstadt seventy years ago, Brod attended a Sparta–Liverpool football match at the Sparta Prague stadium. But before he entered the football grounds, he saw anti-Jewish graffiti on the walls of the grandstand that marks Jews as a threat and the embodiment of evil.[58] One must not forget that the need to create and to compete, essential to the human spirit, draws people like Toman Brod to the game of soccer. The heroism shown by each footballer in Terezín stands as a rejection of anti-Semitism and offers an indelible reminder of human resilience. We have an obligation to listen, reflect, and remember.

9

AFTER THE CATASTROPHE

"Only guard yourself and guard your soul carefully, lest you forget the things your eyes saw, and lest these things depart your heart all the days of your life, and you shall make them known to your children, and to your children's children."—Deuteronomy 4:9

Nothing prepared battle-hardened Allied soldiers for what they would encounter as they drove deep into Nazi Germany in early 1945. Inconceivable horrors greeted the liberators, first as the Soviets reached the major killing centers in Poland. For many who had experienced firsthand the brutality of Nazi Germany on the battlefront and in the faces and stories of those recently released from occupation, shocking scenes awaited. Continuing their genocidal rampage to the very end, Nazi oppressors fled their crimes, leaving abandoned camps, mass graves, boxcars overflowing with corpses, and thousands upon thousands of emaciated, dying prisoners.

The nature of the atrocities faced by Allied liberators is tragically exemplified in the transformation of concentration camp Bergen-Belsen in the final year of the war. At the end of 1944, the camp held fifteen thousand prisoners; by the time the British arrived on April 15, 1945, a massive influx of prisoners, largely from Eastern Europe, had quadrupled the number. Even for those who had endured Auschwitz, Bergen-Belsen offered a staggering measure of suffering beyond comprehension. The Nazis made no effort to house or feed the thousands in the camp. Overcrowding meant that there were no bunks or toilets. Barracks, many half built, fell apart, exposing people to the elements.

Many lost their wits as they were left to die. Cries of thirst and anguished starvation filled the nights.

One Auschwitz survivor named Renee Salt was transported to Bergen-Belsen as a sixteen-year-old. Her first memory of arriving at the camp, after being forced to walk a road littered with the corpses of previous transports, is hellish: "We saw skeletons walking, their arms and legs were like matchsticks—the bones protruding through the remains of their skin. The stench that arose from the camp was terribly overpowering. It seemed that, after all we've been through already, this was something new and horribly different."[1] On the same day that British troops freed Bergen-Belsen, SS officers and camp guards from Ravensbrück and Sachsenhausen marched seventeen thousand women and forty thousand men westward and deeper into the last German-controlled areas.[2] Amid the total collapse of Nazi Germany, these prisoners would not be released.

Similar scenes awaited American liberators at Dachau, Mauthausen, and Buchenwald. Recently liberated captives often could not comprehend the new reality. Enfeebled and terrorized, many inmates struggled to make the transition to freedom. Hundreds died of typhus and other diseases in the days after liberation, assuming they had survived the death marches in the first place. On countless roads and railways across Europe, prisoners died of exhaustion and hundreds more by SS bullets and stray Allied bombs. An estimated 250,000 to 375,000 perished on these forced marches, which continued right up until the German surrender.

The collapse came with a fitting coda. Just over a week before capitulation, Adolf Hitler committed suicide in his vast underground bunker in Berlin. Alongside was his new wife and the ever-faithful propaganda minister Joseph Goebbels, who, with his wife, had carefully poisoned their six children before killing themselves. Thus ended the Nazi revolution, which had proclaimed a triumphant return to national glory just twelve years earlier. Instead, the world suffered death and destruction beyond imagining—an estimated fifty to fifty-five million people died in the Second World War, with almost half of those coming from the Soviet Union alone. Five million German soldiers died, along with nearly six million Jews. It all began with promises of glory, territorial expansion, and the pursuit of racial purification. But it ended in a whimper of cowardice and the ruin of a country widely considered to be among the most civilized in the world.

For those who survived, the end of the war did not mean the end of the Holocaust. Disease and malnourishment claimed thousands after Hitler's defeat. In Bergen-Belsen alone, three hundred inmates died each day over a two week span immediately after liberation. By mid-May 1945, millions of people were on the move, often against their will, as others sought to return to their homelands. These "displaced persons" (or DPs) came to represent the largest migration of people in the shortest amount of time in human history. And the Allied armies were ill prepared to administer the peace. At Dachau and dozens of other former Nazi concentration camps, prisoners remained behind barbed-wire fences, often wearing the same striped camp uniforms that only days prior had been a despicable symbol of Nazi oppression. Worse yet, in some DP camps prisoners lived side by side with Nazi POWs who had been their wartime persecutors.

In the chaotic mix of fugitives and refugees in these places, Jews were but one small minority among a multitude of different peoples looking to restart their lives. Few would categorize the suffering of the Jews as unique in the broader scope of the European catastrophe. Insult followed injury for many. Exiled Jews from the former Reich found themselves treated as "enemy nationals" rather than as victims. They were viewed suspiciously as Germans and Austrians first. Tosia Schneider, a Polish Jew who survived deportation and forced labor, recalled in a 2006 interview, "I tried to lead some kind of a normal life. It was a difficult, confusing time for me. You have to realize: I had lost my whole family, not just the immediate family, but my home town, my neighborhood, my place in the world, there was no time for mourning, and suddenly it all came back and we became aware of all the losses."[3]

Jewish survivors called themselves "She'erith Hapletah," the surviving or spared remnant, a term taken from ancient Hebrew scripture in the Book of Ezra (9:14–15), which speaks of the resilience and vitality of the Jewish people. In these times, the obliteration of Jewish communities across Europe haunted the residents of these assembly centers. Survivors' attempts to rebuild their lives were profoundly interrupted as thousands were prevented from leaving DP camps. The victors imposed strict immigration quotas on refugees seeking to leave Europe for Britain or America. Families torn asunder, survivors usually had nowhere to go. For those who left Germany for the East, the outcomes were no better. In Ukraine and Poland, for example, many Jews saw their Gentile neighbors claim their homes and property, meeting them with hostility and violence upon their return home.

The Germans and their allies had it much better. Prisoner-of-war camps in Europe and in the United States were generally well run and hospitable, in line with the Geneva Conventions. Ex-Nazis and Wehrmacht soldiers played soccer and watched movies, and some even enrolled in college courses. In the Jewish DP camps, survivors of the Holocaust had to fight for extra rations after years of starvation. Shockingly, the medical needs of the DPs were attended to by German doctors and nurses—many of the same people who had inflicted the deadly medicine of the Nazis in their euthanasia and prisoner experimentation programs just weeks earlier. While a few prominent Nazi doctors and medical officials would face justice in the ensuing years, thousands more transitioned seamlessly to service in Allied-run hospitals and clinics. One grotesque example saw more than six hundred medical personnel—doctors, nurses, orderlies, and dentists—join the Allied medical staff at Dachau, the Nazis' first concentration camp and site of the first horrific medical experiments on POWs and political prisoners.[4]

With tens of millions of people migrating in 1945, weary survivors crisscrossed Europe seeking a safe and hopeful landing. Remaining Jews from Hungary tried to return home; ethnic Germans, no longer welcome in western Poland and the Czech Sudetenland, fled north and west; and a motley collection of prisoners of war, demobilized soldiers, and former slave laborers sought relief from their deprivations. Many poured into the western zones of occupation in Germany controlled by the United States, France, and Britain.

Questions of rendering swift justice dominated the attention of the liberators. Attempts to "de-Nazify" Germany were met with evasion and deception. Perpetrators and collaborators went to great lengths to hide their identities. Others made their escape. While survivors struggled with confinement, thousands of Hitler's helpers either blended back into society or fled overseas, to South America or the United States, often with visas in hand. Each "hidden" Nazi who secured a precious exit visa to America meant that one fewer displaced person held in the Allied camps would get out. Seven million stateless people waited while Nazi collaborators, including a small cadre of SS officers, entered foreign countries harbored safely as so-called war refugees. The most notorious of these were Adolf Eichmann and Josef Mengele, two men directly implicated in the deaths of millions. Years after the war, investigations revealed that these Nazi fugitives had considerable assistance from the Vatican and the International Red Cross as they fled through Italy and the Middle East using secret escape routes and falsified travel documents provided by these two powerful institutions.[5] As long as these war criminals claimed to be anticommunist and Catholic, they had friends in high places.

Despite the impossibility of rendering complete justice, the Allies brought to account a handful of the masterminds of the Nazi genocide. In the course of their efforts, leaders of a combatant nation were held responsible for their deeds for the first time. By October 1946, the International Military Tribunal at Nuremberg had rendered historic and precedent-setting verdicts against twenty-one major Nazi criminals for their "crimes against humanity." Not mere "victors' justice" or a measure of revenge, the trials produced vast documentation and crucial eyewitness testimonies leading to meaningful criminal verdicts; some were acquitted, the death penalty came for about half of the Nazi elite, and suicide followed for the most famous defendant, Hitler's named successor and favorite confidante, Reichsmarschall Hermann Göring.

Word filtered back to London and Washington that survivors in the DP camps were suffering under Allied administration. At first, perpetrators, collaborators, bystanders, and victims were often all joined together in liberated camps and refugee centers. Inspections were ordered by President Truman, who sent an emissary, Earl Harrison, the dean of the University of Pennsylvania Law School. Jewish groups also pressed for the inspections. Frightening accounts of squalid living conditions, mistreatment, and abject misery could not be believed. But Harrison's report confirmed anecdotal claims, and the postwar euphoria in America and Britain dimmed a bit. Harrison succinctly concluded: "As matters now stand, we appear to be treating the Jews as the Nazis treated them except that we do not exterminate them."[6] Despite the hopelessness and contempt endured by those contained in DP camps, survivors of the worst genocide in human history responded with the passions they pursued before the war, and the greatest among these was soccer.

By the end of 1946, more than 150,000 Jews remained in German territory, but the proportion increased significantly over the following year to nearly one-third of all DPs living in the Western occupation zones. Organized initially by countries of origin, Jewish DP camps later became hotbeds of Zionist activity, and educational opportunities abounded. Many took to building a new generation: a baby boom exploded in Jewish DP camps, far outpacing others living in Germany.[7] Life prospered in many other ways. As was seen across wartime Europe, from labor camps in Ukraine and concentration camps in Germany to walled-off camps and ghettos in Czechoslovakia and Poland, soccer filled the lives of the people seeking to start anew and searching for hope after so much death.

Soccer in the DP camps was the most popular recreation among those whose political status was in limbo. Boxing also drew fervent support in the detention camps. The European Jewish diaspora proved that life would flourish again. Survivors cultivated their ancient traditions. Converting buildings that were once used to administer suffering, survivors established schools and Yiddish-language newspapers. They returned to Kosher cooking, opened Jewish libraries, and directed theater productions. But sports were far more popular than the rest. Thousands of athletes on hundreds of teams competed on fields across the British and American occupied zones. Curiously, Jewish sports clubs in the British zone were no match for those in the American zone in number, organization, or professionalism. DP camp soccer teams competed within supraregional leagues, and trophies and championship titles were awarded. Soccer was most certainly a distraction in the fight against the monotony of camp life, but it was also an ideological struggle—training for a Zionist future in Israel. We know most about sports that took place in the American zone because newspapers were widely available, serving as the primary sources of documentation.

Every other major camp in the American sector was obsessed with soccer. The Föhrenwald DP camp, third largest behind other Bavarian assembly centers named Landsberg and Feldafing, hosted many games in the DP camp league, which began play in 1946 followed by a formalized championship in 1947. Twelve teams from each of the major camps competed in two rounds, and Föhrenwald finished in fourth place, thirteen points behind winners Landsberg, who won seventeen of their twenty-two matches, suffering only a single loss.[8] In the earliest days of the DP camps, play was rough and spectators uncontrollable; consequently, a rules committee governed play, often enforcing strict league bylaws in stern fashion. One player identified in camps records only as "Steiner," from the second Föhrenwald team, was banned for two months for striking an opponent.

Located near Wolfratshausen, at the confluence of the Isar and Loisach rivers in southern Bavaria, Föhrenwald was originally built on the eve of the war to house IG Farben employees (the company that licensed the patent for deadly Zyklon B, the killing agent in the gas chambers). Föhrenwald would also play an outsized role in the history of post–World War II Europe, as the strongest refugee voice concerning immigration to Palestine came from within the camp.

Later transformed to hold slave laborers, Föhrenwald was hastily converted into a DP camp in June 1945. Streets in the camp were named after American states. Föhrenwald expanded rapidly with the arrival of new refugees and new births. Famously, within a year of its opening, nearly two hundred women were pregnant. Jewish culture proliferated: residents formed a yeshiva (a center for Hasidism) and a synagogue with *mikvah* (Jewish ritual bath); fire and police services and a vocational training institute began; residents could read at least two weekly newspapers; and Allied governors established a youth home, a camp court, and a genuine hospital.

In Landsberg, as in almost every DP facility, nearly all of the residents were between the ages of twenty and thirty-five. Those young and strong enough to survive as workers in the Third Reich filled the camp, with a heartbreaking absence of children and the elderly. At Feldafing, the birth of self-governance for Jewish captives gave American officials a model to use in the dozens of other DP destinations. Set on the shores of a lake and on the road to Innsbruck, with impressive stone buildings and military barracks, Feldafing was once the alpine destination for Hitler Youth members seeking elite training as the future of Nazi Germany.

Time was needed to set up sporting competitions in the tumult of occupation. Survival was first and foremost in the minds of camp administrators and residents. The search for surviving family and friends dominated waking hours. Bulletin boards in each camp held desperate handwritten messages of hope. Residents in the DP camps often lived nearby their places of liberation. Residents in these camps initially were

Poles, Ukrainians, and Latvians, some of whom were Nazi collaborators and included *kapos* from concentration camps. But after August 1945 and the findings of the critical Harrison Report, the camps were segregated for Jews alone.

Soon, everyday life returned, especially at the turn of the new year in 1946. Though it is not possible to pinpoint the start of the zone-wide football competitions, the first recorded match came in early October 1945: the camp newspaper at Landsberg announced a 7–0 victory of Ichud Landsberg over Maccabi Turkheim (the only exclusively Jewish camp in June 1945) with two thousand spectators looking on.[9] Sport clubs in Landsberg were particularly well organized: volleyball, basketball, track and field, table tennis, and boxing were all on offer. Except for soccer, boxing was the most popular competition as it reinforced a combative, pugilistic answer to years of anti-Semitic propaganda portraying Jews as weak and effeminate. Zionist fans embraced boxing as a type of national defense sport. Organized soccer started with friendly matches, and a highly competitive championship encompassing all of southern Germany soon followed.

Waves of Jews fleeing pogroms in Poland and economic depression in 1946 raised the number of Jewish DPs in the American zone from 40,000 to 145,000.[10] Officials worked to cultivate soccer fields, clearing out open spaces and requisitioning American machines to level out future football grounds. Donated equipment came not just from Jewish organizations but also from American charities, including Catholic and Protestant groups.

The DP camp at Bergen-Belsen will be forever associated with the concentration camp where Allied liberators discovered ten thousand unburied dead and sixty thousand prisoners, most barely alive.[11] After the camp stabilized, Jewish leadership began to look after the surviving remnant, Jews from Romania, Hungary, and Poland who accounted for almost seven of every ten residents in Bergen-Belsen. Sports clubs proliferated in track and field, table tennis, handball, and, inevitably, soccer. On July 19, 1946, Belsen's first team, calling themselves Hatikvah (Hope), played Ichud (The One) from Landsberg. So successful was the friendly that Ichud later played Belsen's second team, Hagibor (Hero), made up exclusively of Hungarian Jews. With 2,500 spectators on the sidelines, Ichud Landsberg thrashed Hagibor Belsen 4–0. Such huge attendance at these matches is especially remarkable when one realizes the largest of the DP camps held no more than five or six thousand people. Later, teams in the British-controlled zone, such as Bergen-Belsen, were excluded from the main DP camp league, which was limited to teams from the American sector. But other teams would form in the camp; one Polish team earned a match against British soldiers as early as November 1945.

The most improbable of survivors who played competitive football in Bergen-Belsen was Martin Abraham Stock, a German Jew who three times survived the lethal camps at Płaszów (Poland), Sachsenhausen, and Bergen-Belsen, to go on to become the first-ever Jewish representative on the executive board of the DFB in the postwar years. Stock, born in Hamburg, served in World War I after a successful career as a player and board member of an obscure German football club called Altona-Hamburg. Purged from his club after the Nazi revolution, Martin Stock was deported on November 8, 1941, along with 969 Jews from Hamburg to a ghetto in faraway Minsk. He was among only eight who survived, later shuttling between concentration camps until his liberation day at Bergen-Belsen. Such was his passion for football that he refused to leave Germany. Stock returned to the game, serving the DFB and participating in the fifty-year anniversary of Altona and honoring returned soldiers, some of whom had played for the club but who had also kept the extermination machinery running smoothly for Nazi Germany. When he finally left German football, resigning his post with the DFB in 1950, Martin Abraham Stock was so beloved that Sepp Herberger and the general secretary of the DFB saw him off at the airport on his departure to a new life in Brazil. Largely forgotten in the years that followed, Stock's compelling story has only recently been unearthed by historians.[12]

Soccer dominated the sports reporting in all of the DP camp newspapers. One tournament over Passover between April 18 and 22, 1946, included an opening parade with team flags and three thousand spectators. Qualifying matches, held at the Landsberg camp, reduced twelve teams down to the final two, and Landsberg and Feldafing met in the final. This time, the football grounds swelled with some five thousand watching on. Play was fierce as neither team would back down, and with much of the match remaining play had to be cut short when Feldafing players acted "unsportingly" toward the referee. The tournament went unfinished with no winner declared.

The top league in the American zone included the nine best teams, calling itself the A-Klasse. The opening match for the A-Klasse came on July 13, 1946, and teams were made up of former professionals from Poland and other clubs across Europe. Most accounts give the league a high rating. Matches were evenly contested and the quality of play strong. Tickets to matches provided much-needed revenue for DP clubs. The top matches dominated news coverage. From the summer of 1946, we find this account:

> The match aroused great interest in Stuttgart. All the Jews in Stutt-gart were present at this soccer event. . . . Landsberg started off with strong attacks, and already in the 37th minute Urbach [of Lands-berg] headed a goal from a corner from the outside right Mundek. At the end of the first half it stood at 1–1 to Landsberg. . . . Stuttgart started to attack very aggressively, with the result that goalkeeper Helfing got a bad eye injury and center right Urbach was hit in the foot and couldn't play on at first. . . . It seemed as if Stuttgart wanted to win with sheer might. But the Landsberg defense is in a class of its own. They let nothing get past them, and even in the final minute Urbach managed to head the ball over the goal. . . . The match ended in a 1–1 draw. [13]

Just as in civilian life, events off the pitch affected the game on the field: rowdy and unruly spectators threatened to disrupt play and excess ag-gressiveness resulted in a rash of injuries early on. The disciplinary committee suspended a number of DP players for playing with and against Germans and for teams using Christian players. Many at the time interpreted such outbursts and indiscretions as natural extensions of highly competitive sporting behavior, but others saw them as reflec-tions of the pent-up frustrations of displaced persons unsure of their future.

Nearly two years of peace in Europe brought renewed excitement to the business of living. When winter turned to spring in 1947, sport again took center stage. Rivalries and an increasing sense of professionalism made soccer more popular than ever. Dozens of DP camp teams from the lower ranks fought fiercely for promotion to the A-Klasse. In 1947, the league expanded from nine to twenty-two teams, which were then organized by a northern and southern division with ten and twelve teams, respectively. No team would rise higher than Ichud Landsberg, who became repeat champions.

For many, a lack of work and meaningful diversions behind the barbed wire became unbearable. But players and spectators drew deep meaning from sport. Matches served as an outlet from the temporary, mundane existence lived in the camps. Sport was a type of occupation—it structured daily life and allowed people to channel frustrations and consume time. In the DP centers, gyms and sporting equipment allowed physical renewal.

Many displaced persons saw themselves as strangers in a murderers' land—one common refrain heard on the assembly areas was that "our blood is in their soil." With Jewish cultural foundations destroyed, players and fans took pleasure in renewing their identity as Jews, as they gathered pitch-side to watch and cheer. Matches against occupation forces from the United States and teams representing Switzerland and Poland added powerfully to this growing identity. But never would DPs play against German teams. Sport contributed greatly to the physical restoration of a people. Astute observers called it a "productive forgetting."

Emotional investment was significant for these footballers. A Jewish youth leader in charge of a team of young male Holocaust survivors who found refuge in England remembered the reply of one boy who lost his temper in one match. Rebuking the boy for fighting, the young man replied, "I've lost so much that I can't keep losing."[14]

With the November 1947 UN partition of Palestine and the end of the British Mandate on May 14, 1948, the State of Israel came into existence and the exodus began. DP camps across Germany emptied: the 165,000 Jewish DPs living in the American and British zones in April 1948 would see their numbers plummet to half just five months later.[15] With mass immigration to Israel and the closing of the DP camps, competitive sport came to an abrupt and sudden end. Föhrenwald remained open several more years, becoming the last DP camp to close in 1957.

REBIRTH OF GERMAN FOOTBALL
IN THE OCCUPIED ZONES

Rebuilding German football in the occupied zones depended greatly on where the matches would be played. As the outcome of the war became clear, the leading Allied powers agreed to divide Germany into four regions to be governed by each of the soon-to-be-victorious nations. Once German surrender was complete, each nation set about administering the peace and imposing its will on the defeated. In the Soviet zone, old clubs were banned from reforming and their property confiscated. Stalin had long envisioned a radical reorganization of Germany according to communist ideals, even before Hitler committed suicide. In the eastern half of Germany, large crowds were banned from gathering, and centralized state control of football meant that politics dominated the sport.

The French zone of occupation, in the far southwestern tip of Germany, was run more along the dictates of revenge. With memories of Verdun and yet another German occupation of their country within two decades, military authorities in the French zone, including the long-disputed Saarland, ran German football. The French were in no mood to be sporting: all football activity required approval, and strict travel restrictions were imposed on teams. And usually these applications were turned down. Thus life was generally hardest for the occupied in the Russian and French zones, but in a curious twist of fate, it would be the Americans, who knew the least about the game and its traditions, who reinvigorated German football.

The British rivaled the French in their animosity toward the Germans. In some cases, retribution guided British policy in the northwestern part of Germany. One of the rival clubs to the great Schalke 04 and Dortmund teams, in what was once known as the Gauliga Westfalen in the Nazified 1930s, was Westfalia Herne. The team kept their name but little else under the British, who confiscated all club equipment and the football grounds owned by the club. One English officer even demanded that Herne burn their uniforms.[16] But the British love for the game eventually eased the more punitive aspects of occupation, and by fall 1945 matches featuring the region's best teams against British army sides were the talk of the district. One day in November, thirty-five thousand gathered to watch Schalke 04 play against a team representing the Fifty-Third Army Division in Wuppertal, a match won by the Germans 2–1.

Footballers and club officials returning to their home grounds were devastated to find clubhouses in ruin and craters where playing fields once had been. Shock led to dismay at the sight of baseball diamonds and goalposts for American football standing where once perfectly manicured soccer fields lay. A skeptical pause soon gave way to approval of reorganization of German football clubs. American leniency led to one of the first postwar friendlies, a match featuring Schwaben Augsburg against a team of POWs on July 1, 1945, well before the American war with Japan was over.[17] Smaller football associations in the south of Germany, rich in footballing tradition, scrambled quickly to reform teams with whatever players could be mustered. One of their first actions was to create the Oberliga, a zone-wide league that started play a mere three weeks after its formation.

That Germany was in ruins would not deter these new football pioneers. Teams often played for meat, vegetables, and boxes of coal. Equipment was in very short supply, and most teams only had one ball. The loss of a game ball to a nearby creek or forest usually meant the end of a match. Transportation always presented a problem; some club officials found themselves traveling to meetings in coal cars or with their teams on trains lacking heat and basic food provisions. Material goods were scarce, and clubs often improvised uniforms from scrap fabric. Red shirts were especially popular in these times, despite prohibitions by the Allies. In some cases, club uniforms were made from leftover flags and banners that no one seemed to want anymore. All you had to do was remove the swastikas. And in the small city of Hamm, twenty-five miles northeast of Dortmund in the soccer-mad Ruhr region, a local club used gravestones to bolster the stairs leading to the grandstands, making sure the inscriptions faced downward so as not to disturb arriving fans seeking to escape the deprivations of life under occupation.[18]

Nationwide football returned to greater Germany in the fall of 1947 when the four Oberligen, representing Berlin and the occupation zones in the north, south, and west came together (joined one year later by the French southwest, which struggled under military rule) for a knock-out-round tournament. Winners from each of the zonal playoffs faced off in a two-round playoff to determine the finalists, and when the dust settled FC Kaiserslautern faced off against FC Nürnberg in the first national championship of the postwar era. On the Kaiserslautern side, five childhood mates put on the club shirt, including two sets of brothers, most famously Fritz Walter and brother Ottmar. In a strange irony, Nuremberg, the spiritual home of the National Socialists, was also represented in the final, though the city itself had suffered a particularly devastating bombing campaign because of its prominence in Nazi politics. An animated crowd of seventy-five thousand filled the stands in Cologne on June 21, 1948, and when FC Nürnberg emerged 2–1 winners, the proud club celebrated their return in front of the Nuremberg central train station, with tens of thousands of fans standing on a huge swathe of rubble as if it were a home-ground terrace.

Sepp Herberger waited out the first five years after the war's end. Unlike his fellow DFB colleagues Otto Nerz and Felix Linnemann, both of whom did not survive imprisonment for their Nazi Party associations, Herberger escaped the more serious penalties of de-Nazification after paying a fine and living in a professional wilderness for a time. He had relocated to Cologne, where he could keep an eye on young prospects and craft a living for himself by training future coaches, some of whom would one day bring German football back into the modern world. Herberger had always kept in close contact with his former players. And he waited for his broken country to reappoint him as national team trainer, a mere formality once the timing was right. To Herberger's horror, the job was opened up and advertised by the DFB. Undeterred, the single-minded man from Mannheim lobbied hard for his old job, writing angry letters and calling upon journalist friends whom he believed owed him a favor or two for being such a great interview over the years.[19]

The DFB relented and by January 21, 1950, Germany had a proper football coach, a reinvigorated national football association, and an emerging collection of players ready to represent their partitioned country. Then, nine months later almost to the day, the "new" nation of West Germany rejoined the community of world football when FIFA lifted its ban in late September. Eight weeks later, Switzerland agreed to be the first opponent for post-Nazi Germany, and the ever-reliable Swiss played the role perfectly, going down to their hosts (minus an injured Fritz Walter) 1–0 in front of 115,000 fans in Stuttgart. With Sepp Herberger back at the helm and memories of the power and precision of the Breslau Elf beginning to fade, *Die Mannschaft* was ready to write a new national story. Perhaps unsurprisingly, Germany had a hard time finding opponents during the Allied occupation. Among non-German-speaking nations, only the Republic of Ireland and Turkey agreed to play them in friendly matches between 1951 and 1953.

With the Cold War intensifying in Europe and Germany on the front lines of the battle, football once again took on a political edge. The World Cup tournament had been restarted in 1950 after a twelve-year hiatus, with South American powerhouse Uruguay winning their second championship, beating host Brazil 2–1. Uruguay claimed the newly renamed Jules Rimet Cup, so changed to honor the twenty-fifth anniversary of Rimet's presidency of FIFA. Neutral Switzerland was rewarded with the next world championships, and West Germany's preparations for their first World Cup since the debacle in Italy in 1938—when the national side crashed out in the first round against the Swiss—were erratic at best, but also had the unexpected side effect of producing a thaw in relations with its neighbors. Part of the predicament was the wide range of competition in the various Oberligen in the western zones. The best teams, from which the national team drew players, often beat club rivals by scores of 8–0 and 9–0. Some teams simply weren't tested. In Oberliga Nord, Hamburg tallied more than one hundred goals in the 1951 season, leaving the team unchallenged until the nationwide finals began.

Doubts mounted the next year when Herberger's side lost successive matches to Turkey, Ireland, and, painfully, France, who so thoroughly outplayed the Germans that Fritz Walter considered quitting the team. That the French played with revenge on their minds was lost on Walter. The press started to turn on both coach and team, and only a hard-fought draw in Madrid in December 1952 seemed to save Herberger's job.

When the time came to enter official World Cup qualification, West Germany continued to stumble. An uninspired away draw to Norway was followed by a mediocre 3–0 win against Saarland. The Saarland, still occupied by French troops, had attained independent status within FIFA (until its reabsorption into West Germany in 1956) and competed in qualification matches for the 1954 World Cup. The return match against Norway produced a 5–1 victory in November 1953, boosting hopes among the German faithful. The winter break followed, and in March 1954 West Germany traveled back to Saarland (an away match at home?) for the deciding qualification match. Extra intrigue attended the match: Saarland was managed by Helmut Schön, the former SC Dresden star and a German international under Herberger.

Playing on Sepp Herberger's fifty-seventh birthday, West Germany claimed a 3–1 win, securing passage unconvincingly to the fifth World Cup tournament. Amid lackluster performances and relatively poor preparations, Germany was just happy to continue playing. Awaiting them in their group was pretournament favorite Hungary, who had completely humiliated England 6–3 at Wembley Stadium and 7–1 in Budapest in the lead-up to the championships. No one could conceivably challenge Hungarian supremacy as the Mighty Magyars brought a four-year unbeaten streak to Switzerland. In the minds of most observers, there was only ever going to be one winner of the 1954 World Cup: Hungary.

The very idea of West Germany contending for the Jules Rimet Cup in Switzerland was ludicrous. The nation had been excluded from the 1950 World Cup and successive Olympic games in 1948 and 1952. Their performances gave no indication of being world class. So it was that in their opening match of group play, Germany went down 1–0 to Turkey inside of three minutes. But twelve minutes later, Germany leveled the score and went on to dominate play, finishing the game as 4–1 winners. The second match pitted the Germans against the invincible Hungarians. In the years following this match, analysts have long speculated why Sepp Herberger decided to drop eight players ahead of the contest. Some guessed he wanted to lull the Hungarians into a false sense of supremacy. The national team trainer played it coy, evasively dodging questions about his tactics. The match finished a humiliating 8–3.

The loss brought down condemnations and calls for Herberger's head. In truth, the trainer fielded a reserve team so as to rest his squad for the more pivotal playoff rematch against Turkey three days later. West Germany went on to soundly defeat the Turks 7–2, and after dispatching Yugoslavia in the quarterfinals 2–0, with an own goal and a strike by Helmut Rahn making the difference, West Germany faced Austria in the semifinal. The descendants of the Wunderteam, this version of the Austrian national team outlasted Switzerland in their epic quarterfinal to win 7–5, a match still considered as one of the best ever played in the World Cup. West Germany came into their semifinal riding a wave of momentum, but the old animosities were largely gone for their Teutonic neighbor to the south. As the rains fell on the last day of June, Germany walked off the pitch as 6–1 victors, with four goals coming from set pieces. They played the Austrians "off of the park." German industriousness was replaced with technical brilliance and teamwork built on a familiarity bred in childhood—five of the starting eleven played football together for boyhood club Kaiserslautern. The rains continued to fall on the Swiss countryside, and when the day came for the final match in Berne, the Hungarians would have to battle more than their German counterparts.

When Hungary and West Germany walked out on the pitch at the Wankdorfstadion on Sunday, July 4, 1954, they immediately saw the effects of the heavy rain that had fallen the previous day. Mud clung to players' boots, but the Germans had an extra weapon in their arsenal. Team bootman Adi Dassler, the founder of the Adidas sporting goods company, was on the bench next to Sepp Herberger, and he was well prepared for days like these. Though the weather had remained clear at kickoff, conditions deteriorated rapidly and rain in the second half turned the pitching to a bog in some areas. Dassler had supplied boots to the national squad for years, but in the Berne mud he switched to longer removable studs, giving the Germans a decided advantage.

The Germans still had to play the game, and after nine minutes they went down two quick goals, scored by Ferenc Puskás and Zoltán Czibor. Rather than becoming demoralized, Herberger's men responded immediately. Two minutes after a failed back pass that had gifted Hungary their second goal, Fritz Walter played a first-time ball to Rahn, who sent a blistering cross from the left—meant as a shot—to the goalmouth, where prolific inside right Max Morlock of FC Nürnberg pounced on the slightly deflected pass, just barely tapping the ball inside the left post before the keeper could claim it, for the Germans' first goal. The equalizer came just seven minutes later on a volleyed corner by Helmut Rahn. Before twenty minutes passed, four goals had been tallied, and the teams played late into the match deadlocked at 2–2.

What came next became known as *Das Wunder von Bern*—the Miracle of Berne. The Hungarians dominated long stretches of the second half, but their possession came to naught. The Germans desperately cleared two shots off the goal line and the crossbar, and some heroic goalkeeping saved them other times. Puskás saw his equalizer at the end called offside by the Welsh linesman. But six minutes from time, the inevitability of a Hungarian victory was swept away when Helmut Rahn blasted home the winning goal, a left-footed shot from the edge of the penalty box coming from a poor clearance by the Hungarians.

Equal to the goal in German consciousness was the radio commentary on the day. In this era before television, millions back home anxiously sat by their radios listening intently to the match. Forever imprinted on collective German memory was the ecstatic reporting of German radio commentator Herbert Zimmermann:

> *Schäfer nach innen geflankt . . . Kopfball . . . Abgewehrt . . . Rahn schiessen . . .* ("Schäfer puts in the cross . . . header . . . cleared . . . Rahn shoots . . .")
>
> *Tor! Tor! Tor! Tor!* ("Goal! Goal! Goal! Goal!") [Zimmermann falls silent for eight seconds before he speaks again]
>
> *Tor für Deutschland! Drei zu zwei führt Deutschland. Halten Sie mich für verrückt, halten Sie mich für übergeschnapp!* ("Goal for Germany! Germany lead 3–2. Call me mad, call me crazy!")

Rahn's goal and Zimmerman's call defined a nation and erased, for a time anyway, German shame and the dark days of a humiliating occupation. German football writer Uli Hesse reflected on the power and meaning of the team's victory over the Hungarians to a broken nation still reeling from the Nazi hangover: "Half a century later, every true football fan beyond school age can still recite the words as if they were a poem, knowing that what follows is the voice urging Rahn to try a shot from deep, then realising the player does exactly that. '*Aus dem Hintergrund müsste Rahn schiessen . . . Rahn schiesst!*' [Rahn should shoot from deep . . . Rahn shoots!]"[20] The phrase "Wir Sind Wieder Wer" ("We are somebody again") is commonly mentioned to express the profound meaning of the Miracle at Berne to the German people. From this victory, a new postwar identity emerged for Germany, one which by most accounts would drive the economic miracle that came in the decades that followed.

After the match, ecstatic celebrations erupted across West Germany. The first of many public gatherings and parades came after the German national team's arrival in Munich after the short train ride from Switzerland. An estimated two million people greeted *Die Mannschaft* as they descended onto the Munich train platform. Players were showered with gifts in the week that followed. Holding forth in the Löwenbräukeller beer hall in Munich, DFB president Peco Bauwens joined in the celebrations, offering a speech that was broadcast live by a Bavarian radio station.

Undoubtedly fueled by alcohol, high emotion, and a lingering sense of nationalism, Bauwens offered the usual platitudes about German fortitude and spirit before moving on to darker themes. He continued by suggesting the World Cup victory was inspired by the Nordic god of thunder, Wotan. In his mind, the players had carried the German flag in their hearts. Bauwens's beer-cellar fervor reached a crescendo when he apparently identified the team's success as the result of a loyal allegiance to the *Führerprinzip*—the Nazi-sanctified principle of having one strong man leading the others.[21] Before he could finish his speech, the radio station cut him off. Mysteriously, all tapes and transcripts of the broadcast were lost, but the damage was done. Angry denunciations of the toast, labeled by some as the *Sieg Heil* speech, appeared widely in Bavarian newspapers. The foreign press was aghast when they heard the first two verses of the forbidden national anthem—forever corrupted by the Nazis—"Deutschland über alles," sung by German fans. Peco Bauwens's chilling blend of Aryan mysticism and a nationalism fed by athletic triumph was too much to take. Nine years removed from the end of the war and like the nation, the German Football Association still had much work to do to come to terms with the war and the Holocaust.

Pitchside in Berne, West German captain Fritz Walter took possession of the 1954 version of the Coupe du Monde, handed to him by the cup's eponymous namesake, FIFA president Jules Rimet. Four years earlier, few were sure that the tournament would ever resume after twelve years of devastating war and occupation. As Walter held the trophy aloft for all to see, the modernist figurine created by French sculptor Abel Lafleur had already taken a long, winding path to Berne. The story of the Jules Rimet Cup reads like a gangster caper. Only in this tale, the gangsters ransacked an entire continent. But for a solitary Italian football official, the Rimet would have ended up in Nazi hands, yet another priceless object hoarded by history's greatest thieves.

During the Nazi reign of terror, Europe's artistic and cultural heritage came under relentless attack, orchestrated much like the Blitzkrieg warfare of the German army. In every country they conquered, Nazi military and political officials looted central banks and pillaged national museums and private collections, sending confiscated gold reserves and other treasures back to Germany. Hitler's racial and military crusades enabled an art and money plundering operation unparalleled in modern times. The Jules Rimet Cup became a target in this massive search-and-seizure operation. Thwarted on the pitch in the 1938 World Cup in France, Nazi Germany essentially gave up on football as a reliable means of statecraft. Envying the success of Mussolini's fascists in winning successive world championships in 1934 and 1938, the Nazis turned to the next best option for securing the trophy: they would steal it. With ally Italy in possession of the cup, the mission seemed simple. But the changing fortunes of war saw Mussolini ousted and the Nazis forced to occupy the Italian Peninsula.

Paying close attention to the rapidly changing events in his country, Italian Football Federation official Ottorino Barassi took matters into his own hands. Word of Nazi plans to seize the Rimet trophy, along with other priceless Italian artifacts, reached Barassi, and he secretly removed the trophy from a Rome bank, taking it back to his hometown of Cremona in northern Italy. Weighing just over thirteen and a half pounds and measuring fourteen and a half inches tall, the gold-plated, sterling silver Coupe du Monde was an Art Deco masterpiece sculpted in the likeness of Nike, the Greek goddess of victory. Her arms, spread as though they were the shining source of the light of the sun, held a simple, chalicelike cup.

The stature of this trophy grew with the phenomenal success of the World Cup tournament. Hiding it in a town that was a symbol of fascist domination likely emboldened Barassi. Nazi soldiers eventually appeared at Barassi's house, searching thoroughly for the statuette, world football's Holy Grail. Shockingly, they failed to search under Barassi's bed. If they had, they would have found an old shoebox containing the most coveted prize in the game. A few years later, Ottorino Barassi looked on as FIFA chief Jules Rimet handed the cup over to winners Uruguay as the World Cup restored the possibility of sport and peace over war and domination. Rising from the cataclysms of war, the reborn tournament, hosted brilliantly by Brazil, set into motion the spectacle and passion that now defines the quadrennial event celebrated by the entire planet.

In a dramatic postscript to this story, the Jules Rimet Cup would change hands many more times in the coming years, beyond the footballers who earned it. On the eve of the 1958 World Cup in Sweden, Germany returned the cup but, mysteriously, it now had a new base and was a few centimeters taller. Speculation was that the original was lost and a replica had been produced by the Germans for the next competition. The mystery went unsolved.

Several years passed, and four months before England hosted the 1966 competition, the trophy once again went missing, nicked from a one-day sport stamp exhibition where it was on display. A ransom note for fifteen thousand pounds led to the quick arrest of a middleman by Scotland Yard, but the cup remained missing—that is, until a week later, when barge worker Dave Corbett was walking his black-and-white Collie "Pickles" in his local park and stopped to make a phone call at the public phone box. As the dog scratched around, Corbett noticed that his furry companion had torn open a newspaper-wrapped parcel hidden in a nearby bush. Seeing the glint of gold and the words "Brazil 1962," an astonished Corbett could not believe his eyes. Pickles had found the World Cup and, by doing so, saved an embarrassed nation. Later that summer, England won their first Jules Rimet Cup, famously paraded around by team captain Bobby Moore as he was carried around the Wembley pitch on teammates' shoulders.

But the perilous journey of the trophy did not end there. At the 1970 World Cup in Mexico, Brazil defeated fellow two-time champions Italy 4–1 to win the world title and the right to take permanent possession of the Jules Rimet. This is the tournament of the incomparable Pelé, the Golden Ball winner as most valuable player and inspirational leader who scored and assisted twice in the final. This 1970 Brazil team is widely considered to be the best World Cup squad ever to take the field. But thirteen years later, thieves once again made off with the trophy, stealing it from the poorly guarded headquarters of the Brazilian Football Federation in Rio de Janeiro. It has never been seen again.

Sepp Herberger had endeared himself to players, fans, and journalists over the years with his quirky, gurulike sayings that later became embedded in German culture. Herberger's most famous and pithy utterances served to remind whoever was within earshot that football is an unpredictable, difficult-to-control game and that you must never let your guard down. Herberger enjoyed the longest tenure of any national team trainer—he managed a total of twenty years, six during the Nazi era, retiring in 1964 and handing over the reins to former player and acolyte Helmut Schön (who also took West Germany to their second World Cup title as hosts in 1974). Perpetuating the spirit of *Kampf*, the soldierly struggle glorified during the 1930s, Herberger's miracle team beat the more skilled Hungarians in the mud of Berne because they were more fit and outworked every opponent. For those twenty years, Sepp Herberger's influence on the development of German football was enormous, and he linked prewar squads to the team that reached the pinnacle of the world game. Generations of German soccer players and coaches learned to play football in a style first developed under Adolf Hitler.[22]

After the World Cup win, Sepp Herberger was lionized in Germany along with his players. Decades passed and his reputation only grew. Herberger became a household name and a cultural icon, remarkable for the fact he had joined the Nazi Party in the 1930s and survived the reckoning that followed largely unscathed. But he is best remembered for his succinct sayings that are spiritual cousins to well-worn football maxims known today, like "Play to the final whistle" and "The best team doesn't always win." Every German of a certain age knows Herberger's now famous lines, "Der Ball ist rund" (The ball is round), "Das Spiel dauert 90 Minuten" (The game lasts for ninety minutes), and "Nach dem Spiel ist vor dem Spiel" (After the game is before the game). He demanded simple obedience to these maxims; they prevented complacency and guaranteed dedication and supreme effort among his players.

To a nation stepping out of the long shadow of war, Herberger and his soccer teams meant a great deal. Each of their first three world championships represented a milestone in German national identity and a frightful reminder of German unity and strength to its neighbors. The win in 1974 as host nation over Johan Cruyff and the *Brilliant Oranje* of the Netherlands lingered long in the collective Dutch memory of the occupation. Years later, England striker Gary Lineker, after losing the 1990 World Cup semifinal to eventual champion Germany on penalties, channeled the legendary German coach with his own cheeky twist: "Football is a simple game; twenty-two men chase a ball for ninety minutes, and at the end, the Germans win." The 1990 World Cup win in Italy came on the eve of German reunification, at a time when many experts expected the reconstituted German team to dominate for years. Such predictions didn't come to pass. It would be another twenty-four years until Germany returned from the footballing wilderness to claim another World Cup title, overcoming Argentina in extra time in the Estádio do Maracanã in Rio de Janeiro, becoming the first European country to win a World Cup in South America.

RECONCILING THE PAST

The return of Germany to the community of civilized nations happened faster than anyone would imagine. Success on the football pitch enhanced the rebuilding of the nation, renewed with postwar economic vigor. Yet it would take several decades for the national football association to come to terms with the past. When the DFB began preparations to host the 2006 World Cup, they recognized that the eyes of the world would be fixed on Germany and the past would be questioned.

DFB accounts of the Nazi period whitewashed the close relationship enjoyed by the DFB and the National Socialists. But with centenary celebrations of the founding of the German FA in 2000 came mounting pressure on the DFB to open up its archives, and in turn, the DFB offered to sponsor a self-investigation. Many players and association officials had been labeled as "fellow travelers" by German courts after the war, in effect exonerating them of any serious guilt. At the club level, Borussia Dortmund was the first to respond to requests from the DFB to critically evaluate the past. Like many Rhineland clubs, Dortmund was full of socialist and communist loyalists among the players and club officials, the first targets of Nazism. German historians had already revealed that well into the 1970s, nearly half of the DFB governing committee at the time had been NSDAP members. Shockingly, one member of the DFB executive board was a man who served two years in prison for SS war crimes.

From its very founding, the Deutscher Fußball-Bund was a deeply conservative organization that was easily pulled into the nationalistic aims of Nazism. DFB national team trainer Sepp Herberger allowed himself to be used by the Nazis in their propaganda machinery; his active cooperation, including a cameo role, with the popular football film *Das Grosse Spiel* (*The Big Game*, 1942) contributed to the stability of the regime. Guilt was be shared and Herberger's reputation diminished. The concept that gained hold in this period of reflection and accountability was "seduction"; like many professional fields in Nazi Germany, football joined with lawyers, doctors, and teachers in being seduced by Nazism. True, there were ideologues and true believers in every walk of life, but opportunism, passive acceptance, careerism, and blind ambition were more typical explanations of this deeply rooted complicity.

The most decorated and prominent club in German football is Bayern Munich. For decades, the Bavarian outfit was seen as the club of the beer halls and the Brownshirts. Because Munich was the birthplace of National Socialism, Bayern Munich was tainted by association in the public eye. The truth was quite the opposite.

In the years leading up to the Nazi revolution, Bayern was a provincial club with few successes to trumpet. But it was a stout Jewish man named Kurt Landauer who brought Bayern Munich to the heights of German football. The forceful Landauer brought a number of innovations to the Bavarian side. The youth academy flourished under his watch, and fiscal responsibility kept the team afloat in the depths of economic depression in the early 1930s.

A progressive philosophy brought beautiful football to Bayern. When others imitated the English style, Kurt Landauer was inspired by the Hungarian style not-so-coincidentally played by the best Jewish footballers in central Europe. The Bayern chairman rejected the notion of *Kampfgeist*, the "spirit of struggle" so enthusiastically embraced by the Nazis. Instead of a martial struggle, he saw football as a game of artistry and joy, played by men who sought to display their creativity with the ball. Landauer took the helm as club president in 1919 and for the next decade built a team to rival German giants Schalke 04, FC Nürnberg, and FC Saarbrücken.

With a membership and a board of directors with strong Jewish influence, Bayern Munich would be denounced later as a *Judenklub*. Yet Bayern never gave in to prevailing political sentiments of the time. Such sly resistance did not last long, especially in the birthplace of Nazism. On the very day Dachau was established on the outskirts of Munich, Kurt Landauer was forced to resign his position in the nationwide Nazi purge of sport and education. During the Nazi period, it was actually local rivals 1860 Munich who collaborated with the National Socialists and not Bayern, who resisted by appointing non-Nazis, answering secretly to Landauer, who ran the club behind the scenes. A few years later, he was arrested on *Kristallnacht* in 1938 and sent to Dachau like tens of thousands of other Jewish men. Landauer stayed in Dachau just thirty-three days, owing his quick release to his military service in World War I.

Loyalty to the club remained strong despite Nazi anti-Semitism, and when Bayern Munich, now officially *Judenfrei*, traveled to Zurich to play a friendly against a Swiss club, one of the few instances of open rebellion by a German football club made the news. Bayern players, forbidden by the Gestapo to meet officially with Landauer, who had fled to Switzerland, instead spotted their former club president in the stands and lined up to applaud the man who brought Bayern from anonymity to their first of many championships in 1932. After the war, Landauer returned to Munich and to the post of club president, going on to become the longest-tenured chief executive in club history.

In the postwar years, like so many German institutions, FC Bayern Munich ignored the Nazi period in official club accounts, in essence repressing the horrors of the Holocaust. More often, club officials simply deflected questions about the Nazi era, relying on the euphemistic phrase "the political events between 1933 and 1945." But after the 2006 World Cup, Bayern and many other clubs looked more critically at their histories, and in time forgotten heroes were brought back to the forefront and finally given the honor they deserved. In 2009, on the 125th anniversary of his birth, Kurt Landauer was recognized as the father of the modern Bayern Munich with a memorial ceremony at the concentration camp of Dachau, located just seventeen miles from the club's new modern training ground and stadium.

Hundreds of Jewish footballers and club officials essentially disappeared in the Nazi period, and few within the DFB ever asked questions about their status. Several were especially well known as soccer grew into a mass phenomenon in Germany and across Europe between the wars. Two names stand above the rest. Julius Hirsch and Gottfried Fuchs together formed the most fearsome strike force in the early years of German football, propelling Karlsruhe FV to their first and only domestic championship in 1910. Hirsch was the first Jewish player to represent the national team. Fuchs's claim to glory was the ten goals he scored against Russia in a group match at the 1912 Olympics in Stockholm, a German record that stands to this day. Both men were erased from DFB archives in the Nazi years.

The best player of his generation, Gottfried Fuchs was later compared to Fritz Walter. Fuchs escaped the clutches of Nazi Germany, immigrating to Canada after 1937. Julius Hirsch did not escape. Troubled by personal problems in the intervening years, including multiple suicide attempts before his deportation to Auschwitz in March 1943, Hirsch was declared dead in May 1945, another victim of the Nazi death factory.

It wasn't until sixty years later that the Deutscher Fußball-Bund formally acknowledged the fate of Hirsch and other Jewish footballers. Recognizing the close relationship between the DFB and the Nazis, Julius Hirsch was honored posthumously with an award granted to individuals and clubs that actively advance human rights. Dubbed the Julius-Hirsch-Preis, the first prize was awarded in 2005 to celebrate efforts to combat racism, anti-Semitism, and xenophobia, and it went to Bayern Munich for its staging of a friendly, a "match of peace," between its under-seventeen team and an Israeli-Palestinian youth squad. While nothing can truly make amends for the appalling indifference and obfuscation of a complicit past, German football is moving forward, like much of the rest of Germany, offering a genuine remembrance of a complicated and tragic history.

REMEMBRANCE OF SURVIVAL AND RESISTANCE

"To resist the dehumanizing, brutalizing force of evil, to refuse to be abased to the level of animals, to live through the torment, to outlive the tormentors, these too were acts of resistance. Merely to give witness by one's own testimony was, in the end, to contribute to a moral victory. Simply to survive was a victory of the human spirit."—Sir Martin Gilbert, eminent twentieth-century historian, on survival during the Holocaust[23]

Impenetrable. The Holocaust seemingly falls beyond our human capacity to understand it. The enormity of events that came together to make the war and genocide that followed seems out of reach to the modern observer. But it is the individual stories revealed here that illuminate and explain. Soccer under the swastika helped preserve a more civilized existence. When stripped of propagandistic and nationalistic aims, soccer in the Nazi era affirmed human agency, lived out in hope, strength, and perseverance. The motivations shown by the countless men, women, and children who picked up a football and started playing wherever they found themselves ensnared in Nazi-occupied Europe are myriad. Like all who fell captive to the Nazis, their imprisonment created confusion, uncertainty, and, bizarrely, opportunity.

In the debased moral landscape of the camps, each prisoner had to consider his or her own survival above everything else. One pathway to survival, as we have seen, was football. But the games were so much more; they meant defiance, resistance, and rebellion against one of the most heinous political ideas in human history. Others played simply to reclaim an element of their humanity in an expression of pleasure and entertainment. Clearly, there was a redemptive element to the suffering endured by those held captive and murdered by Nazi criminals. For as many surviving heroes as we identify in these stories, we also find many more who perished.

The loudest voices should be those that have been silenced forever: the millions murdered by starvation and by disease brought on by ghettoization, those who perished by bullet and by gas chamber. Millions were denied the right to experience life and fulfill their dreams. While many embraced life as fully as possible in the camps and ghettos, others gave in to despair or the darker impulses of their nature. One Auschwitz survivor reminds us of these blurred lines between prisoner destinies in the Nazi universe.

Young Dutch Holocaust survivor Louis de Wijze was just the right age to avoid being killed outright for being a Jewish child and thus deemed unworthy of life as the future of the Jewish people. De Wijze was also a soccer player who made his debut for a top-division side in Holland as a seventeen-year-old but soon after the occupation was deported to Westerbork. He stayed in the transit center about eighteen months, earning an assignment to a favored labor detail in the camp where he was fed well, working his way into excellent physical condition. This conditioning later allowed de Wijze to endure starvation rations and murderous labor at Auschwitz-Monowitz, his destination after Westerbork. De Wijze admits that this combination of blind luck, endurance, and his own resourcefulness led to his survival when everyone around him died. De Wijze outlasted the vast majority who entered the camps at Westerbork, Auschwitz, and finally Buchenwald. But his own admission in the following passage is tempered by another revelation long after the war:

> Everyone lives for himself. Our one and all-encompassing credo is: Survive! Between the outer limits of life and death, previous values and norms lose their meaning, and our spiritual baggage gradually erodes. The only norm that counts is "I." All our senses, thoughts, and deeds are used only for our own benefit. A large part of our previous vocabulary has disappeared. New meanings are filling the empty spaces. Nobody ever again talks about "stealing." The way we manage to obtain extra bread, feet covers, better wooden shoes, or objects to swap through all kinds of creative ways is now called "organizing," irrespective of whether you can call it "legal."
>
> That is how we live from day to day, from one piece of bread to the next bit of soup. We don't think any farther than tomorrow; yesterday is gone. And when Sunday comes and your unit, thank God, doesn't have to work that day, the hours slip away like water in your hand. Those who still can, walk in small groups through the camp. One day without yelling kapos, beating guards. But for most people, a single day to regain one's strength is insufficient. Sunday, for a lot of people, is just a day to start worrying about Monday. When I put on my squeaky clean, freshly ironed soccer attire and walk on the pitch with my teammates, I feel incredibly privileged compared with the masses. During that hour and a half of sports competition, nothing matters but the leather ball and the goal, just like old times.[24]

Just a few pages later in this same memoir we learn that Louis de Wijze passed a deadly selection (his second) at Auschwitz-Monowitz only to step back in line after handing off his bundle of clothing to an emaciated Czech prisoner named Hugo and pushing the stunned man back into the "line of life." Certain death would have followed his deception had he been caught.

Selflessness and survival. Many memoirists from the Holocaust acknowledge an inescapable contradiction about life in the camps. Opportunism and luck intermingled with capricious executions, random beatings, and torture. Many who survived by playing football were self-interested but also self-sacrificing. Heroic behavior was on display, though it was less likely to be confessed because of survivors' guilt. In the space between heroism and selfishness lies remembrance. The legacy of these witnesses has forced entire nations to confront the near-distant past. Yet one disturbing reality still confounds: what is to be made of the innumerable bystanders to this devastating history?

THE LEGACY OF INDIFFERENCE

"This was the thing I wanted to understand ever since the war. Nothing else. How a human being can remain indifferent. The executioners I understood; also the victims, though with more difficulty. For the others, all the others, those who were neither for nor against, those who sprawled in passive patience, those who told themselves, 'The storm will blow over and everything will be normal again,' those who thought themselves above the battle, those who were permanently and merely spectators—all were closed to me, incomprehensible."—Auschwitz survivor and Nobel laureate Elie Wiesel[25]

The Holocaust is a tear in the fabric of Western Civilization that has never quite been repaired. Millions were thrown into the storm of steel and mechanized death. Seemingly, little has changed in the years since. Indifference still plagues humanity. Genocide has not abated; if anything, it marches on unhindered. Complicated and deeply entrenched historical and political conflicts also make prevention of genocide in contemporary times exceedingly difficult. But it doesn't have to be this way.

We must engage our moral imagination. With the passing of seventy years since the end of the Holocaust, we can easily forget the struggle. Testimonies of soccer survival can inspire us to resist apathy. With history as a guide, we can stand collectively in the breech between goodness and the twin evils of authoritarianism, which is obvious, and passive indifference, which is more obscure. In occupied France, for example, we know that about 10 percent of French citizens aided the resistance while another 10 percent actively collaborated with the Nazis in tracking down and deporting their fellow citizens. The silent 80 percent did neither, choosing inaction and, ultimately, deciding to self-protect. This pattern repeated in nearly every country touched by the Holocaust. It is a choice between action and inaction. In the popular parlance, we can become "upstanders." Moving from a place of uncertainty and unconcern begins with remembrance.

The last twenty years have seen a proliferation of Holocaust memorials across Germany. Shame and denial are being replaced by an honest national self-reflection on the past. The most famous of these memorials sits in the shadow of the Brandenburg Gate, not far from the Reichschancellery building where the final vestiges of the Nazi empire collapsed so many years ago. This Memorial to the Murdered Jews of Europe is an impressive field of over 2,700 monolithic concrete blocks that to some resemble rectangular burial vaults. These stelae of various sizes are spread across nearly five acres of undulating ground in the very heart of Berlin.

As monumental as places like these are, a different type of memorial has also sprung up across Europe, one that is more intimate and personal. Blocks on a much smaller scale fill sidewalk spots in front of the last known residence of Jews deported to their deaths between 1933 and 1945. Known as *stolpersteine* (stumbling stones), these four-inch cubes of granite are covered with a brass plate that is stamped with details of the individual lost to Nazi hate: the name, birth date, and known fate of the person or group, and the dates of deportation and death, if they are known. The creation of German artist Gunter Demnig, more than fifty thousand *stolpersteine* have currently been laid in eighteen different countries, with the first stone placed in a Cologne sidewalk in 1992. Each stone is a commemoration of a single life. Passersby are often caught off guard when they encounter them on the streets, elevated ever so slightly above street level. Jewish footballers have found a place in these memorials. Prewar German player Julius Hirsch was honored with a stone on November 9, 2006, in Karlsruhe, Germany, on the very same day *Kristallnacht* is remembered. *Stolpersteine* were laid for Sally Meyer and Julie Lichtmann in Gelsenkirchen, the victims who lost their textile business to Aryanization and the opportunism of Schalke 04 star Fritz Szepan. Famous Dutch football figures were honored in 2009—the final homes of radio announcer Han Hollander (on Amstelkade 118 in Amsterdam) and goalkeeper Juda de Vries serve as de facto sites of tribute in a country where collaboration and indifference reigned.

Short is the time for hearing those who bear witness. For those still alive as witnesses to the Holocaust, the opportunity to experience justice has largely passed. We are now left with remembering. There is no reckoning with the enormity of the events, but we can account for the individual stories because in them we find meaning. Some have rejected this notion of finding meaning in the Holocaust. This is patently false as one does not have to find meaning in the suffering. That would be offensive to the memory of those who suffered and perished. But we can find meaning in these extraordinary tales of resilience and resistance. And in ordinary stories of soccer. We are at the end of the survivor era. The witnesses are fading away with each passing day. Almost all of those who left behind their testimonies are now gone. The accounts found here offer a legacy of remembrance. Football takes on significance beyond the pitch. Today the modern game is a spectacle; in the Nazi era it actually meant life and death.

It is most fitting to give the final word on soccer under the swastika to a survivor of the Holocaust. With so many voices silenced forever, and with the haunting realization that the last living witnesses to the Holocaust will soon fade into history, we celebrate the strength of those who lived to see the end of the deadliest war in human history. And we rejoice in the beauty of a game that inspired people standing at death's door to play without thought of what tomorrow would bring.

A onetime goalkeeper in the concentration camps, Czech Jewish novelist Arnošt Lustig survived a death march back into Germany after enduring the horrors of Terezín and Auschwitz as a young man. After his liberation from Buchenwald, Lustig went on to become a professor of literature at American University in Washington, DC, where he was well known for joining in pickup soccer games with international students well into his seventies. One of the foremost novelists of the Holocaust, Lustig elevates this child's game in his writing to a place of reverence and inspiration as it was played in Nazi Europe. Just two years before his death, the writer reflected on the power of the game to serve as a symbol of defiance and a pathway to preserving humanity:

> Soccer is a marvelous game. Something between art and exercise, a test of fast thinking, judgment, the ability to combine. It is creative, fast; thinking and imagination predominate. . . . The effort to pass or score, it corresponds to the ancient instinct of man to fight your way through, to free yourself, to reach the goal. Through soccer, one reaches intoxication like in works of art or sex, fulfillment that boosts your confidence for a bit. It erases or restricts feelings of inferiority.

Soccer is a joyous and a cheerful game. It encourages those who are playing and even those who are watching. . . . During existential circumstances when one is under pressure and close to death, soccer turns into a symbol of defiance, longing for beauty, the possibility of living. It's a shame that 99 players out of a hundred died and they didn't live to see the end and peace, the opportunity to live and play or to watch soccer. Soccer is joy and peace, a beautiful game that changes life into joy, the gratification of defiance. Thoughts about soccer in Terezin and anywhere else I would conclude with two sentences: Let the game called soccer live. While it is played, a person on this earth will stay human.[26]

NOTES

INTRODUCTION

1. Donn Risolo, *Soccer Stories: Anecdotes, Oddities, Lore, and Amazing Feats* (Lincoln: University of Nebraska Press, 2010), 89.

2. Werner Skretny, *Julius Hirsch. Nationalspieler. Ermordet. Biografie eines jüdischen Fußballers* (Göttingen: Verlag Die Werkstatt, 2012), 5. Translated into an abbreviated English book titled *Gotti and Juller.*

3. Doris Bergen, *War and Genocide: A Concise History of the Holocaust* (Lanham, MD: Rowman & Littlefield, 2009), vii.

4. From the April 10, 1938, edition of the *Völkischer Beobachter*, translated from original cited in Frank Veröffentlicht Bajohr, "Fritz Szepan: Fußball-Idol und Nutznießer des NS-Regimes," in *Sportler im "Jahrhundert der Lager": Profiteure, Widerständler und Opfer*, ed. Diethelm Blecking and Lorenz Peiffer (Göttingen: Die Werkstatt, 2012), 110.

5. Simon Kuper, *Ajax, the Dutch, the War: The Strange Tale of Soccer during Europe's Darkest Hour* (New York: Nation Books, 2012), 57.

6. Ibid., 64.

7. Ibid., 61.

8. Ibid., 65.

9. Timothy Snyder, *Bloodlands: Europe between Hitler and Stalin* (New York: Basic Books, 2010), xv.

I. SOCCER UNDER THE SWASTIKA

1. Eduardo Galeano, *Football in Sun and Shadow* (New York: Nation Books, 2013), 18.

2. Quoted in Ulrich Hesse-Lichtenberger, *Tor! The Story of German Football* (London: When Saturday Comes Books, 2003), 99.

3. Wolfram Pyta, "German Football: A Cultural History," in *German Football: History, Culture, Society*, ed. Alan Tomlinson and Christopher Young (New York: Routledge, 2006), 3.

4. David Goldblatt, *The Ball Is Round: A Global History of Soccer* (New York: Riverhead Books, 2008), 230.

5. Pyta, "German Football," 7.

6. United States Holocaust Memorial Museum, "The Nazi Olympics: Historical Quotes," https://www.ushmm.org/information/press/press-kits/traveling-exhibitions/nazi-olympics/historical-quotes.

7. Arnd Krüger, "Der Einfluss des faschistischen Sportmodells Italiens auf den nationalistischen Sport," in *Sport und Politik 1918–1939/40: Proceedings, ICOSH Seminar*, ed. A. Morgan Olsen (Otta, Norway: Engers Boktrykkeri A/S, 1986), 55.

8. Arnd Krüger, "The Role of Sport in German International Politics," in *Sport and International Politics: The Impact of Fascism and Communism on Sport*, ed. J. Riordan and P. Arnaud (London: Routledge, 1998), 89.

9. Kuper, *Ajax*, 169.

10. Barbara Keys, *Globalizing Sport: National Rivalry and International Community in the 1930s* (Cambridge, MA: Harvard University Press, 2006), 129.

11. Kuper, *Ajax*, 29.

12. Quoted in Hesse-Lichtenberger, *Tor!*, 63.

13. Quoted in Angela Teja, "Italian Sport and International Relations under Fascism," in Riordan and Arnaud, *Sport and International Politics*, 162.

14. Hesse-Lichtenberger, *Tor!*, 81.

15. Kuper, *Ajax*, 184.

16. Goldblatt, *Ball Is Round*, 328.

17. Hesse-Lichtenberger, *Tor!*, 89.

18. Goldblatt, *Ball Is Round*, 330.

19. Quoted in Hesse-Lichtenberger, *Tor!*, 93.

2. WAR MINUS THE SHOOTING

1. Friedrich W. Nietzsche, *Human, All Too Human* (Lincoln: University of Nebraska Press, 1984), 51.
2. Anthony R. Pratkanis and Elliot Aronson, *Age of Propaganda: The Everyday Use and Abuse of Persuasion* (New York: Freeman, Holt and Company, 2001), 318.
3. Ibid., 179.
4. Hilmar Hoffmann, *The Triumph of Propaganda: Film and National Socialism* (Providence, RI: Berghahn, 1996), 90.
5. Garth S. Jowett and Victoria O'Donnell, *Propaganda and Persuasion*, 6th ed. (Thousand Oaks, CA: Sage, 2014), 264.
6. Hoffmann, *Triumph of Propaganda*, 94.
7. Pratkanis and Aronson, *Age of Propaganda*, 323.
8. Jowett and O'Donnell, *Propaganda and Persuasion*, 265.
9. Goldblatt, *Ball Is Round*, 307.
10. Simon Martin, *Football and Fascism: The National Game under Mussolini* (New York: Berg, 2004), 76.
11. Ibid., 185.
12. Quoted in ibid., 190.
13. Quoted in Peter J. Beck, *Scoring for Britain: International Football and International Politics, 1900–1939* (London: Routledge, 1999), 194.
14. Quoted in David C. Large, *Nazi Games: The Olympics of 1936* (New York: W. W. Norton, 2007), 103.
15. Duff Hart-Davis, *Hitler's Games: The 1936 Olympics* (London: Harper & Row, 1986), 89.
16. Quoted in Rob Steen, *Floodlights and Touchlines: A History of Spectator Sports* (London: Bloomsbury, 2014), 350.
17. Quoted in Allen Guttmann, "Berlin 1936: The Most Controversial Olympics," in *National Identity and Global Sports Events: Culture, Politics, and Spectacle in the Olympics and the Football World Cup*, ed. Alan Tomlinson and Christopher Young (Albany: SUNY Press, 2006), 45.
18. Large, *Nazi Games*, 5.
19. Ibid., 198.
20. Ibid., 275.
21. Tobias Jones, *The Dark Heart of Italy* (New York: North Point Press, 2004), 75.
22. Quoted in Goldblatt, *Ball Is Round*, 310.
23. Quoted in Steen, *Floodlights and Touchlines*, 358.
24. Large, *Nazi Games*, 309.

25. Lutz Koepnik, "0–1: Riefenstahl and the Beauty of Soccer," in *Riefen-stahl Screened: An Anthology of New Criticism*, ed. Neil Christian Pages, Mary Rhiel, Ingeborg Majer-O'Sickey (New York: Continuum, 2008), 64.

26. Ibid., 65.

27. Beck, *Scoring for Britain*, 9.

28. Winston Churchill, "Sport Is a Stimulant in Our Workaday World," *News of the World*, September 4, 1938.

29. Quoted in Kuper, *Ajax*, 39.

30. Ibid., 17.

31. Eddie Hapgood, *Football Ambassador: The Autobiography of an Arsenal Legend* (London: GCR Books, 2009), 40.

32. George Orwell, "The Sporting Spirit," *Tribune*, December 14, 1945, in Sonia Orwell and Ian Angus, eds., *The Collected Essays, Journalism and Letters of George Orwell*, vol. 4: *In Front of Your Nose, 1945–1950* (London: Seeker & Warburg, 1968), 42.

3. THE MATCH OF DEATH

1. Galeano, *Football in Sun and Shadow*, 39.

2. Karel C. Berkhoff, *Harvest of Despair: Life and Death in Ukraine under Nazi Rule* (Cambridge, MA: Belknap Press, 2004), 91.

3. Kurt Werner was a member of Sonderkommando 4a of Einsatzgruppen C. His testimony comes from Ernst Klee, Willi Dressen, and Volker Reiss, eds., *"The Good Old Days": The Holocaust as Seen by Its Perpetrators and Bystanders* (New York: Free Press, 1991), 66.

4. James Waller, *Becoming Evil: How Ordinary People Commit Genocide and Mass Killing*, 2nd ed. (New York: Oxford University Press, 2007), 95.

5. Berkhoff, *Harvest of Despair*, 166.

6. Ibid., 164.

7. Andy Dougan, *Dynamo: Triumph and Tragedy in Nazi-Occupied Europe* (Guilford, CT: Lyons Press, 2002), 127.

8. Ibid., 136.

9. Ibid., 131.

10. Ibid., 132.

11. Ibid., 147.

12. Ibid., 151, and Andrew Gregorovich, *Forum: A Ukrainian Review* (Spring–Summer 1994): 18.

13. Dougan, *Dynamo*, 162.

14. Ibid., 164.

15. I. Konunchuk and I. Korolkov, "Chi bur 'match smerti' u Kievi?," *Ukraina moloda*, December 12, 1996, 8.

16. Dougan, *Dynamo*, 171.

17. Ibid., 178.

18. Gregorovich, *Forum*, 18, and Anatoly Kuznetsov, "The Dynamo Team: Legend and Fact," in *The Global Game: Writers on Soccer*, ed. John Turnbull, Thom Satterlee, and Alon Raab (Lincoln: University of Nebraska Press, 2008), 227.

19. Dougan, *Dynamo*, 179.

20. Ibid., 185.

21. Ibid., 187.

22. Berkhoff, *Harvest of Despair*, 305.

23. James Riordan, "The Match of Death: Kiev, 9 August 1942," *Soccer and Society* 4, no. 1 (Spring 2003): 90.

24. Gregorovich, *Forum*, 17.

25. Dougan, *Dynamo*, 229–31.

26. Martin Winstone, *The Holocaust Sites of Europe: An Historical Guide* (London: IB Taurus, 2010), 373.

4. THE BEAUTIFUL GAME IN THE KZ

1. Viktor E. Frankl, *Man's Search for Meaning* (Boston: Beacon Press, 2006), 65–66.

2. Winstone, *Holocaust Sites of Europe*, 121.

3. Laurence Rees, *Auschwitz: A New History* (New York: MJF Books, 2005), 6.

4. *Deutschland Berichte der Sopade*, no. 5 (1937): A-183.

5. The details of this story appeared in *Rund* magazine on May 5, 2007.

6. Personal correspondence, Dachau Memorial archives.

7. Krzysztof Dunin-Wąsowicz, *Resistance in the Nazi Concentration Camps, 1933–1945* (Warsaw: PWN Polish Scientific Publishers, 1982), 295.

8. Veronika Springmann, "Fussball im Konzentrationslager," in *Hakenkreuz und rundes Leder*, ed. Lorenz Peiffer and Dietrich Schulze-Marmeling (Göttingen: Verlag die Werkstatt, 2008), 502.

9. Quoted in ibid., 500.

10. Translated testimony of Franz Orzyschek from the Archiv Gedenkstätte und Museum Sachsenhasuen/Siftung Brandenburgische Gedenkstätten, record number (AS) R41/25.

11. Odd Nansen, *From Day to Day* (New York: G.P. Putnam's Sons, 1949), 377.

12. Skretny, *Julius Hirsch*, 236.

13. Ibid., 238.

14. Ibid., 236.

15. Ibid., 237.

16. David A. Hackett, *The Buchenwald Report: Report on the Buchenwald Concentration Camp near Weimar* (Boulder, CO: Westview Press, 1995), 266.

17. Buchenwald archives testimony, signature BwA 31/332 B1A.

18. Testimony first appeared in Hackett, *Buchenwald Report*, 266.

5. GENIUS ON THE DANUBE

1. Quoted in Carl E. Schorske, Fin-de-Siècle *Vienna: Politics and Culture* (New York: Alfred A. Knopf, 1980), 200.

2. James Wilson, *Inverting the Pyramid: The History of Soccer Tactics* (New York: Nation Books, 2013), 55.

3. *Welt am Montag*, March 22, 1948.

4. Quoted in Goldblatt, *Ball Is Round*, 198.

5. Quoted in Wilson, *Inverting the Pyramid*, 56.

6. Goldblatt, *Ball Is Round*, 258.

7. Franklin Foer, *How Soccer Explains the World* (New York: HarperCollins, 2004), 75.

8. *Völkischer Beobachter* (Wiener Ausgabe), October 4, 1937, 17.

9. Quoted in Hesse-Lichtenberger, *Tor!*, 82.

10. Matthias Marschik, "Between Manipulation and Resistance: Viennese Football in the Nazi Era," *Journal of Contemporary History* 34 (April 1999): 223.

11. Quoted in Thomas Weyr, *The Setting of the Pearl: Vienna under Hitler* (New York: Oxford University Press, 2005), 226–27.

12. Gordon J. Horwitz, *In the Shadow of Death: Living outside the Gates of Mauthausen* (New York: Free Press, 1990), 24.

13. Testimony of Josef Herzler, Mauthausen Memorial Museum record number AMM V/3/22.

14. According to Speer's brother, Hermann, overheard in conversation. Quoted in Rees, *Auschwitz*, 24.

15. Stefan Krukowski, *Byłem kapo* (I was a kapo) (Warsaw: Książka i Wiedza, 1963), 71.

16. Testimony of Oskar Schlaf, Mauthausen Memorial Museum record number AMM F/9a/1/3.

17. Match reports have been translated, paraphrased, and excerpted from Mauthausen Memorial Museum records.

18. Quoted in Michel de Bouard, "Mauthausen," *Revue d'histoire de la Deuxième Guerre mondiale*, no. 15–16 (July–September 1954): 60.

19. See BBC interview from April 19, 2013, as told by daughter Manuela Valletti.

20. Ferdinando Valletti died in 2007, keeping secret his story from his family to the very end. See the recent biography of Valletti, written in Italian by his daughter Manuela, and published under the title *Deportato 157633: Voglia di Non Morire* (Deported 157633: A Wish Not to Die).

21. *The Mauthausen Concentration Camp in 1938–1945: Catalog to the Exhibition at the Mauthausen Memorial* (Vienna: New Academic Press, 2013), 80.

22. Primo Levi, *The Drowned and the Saved* (New York: Vintage, 1988), 37.

23. Ibid.

24. The obituary appeared in the *Pariser Tageszeitung*, January 25, 1939; quoted in Goldblatt, *Ball Is Round*, 258.

25. Wilson, *Inverting the Pyramid*, 76.

26. David Art, *The Politics of the Nazi Past in Germany and Austria* (Cambridge: Cambridge University Press, 2006), 43.

6. FOOTBALL IN THE
POLISH KILLING FIELDS

1. Dante Alighieri, *The Divine Comedy of Dante Alighieri, Inferno* (Cambridge, MA: Harvard University Press, 1918), 27.

2. Imre Kertész, *Fatelessness* (New York: Vintage, 2004), 89.

3. Ibid., 110.

4. Quoted in Marta Bogacka, *Bokser z Auschwitz: Losy Tadeusza Pietrzykowskiego* (The Auschwitz Boxer) (Warsaw: Demart SA , 2012).

5. Rees, *Auschwitz*, 86.

6. Wolfgang Sofsky, *The Order of Terror: The Concentration Camp* (Princeton, NJ: Princeton University Press, 1997), 151.

7. Andrzej Krajewski, "Piłkarski mecze w Auschwitz: Futbol w piekle," *Polityka*, May 27, 2013, http://www.polityka.pl/tygodnikpolityka/historia/1543645,1,pilkarski-mecze-w-auschwitz.read.

8. Uri Talshir, "Holocaust Remembrance Day Profile: The Goalkeeper of Theresienstadt," *Haaretz.com*, April 12, 2010, http://www.haaretz.com/print-edition/sports/holocaust-remembrance-day-profile-the-goalkeeper-of-theresienstadt-1.284077.

9. Ibid.

10. Don Moore, "William Schick Survived Auschwitz," *Charlotte Sun*, January 1, 2006.

11. Ibid.

12. Levi, *Drowned and the Saved*, 62–63.

13. Ibid., 53.

14. Miklós Nyiszli, *Auschwitz: A Doctor's Eyewitness Account* (New York: Arcade Publishing, 2011), 68.

15. Jean-Claude Pressac, *Auschwitz: Technique and Operation of the Gas Chambers* (New York: Beate Klarsfeld Foundation, 1989), 509.

16. Tzvi Ben Gedalyahu, "The Auschwitz Boxer: A Surviving Holocaust Story," *Israel National News*, December 26, 2012, http://www.israelnationalnews .com/News/News.aspx/163582#!.

17. Levi, *Drowned and the Saved*, 55.

18. Ibid.

19. Walter Stanoski Winter, *Winter Time: Memoirs of a German Sinto Who Survived Auschwitz* (Hertfordshire, UK: University of Hertfordshire Press, 2004), 143.

20. Ibid., 148.

21. Roll-call leader Hartmann is likely SS Sturmann Kurt Hartmann, who was expelled from the SS and forced to serve four months in prison by an SS court in Breslau for his preferential treatment of prisoners (see Hermann Langbein, *Menschen in Auschwitz* [Frankfurt am Main: Ullstein-Verlag, 1980], 487). Winter's fond recollection of this "lance corporal" appears to be justified.

22. Winter, *Winter Time*, 55.

23. Pozsár Gábor, "Nekem emberebb embernek kell lennem," *Hetek*, April 25, 1998, http://www.hetek.hu/riport/199804/nekem_emberebb_embernek _kell_lennem.

24. Auschwitz State Museum, Statement (vol. 75, k., 93–94) from former prisoner Bronisław Cynkar (prisoner no. 183).

25. Auschwitz State Museum, Zespół Oświadczenia (vol. 133, 87–88), relacja byłego więźnia Kurt Hacker (prisoner no. 130029).

26. Auschwitz State Museum, Statement (vol. 94, 193) from former prisoner Mieczysław Pietrzak.

27. Donn Risolo, *Soccer Stories: Anecdotes, Oddities, Lore, and Amazing Feats* (Lincoln: University of Nebraska Press, 2010), 167.

28. United States Holocaust Memorial Museum, interview transcript from John Komski.

29. Arnošt Lustig, *Fire on Water: Porgess and the Abyss* (Evanston, IL: Northwestern University Press, 2005), 143.

30. Ron Trucks and Arnošt Lustig, "A Conversation with Arnošt Lustig," *New England Review* 20, no. 4 (Fall 1999): 75.

31. Auschwitz State Museum, Statement (vol. 82, pp. 65–66) from former prisoner Władysław Plaskura.

32. *Auschwitz 1940–1945* (Oświęcim: Auschwitz-Birkenau State Museum, 2000), 1:103.

33. Rees, *Auschwitz*, 171.

34. Tobias Jones, *The Dark Heart of Italy* (New York: North Point Press, 2004), 73.

35. Archiwum Państwowego Muzeum Auschwitz-Birkenau, Zespół Oświadczenia, Testimonies Fond, vol. 44, 47.

36. United States Holocaust Memorial Museum, "Gross-Rosen," Holocaust Encyclopedia, http://www.ushmm.org/wlc/en/article.php?ModuleId=10005454.

37. Winstone, *Holocaust Sites of Europe*, 304.

38. Ibid., 305.

39. See the website of the Gross-Rosen Museum, Rogoźnica, Poland, http://en.gross-rosen.eu/.

40. Ibid.

41. Ibid.

42. Michael Kowalski, "Piłkarze z piekła na ziemi. To oni wygrali z Niemcami," EuroSport.Onet.pl, August 1, 2012, http://eurosport.onet.pl/pilka-nozna/pilkarze-z-piekla-na-ziemi-to-oni-wygrali-z-niemcami/mn9q1.

43. Krajewski, "Piłkarski mecze w Auschwitz."

44. "Herosi w pasiakach," Gross-Rosen Museum, June 6, 2012, http://www.gross-rosen.eu/herosi-w-pasiakach-nieznana-historia-pilki-noznej-w-kl-gross-rosen.

45. From the archives of the Gross-Rosen Museum, Rogoźnica, Poland.

46. Exhibition video produced by Gross-Rosen Museum, Rogoźnica, Poland.

47. Testimony of Wladyslaw Boczon, archives of the Gross-Rosen Museum, Rogoźnica, Poland.

48. Arnold Mostowicz, *With a Yellow Star and a Red Cross: A Doctor in the Lodz Ghetto*, trans. Henia Reinhartz and Nochem Reinhartz (Portland, OR: Vallentine Mitchell, 2005), 185.

49. Ibid.

50. Ibid., 184.

51. Tadeusz Borowski, *This Way for the Gas, Ladies and Gentlemen* (New York: Penguin, 1976), 83.

7. THE CURIOUS STORY OF DUTCH SOCCER DURING NAZI OCCUPATION

1. David Winner, *Brilliant Orange: The Neurotic Genius of Dutch Soccer* (New York: Overlook Press, 2008), 110.

2. Journalist Simon Kuper's fantastic book *Ajax, the Dutch, the War* (2012) stands as an essential and highly engaging resource on Dutch football during World War II. Kuper spent his childhood in Holland, and his trenchant analysis and poignant interviews with actual survivors of the period is a must-read for anyone wanting to understand the intersection of history and football culture from this time.

3. Winner, *Brilliant Orange*, 130.

4. Ibid., 212.

5. Quoted in the Jewish Historical Museum (Amsterdam) exhibit publication on the Hollandsche Schouwburg (http://www.jhm.nl/)

6. Winstone, *Holocaust Sites of Europe*, 41.

7. Horwitz, *In the Shadow of Death*, 53.

8. Chris van der Heijden, quoted in Kuper, *Ajax, the Dutch, the War*, 98.

9. Winner, *Brilliant Orange*, 213.

10. Quoted in ibid., 214.

11. Verzetsmuseum (Dutch Resistance Museum [DRM]), Season '40–'45 exhibit, section 3.5, April 29, 2009, to April 11, 2010.

12. Kuper, *Ajax, the Dutch, the War*, 95.

13. DRM, Season '40–'45 exhibit, section 9.3.

14. Kuper, *Ajax, the Dutch, the War*, 72.

15. Ibid., 75–78.

16. Ibid., 84.

17. DRM, Season '40–'45 exhibit, section 7.2.

18. Goldblatt, *Ball Is Round*, 326.

19. DRM, Season '40–'45 exhibit, section 5.2.

20. Kuper, *Ajax, the Dutch, the War*, 120.

21. DRM, Season '40–'45 exhibit, section 7.1.

22. Kuper, *Ajax, the Dutch, the War*, 101.

23. DRM, Season '40–'45 exhibit, section 4.7.

24. Kuper, *Ajax, the Dutch, the War*, 94.

25. DRM, Season '40–'45 exhibit, section 3.1.

26. Bas Kortholt, Guido Abuys, and Dirk Mulder, *Het Verdwenen Elftal: Voetbal in Kamp Westerbork* [The Vanished Eleven: Football in Camp Westerbork] (Hooghalen, Netherlands: Herinneringscentrum Kamp Westerbork, 2012), 12.

27. Ibid., 13.

28. Ibid., 15.

29. Kuper, *Ajax, the Dutch, the War*, 103.

30. Kortholt, Abuys, and Mulder, *Het Verdwenen Elftal*, 25.

31. See Louis de Wijze, *Only My Life: A Survivor's Story* (New York: St Martin's Press, 1997), 68.

32. Ibid., 45–46.

33. DRM, Season '40–'45 exhibit, section 4.9.

34. Ibid., section 9.4.

35. Ibid., section 9.10.

36. Quoted in Kuper, *Ajax, the Dutch, the War*, 104.

37. Ibid., 53.

38. Ibid.

39. Ibid.

40. Quoted in Manfred Gerstenfeld, "Wartime and Postwar Dutch Attitudes toward the Jews: Myth and Truth," *Jerusalem Letter*, no. 412 (August 1999), http://www.jcpa.org/jl/vp412.htm.

41. See Lawrence Langer, "The Dilemma of Choice in the Death Camps," *Centerpoint: A Journal of Interdisciplinary Studies* 4 (Fall 1980): 53–59.

8. GHETTO SOCCER IN LIGA TEREZÍN

1. Pavel Friedmann was a twenty-one-year-old captive in Terezín. Personal translation of original poem from the archive of the Jewish History Museum in Prague; DOCUMENT.JMP.SHOAH/T/2/A/10j/326/017/003 and inventory number: 326.

2. Winstone, *Holocaust Sites of Europe*, 158.

3. Saul Friedländer, *Nazi Germany and the Jews, 1933–1945* (New York: HarperCollins, 2009), 389.

4. Ludmila Chládková, *The Terezín Ghetto* (Prague: Památník Terezín, 2005), 4.

5. Friedländer, *Nazi Germany and the Jews*, 411.

6. Karel Margry, "Theresienstadt (1944–1945): The Nazi Propaganda Film Depicting the Concentration Camp as Paradise," *Historical Journal of Film, Radio and Television* 12, no. 2 (1992): 145.

7. Chládková, *Terezín Ghetto*, 15.

8. Friedländer, *Nazi Germany and the Jews*, 297.

9. See Anna Hájková, "The Fabulous Boys of Theresienstadt: Young Czech Men as the Dominant Social Elite in the Theresienstadt Ghetto" in *Im Ghetto: Neue Forschungen zu Alltag und Umfeld*, Contributions to the History of Na-

tional Socialism 25 , ed. Christoph Dieckmann and Babette Quinkert (Göttingen: Wallstein Verlag, 2009), 134.

10. Goldblatt, *Ball Is Round*, 259.

11. Susie Davidson, *The Music Man of Terezín: The Story of Rafael Schaechter* (Somerville, MA: Ibbetson Street Press, 2012), 11.

12. See the 2012 documentary film, first aired on PBS, *Defiant Requiem*, from Partisan Pictures. The film includes dramatic reenactments of ghetto experiences and performances of Verdi by a modern choir in Terezín led by American maestro Murry Sidlin.

13. Margry, "Theresienstadt," 146.

14. Vera Schiff, *The Theresienstadt Deception* (Lewiston, NY: Edwin Mellen Press, 2012), 16–17.

15. Quoted in Friedländer, *Nazi Germany and the Jews*, 388.

16. Chládková, *Terezín Ghetto*, 31.

17. Margry, "Theresienstadt," 153.

18. Ibid., 151.

19. Ibid., 154.

20. Foer, *How Soccer Explains the World*, 76–77.

21. Mike Schwartz and Avi Kanner, *Liga Terezín*, directed by Avi Kanner (Givat Haim Ihud, Israel: Beit Theresienstadt, 2013), DVD.

22. Ibid.

23. Karel Margry, "The First Theresienstadt Film (1942)," *Historical Journal of Film, Radio and Television* 19, no. 3 (1999): 303.

24. Margry, "Theresienstadt," 155.

25. Schwartz and Kanner, *Liga Terezín*.

26. Nicola Schlichting, "Kleiderkammer schlägt Gärtner 9:3, Fußball in Theresienstadt," in *Schwerpunktthema: Fußball; Jahrbuch des Nürnberger Institutes für NS-Forschung und jüdische Geschichte des 20. Jahrhunderts*, ed. Jim G.Tobias and Peter Zinke (Nuremberg: ANTOGO Verlag, 2006), 82.

27. Yad Vashem Archives, transcript from interview with Ludvik Steinberg, Nationales Hilfskomitee für Deportierte [National Relief Committee's Home for the Deported], June 21, 1945, Budapest, no. 20, O15E.

28. Archives of the Memorial Theresienstadt (Památník Terezín), collection PT 4009.

29. *Beit Terezín Memorial Newsletter*, January 2011, 11, http://www.bterezin.org.il/120869/Newsletters---New-Format.

30. František Steiner, *Fotbal Pod Zlutou Hvezdou* [Soccer Under the Yellow Star] (Prague: Olympia, 2009), 43.

31. Hájková, "Fabulous Boys of Theresienstadt," 130.

32. Schlichting, "Kleiderkammer schlägt Gärtner 9:3," 85.

33. Archives of the Memorial Theresienstadt (Památník Terezín), collection PT 4246-6.

34. Translated from Steiner, *Fotbal Pod Zlutou Hvezdou*, 36.

35. First published in *Rim, Rim, Rim*, no. 4, from the archives of the Memorial Theresienstadt (Památník Terezín), collection A-1189. Translated from Schlichting, "Kleiderkammer schlägt Gärtner 9:3," 73.

36. Hana Volavkova, ed., *I Never Saw Another Butterfly: Children's Drawings and Poems from Terezín Concentration Camp, 1942–1944* (New York: Schocken Books, 1993), 1.

37. Pavel Weiner, *A Boy in Terazin* (Evanston, IL: Northwestern University Press, 2012), 121.

38. Steiner, *Fotbal Pod Zlutou Hvezdou*, 78.

39. Ibid., 45.

40. Archives of the Memorial Theresienstadt (Památník Terezín), diary of Willy Mahler, July and August 1944.

41. Yad Vashem, "Between the Worlds: Social Circles in the Theresienstadt Ghetto," https://www.yadvashem.org/yv/en/education/learning_environments/terezin/.

42. Hájková, "Fabulous Boys of Theresienstadt," 130.

43. Steiner, *Fotbal Pod Zlutou Hvezdou*, 40.

44. Burka's memoir is an album with pictures painted by him and other Terezín artists and published in 2007. See Dahlia Karpel, "Even SS Officers Applauded the Jewish Players of the Soccer League in Terezín," *Haaretz*, April 17, 2009, http://bterezin.brinkster.net/LIGA_TEREZIN/2009-04-17_Haaretz_LIGA_TEREZIN-English.pdf.

45. Ibid.

46. Steiner, *Fotbal Pod Zlutou Hvezdou*, 64.

47. Arnošt Lustig, *The Unloved: From the Diary of Perla S.* (Evanston, IL: Northwestern University Press, 1996), 24–25.

48. Karpel, "Even SS Officers Applauded."

49. Petr Erben, *In My Own Footsteps* (Konstanz, Germany: Hartung-Gorre, 2001), 39.

50. *Beit Terezín Memorial Newsletter*, August 2009, http://www.bterezin.org.il/120869/Newsletters---New-Format.

51. Karpel, "Even SS Officers Applauded."

52. Steiner, *Fotbal Pod Zlutou Hvezdou*, 93.

53. *Beit Terezín Memorial Newsletter*, August 2009.

54. Chládková, *Terezín Ghetto*, 9.

55. Winstone, *Holocaust Sites of Europe*, 169.

56. Schiff, *Theresienstadt Deception*, 59.

57. Schwartz and Kanner, *Liga Terezín*. Note: Their film is part of an excellent program at the Israeli memorial Beit Theresienstadt. Created and maintained by Oded Breda, nephew of the murdered Pavel Breda mentioned previously in this chapter, the project carefully documents soccer in Terezín. The program includes public exhibitions, educational outreach, and a memorial soccer tournament each year.

58. Ibid.

9. AFTER THE CATASTROPHE

1. Quoted in Rees, *Auschwitz*, 266.

2. Bergen, *War and Genocide*, 229.

3. Testimony from the permanent exhibition of the Buchenwald and Mittelbau-Dora Memorials Foundation (2010).

4. Eric Lichtblau, *The Nazis Next Door: How America Became a Safe Haven for Hitler's Men* (New York: Houghton Mifflin Harcourt, 2014), 4.

5. Ibid., 8, n. 8.

6. Quoted in ibid., 4–5.

7. Bergen, *War and Genocide*, 240.

8. Angelika Königseder and Juliane Wetzel, *Waiting for Hope: Jewish Displaced Persons in Post–World War II Germany*, trans. John A. Broadwin (Evanston, IL: Northwestern University Press, 2001), 127.

9. Philipp Grammes, "Sports in the DP Camps, 1945–1948," in *Emancipation through Muscles: Jews and Sports in Europe*, ed. Michael Brenner and Gideon Reuveni (Lincoln: University of Nebraska Press, 2006), 190.

10. Ibid., 191.

11. Königseder and Wetzel, *Waiting for Hope*, 168.

12. See Arthur Heinrich, *A Jew in German Football: The Three Lives of Martin Abraham Stock* (Göttingen: Verlag Die Werkstaat, 2014).

13. *Landsberger Lager-Caitung*, no. 41, July 26, 1946, 7.

14. Quoted in Martin Gilbert, *The Boys: Triumph over Adversity* (London: Weidenfeld & Nicolson, 1996), 380.

15. Grammes, "Sports in the DP Camps," 202.

16. Hesse-Lichtenberger, *Tor!*, 105.

17. Ibid.

18. Ibid., 107.

19. Ibid., 115.

20. Ibid., 125.

21. Goldblatt, *Ball Is Round*, 354.

22. Kuper, *Ajax, the Dutch, the War*, 185.

23. Martin Gilbert, *The Holocaust: A History of the Jews of Europe during the Second World War* (New York: Holt, Rinehart and Winston, 1985), 828.

24. De Wijze, *Only My Life*, 67.

25. Originally from the essay "The Town Beyond the Wall," quoted in Robert McAfee Brown, *Elie Wiesel: Messenger to All Humanity* (Notre Dame, IN: University of Notre Dame Press, 1983), 71–72.

26. Steiner, *Fotbal Pod Zlutou Hvezdou*, 89–90.

BIBLIOGRAPHY

BOOKS AND CHAPTERS

Art, David. *The Politics of the Nazi Past in Germany and Austria*. Cambridge: Cambridge University Press, 2006.

Bajohr, Frank. "Fritz Szepan: Fußball-Idol und Nutznießer des NS-Regimes." In *Sportler im "Jahrhundert der Lager": Profiteure, Widerständler und Opfer*, edited by Diethelm Blecking and Lorenz Peiffer, 110–15. Göttingen: Verlag Die Werkstatt, 2012.

Beck, Peter J. *Scoring for Britain: International Football and International Politics, 1900–1939*. London: Routledge, 1999.

Bendersky, Joseph W. *A History of Nazi Germany*. Chicago: Nelson-Hall, 1985.

Bergen, Doris. *War and Genocide: A Concise History of the Holocaust*. Lanham, MD: Rowman & Littlefield, 2009.

Berkhoff, Karel C. *Harvest of Despair: Life and Death in Ukraine under Nazi Rule*. Cambridge, MA: Belknap Press, 2004.

Biber, Jacob, *Risen from the Ashes: A Story of Jewish Displaced Persons in the Aftermath of World War II*. San Bernardino, CA: Borgo, 1990.

Bogacka, Marta. *Bokser z Auschwitz: Losy Tadeusza Pietrzykowskiego* [The Auschwitz Boxer]. Warsaw: DeMart SA, 2012.

Borowski, Tadeusz. *Bei uns in Auschwitz. Erzahlungen*. Munich: Piper, 1982.

———. *This Way for the Gas, Ladies and Gentlemen*. New York: Penguin, 1976.

Brenner, Michael. "Why Jews and Sports." In *Emancipation through Muscles: Jews and Sports in Europe*, edited by Michael Brenner and Gideon Reuveni, 1–13. Lincoln: University of Nebraska Press, 2006.

Brown, Robert McAfee. *Elie Wiesel, Messenger to All Humanity*. Notre Dame, IN: University of Notre Dame Press, 1983.

Burns, Jimmy. *La Roja: How Soccer Conquered Spain and How Spanish Soccer Conquered the World*. New York: Nation Books, 2012.

Chládková, Ludmila. *The Terezín Ghetto*. Prague: Památník Terezín, 2005.

Davidson, Susie. *The Music Man of Terezín: The Story of Rafael Schaechter*. Somerville, MA: Ibbetson Street Press, 2012.

Deutscher Fußball Bund. *100 Jahre DFB: Geschichte des Deutschen Fußball Bundes*. Berlin: SVB Sportverlag Berlin, 1999.

de Wijze, Louis. *Only My Life: A Survivor's Story*. New York: St. Martin's Press, 1997.

Dougan, Andy. *Dynamo: Triumph and Tragedy in Nazi-Occupied Europe*. Guilford, CT: Lyons Press, 2002.

Dunin-Wąsowicz, Krzysztof. *Resistance in the Nazi Concentration Camps, 1933–1945*. Warsaw: PWN-Polish Scientific Publishers, 1982.

Erben, Petr. *In My Own Footsteps*. Konstanz, Germany: Hartung-Gorre, 2001.

Foer, Franklin. *How Soccer Explains the World*. New York: HarperCollins, 2004.

Frankl, Viktor E. *Man's Search for Meaning*. Boston: Beacon Press, 2006.

Friedländer, Saul. *Nazi Germany and the Jews, 1933–1945*. New York: HarperCollins, 2009.

Galeano, Eduardo. *Football in Sun and Shadow*. New York: Nation Books, 2013.

Gilbert, Martin. *The Boys: Triumph over Adversity*. London: Weidenfeld & Nicolson, 1996.

———. *The Holocaust: A History of the Jews of Europe during the Second World War*. New York: Holt, Rinehart and Winston, 1985.

Goldblatt, David. *The Ball Is Round: A Global History of Soccer*. New York: Riverhead Books, 2008.

Grammes, Philipp. "Sports in the DP Camps, 1945–1948." In *Emancipation through Muscles: Jews and Sports in Europe*, edited by Michael Brenner and Gideon Reuveni, 187–212. Lincoln: University of Nebraska Press, 2006.

Greif, Gideon. *We Wept Without Tears: Testimonies of the Jewish Sonderkommando from Auschwitz*. New Haven, CT: Yale University Press, 2005.

Guttmann, Allen. "Berlin 1936: The Most Controversial Olympics." In *National Identity and Global Sports Events: Culture, Politics, and Spectacle in the Olympics and the Football World Cup*, edited by Alan Tomlinson and Christopher Young, 65–81. Albany: SUNY Press, 2006

Hackett, David A. *The Buchenwald Report: Report on the Buchenwald Concentration Camp near Weimar*. Boulder, CO: Westview Press, 1995.

Hájková, Anna. "The Fabulous Boys of Theresienstadt: Young Czech Men as the Dominant Social Elite in the Theresienstadt Ghetto." In *Im Ghetto: Neue Forschungen zu Alltag und Umfeld*, Contributions to the History of National Socialism 25, edited by Christoph Dieckmann and Babette Quinkert, 116–35. Göttingen: Wallstein Verlag, 2009.

Hapgood, Eddie. *Football Ambassador: The Autobiography of an Arsenal Legend*. London: GCR Books, 2009.

Hart-Davis, Duff. *Hitler's Games: The 1936 Olympics*. London: Harper & Row, 1986.

Havemann, Nils. *Fußball unterm Hakenkreuz: Der DFB zwischen Sport, Politik und Kommerz*. Bonn: Bundeszentrale für politische Bildung, 2006 [summary English version].

Heinrich, Arthur. *A Jew in German Football: The Three Lives of Martin Abraham Stock*. Göttingen: Verlag Die Werkstaat, 2014.

Hesse-Lichtenberger, Ulrich. *Tor! The Story of German Football*. London: When Saturday Comes Books, 2003.

Hoffmann, Hilmar. *The Triumph of Propaganda: Film and National Socialism*. Providence, RI: Berghahn, 1996.

Horwitz, Gordon J. *In the Shadow of Death: Living outside the Gates of Mauthausen*. New York: Free Press, 1990.

Jones, Tobias. *The Dark Heart of Italy*. New York: North Point Press, 2004.

Jowett, Garth S., and Victoria O'Donnell. *Propaganda and Persuasion*. 6th ed. Thousand Oaks, CA: Sage, 2014.

Kertész, Imre. *Fatelessness*. New York: Vintage, 2004.

Keys, Barbara. *Globalizing Sport: National Rivalry and International Community in the 1930s*. Cambridge, MA: Harvard University Press, 2006.

Klee, Ernst, Willi Dressen, and Volker Reiss, eds. *The Good Old Days: The Holocaust as Seen by Its Perpetrators and Bystanders*. New York: Free Press, 1991.

Koepnik, Lutz. "0–1: Riefenstahl and the Beauty of Soccer." In *Riefenstahl Screened: An Anthology of New Criticism*, edited by Neil Christian Pages, Mary Rhiel, and Ingeborg Majer-O'Sickey, 52–70. New York: Continuum, 2008.

Königseder, Angelika, and Juliane Wetzel. *Waiting for Hope: Jewish Displaced Persons in Post–World War II Germany*. Translated by John A. Broadwin. Evanston, IL: Northwestern University Press, 2001.

Kortholt, Bas, Guido Abuys, and Dirk Mulder. *Het Verdwenen Elftal: Voetbal in Kamp Westerbork* [The Vanished Eleven: Football in Camp Westerbork]. Hooghalen, Netherlands: Herinneringscentrum Kamp Westerbork, 2012.

Kruger, Arnd. "Der Einfluss des faschistischen Sportmodells Italiens auf den nationalistischen Sport." In *Sport und Politik 1918–1939/40: Proceedings, ICOSH Seminar*, edited by A. Morgan Olsen, 226–32. Otta, Norway: Engers Boktrykkeri A/S, 1986.

———. "The Role of Sport in German International Politics." In *Sport and International Politics: The Impact of Fascism and Communism on Sport*, edited by Pierre Arnaud and James Riordan, 79–96. London: Routledge, 1998.

Krukowski, Stefan. *Byłem kapo* [I was a *kapo*]. Warsaw: Książka i Wiedza, 1963.

Kuper, Simon. *Ajax, the Dutch, the War: The Strange Tale of Soccer during Europe's Darkest Hour*. New York: Nation Books, 2012.

———. *Football Against the Enemy*. London: Orion Books, 1994.

Kuznetsov, Anatoly. "The Dynamo Team: Legend and Fact." In *The Global Game: Writers on Soccer*, edited by John Turnbull, Thom Satterlee, and Alon Raab, 189–94. Lincoln: University of Nebraska Press, 2008.

Langbein, Hermann. *Menschen in Auschwitz*. Frankfurt am Main: Ullstein-Verlag, 1980.

Large, David C. *Nazi Games: The Olympics of 1936*. New York: W. W. Norton, 2007.

Levi, Primo. *The Drowned and the Saved*. New York: Vintage, 1988.

Lichtblau, Eric. *The Nazis Next Door: How America Became a Safe Haven for Hitler's Men*. New York: Houghton Mifflin Harcourt, 2014.

Lustig, Arnošt. *Fire on Water: Porgess and the Abyss*. Evanston, IL: Northwestern University Press, 2005.

———. *The Unloved: From the Diary of Perla S.* Evanston, IL: Northwestern University Press, 1996.

Margry, Karel. "The Concentration Camp as Idyll: Theresienstadt—a Documentary from the Jewish Settlement Area." In *Geschichte, Rezeption und Wirkung: Jahrbuch 1996 zur Geschichte und Wirkung des Holocaust*, 319–52. Frankfurt am Main: Fritz Bauer Institut, 1996.

Maršálek, Hans. *Die Geschichte des Konzentrationslager Mauthausen. Dokumentation. 4. Auflage*. Vienna: Edition Mauthausen, 2006.

Martin, Simon. *Football and Fascism: The National Game under Mussolini*. New York: Berg, 2004.

Mostowicz, Arnold. *With a Yellow Star and a Red Cross: A Doctor in the Lodz Ghetto*. Translated by Henia and Nochem Reinhartz. Portland, OR: Vallentine Mitchell, 2005.

Murray, Bill. *The World's Game*. Chicago: University of Chicago Press, 1996.

Nansen, Odd. *From Day to Day*. New York: G. P. Putnam's Sons, 1949.

Nietzsche, Friedrich W. *Human, All Too Human*. Lincoln: University of Nebraska Press, 1984.

Nyiszli, Miklós. *Auschwitz: A Doctor's Eyewitness Account*. New York: Arcade, 2011.

Orwell, George. "The Sporting Spirit, Tribune, 14 Dec. 1945." In *The Collected Essays, Journalism and Letters of George Orwell*, vol. 4: *In Front of Your Nose, 1945–1950*, edited by Sonia Orwell and Ian Angus. London: Secker & Warburg, 1968.

Pennachia, Mario. *Generale Vaccaro*. Rome: Nuove Idee, 2008.

Pinsky, Robert. *The Inferno of Dante: A New Verse Translation*. New York: Farrar, Straus and Giroux, 1994.

Pratkanis, Anthony R., and Elliot Aronson. *Age of Propaganda: The Everyday Use and Abuse of Persuasion*. New York: Freeman, Holt and Company, 2001.

Pressac, Jean-Claude. *Auschwitz: Technique and Operation of the Gas Chambers*. New York: Beate Klarsfeld Foundation, 1989.

Pyta, Wolfram. "German Football: A Cultural History." In *German Football: History, Culture, Society*, edited by Alan Tomlinson and Christopher Young, 1–22. New York: Routledge, 2006.

Rees, Laurence. *Auschwitz: A New History*. New York: MJF Books, 2005.

Riordan, James. *Match of Death*. New York: Oxford University Press, 2003.

Risolo, Donn. *Soccer Stories: Anecdotes, Oddities, Lore, and Amazing Feats.* Lincoln: University of Nebraska Press, 2010.

Schiff, Vera. *The Theresienstadt Deception.* Lewiston, NY: Edwin Mellen Press, 2012.

Schlichting, Nicola. "Kleiderkammer schlägt Gärtner 9:3, Fußball in Theresienstadt." In *Schwerpunktthema: Fußball; Jahrbuch des Nürnberger Institutes für NS-Forschung und jüdische Geschichte des 20. Jahrhunderts,* edited by Jim G.Tobias and Peter Zinke. Nuremberg: ANTOGO Verlag, 2006.

Schorske, Carl E. Fin-de-Siècle *Vienna: Politics and Culture.* New York: Alfred A. Knopf, 1980.

Skretny, Werner. *Julius Hirsch. Nationalspieler. Ermordet. Biografie eines jüdischen Fußballers.* Göttingen: Verlag Die Werkstatt, 2012.

Snyder, Timothy. *Bloodlands: Europe between Hitler and Stalin.* New York: Basic Books, 2010.

Sofsky, Wolfgang. *The Order of Terror: The Concentration Camp.* Princeton, NJ: Princeton University Press, 1997.

Springmann, Veronika. "Fussball im Konzentrationslager." In *Hakenkreuz und rundes Leder,* edited by Lorenz Peiffer and Dietrich Schulze-Marmeling, 489–503. Göttingen: Verlag die Werkstatt, 2008.

Steen, Rob. *Floodlights and Touchlines: A History of Spectator Sports.* London: Bloomsbury, 2014.

Steiner, František. *Fotbal Pod Zlutou Hvezdou* [Soccer Under the Yellow Star]. Prague: Olympia, 2009.

Teja, Angela. "Italian Sport and International Relations under Fascism." In *Sport and International Politics: The Impact of Fascism and Communism on Sport,* edited by Pierre Arnaud and James Riordan, 147–70. London: Routledge, 1998.

Urban, Thomas. *Schwarze Adler, Weiße Adler. Deutsche und Polnische Fußballer im Räderwerk der Politik.* Göttingen: Die Werkstatt, 2011.

Volavkova, Hana. . . . *I Never Saw Another Butterfly* . . . *: Children's Drawings and Poems from Terezín Concentration Camp, 1942–1944.* New York: Schocken Books, 1993.

Wachsmann, Nikolaus. *KL: A History of the Nazi Concentration Camps.* New York: Farrar, Straus and Giroux, 2015.

Waller, James. *Becoming Evil: How Ordinary People Commit Genocide and Mass Killing.* 2nd ed. New York: Oxford University Press, 2007.

Walter, Fritz. *11 rote Jäger : Nationalspieler im Kriege.* Munich: Copress-Verlag, 1959.

Weiner, Pavel. *A Boy in Terezin.* Evanston, IL: Northwestern University Press, 2012.

Welch, David. *The Third Reich: Politics and Propaganda.* New York: Routledge, 1993.

Weyr, Thomas. *The Setting of the Pearl: Vienna under Hitler.* New York: Oxford University Press, 2005.

Wilson, James. *Inverting the Pyramid: The History of Soccer Tactics.* New York: Nation Books, 2013.

Winner, David. *Brilliant Orange: The Neurotic Genius of Dutch Soccer.* New York: Overlook Press, 2008.

Winstone, Martin. *The Holocaust Sites of Europe: An Historical Guide.* London: IB Taurus, 2010.

Winter, Walter Stanoski. *Winter Time: Memoirs of a German Sinto Who Survived Auschwitz.* Hertfordshire, UK: University of Hertfordshire Press, 2004.

Zuckmayer, Carl. *A Part of Myself.* New York: Carroll & Graf, 1984.

ACADEMIC PAPERS, JOURNALS, AND TRANSCRIPTS

Beck, Peter J. "England v Germany, 1938." *History Today* 32 (1982): 29–34.

Beit Terezín Memorial Newsletter. August 2009. http://www.bterezin.org.il/120869/Newsletters---New-Format.

Beit Terezín Memorial Newsletter. January 2011. http://www.bterezin.org.il/120869/Newsletters---New-Format.

Brustein, William. "Who Joined the Nazis and Why." *American Journal of Sociology* 103 (July 1997): 216–21.

de Bouard, Michel. "Mauthausen." *Revue d'histoire de la Deuxième Guerre mondiale,* nos. 15–16 (July–September 1954): 41–80.

Ferenc, Jakub. "Football in Occupied Poland (1939–1945)." *Revista de Psicologia, Ciéncies de l'Educacio i de l'Esport* 32, no. 2 (2014): 47–52.

Gerstenfeld, Manfred. "Wartime and Postwar Dutch Attitudes toward the Jews: Myth and Truth." *Jerusalem Letter,* August 15, 1999.

Gregorovich, Andrew. *Forum: A Ukrainian Review* (Spring–Summer 1994): 17–18.

Konunchuk, I., and I. Korolkov. "Chi bur 'match smerti' u Kievi?" *Ukraina moloda,* December 12, 1996, 8.

Lee, Johnny K. "Playing for Life: Survival Soccer in 1942." *Soccer and Society* 7, no. 4 (December 2006): 486–93.

Margry, Karel. "The First Theresienstadt Film (1942)." *Historical Journal of Film, Radio and Television* 19, no. 3 (1999): 303–37.

———. "Theresienstadt (1944–1945): The Nazi Propaganda Film Depicting the Concentration Camp as Paradise." *Historical Journal of Film, Radio and Television* 12, no. 2 (1992): 145–62.

Marschik, Matthias. "Between Manipulation and Resistance: Viennese Football in the Nazi Era." *Journal of Contemporary History* 34 (April 1999): 215–29.

Riordan, James. "The Match of Death: Kiev, 9 August 1942." *Soccer and Society* 4, no. 1 (Spring 2003): 87–93.

Trucks, Ron, and Arnošt Lustig. "A Conversation with Arnošt Lustig." *New England Review* 20, no. 4 (Fall 1999): 68–76.

Voices of the Holocaust Project. "David P. Boder Interviews Friedrich Schlaefrig, 23 August 1946." http://voices.iit.edu/interviewee?doc=schlaefrigF.

Yad Vashem Archives. Transcript from Interview with Ludvik Steinberg, Nationales Hilfskomitee für Deportierte [National Relief Committee's Home for the Deported], June 21, 1945, Budapest, no. 20, O15E.

ARCHIVES AND MEMORIALS

Auschwitz-Birkenau State Museum, Oświęcim, Poland.
Beit Theresienstadt (Terezín) Martyrs Remembrance Association, Israel.
Dachau Concentration Camp Memorial Site, Dachau, Germany.
Ghetto Fighters' House Museum Archive, Israel.
Gross-Rosen Museum, Rogoźnica, Poland.
Jewish Historical Museum, Amsterdam, Netherlands.
Jewish Museum of Prague, Czech Republic.
Mauthausen Memorial, Mauthausen, Austria.
Sachsenhausen Memorial and Museum, Oranienburg, Germany.
Terezín (Theresienstadt) Memorial, Terezín, Czech Republic.
United States Holocaust Memorial Museum, Washington, DC.
Verzetsmuseum (Dutch Resistance Museum), Amsterdam, Netherlands.
Westerbork Memorial (Herinneringscentrum Kamp Westerbork), Hooghalen, Netherlands.
Yad Vashem, the Holocaust Martyrs' and Heroes' Remembrance Authority, Jerusalem, Israel.

PERIODICALS, NEWSPAPERS, AND FILM

Charlotte Sun, January 1, 2006.
Defiant Requiem. DVD. Produced by Whitney Johnson, Tomas Krejci, and Peter Schnall. Directed by Doug Schultz. New York: Partisan Pictures, 2012.
Deutschland Berichte der Sopade, no. 5 (1937): A-183.
Gábor, Pozsár. "Nekem emberebb embernek kell lennem." *Hetek*, April 25, 1998. http://www.hetek.hu/riport/199804/nekem_emberebb_embernek_kell_lennem.
Interview with Laszek Rylski, *Agence France-Presse*, June 7, 2012.
Karpel, Dahlia. "Even SS Officers Applauded the Jewish Players of the Soccer League in Terezín." *Haaretz*, April 17, 2009. http://bterezin.brinkster.net/LIGA_TEREZIN/2009-04-17_Haaretz_LIGA_TEREZIN-English.pdf.
Landsberger Lager-Caitung, no. 41 (July 26, 1946): 7.
Schwartz, Mike, and Avi Kanner. *Liga Terezín*. DVD. Directed by Avi Kanner. Givat Haim Ihud, Israel: Beit Theresienstadt, 2013.
Völkischer Beobachter (Vienna Edition; Wiener Ausgabe), April 10, 1937, and April 10, 1938.
Welt am Montag, March 22, 1948.

INDEX

ABOUT THE AUTHOR

Kevin E. Simpson is a professor, former college soccer player, and the recipient of numerous fellowships and grants from the United States Holocaust Memorial Museum, Yad Vashem (Israel), the Defiant Requiem Foundation, and the Holocaust Education Foundation of Northwestern University (Illinois). He completed his PhD in counseling psychology at the University of Denver in 1999, going on to teach for twelve years at Concordia University, Portland. He was a visiting professor in London (2007) and later in Vienna (2011), where he taught on the psychology and history of the Holocaust in Austria. Dr Simpson has published and presented widely to academic and popular audiences on topics including sport psychology, propaganda and persuasion, comparative genocide, Christianity and bystander factors during the Nazi era, and teaching the psychology of the Holocaust. He has also conducted archival research and fieldwork across Eastern Europe, including at almost all of the key concentration camps and Holocaust memorial sites in Poland, Germany, Austria, and the Czech Republic. He is professor of psychology at his alma mater, John Brown University, in Siloam Springs, Arkansas, where he makes his home.